The Complete Manual *of* Typography

The Complete Manual *of*

Typography

A GUIDE TO SETTING PERFECT TYPE

JAMES FELICI

The Complete Manual of Typography
James Felici
Copyright © 2003 by James Felici

This Adobe Press book is published by Peachpit Press.
For information on Adobe Press books, contact:

Peachpit Press
1249 Eighth Street, Berkeley, CA 94710
Tel: 510.524.2178 Fax: 510.524.2221
http://www.peachpit.com

To report errors, please send a note to errata@peachpit.com
Peachpit Press is a division of Pearson Education. For the latest on Adobe Press books,
go to http://www.adobe.com/adobepress

Editor Serena Herr
Production Coordinator David Van Ness
Cover and Book Design Frances Baca
Compositor Frances Baca
Copyeditor and Proofreader Karen Seriguchi
Indexer Jack Lewis
Printer Von Hoffmann Corporation

This book is set in Monotype Perpetua and Linotype Syntax, both from Adobe Systems.
Perpetua is a trademark of the Monotype Corporation registered in the U.S. Patent and
Trademark Office and may be registered in certain other jurisdictions. Syntax is a registered
trademark of Linotype-Hell AG and/or its subsidiaries.

ISBN 0-321-12730-7
12

Printed and bound in the United States of America

for Jennifer

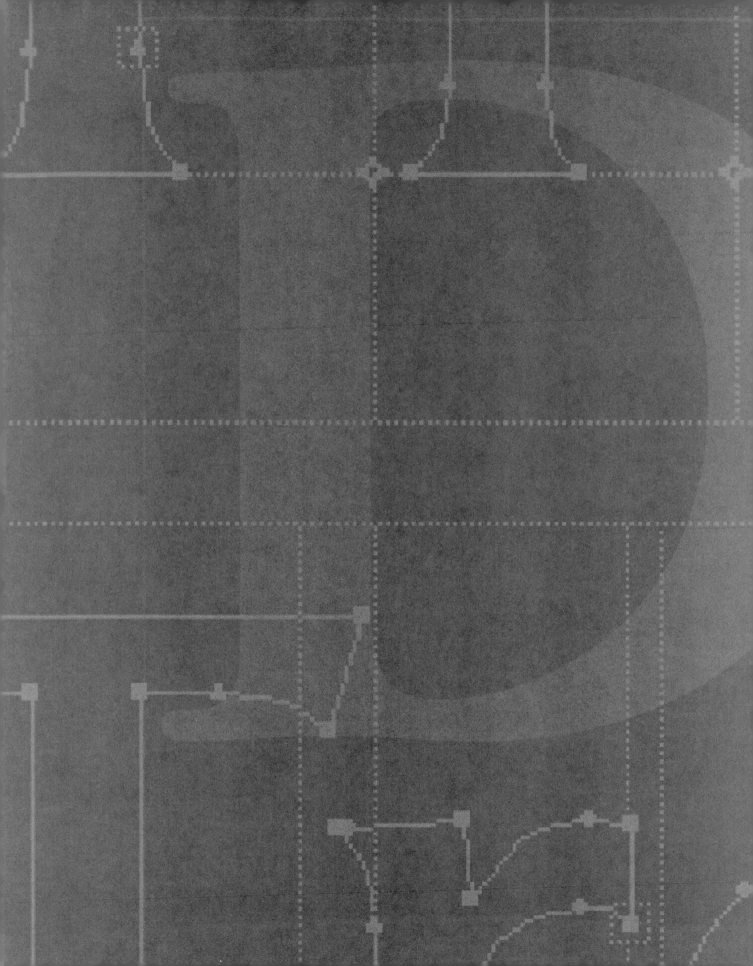

Foreword

Give me that old-time typography.

Gutenberg was the last person to get away with bad typography. Since type as such didn't exist before him, he was the last person to escape typographic criticism. All of you have no excuse: you will produce great typography because 550 years of experience and this great book are at your fingertips.

Type and typography—what you do and how you do it—are both science and art. There are rules, most of which get ignored. There are tools, most of which are not used. But now you have the ultimate typographic tool: Jim Felici's knowledge.

Type is Jim's life, and Jim's life has followed the evolution of the industry. He learned to kern at his pappy's knee and made the transition from hot metal to cold type. He melted lead pigs and slung Linotype slugs, juggled "golf balls" on strike-on IBM Composers, and punched paper tape for photographic typesetting. He had glass fonts and plastic fonts and film fonts and then digital fonts on a disk.

When the personal computer came along he jumped on the bandwagon. Set type with Tandy or Kaypro? Give him Big Blue on a desktop. Then came the Macintosh. Finally, a machine that dealt with type onscreen and off. It actually had menu items for font and size and style and knew what italic and bold were all about. Type became so simple that everyone overdid it. The result was ransom-note typesetting.

Jim progressed from character printer to dot matrix printer to laser printer and then imagesetter and platesetter and even digital printing. He advanced from monochrome to color. 300 dpi became 600 dpi and some output hit 3,000 dpi. PostScript became the universal language of printing.

He started with 13 fonts and went to the standard 35. New fonts proliferated like little electronic rabbits and he bought them by the dozen. The library grew and he needed bigger disks and special software to manage a fount of fonts. Who needs six versions of Garamond? He does. Then there were new versions of every program—revision 1.0, revision 2.0—"revision," from some language meaning "to squeeze again." Along the way, spelling checkers destroyed our ability to spell and online thesauri put us at a loss for words.

In only a few years we wiped out the entire typesetting industry, and typesetting moved to the creative originator. Now the most demanding type buyers became less demanding. We started to see inch marks instead of real quotes and two hyphens substituting for em dashes. Forget about en dashes and real small caps and good H&J. Eventually, though, the industry did give us professional font sets, and programs automated some typographic processes.

So here we are. At this point, most people who work with type have to catch up with both what is old and what is new in typography. Fortunately, you have the solution in your hands: a concise, beautiful book that pulls together everything you need to produce great typography.

—FRANK ROMANO
Roger K. Fawcett Professor
Rochester Institute of Technology
School of Print Media

Contents at a Glance

Foreword vii
Introduction xxi

PART ONE Typographic Basics

1   The State of the Art and How We Got Here 3
2   Units of Typographic Measurement 21
3   About Typefaces 29
4   About Fonts 49
5   The Basics of Using Typefaces 67
6   Typesetting versus Typewriting 79
7   Setting Type on a Personal Computer 89
8   What Makes Good Type Good (and Bad Type Bad) 103

PART TWO How to Set Type

9   Measure, Point Size, and Leading 115
10 Controlling Hyphenation and Justification 133
11 Kerning and Tracking 165
12 Managing Indention and Alignment 177
13 Special Characters and Special Situations 195
14 Document Structures and Typographic Conventions 215
15 Tables 237
16 Language-Specific Issues 259
17 Typesetting with Style Sheets 271
18 Output-Resolution Issues 281

PART THREE References

Glossary 293
Index 325
Further Reading 361

Table of Contents

Foreword vii

Introduction xxi

PART ONE Typographic Basics

1   The State of the Art and How We Got Here 3

The Building Blocks of Type 3
    Bounding Boxes and Spaces 5
    Type Design as a Function of Size 5
Evolution and Automation 6
    The Typewriter: The First Desktop Publishing Tool 7
        Escapement • Monospaced Type • Proportional Type
    Monotype: Counting Character Widths 9
    The Changing Definition of *Font* 10
        Photographic Fonts • Electronic Fonts
Desktop Publishing Alters the Rules 13
    The PostScript Model 13
        Raster Image Processing • Device Independence
        PostScript Fonts • Imaging PostScript Fonts
Output Resolution and Type Quality 16
    The Dark Side of WYSIWYG 17
        Near WYSIWYG
    The Shadow of the Word Processor 19

2   Units of Typographic Measurement 21

Absolute Measurements 21
    Uses for Picas and Points 22
        The Definition of *Point Size* • Notation Conventions
    Use of English and Metric Units 24

Relative Units 24
    The Em 24
        Em-based Character Widths • Em-based White-Space Adjustments
        Em-based Spacing Units • The Word Space
Other Units of Measure 27
    Ciceros 27
    Agates 27

3   About Typefaces 29

Definitions: *Font* versus *Typeface* 29
Type Design and the Em Square 30
    The Baseline 30
    x-Height 32
Type Anatomy 32
    Calligraphic Influences 32
    Serifs 33
        Bracketed Serifs • Unbracketed Serifs • Slab Serifs
        Hairline Serifs • Wedge Serifs
    Ascenders and Descenders 36
    Vestigial Features: Ink Wells 36
Optical Aspects of Typeface Design 37
Size Changes Everything 37
    Master Character Designs 38
        Multiple Master Fonts
Principal Features of Typefaces 40
    Seriffed and Sans Serif 40
    Variations in Typeface Weight 41
        Degrees of Boldness
    Romans and Italics 42
        Obliques
    Variations in Typeface Width 43
    Typeface Families 43
Typefaces as Role Players: Text, Display, and Decorative 44
    Nonalphabetic Fonts 44
Classifying Typefaces by Historical Period 45
    Old-Style Typefaces 45
    Transitional Typefaces 46
    Modern Typefaces 46
Typeface-Naming Issues 47

4   About Fonts 49

The Two Basic Kinds of Fonts: Outline and Bitmapped 49

What's in a Font? 51

  Font Formats 52
        PostScript Fonts • TrueType Fonts • OpenType Fonts

Cross-Platform Font-Compatibility Issues 54

  Character-Set Issues 55

  ASCII and Unicode 55

  Font-Encoding Issues 56
        The Mac's "Borrowed Characters"

Finding the Characters You Need 57

  Using Windows' Character Map 57

  Using the Macintosh's Key Caps 58
        The Mac os and Unicode

  "Expert Sets" and Alternate Fonts 59

  Characters outside the Unicode Standard 60

Identifying Font Formats 61

  Identifying the Formats of Macintosh Fonts 62

  Identifying the Formats of Windows Fonts 62

The Basics of Font Management 64

Font-Editing Programs 64

5   The Basics of Using Typefaces 67

Readability 67

Traditional Roles for Seriffed and Sans Serif Types 68

  Common Features of Text Faces 69

Expressing Emphasis 71

  Uses for Bold and Other Type Weights 71

  Uses for Italics 72

Uses for Condensed and Extended Faces 73

  Problems with Electronic Expanding and Condensing 73

Using Display Type 74

Using Decorative Type 75

Type in Color 75

Reverses 76

6   Typesetting versus Typewriting 79

Page Sizes and Line Lengths 79
Word Spaces 80
Line Endings and Carriage Returns 81
   Quads 82
Typeface Choice and Point Size 83
   Forms of Emphasis and Highlighting 84
Unavailable Characters 85
   Hyphens and Dashes 85
   Quotation Marks 86
      Primes
   Fractions 86
Tabs 87

7   Setting Type on a Personal Computer 89

Typesetting and the Word Processing Legacy 89
   Assigning Typographic Attributes 90
      The Problem with "Selections"
How WYSIWYG Works 91
   Bitmapped Fonts for Screen Display 92
      PostScript Screen Type and ATM • Type and the "Style" Menu
      Screen Rendering When Fonts Are Missing • TrueType-based Screen Type
How Operating Systems Manage Fonts 95
   Problem: Corrupted Fonts 96
   Problem: Missing Fonts 97
   Problem: Duplicate Fonts 98
   Problem: Duplicate Font Numbers 99
Font Embedding 99
   Embedded Subsets of Fonts 100
Font Copyright Issues 100

8   What Makes Good Type Good
    (and Bad Type Bad) 103

Legibility and Readability 103
Type Color 104
   Overly Tight Spacing 105
   Overly Loose Spacing 107
   Unbalanced Spacing 107

Long Lines and Tight Leading 109

Narrow-Measure Problems 109

Optical Effects and Alignment Problems 110

The Eyes Have It 111

PART TWO   How to Set Type

9   Measure, Point Size, and Leading 115

Line Length, or Measure 115

Point Size and Measure 120

Leading 120

Automatic Leading 122

Leading in Text Frames 123

Changing Leading as Type Size Changes 124
Line Spaces and Space Bands

The "Baseline Shift" 126

Leading in Reversed Type 127

Asymmetrical Leading in Display Type 127

Leading in Non-text Settings 128

Leading Considerations in Multicolumn Settings 128

Typeface-Specific Considerations 128

Seriffed Typefaces, Point Sizes, and Measures 129
The Effect of x-Height • The Effect of Character Width
The Effect of Stroke Weight

Sans Serif Typefaces, Point Size, and Measure 131

Typefaces and Leading 131

10   Controlling Hyphenation and Justification 133

What *Hyphenation and Justification* Means 133

How H&J Works 134
Character-by-Character Calculations

Problems with Line-at-a-Time H&J 137

Hyphenating and Justifying a Range of Lines 137
Defining a Range for Multiline H&J

Line-Break Points 139

Controlling Word and Letter Spaces 140

Controlling Hyphenation 141
    Hyphenation Zones • Choosing a Means of Hyphenation • Kinds of Hyphens
    Hyphenation Style • Adding to the Hyphenation Dictionary
How Measure Affects H&J 145
Specifying Word-Space Ranges in Ragged-Margin Type 145
Specifying Word-Space Ranges in Text with Justified Margins 146
Specifying Letter-Space Ranges 150
    Letterspacing and Forced Justification 151
        Letterspacing Tricks and Problems
Altering Character Widths during H&J 152
Testing Your H&J Values 154
    About Program Defaults 154
Fixing and Avoiding Composition Problems 154
    Loose Lines/Tight Lines 154
        Tweaking the Hyphenation • Tweaking the Spacing
    Paragraph Color Problems 156
    Widows and Orphans 157
        Rescuing Widows • Helping Orphans
    Vertical Justification 159
        Frame-at-a-Time Vertical Justification
    Rivers 161
Aesthetic Rags 162

11   Kerning and Tracking 165

Definitions: *Kerning* and *Tracking* 165
Kerning in Practice 166
    Manual Kerning 168
        Manual Kerning Strategies • Kerning Italic-Roman Character Combinations
    Algorithmic Kerning 170
    Creating Custom Kerning Tables 170
        Kerning Numerals
Using Tracking Controls 172
    Special Tracking Situations 173
        Character Spacing and Script Faces
    Text on Curved Baselines 175

12   Managing Indention and Alignment 177

Kinds of Indents 177
    Indents as Paragraph Attributes 178
    Running Indents 179
        Orphans and Running Indents
    First-Line Indents 180
        First-Line Indents in Rag-Left Text • Sidestepping First-Line Indents
    Hanging Indents 182
    Indents on a Point or Character 183
Skews and Wraps 183
    Setting Skews 183
    The Basics of Setting Wraps 184
        Rectangular Wraps • Wrapping Irregular Shapes
Alignments of Characters and Text Blocks 188
    Page and Baseline Grids 188
        Text Frames and Grid Alignment
    Vertical Alignment: Top, Center, and Bottom 189
        Top Alignment • Center Alignment • Bottom Alignment
    Hanging Characters 191
Visual Alignment 191
    Troublesome Alignments with Ragged Margins 191
        Problems with Centered Text
    Aligning Oversized Characters 193

13   Special Characters and Special Situations 195

Extended Character Sets 195
Small Capitals 197
    Uses for Small Caps 198
Old-Style Numbers 198
Ligatures, Logotypes, and Diphthongs 199
    Automatic Ligature Substitution 200
    Ligatures in Display Type 201
Swash Characters 201
Superiors, Inferiors, and Ordinals 201
Fractions 202
    Building Fractions by Hand 203
    Fraction Form 204
Dashes 204

Points of Ellipsis 205
    Points of Ellipsis and Line Breaks 206
Common Pi Characters 207
    Hard-to-Find Characters 207
        Primes • Minus and Multiplication Signs
Accented Characters 208
    The Dotless *i* 209
Character-Specific Spacing Issues 209
Initial Capitals 210
    Drop Caps 211
        Difficult Drop-Cap Characters • Readability Issues with Drop Caps
    Standing Initial Caps 212

**14 Document Structures
and Typographic Conventions** 215

Structural Elements 215
    Chapter Headings 217
    Subheadings 217
        Subhead Spacing Issues • Subhead Indention • Cut-In Subheads
    Extracts 221
    Outline Formats and Tables of Contents 221
        Outline Form • Table-of-Contents Form
Navigation Tools 224
    Page Numbers, or Folios 224
    Running Heads 225
    Jump Lines 226
        End Marks
Independent Text Units 227
    Captions and Legends 227
    Footnotes and Endnotes 228
        Footnote Point Size and Leading • Footnote Alignment • Footnote Symbols
Indexes 231
    Index Typefaces and Point Sizes 232
    Index Indention Styles 232
        Run-In Index Style • Indented Index Style
    Page-Break Issues in Indexes 233
Bibliographies 234

15 Tables 237

The Structure of Tables 237
    How Table Structures Are Specified 239
        Problems with the Spreadsheet Table Metaphor
    Typeface, Point Size, and Leading Specifications 243
    Alignments in Tables 244
        Indention in Tab Entries
    Rules in Tables 244
Table-Setting Techniques 245
    Balancing Column Widths and Gutters 246
    Leading in Tables 247
        Leading of Rules • Centering Text between Rules
    Aligning Heads and Tab Entries 250
    Alignment Issues in Numeric Tables 252
        Hanging Characters in Numeric Tables
        Aligning Currency Symbols in Tables
    Void or "Missing" Entries 255
Faking It 256

16 Language-Specific Issues 259

Character Sets 259
Hyphenation 260
Time Expressions 260
Currency Symbols 261
British English versus American English 262
    American and British Quotation Styles 262
    American and British Abbreviation Styles . , , ... 263
    American and British Temperatures 263
French Typographic Conventions 263
    French Punctuation Style 263
        French Quotation Style • French Punctuation Spacing
    French Accents 265
    French Capitalization 265
    French Numeric Expressions 266
Spanish Typographic Conventions 266
Italian Typographic Conventions 267
German Typographic Conventions 267

17   Typesetting with Style Sheets 271

How Style Sheets Work 271
    Printing Style Sheets 272
    Paragraph versus Character Styles 273
        Follow-On Paragraph Styles
Creating Style Sheets 274
    Parent-Child Style Sheets 274
    Creating Style Sheets from Existing Text 274
Using Style Sheets 277
    Removing Style Sheets 277
    Setting Overrides 278
        Using Style Sheets to Create Overrides
    Searching and Replacing Styles 278
    Paragraph Style Sheets and Document Structures 279
    Importing Style Sheets 279

18   Output-Resolution Issues 281

The Advantages of High-Resolution Output 281
    Factors That Influence Print-Type Clarity 283
    Adapting to Low Print Resolutions 283
        Avoid Small Point Sizes • Avoid Reverses and Type over Backgrounds
        Avoid Angled Type at Text Sizes and Below
Type Onscreen 284
    Typefaces for Screen Display 285
    Other Onscreen Legibility Enhancements 286
Typography and the World Wide Web 287
    The Promise of Cascading Style Sheets 288
        What Cascading Style Sheets Can Do

PART THREE   References

Glossary 293
Index 325
Further Reading 361

Introduction

This book is about how type should look and how to make it look that way; in other words, how to set type like a professional. It primarily covers type in print, although people who read on computers need all the typographic help they can get, so setting type for screen display also gets its due.

The book is organized so that you can approach it in two ways: as a textbook to read from cover to cover, or as a reference guide to jump into at any point as need dictates. It has a wonderful index.

This is not a style guide, but an execution guide. It doesn't explain why you might choose to use the typeface Bembo over Garamond, but rather, having made that choice, how you can set Bembo in the best possible way. Good design hinges on well-set type.

The rules of typography are centuries old, and although the technologies have changed, the goal has always remained the same: beautiful settings in the service of a pleasant and fruitful reading experience. So while this book explains in very practical terms how to use today's computerized tools, I've written it to outlast them. References to specific programs have been kept to a minimum (although the capabilities of all the major programs have been taken into account). Programs change, but the lessons in this book will be just as applicable to version 20.0 of your software as they are to the version you use today.

Not all of the capabilities discussed in this book exist in every program or system. But none of them are fantasies—they all exist somewhere. Every typographer and typesetter has to hope that they all will converge in one program as soon as possible. In the meantime, I've included scores of workarounds to wring good type out of uncooperative programs.

Beautiful type comes from attention to myriad tiny details. It's built up a fraction of an em at a time, through hundreds of decisions whose geometry belies their gravity. It requires, as a colleague once wrote, a heart hardened against accusations of being too fussy.

—JAMES FELICI

PART ONE Typographic Basics

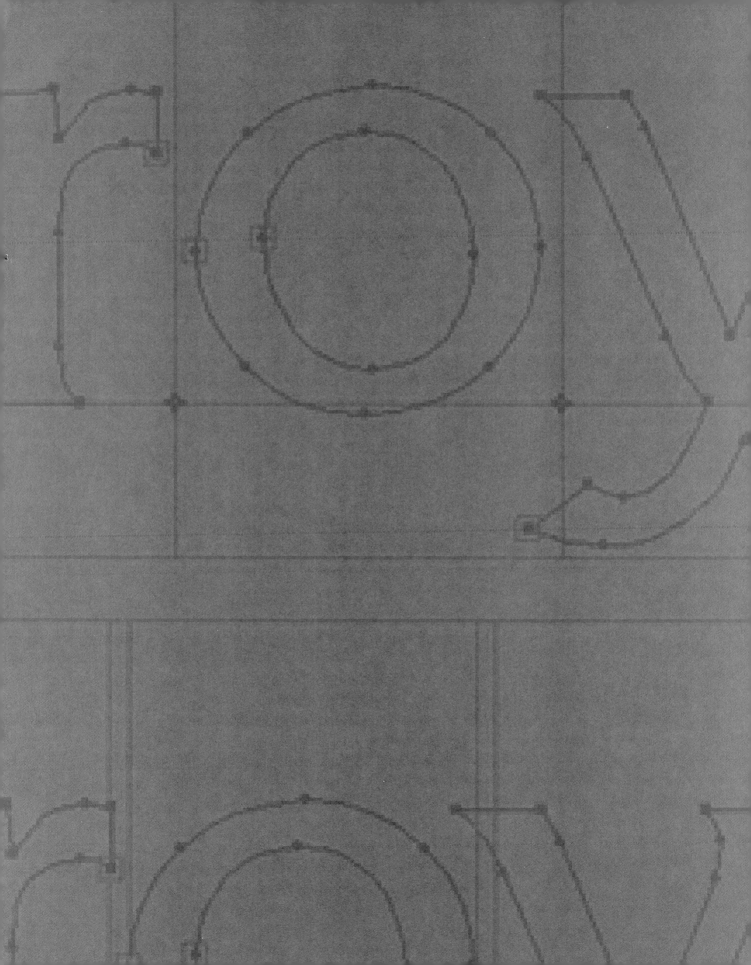

CHAPTER 1

The State of the Art and How We Got Here

THE BUILDING BLOCKS OF TYPE

EVOLUTION AND AUTOMATION

MONOSPACED AND PROPORTIONAL TYPE

THE CHANGING DEFINITION OF "FONT"

THE POSTSCRIPT MODEL

OUTPUT RESOLUTION AND TYPE QUALITY

The way we set type today—and the language we use to talk about the process—comprise a hodgepodge of technologies, techniques, and influences that have accumulated for more than 500 years, ever since Johannes Gutenberg developed his printing system based on the notion of movable type. A surprising number of his innovations and refinements are still at work behind the curtains of today's slick computerized typesetting systems (as well as the most modest of word processors). You can't talk about type without using words that have roots in German, French, and Italian.

And despite typesetting's evolution over the years, most of its fundamental concepts can be understood best by looking at how Gutenberg figured out how to set type. This chapter explains the essentials of typesetting in the historical settings that spawned them.

The Building Blocks of Type

The basic idea of movable type is that every letter of the alphabet, every punctuation mark, and every numeral and symbol is molded in high relief on its own metal block. These blocks are set in rows to form lines of text, and the raised

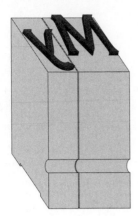

The State of the Art
and How We Got Here

FIGURE 1.1 Gutenberg's system of movable type was based on the casting of each character on its own metal block. Of the blocks' dimensions, only the widths varied to accommodate each character. Word spaces were created with shorter blocks that didn't come up to the level at which the printing blocks were inked. The "nick" on the front of each block is an orientation aid, helping the hand typesetter to quickly distinguish, for example, between a *d* and an upside-down *p*.

shapes of the letters get inked and pressed onto paper. The common rubber stamp uses the same principle, but the type isn't movable.

Credit for inventing movable type probably belongs to the Koreans, who, centuries before Gutenberg, were printing with reusable type blocks made from ceramic. Gutenberg's genius was to work the concept into a complete typesetting and printing system (combining a press design borrowed from winemakers with metal-casting techniques borrowed from jewelers). The fundamental element was standardizing the dimensions and manufacture of those little printing blocks (Figure 1.1).

To set type using Gutenberg's technique, the blocks—cast from a lead alloy—were arranged in rows, as shown schematically in Figure 1.2. (To be printed correctly, the images of the characters were reversed and had to be set in lines reading from right to left—one aspect of the old system that fortunately has been left behind.) Those rows of letter blocks—lines of type—were stacked one below the other to form a page, and then the whole rectangular mass was locked in place by a frame that pressed in on all sides. To add space between the lines, thin strips of metal were inserted between the rows, a process called *adding lead*. Today the term *leading* is still used to describe the distance between one line of type and the one above or below it.

Just as important as the printing blocks in this scheme were the nonprinting blocks, whose job it was to secure the positions of the others. These "blanks" were used, for example, to form indents and to fill out incomplete lines like those at the end of a paragraph.

Although this system of setting type was later automated and eventually computerized—replacing the metal printing blocks altogether—the concepts of letter blocks and spacing blocks persist in digital typesetting. They are, in fact, the keystones of the entire system.

FIGURE 1.2 This schematic view of a body of handset metal type makes visible what's going on behind the scenes in a modern computerized typesetting system. Rows of characters are stacked as lines of text, and the ends of the lines (as well as indents) are filled out with spaces. In handset type, the spaces are necessary for the type to be "locked up," held in place in a tight rectangle so that the block can be moved around as a unit and printed without individual characters moving around.

Bounding Boxes and Spaces

Within a computerized typesetting system, every character and symbol is conceived of as existing in a box whose dimensions are analogous to the surface of those old metal printing blocks (Figure 1.3). Just as in Gutenberg's day, this *bounding box* defines the space each letter takes up on a printed page. The space between the character image itself and the edge of the bounding box—called the *side bearing*—defines how far that character's image will be from the image of a character set next to it. Likewise, the upper and lower limits of the bounding box define where the lines of type above and below it will be set.

The big difference between metal type and digital type, of course, is that bounding boxes—being virtual boundaries, not physical ones like the edges of a piece of metal type—can now be manipulated so that they overlap (Figure 1.4). Typesetters in the digital age can position every character with infinite freedom and control. This is much easier than hacking at tiny metal blocks with a file to change their shapes and alter their spacing relative to their neighbors.

Like handset type, digital type must also take into account spaces within and between lines, such as paragraph indents or the extra space between a headline and the text below it. Although those areas appear blank on the printed page, it's important to think of them as filled with spaces rather than as simple voids.

If there is an essential truism in typesetting, it is that a page contains no voids, only spaces between printed elements. The essence of typesetting is regulating the size of those spaces to control the balance and rhythm between black and white. This is the key to a graphically harmonious page—one with good *type color*—as well as to text that is pleasing and easy to read.

Type Design as a Function of Size

Gutenberg may have created a system for the reproduction of printed pages, but the visual system he was imitating—calligraphy—was already highly evolved. To meet the expectations of readers, Gutenberg and the printers that followed him were obliged to follow type design, book design, and calligraphic conventions very closely.

Calligraphers already knew, for example, that characters rendered in different sizes should be proportioned differently. Type in small sizes is more legible if the characters are somewhat wider and somewhat heavier. In large sizes, letters corresponding to the same design can be more finely modeled: thinner, lighter, and more nuanced (Figure 1.5). When various sizes are used together, such subtle design variations are not apparent and the design of the characters seems consistent throughout.

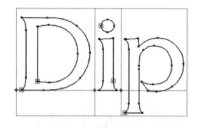

FIGURE 1.3 Seen from inside a font-editing program, character outlines appear in individual bounding boxes. The points along the outlines indicate where curves and line segments meet.

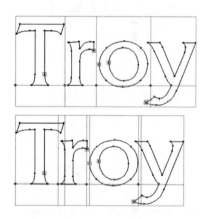

FIGURE 1.4 Drawn from within a font-editing program, this illustration shows (at top) how characters fit together when typed without adjustments to the spacing. When the spaces between characters have been adjusted to compensate for the shapes they present to their neighbors (bottom), you can see how the bounding boxes of the characters overlap.

In the top sample, you can see that the *y* in this typeface is a *kerning character;* that is, parts of it extend beyond its bounding box. Kerning characters are created this way to prevent unsightly gaps from appearing between them and the letters set next to them.

Master Master Master

FIGURE 1.5 These three samples represent the same typeface, but they've been created using different master designs. The one at the top is based on a design for small type—footnotes, for example—and of the three it clearly has the heaviest bulk and greatest width, features that make it more legible despite its small stature on the page. The middle sample is drawn from a master designed for text-sized type. The bottom sample is from a display-sized master, and its narrower width and lighter weight are specifically tailored for large sizes.

Because metal type foundries needed to create separate sets of printing blocks for every type size that printers wanted to use, it was easy enough for them to follow this calligraphic tradition. The practice continued into the latter half of the twentieth century, when ironically, technological progress threatened this highly sophisticated system. First by means of photographic lenses and later through mathematical scaling, typesetting technologists discovered techniques by which a single type design could be shrunk or enlarged to a range of sizes. A single *master* image, then, could generate type for footnotes as well as newspaper headlines.

Vendors of typesetting systems were happy they didn't have to design type over and over for every size they wanted to produce, but it was a setback for the quality of printed material. When all sizes of type were produced from a single master (usually a size designed for standard book-text use), small type became pinched looking and hard to read, and large type looked bulky and sprawling. As a result, wholly separate typesetting systems came to be used for text-sized type and for larger *display* type. Technological solutions to these problems are only starting to appear (see "Multiple Master Fonts," in Chapter 3).

Evolution and Automation

The ink wasn't dry on Gutenberg's Bible before imitators came up with similar typesetting and printing systems. Type styles proliferated and popular styles were mercilessly plagiarized (another typographical tradition still honored today). There were no universal standards for the proportions or dimensions of the type blocks used to set type.

For almost 400 years, though, the processes of typesetting and printing very much resembled those practiced by Gutenberg. Type was set letter by letter, and after a print run the type was dumped in a pile to be sorted and redistributed into its cases by a host of sorry apprentices. Those poor souls had to unfailingly differentiate *1*s from *l*s and *0*s from *O*s, judging by the reversed images on tiny lead blocks whose faces were typically no larger than a match head. Each cabinet where the type was stored had multiple drawers, or cases; capital letters—*majuscules*—were put in the *upper case,* and the small, *minuscule,* letters were put in the *lower case.* Woe betide the poor worker who sorted more slowly than his boss set type, leaving his master angry and *out of sorts.*

The latter half of the nineteenth century saw three major developments that changed the shape of how type was set. Within a decade the Linotype and Monotype machines had sounded the death knell for large-scale commercially handset type.

6-point type, 6-point master

If it had been intended to leave it in the discretion of the legislature to apportion the judicial power between the supreme and inferior courts according to the will of that body, it would certainly have been useless to have proceeded further than to have defined the judicial power and the tribunals in which it should be vested. The subsequent part of the section is mere surplusage—is entirely without meaning—if such is to be the construction. If Congress remains at liberty to give this court appellate jurisdiction, where the Constitution has declared their jurisdiction will be original, and original jurisdiction where the Constitution

6-point type, 11-point master

If it had been intended to leave it in the discretion of the legislature to apportion the judicial power between the supreme and inferior courts according to the will of that body, it would certainly have been useless to have proceeded further than to have defined the judicial power and the tribunals in which it should be vested. The subsequent part of the section is mere surplusage—is entirely without meaning—if such is to be the construction. If Congress remains at liberty to give this court appellate jurisdiction, where the Constitution has declared their jurisdiction will be original, and original jurisdiction where the Constitution has declared it shall be appellate, the

8-point type, 6-point master

If it had been intended to leave it in the discretion of the legislature to apportion the judicial power between the supreme and inferior courts according to the will of that body, it would certainly have been useless to have proceeded further than to have defined the judicial power and the tribunals in which it should be vested. The subsequent part of the section

8-point type, 11-point master

If it had been intended to leave it in the discretion of the legislature to apportion the judicial power between the supreme and inferior courts according to the will of that body, it would certainly have been useless to have proceeded further than to have defined the judicial power and the tribunals in which it should be vested. The subsequent part of the section is mere surplusage—is entire-

The Typewriter: The First Desktop Publishing Tool

The first of those innovations was the Remington typewriter. It incorporated several concepts that are key to modern typesetting systems, and it paved the way for what could be called "office typesetting," which evolved into computerized word processing.

ESCAPEMENT

A primary feature of the typewriter is the movement of the printing element relative to the paper it's printing on. In virtually all manual typewriters the carriage bearing the paper moves from side to side, and the printing element is stationary. In electronic typewriters, it's usually the printing head that moves.

The principle of such movement—called *escapement*—is applied in virtually every typesetting technology. After a manual typewriter key is struck, the paper moves—escapes—relative to the print mechanism. This puts the paper in position to receive the next character. When you type on a computer, the same thing occurs: After the character you type appears onscreen, the cursor moves to the right a distance equivalent to the width of that character.

Although it's no longer common practice in desktop typesetting programs, dedicated electronic typesetting systems routinely suspended the escapement motion to allow one character to be superimposed on another. Accented characters, for example, were commonly set by imaging one letter but suspending its normal escapement until another character—the accent—had been imaged on top of it. Then the escapement due the letter would be applied and normal typesetting would continue.

FIGURE 1.6 The left-hand samples above show type generated from a master design for small sizes. Compared with the samples on the right (based on a design for normal text-sized type), the small-master type is darker, it looks somewhat larger, and it sets wider, which you can see by comparing the line endings. The darker color of the small-master type will also blend better with that of other type on the page. Ultimately, type generated from the appropriate master designs will be easier to read than type—like that on the right—scaled out of its optimal size range.

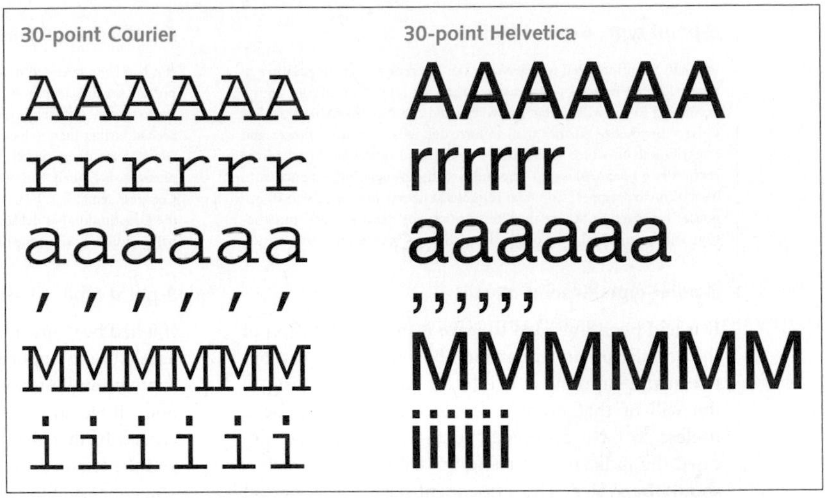

FIGURE 1.7 In monospaced type-faces such as Courier, all characters take up the same amount of horizontal space on the line. Monospacing can be achieved through exaggerated side bearings (the white spaces flanking each character), as it is in the commas shown here, or by distortions in the character shapes themselves to make them fit the one-size-fits-all scheme. Proportionally spaced typefaces, such as Helvetica, allow characters to take on their "natural" proportions and widths.

30-point Courier   30-point Helvetica

MONOSPACED TYPE

The letters of the Latin alphabet (on which most European languages are based) have varying widths. The diverse shapes and widths of these letters, in fact, are a major reason why the practice of typography is so complex. These shapes have evolved over millennia to become part of the enormously subtle and sophisticated visual system of reading. They were not designed with typesetting in mind, and efforts to modernize the alphabet to make its character shapes more mechanically apt or more stylistically consistent have generally been resounding flops.

Typewriters, though, are crude devices (especially that first 1879 model), and it was impractical to design one that could have a unique escapement for every letter of the alphabet. So instead of adapting the machine to the alphabet, typewriter manufacturers adapted the alphabet to the typewriter, and *monospaced* type was born.

In a monospaced typeface, all the characters have the same width, so the typesetting machine (whatever it is) accords them all the same escapement. No matter which letter you type, the typewriter carriage moves the same distance. The common computer typeface Courier is in fact a typewriter typeface, and all its characters have the same width (Figure 1.7). In these monospaced types, where it was impractical to make the printed letterforms the same width, narrower ones—such as *l, i,* and punctuation—were given exaggerated features and side bearings so that the escapement was appropriate. Normally wider characters—*M,W, O*—had to be squeezed onto that same Procrustean bed.

Although monospaced fonts distort the natural forms of characters, such typefaces do have practical roles. Monospaced types continue to be used in applications where it's desirable to have the characters in each line align in neat vertical rows, as in some computer program displays. In addition, the numbers in most typefaces have the same character width—you could call them a mono-spaced subset of the larger character set—so that numbers will align neatly in financial and numerical tables (Figure 1.8). When a computer typesetting system or printer can't image a particular typeface for some reason, it will often substitute the monospaced Courier, simply because Courier looks so different and so wrong that the error can't be overlooked. (In theory, anyway. If you start looking—particularly at ads—you'll often see Courier appearing in what are quite clearly erroneous but unnoticed substitutions.)

PROPORTIONAL TYPE

Monospacing was a dead end, but the idea of giving characters a limited number of specified numerical widths was appealing. Machine manufacturers still had to deal with the issue of escapement, but allowing every character to have a unique width would make for a very precise and complicated machine. Inventors of early typesetting systems tried dividing the characters in a typeface into a fixed number of categories, sorted by width. The narrowest ones would go in one group, the widest in another, and the rest in steps in between. If there were five such categories, the widths of the characters could be expressed as being from one to five units. In this scheme, all the characters would be designed to fit one of five widths, and the typesetting machine would translate those widths into one of five corresponding escapements. But to shoehorn all the characters of a typeface into such a small number of widths still meant distorting their designs. To make better *proportionally spaced type*—that is, type that copied historical, handset models—the number of width categories had to be increased. This was what the Monotype and Linotype systems did.

Monotype: Counting Character Widths

The Monotype machine was an automated type foundry, which from a cauldron of hot metal cast individual letter blocks one at a time (at surprising speed) and spit them out into composed lines, just as if they had been set by hand. It could compose whole pages this way—starting from the bottom up—stacking one line upon another, eliminating huge amounts of handwork. When the job was done, the type was melted down and recycled—no more sorting.

A principal Monotype innovation was to allow someone working on a keyboard to record keystrokes and formatting commands—line length, indents, etc.—on a punched paper tape. The tape was then used to drive the typecasting machine, the way a punched paper scroll drives a player piano.

The information recorded on the paper tape was essentially the same as that recorded by today's computer programs as you type into a word processor or

1,711,093,655
935,101,394
722,620
48,825,903

1,711,093,655
935,101,094
722,621
48,825,903

FIGURE 1.8 Most typefaces include *lining figures,* as shown at the top here. These are numerals that all have the same height and, most important, character width. They are, in effect, a monospaced subset of the characters within a typeface. This monospacing allows numbers in tables to align neatly in columns. As in all monospaced systems, there are some spacing problems, and the *1* usually appears to be set a little too loose.

The sample at the bottom is set with old-style figures (sometimes called *lowercase figures*), which in this example have unique character widths, making them less desirable for financial reports and tables, where the lack of vertical alignment can create a disorganized impression.

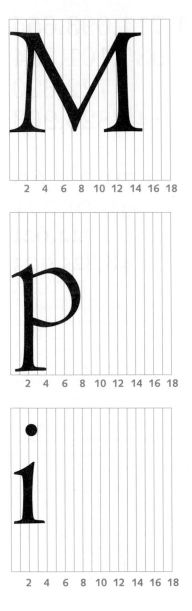

FIGURE 1.9 In the 18-unit character-width scheme used by Monotype casting systems, every character had to fit within one of the prescribed width categories. In this representation, the *M* on the top is 15 units wide, the *p* is 8 units wide, and the *i* only 4 units wide.

page layout program. First, it recorded the width of every letter typed—the escapement, as it were—adding those widths together until their sum approached the specified length of the line being set. At the end of each line, the operator had to decide what to do with any small amount of space left over: leave it at the end of the line (as on a typewriter) or distribute it evenly between the words of the line, spreading the line to its maximum allowable length. (This process, called *justification,* is discussed in detail in Chapter 10.)

To accomplish this separation of input and output, every typeface for the Monotype system had to be designed with a standard way of expressing the widths of its characters. These widths were expressed in units, with the widest characters—often the *M* and *W*—being 18 units wide, and narrower characters correspondingly fewer, as seen in Figures 1.9 and 1.10.

The Monotype tape, like a modern computer disk, was recording two things as the typist worked: what keystrokes and spaces were called for and how wide they should be. The principal difference in this regard between now and then is that the widths of modern typefaces are measured not in one of 18 possible widths, but one of a thousand or more. Contemporary typeset characters can thus adhere even more closely to their natural, historical proportions. Typeface designers no longer have to worry about aesthetic restrictions imposed by the limitations of a typesetting system.

The Linotype machine, which appeared about the same time, used a similar counting system but took a different tack. Instead of casting letters one by one, it assembled the molds for a line's worth of characters and cast them all at once in one piece—a line o' type. This *linecasting* machine was a "direct-input machine": keystrokes were translated directly into machine action, not recorded in advance for output later.

The Changing Definition of *Font*

In the days of handset type, a *font* (a term that comes from an early French word meaning "molding" or "casting") comprised one or more drawers full of type blocks in a single size. With the advent of the Monotype and Linotype machines, a font then became a set of molds (or *matrices*) from which type could be cast as it was needed, on the fly.

All of this type was destined for a specific kind of printing press, the *letterpress.* On a letterpress the printed impression is created by inking a raised surface (which can be a photographic image as well as type) whose image is transferred under pressure to the paper. Recessed areas—those below *type-high*—receive no ink, do not come into contact with the paper, and so create the "blank" areas of the page.

5	☐	☐	*l*	*t*	'	'	.	,	☐	l	i	]	[	'	☐
6	*j*	*f*	*i*	!	:	;	-	*j*	*f*	I	*!*	:	;	☐	☐
7	*c*	*r*	*s*	*e*	)	(	'	'	r	s	t	J	v	º	z
8	‡	*q*	*	*b*	*g*	*o*	?	I	z	c	e	z	s	†	?
9	*I*	☐	*9*	*7*	*5*	*3*	*1*	*0*	.	9	7	5	3	1	0
9	¢	☐	☐	*8*	*6*	*4*	*2*	*$*	-	$	8	6	4	2	☐
9	*x*	*k*	*y*	*d*	*h*	*a*	x	J	g	o	a	P	F	L	T
10	A	*fi*	*u*	*n*	.	S	v	y	p	u	n	Q	B	O	E
10	D	☐	*fl*	*p*	fi	fl	q	k	b	h	d	V	Y	G	R
11	H	&	*J*	*S*	œ	æ	*ff*	☐	Z	☐	ff	x	U	K	N
12	*O*	*L*	*C*	*F*	w	£	æ	L	P	F	¶	M	*Z*	*Q*	*G*
13	*E*	*&*	*Q*	*V*	*C*	*B*	*T*	*O*	*E*	*A*	w	*P*	*T*	*R*	*B*
14	*D*	*A*	*Y*	ffl	ffi	*m*	œ	Y	U	G	R	Œ	Æ	w	*V*
15	*K*	*N*	*H*	ffl	ffi	X	D	N	K	H	m	&	☐	*X*	*U*
18	Œ	Æ	¾	¼	½	*W*	*M*	—	...	M	W	%	Œ	Æ	☐

FIGURE 1.10 This schematic layout shows how a Monotype font (or matrix) arranged characters in categories according to their relative widths, indicated on the scale at the left. Most of them are 9 or 10 units wide. Although the character set in this illustration is correct, the widths of the characters shown (drawn from a modern digital font) are only approximate.

But by the middle of the twentieth century, offset lithography was becoming an increasingly popular printing medium because of its radically lower costs. Offset litho is essentially a photographic process in which the image of a page is projected onto a thin, flexible printing plate covered with a photographic emulsion. When this plate is "developed" like film, the printing areas take on a quality that repels water but allows ink to adhere. When the plate is mounted onto the rotating drums of a press, it is first wet with water and then smeared with ink. The oily ink is repelled by the wet parts of the plate (the blank parts of the page), but it adheres to the parts that form the printed image. The image is "offset"—printed, in effect—onto an intermediate roller, and that roller transfers the image in ink onto paper.

This double printing process may seem inefficient, but it has a very important consequence: It allows the image on the printing plate to be *right-reading*, just like the final page. On a letterpress, where ink is transferred directly to paper, the printing surface has to be a mirror image of the final page, just like a rubber stamp. That makes page composition much more complicated.

The development of offset lithography meant that printers no longer needed to stamp type physically to image it; all they needed was a photographic image of the type that could be transferred onto the printing plate. Metal type was pushed out of the picture. Phototypesetting was born.

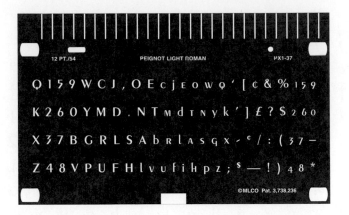

FIGURE 1.11 This is a life-size representation of a photographic film font used on a Mergenthaler VIP phototypesetter from the 1970s. Along with several other fonts, it was mounted on a drum that spun at high speed. A beam of light inside the drum was flashed through the appropriate character images as they whirled into position. The images were exposed onto photographic film.

PHOTOGRAPHIC FONTS

Early phototypesetting machines looked very much like Linotype and Monotype machines. But in place of the array of molds into which hot metal was poured for casting, these newer machines substituted small photographic negatives bearing the images of characters. A light shining through these negatives—one character after another—cast their images on photographic paper that, as on a typewriter, was advanced horizontally to build lines and then vertically to build pages or columns of type.

From a typesetting standpoint, the brilliant thing about photo type (quite apart from the absence of that cauldron of molten lead at your side all day) was that the type could be scaled to various sizes through a series of lenses. A range of type sizes could be generated from a single set of master images, a single font. Refinements in technology eventually reduced the size of these film fonts to a single negative of about 2 by 3 inches (Figure 1.11). But the type could still be enlarged only so far before it lost sharpness. Headline type, for example, had to be set on a machine equipped with much larger fonts.

ELECTRONIC FONTS

Efforts to improve the scaling of photographic fonts led in the 1950s to experiments with cathode-ray tubes (like those in TVs and computer monitors) to sharpen the images of type. Although that effort fizzled, by the 1960s a variety of typesetting machines appeared that could image type directly from a CRT onto photographic film. Images of the characters were not generated by photographs of letters; instead, mathematical formulas electronically generated the images on the screen. These were the first electronic fonts.

The most successful approach was to describe the outlines of characters, which were then filled in onscreen. But in those early days, most of the outlines were described as large numbers of straight lines and the simplest of curves.

Setting large type was still a problem, as parts of letters were marred by noticeable flat areas and facets. This scalable outline technology, though, has been refined, and it is now the standard on all typesetting systems (Figure 1.12).

Desktop Publishing Alters the Rules

In the early 1980s a sudden series of technological changes revolutionized typesetting. First, desktop computers appeared that had enough memory and computing power to do the same work as those running dedicated typesetting systems, but at a fraction of the price. (A typical minicomputer for a dedicated typesetting system had only 768 kilobytes of memory.) The first of those dedicated systems was "ported" to a desktop computer in 1985.

Second, laser printers appeared that could function as low-cost desktop typesetters. Similar laser technology was soon applied to high-resolution phototypesetters, replacing the CRT-based generation of machines. At this point—when the laser began imaging—these machines stopped being mere typesetting machines and became *imagesetters,* as adept at rendering artwork as type.

Third, desktop computer operating systems inspired by concepts created at the Xerox Palo Alto Research Center (PARC) started using the screen to give an accurate preview of the printed page. This feature, called WYSIWYG (what you see is what you get), meant among other things that someone could set type without having to learn a huge vocabulary of arcane formatting commands. If you could make it look pretty on the screen, it would look pretty on the page.

Fourth, and perhaps most important, was PostScript, a computer language designed to describe any printed "event" on a page. Developed by Adobe Systems, PostScript was one of many *page description languages* (PDLS) that appeared, but it was the most complete and the most promising, and—significantly—it had won commercial contracts with Apple Computer and Mergenthaler-Linotype, a leading manufacturer of high-end typesetting systems.

The PostScript Model

Probably the most notable aspect of PostScript—quite apart from the technology behind the language and all the things it could do—was that it was not linked to any specific computer or printer; nor was it linked to a particular operating system or other software. It was totally *device independent.* In theory, a page described in PostScript code (which could be written in universally readable ASCII format) could be created on any computer and imaged on any printer, any monitor screen, or any unforeseeable other imaging device. Any computer program could express itself in PostScript code.

FIGURE 1.12 The outline of a character in a digital font (represented on the left) is composed of a relatively small number of straight-line and curved paths, or vectors, as shown in the disassembled version of the outline on the right. The entire outline can be scaled to any size while preserving its original proportions.

FIGURE 1.13 In a raster device such as an imagesetter or computer monitor, characters are drawn by a beam sweeping across the "page," blinking on and off as it goes. In this illustration, the beam has already swept horizontally across the page many times, drawing a slice of the character during each successive pass.

PostScript described everything it could as a scalable, *vector-based* object. That is, it defined objects as outlines or paths—vectors—that users could resize at will and image at any resolution. Prior to PostScript, most computer graphics—as well as type—were *bitmaps,* images drawn dot for dot (each one represented by one *bit* of computer data) for a particular resolution. Under the new regime, type became just another kind of scalable graphic.

RASTER IMAGE PROCESSING

To convert a page description written in PostScript into a printed page, those PostScript commands had to be interpreted and expressed for a specific output device. Theoretically, this *PostScript interpreter* could be a software program running on a desktop computer. But because the computing process was so complex, the interpreter more often was (and still is) a "black box," a separate computer dedicated solely to translating PostScript commands into directions that told an output device—a laser printer, for example—how to image a page.

This black box is commonly called a *raster image processor,* or RIP. The name is based on old television-industry jargon. It refers to the way an image is created on a CRT screen, one horizontal line at a time, by a narrow beam that scans from side to side in so-called raster lines (*raster* comes from a Latin word meaning "rake"), as shown in Figure 1.13. These horizontal lines are drawn from top to bottom on the screen at very high speed.

The beam—a stream of electrons in a CRT, a laser beam in a laser printer or imagesetter—blinks on and off to create the dark and light spots you see onscreen or on a printed page. The fineness of the beam and the rate at which it can blink on and off as it travels determine the *resolution* of the device, that is, the number of apparent dots it can create per inch or centimeter.

The number of dots whose position a RIP has to calculate on each page is formidable. A page from a desktop laser printer with a resolution of 300 dots per inch (*dpi*) contains more than a million dots. At 600 dpi, the number shoots up to nearly 4 million. At even the low end of common imagesetter resolutions, that number soars to 16 million dots per page.

DEVICE INDEPENDENCE

Device independence of the kind PostScript offered was revolutionary. In the centuries after Gutenberg, any type you bought had to match the press equipment you were using. Until the late nineteenth century, there weren't even any commonly accepted standards for the basic units of typographic measurement. When the rise of photocomposition led to an explosion in the number of companies selling typesetting systems, each system vendor had its own proprietary font technology. Once you bought a system, you were obliged to buy that vendor's fonts, and they cost a fortune, often nearly as much as the hardware they worked with.

In addition, once a job was typeset on one system, it was wedded to that system forever, unless someone was willing to retype and reformat the entire thing. With very few exceptions, jobs created on one brand or model of typesetting system could not be used on another. It was no wonder that many publishers rushed to adopt a desktop publishing system—even with its more limited capabilities—just to be out from under the yoke of a single vendor and the cost of being locked in to a single proprietary technology. PostScript's promise of device-independent fonts was another irresistible siren call.

POSTSCRIPT FONTS

To make its device independence work, PostScript had to create a complete floating world of its own, free of proprietary technologies that kept existing systems incompatible with one another. Fonts were a key part of the equation; indeed, they proved to be one of the most complicated parts of the puzzle. Although its founders didn't foresee this development, Adobe soon became one of the leading font companies in the world.

PostScript fonts store the images of characters as outline drawings. The outlines are in turn built out of straight-line and curved segments. The curves—called *Bézier curves,* after the French automotive mathematician who discovered this compact way of describing complex curves—are the same as those used in popular drawing programs. When type of a certain size needs to be created, outlines for the characters are copied from the font, scaled to size by the RIP, and "colored in" (Figure 1.14) by the output device—usually a computer monitor, printer, or imagesetter—according to the resolution of the device.

IMAGING POSTSCRIPT FONTS

Determining which dots, or *pixels,* become part of this coloring-in is complicated. The PostScript interpreter looks at the whole page as a grid of pixels. The process by which character outlines are superimposed on that grid, and decisions made about which pixels are to be imaged, is called *grid fitting.*

At its simplest, grid fitting consists of laying the outline of a character over the grid at its appointed location (the one specified by the typesetting commands that describe the page) and coloring in those pixels whose centers fall on or within the outline. As shown in Figure 1.15, though, this doesn't always create perfect visual results, especially at lower resolutions (as on a computer monitor screen), where the eye can make out individual pixels and where even

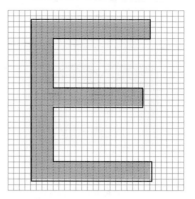

FIGURE 1.14 In this simplified illustration, a raster image processor lays the outline of a character over a grid representing all the possible pixels on a page and "colors in" those pixels whose centers fall within the outline. At this point, the imaged character is said to have been *rasterized.*

a single misplaced one can be distracting. In some cases, pixels may drop out, causing gaps in the bitmapped image. Sometimes subtly adjusting the position of the outline on the grid will create a more felicitous alignment of character form and pixels.

More often, the outline itself has to be reshaped to assure that appropriate pixels are turned on and the character shape is reproduced with maximum fidelity. To accomplish this, programming instructions popularly called *hints* are added to fonts. These improve the clarity and form of characters rendered with relatively small numbers of pixels, in situations where they're being set at small sizes or at modest resolutions.

From the outset, Adobe Systems had its own system of hinting for PostScript fonts, but it would not give that system away for free, as it did with other details of how to create PostScript fonts. Other font vendors could create PostScript-compatible fonts, but those fonts wouldn't look as good as Adobe's except at very high resolutions. Some elements of the computing and publishing communities felt abused by this arrangement, and eventually Apple and Microsoft collaborated to create a new outline font format, TrueType.

PostScript, TrueType, and a new fusion font format combining the two—OpenType—are discussed and compared in detail in Chapter 4.

Output Resolution and Type Quality

Images of contemporary digital type are composed of dots. On a computer monitor screen, with a resolution of 72 or 96 dpi, individual dots are big enough to see clearly. In this environment, it's very difficult to identify a particular typeface onscreen at common text sizes. There just aren't enough pixels available to draw a sufficiently detailed picture (Figure 1.16). To see type onscreen as clearly as it appears on the cheapest laser printer means zooming in to at least 300 percent magnification, at which point you don't get a good view of the page anymore.

As resolution increases, pixels become smaller, and the details and nuances of character shapes can be more clearly and accurately rendered. Equally important, at higher resolutions the crucial spaces between characters can be more rigorously controlled, resulting in far more legible and readable type. It's only above 1,000 dpi that you enter the realm of what's often called *typeset quality.*

But how the pixels are imaged is as important as their size. Photographic film is still the preferred substrate for commercial typesetting because the pixels imaged on it are exactly formed and crisply defined. The grains of the silver compounds that change color when the film is exposed are minute, so the images of the pixels are sharply focused and hard-edged. By comparison, type

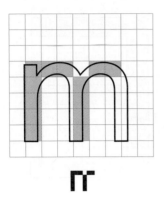

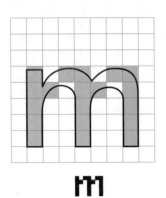

FIGURE 1.15 Character outlines rarely align as neatly on the grid as they do in Figure 1.14. Particularly at low resolutions (like the computer-screen resolution represented here), the outlines often fall at inconvenient locations. In the top grid, so few pixel centers fall within the outline that the character (shown as it would be imaged) is only half formed. For this reason, font engineers add instructions, or *hints,* to font coding that cause the outlines to change shape, assuring that the proper pixels are turned on, as shown in the lower grid.

FIGURE 1.16 Bodoni at three resolutions: Giambattista himself above, and the typeface that bears his name below. The more pixels available to image a photo or a typeset character, the clearer and more faithful the final representation will be. The three magnifications here could be likened to screen, desktop printer, and image-setter resolutions.

created by high-resolution inkjet or laser printers on plain paper (even though the paper may be coated to make it smoother) is not as crisp because neither of those technologies can make as hard-edged a dot. The dots may be small, but they tend to spread or have a fuzzy edge or halo.

To reduce the jaggedness of type produced at modest (sub-1,000 dpi) resolutions, some laser printers use a technology called *variable dot size.* By modulating the power of the laser, these printers can create smaller-than-normal dots. When these are positioned along the edges of characters, they fill in the apparent stairstep effect created by the visible pixels along curves and diagonals, thus giving the characters a smoother appearance, as though the text were set at a higher resolution.

The Dark Side of WYSIWYG

At the dawn of the desktop publishing revolution, the typographic and graphic arts establishments were rightly alarmed by the barbarians at the gates. The trench fighters of the revolution were largely untrained, and their weapons— rudimentary page layout programs with little more typographic capability than a word processor—could hardly be expected to maintain the quality standards of the *ancien régime.*

It has, in fact, taken a long time for typesetting tools to catch up with the "dinosaur" systems they replaced. (The computerized photographic and darkroom tools, by comparison, have long since outstripped their "old world" counterparts.) In several important ways the latest generation of digital typographic tools still lacks basic features that even low-end dedicated systems had, such as competent tools for setting tables.

Adobe Garamond

ITC New Baskerville

Linotype Bodoni

ITC Galliard

Monotype Janson

Palatino

Times Roman

Adobe Garamond

ITC New Baskerville

Linotype Bodoni

ITC Galliard

Monotype Janson

Palatino

Times Roman

Adobe Garamond

ITC New Baskerville

Linotype Bodoni

ITC Galliard

Monotype Janson

Palatino

Times Roman

FIGURE 1.17 Because of a poverty of pixels, screen type bears only a vague resemblance to the typeface it alleges to represent. The situation is particularly bad with black-and-white bitmaps, as shown on the left. It would be a challenge to identify any of these typefaces without some clues. The anti-aliased type on the right (bitmaps enhanced with gray pixels to modulate their hard edges) does a better job of representing the typefaces, but for typesetting purposes, it still provides an inadequate preview of how the type is being set.

Much of the blame for that inadequacy is directed toward the adoption of word processing standards in the page makeup programs that became the new typesetting systems. That there was no longer a seat for someone whose specialty was setting type—page makeup typically being the province of the graphic designer and pasteup artist—only complicated the problem.

Basically, for all their ease of use for beginners, menu-driven, mouse-based interfaces aren't ideal for typographic formatting. First, they're too slow. In the old code-driven systems, typographic formatting could be done at typing speeds, which is much faster than the point-and-click, drag-to-select technologies used in most of today's desktop programs. Second, many kinds of typographic controls are simply easier to apply with keystroked codes. For example, you can use a program's search-and-replace function to replace all the indents created with the Tab key with paragraph indents of a specified depth.

Nevertheless, with the exception of a few very high-end typesetting systems used by large publishers, the WYSIWYG menu-and-dialog-box interface is how type is now set. An unfortunate result is that typographic capabilities that don't fit well into this scheme have simply been left out of the toolbox.

NEAR WYSIWYG

Holding a typeset page next to its onscreen equivalent is ample evidence that What You Got is at best a close approximation of What You Saw when you created it. The low screen resolution makes an accurate preview impossible. At 100 percent magnification—that is, at real size—the finest increment by which you can adjust the spacing between characters is at least ten times coarser than the increments used by the typesetter that will image your page.

Likewise, the pixels that build the image of type onscreen are far too large to represent character shapes accurately. In Figure 1.17, any similarity between the bitmapped characters on the left and their high-resolution versions in the middle column might seem to be strictly coincidental. Even the *anti-aliased,* or *smoothed,* versions on the right (created by adding an aura of gray pixels to jagged edges) are crude and blurry approximations of the real thing.

As type size increases beyond text size, the renditions of the screen characters add pixels. At some point, the thin strokes of characters go from one pixel wide to two pixels wide. At such thresholds, distortion of the type becomes acutely visible: Type just below the threshold is clearly too light, and type just over the threshold is clearly too heavy. This effect is largely ameliorated by anti-aliasing, which offers visual gradations between simple one- and two-pixel stem weights (Figure 1.18). Anti-aliased type may be fatiguing to read because of its blurriness (your eyes are always trying to bring it into focus), but it's a boon for a more realistic screen preview.

For some typesetting operations—adjusting the spacing between two characters, for example—zooming in for a closer look effectively increases the resolution of the type as it becomes larger onscreen. This gives a much better view of the actual spatial relationships, one that more closely resembles what will be on the printed page. But at the same time, the view is deceptive because the type is large and the eye perceives the spacing of large type to be much looser than that of small type. In other words, zooming in gives you a good view of the trees, but you can't see the forest, and that's the view your readers will have.

The Shadow of the Word Processor

Competent page layout programs are becoming more typographically savvy, but their connections to word processing conventions still weigh on them. Many of these conventions are antithetical to traditional typesetting practice. Divorcing the two is complicated, though, especially because many publishing systems rely on commercial word processors for the editorial "front ends." This reliance would seem to assure word processing's continuing influence on typesetting and page composition. Ultimately, the problem is that word processing is a volume-oriented application, not a quality-oriented one. To be fair, word processing vendors did not pretend to be creating typesetting programs when they started out. They've been dumped into this position by default.

Fortunately, page layout application vendors are returning to type as an area in which they can add value to their products and differentiate themselves from their competitors. This book, then, will not dwell on what can't be done typographically, but on what should be done. Today's programs can—one way or another—do nearly everything a good dedicated typesetting system used to do, and I'm optimistic that the rest will follow in fairly short order, assuming the public continues to demand better.

Adding pixels to stem weights can cause anomalies.

Adding pixels to stem weights can cause anomalies.

Adding pixels to stem weights can cause anomalies.

Adding pixels to stem weights can cause anomalies.

FIGURE 1.18 At some point as screen type is being scaled up in size, its stem weight—the thickness of its vertical strokes—must go from one pixel to two. In the sample at the top, this threshold is passed when going from 17-point type (the first three lines) to 18-point. The difference is so gross that you'd never guess there was such a small difference in point size between the two. In the bottom sample, the effect has been ameliorated by anti-aliasing, or smoothing, as gray pixels obscure the thresholding effect.

CHAPTER 2

Units of Typographic Measurement

ABSOLUTE MEASUREMENTS: PICAS AND POINTS

RELATIVE UNITS: EM-BASED, WORD SPACE

OTHER UNITS OF MEASURE

Typesetting is a game of controlling spaces, so its tools are all keyed to precise measuring. Because of the intimate scale in which typographic adjustments are made, type's measurements have evolved independently of the coarser units used for other forms of artisanship or commerce. Although the metric system has made some inroads into popular typographic practice—especially in Europe—type's own unique measuring sticks are still the standard.

Absolute Measurements

The measurements you use every day—whether they're inches and feet or centimeters and meters—are *fixed,* or *absolute,* measurements. That is, an inch is always an inch and a meter is always a meter. Type has its own equivalents, which are *picas* and their subdivisions, *points.*

The modern point used as a standard today in almost all typesetting systems is relatively new, having been created by Adobe Systems in the course of developing the PostScript page description language (for more about PostScript, see pages 13–16). Although typographer's points had existed for centuries before that, no standard definition of exactly how wide a point was stuck until 1883, when the U.S. Type Founders Association came to the sage decision that a point should equal exactly .0138 inch, or round about ¹/₇₂ inch. This is the so-called

FIGURE 2.1 At the top, the three rulers demonstrate the advantage of using points and picas for measuring type: the fineness of their increments. They lack the decimal ease of calculating in millimeters, but they're far more useful than the English system, with its inches and nondecimal fractions.

Below, the two bars demonstrate the noticeable difference in the size of American and PostScript points and picas. When working with legacy documents, it's important to know whether or not they were created on PostScript-based systems.

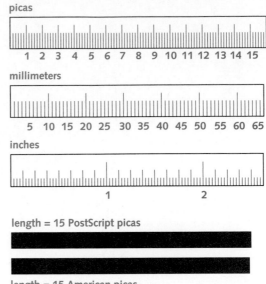

picas

1 2 3 4 5 6 7 8 9 10 11 12 13 14 15

millimeters

5 10 15 20 25 30 35 40 45 50 55 60 65

inches

1　　　　2

length = 15 PostScript picas

length = 15 American picas

American point. Adobe did everyone a favor by rounding that off to *exactly* ¹⁄₇₂ inch (the *PostScript point*), making possible a graceful translation between typographic and English measuring systems. No such handy conversion factor between points and the metric system exists (see Figure 2.1).

Because there are still millions of documents around that were designed using American points, it may sometimes be preferable to reset your typesetting program from PostScript points to American points. Programs that allow this change generally enable it in their Preferences settings.

A PostScript pica is composed of 12 points, which means that there are exactly 6 picas to the inch. How *pica* came to mean 12 points is hazy, but it's had that meaning for centuries. Apparently the Latin word for magpie—*pica*—became associated with the Roman Catholic church because its black-and-white coloration reminded people of the garb of priests and nuns. Somehow *pica* then became associated with certain church rules and regulations, and from there it was used as a name for a standard text-sized type. (Until the nineteenth century, types in various sizes were commonly given proper names—*English* and *St. Augustine,* for example—rather than numerical labels. Some of these names are shown in Figure 2.2.)

Uses for Picas and Points

In general, picas are used for measuring page dimensions and the dimensions of page elements. The widths of columns of type, for example, are typically expressed in picas (or picas and points), as are page margins and the locations of graphics or other elements on the page.

Smaller distances are measured in points alone. Paragraph indents, for example, are often expressed in points, even when they are more than a pica deep. An indent, then, is likely to be said to be 18 points deep rather than 1 pica and 6 points, or a pica and a half, deep. Line spacing—or *leading*—is also expressed solely in points, never picas.

The size of type is measured exclusively in points (and with the advent of computer systems, fractions of points), although in Europe millimeters are increasingly being used in this role. In general, though, the terms *point size* and *type size* are synonymous.

THE DEFINITION OF "POINT SIZE"

The definition of *point size* goes back to the days of handset type (described briefly at the beginning of Chapter 1). When each letter was cast on its own block, that block had to be slightly taller and usually slightly wider than the impression of the letter itself. This slight gap on all four sides prevented the printed images of letters from touching those above, alongside, or below them. The point size of the type was defined by the height of the blocks, from just above the *apex* of the tallest character to just below the limit of the lowest-reaching one (Figure 2.3). When fonts went digital, the point size of the type became the height of the bounding box that surrounded each letter. (For more on bounding boxes, see page 5.)

NOTATION CONVENTIONS

For measurements in picas and points, a false decimal point is often used. The measurement "6 picas, 11 points," then, is often written "6.11 picas" or simply "6.11 p." For fear of confusing newcomers to typesetting, computer programs have often created syntaxes of their own to get around the false decimal point, using such constructions as "6p11" to mean "6 picas, 11 points." Because computerized type systems have allowed modern typesetters to subdivide points in ways unimaginable to metal typesetters, this newer locution makes it easier to describe fractions of a point, using true decimal expressions. For example, "6p11.5" means "6 picas and 11 ½ points."

Sometimes the equals sign is used as a symbol for picas, so 24 picas may be written "24=."

When expressing measurements in points, the word is commonly either spelled out—"12-point type"—or represented by a single prime: "12′ type."

Pearl [5′]
Agate [5½′]
Nonpareil [6′]
Minion [7′]
Brevier [8′]
Bourgeois [9′]
Long Primer [10′]
Small Pica [11′]
Pica [12′]
English [14′]
Great Primer [18′]

FIGURE 2.2 Listed here are the names for some of the common sizes used by English-speaking typesetters (although some of the names are French). Before trying to impress your colleagues, remember that most of these names predate current standards, so the point-size equivalents here are in some cases only approximate.

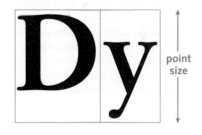

FIGURE 2.3 The point size of type is measured the same way in both metal type and digital type. The rectangles shown here could represent the faces of two metal printing blocks or they could represent the bounding boxes used by digital fonts to define the space that characters take up on the page.

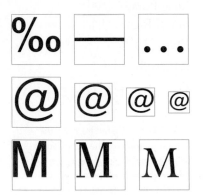

FIGURE 2.4 In ITC Friz Quadrata these four symbols—the per-thousand sign, the em dash, points of ellipsis, and the at sign—are all a full em wide. The four sizes of the at sign show that despite changes in point size, the character always has the same 1-em width. Its absolute width changes, but its width relative to the em square is constant. The *M*s in the bottom row (each shown within an em square corresponding to its typeface and point size) illustrate that the width of an em has nothing to do with the width of an *M*.

Use of English and Metric Units

It's common for English and metric measurements to be used for certain page dimensions, especially the *trim size* of a page (the size of a book or magazine page after it has been cut down to final size after binding). For measuring distances within a page, though, the English system is seldom used, mainly because its basic unit—the inch—is too coarse, and using fractions of an inch is too much work. Although using decimal inches is a common typesetting program option, it's a bit confusing, since rulers and the English measuring tradition have always relied on halves, quarters, eighths, and sixteenths, rather than their decimal equivalents (which often run to three decimal places). The metric system is more commonly used for expressing page dimensions, not only because its units are finer, but also because its reliance on the decimal system makes it far more compatible with the ways computers measure things.

Relative Units

Relative units have no fixed value in terms of absolute units such as picas, inches, or millimeters. These units of measure grow or shrink in size proportionately as the objects they measure shrink or grow. Such units are useful in maintaining size relationships between objects as their dimensions change. By defining one object as being 9 units tall and the one next to it 10 units tall, you can be sure that as they are scaled to a new size the one will always be 10 percent shorter than the other. If you give them discrete dimensions using absolute measurements, the math involved in making sure their relative heights remain in tune becomes much more complicated.

The Em

The fundamental relative unit in typography is the *em*. An em is the same size as the type currently being set, so if you're setting 11-point type, an em equals 11 points. Despite the sound of its name, an em is not the width of an *M;* in fact, an *M* is rarely a full em wide (see Figure 2.4).

EM-BASED CHARACTER WIDTHS

In typography more distances are expressed in fractions of an em than are expressed in picas and points. The widths of typeset characters are a good example. As noted in the previous chapter (see "Proportional Type"), the characters in a typeface are measured in relative units, and these units are fractions of an em. The Monotype system originally used a character-spacing scheme based on 18 units to the em, which meant that characters (and spaces) could have any one of 18 possible widths. The widths of the characters, then, were defined in terms of the em square—and de facto by the width of each other—rather than by a number of absolute units such as points. Once the Monotype system was told what point size was going to be used—that is, how large an em would be—it could calculate the absolute length of the line it was setting, with characters sized accordingly.

The brilliance of this system lay in its separation of the design of the characters in a font from any absolute measurement of the characters. Without it, for every size of type you wanted to use, you would need a separate listing of the absolute width values for each and every character. This system of proportional widths is still employed today, and the widths of characters recorded within a digital font are still expressed as fractions of an em (Figure 2.5).

The original Monotype scheme and the one used in today's digital fonts differ primarily in the number of units they use per em. PostScript fonts are based on a system of 1,000 units per em. This allows type designers to create nearly any character shape without having to shoehorn it into one of a limited number of possible widths. The TrueType format advances this to a maximum possible 32,000 units per em. (For more on font formats, see Chapter 4.)

Like the old Monotype system, a computerized system only needs to know what point size has been specified—that is, what the definition of an em is in a particular circumstance—and it can calculate the widths of characters by multiplying their fraction-of-an-em widths by the width of an em.

EM-BASED WHITE-SPACE ADJUSTMENTS

The spaces between letters are also measured in relative units: fractions of an em. This assures that if, for example, 12-point type is resized to 14-point, any spaces between characters that have been adjusted will also be resized proportionately, and those adjustments will be correct at the new type size.

One such adjustment is *kerning,* the adjustment of spacing between particular letter pairs to correct problems arising from the shapes of those letters. The letters in *To,* for example, are usually kerned closer together, because the empty space under the crossbar of the *T* creates a gap between it and the *o* next to it. Likewise, *rn* in some typefaces have to be kerned apart to avoid having them look like an *m.* Electronic fonts generally have tables of kerning information built into them, as shown in Figure 2.6. These tell the typesetting program that every time certain letters appear next to each other, kerning adjustments have to be made. These adjustments are expressed in relative units.

If absolute units were used to express these kerning adjustments, a separate table would have to be built for every point size at which that font might be used.

```
C 42 ; WX 500 ; N asterisk
C 43 ; WX 833 ; N plus
C 44 ; WX 248 ; N comma
C 45 ; WX 331 ; N hyphen
C 46 ; WX 248 ; N period
C 47 ; WX 278 ; N slash
C 48 ; WX 495 ; N zero
C 49 ; WX 495 ; N one
C 50 ; WX 495 ; N two
C 51 ; WX 495 ; N three
C 52 ; WX 495 ; N four
C 53 ; WX 495 ; N five
C 54 ; WX 495 ; N six
C 55 ; WX 495 ; N seven
C 56 ; WX 495 ; N eight
C 57 ; WX 495 ; N nine
C 58 ; WX 272 ; N colon
C 59 ; WX 272 ; N semicolon
C 60 ; WX 833 ; N less
C 61 ; WX 833 ; N equal
C 62 ; WX 833 ; N greater
C 63 ; WX 365 ; N question
C 64 ; WX 986 ; N at
C 65 ; WX 752 ; N A
C 66 ; WX 595 ; N B
C 67 ; WX 683 ; N C
C 68 ; WX 741 ; N D
C 69 ; WX 562 ; N E
C 70 ; WX 527 ; N F
C 71 ; WX 722 ; N G
C 72 ; WX 771 ; N H
C 73 ; WX 321 ; N I
```

FIGURE 2.5 This is how the widths of characters appear within the coding of a PostScript font (only a partial listing is shown here). In the first column, the *C* stands for *character* and is followed by the encoding number of the character (which in this range is an ASCII number). *WX* stands for *width metrics,* and the number that follows it is the width of the character expressed in thousandths of an em. In the right-hand column, *N* stands for *name* and lists the name of the character in plain (or semiplain) English.

You can see that the numerals have the same width, so they'll align neatly in vertical columns. The capital letters that appear at the bottom of the list, though, have unique widths.

kerning turned off

kerning turned on

To

```
KPX T o -148
KPX T r -130
KPX T s -130
KPX T u -148
KPX T w -167
KPX T y -148
KPX T guillemotleft -167
KPX T guilsinglright -111
KPX T quotesinglbase -111
KPX T quotedblbase -111
KPX T guillemotright -111
KPX T ae -148
KPX T oslash -148
KPX T oe -148
KPX T Aring -56
KPX U comma -60
KPX U hyphen -28
KPX U period -60
KPX U colon -32
KPX U semicolon -32
KPX U A -37
```

FIGURE 2.6 The two samples at the top show the effect of kerning. Here, the void under the crossbar of the *T* will leave a gap in the line unless the *o* is kerned closer to it.

The list below shows part of a kerning table from within a digital font. *KPX* stands for *kerning pair metrics,* and it's followed by the kerning pair to be adjusted, written in plain English. Following that is the adjustment expressed in thousandths of an em. The first is the *To* illustrated above, with its kerning adjustment of minus 148 thousandths of an em. Kerning adjustments can have positive values as well, which would cause the two characters to be spread farther apart.

With adjustments expressed in relative units, the program can use a single table of kerning data for all point sizes—all it has to know is the size of the specified type, the size of an em. For more on kerning, see Chapter 11.

EM-BASED SPACING UNITS

A number of other relative spaces are based on the em:

- The *en space* is equal to half an em space (and does not necessarily relate to the width of an *N*).

- The *thin space* is often defined as half an en space (or one-quarter of an em), but its relationship to an em can usually be defined within most computer typesetting programs.

- A *figure space* is equal to the width of the numerals in a typeface (which are usually all the same width so they'll align vertically in tables). It is used as a placeholder in settings like that shown in Figure 2.7. Because the numerals in different typefaces are of different widths (although many are 1 en wide), the width of a figure space will vary from typeface to typeface. For this reason, the figure space should properly be part of the character set of each font, although it has never become a standard feature of popular fonts. Chapter 15, about setting tables, explains how you can create a figure space for tabular settings.

Although the widths of these spaces—as well as the em—are relative, they are nevertheless referred to as *fixed spaces* because their widths are invariable unless the point size of the type changes. One of the methods that typesetting software uses to fit type into lines is to compress or stretch the spaces between letters and words. Fixed spaces—ems, ens, thins, and figure spaces—are constant and are not affected by the composition process. They will change size only when the size of the type in which they're embedded changes. Word spaces, in contrast, can vary in width as text is composed.

THE WORD SPACE

The width of the *word space,* or *space band,* is also defined as a fraction of an em, but it is different in two important ways from the fixed spaces listed above. First, its width is defined within each font, as shown in Figure 2.8. This is because the widths of characters vary from typeface to typeface. The widths of the word spaces when these typefaces are set have to be adjusted accordingly. The easiest way to do this is to have the designer of the typeface decide how wide its word spaces should be and to enshrine that width in the font for that face.

Also, as mentioned above, word-space widths can be expanded or compressed to meet composition goals and to fit words into lines. This process, called *justification,* is explained in detail in Chapter 10.

Other Units of Measure

International industrial standards are relatively new. With such a long and checkered history, it's not surprising that typesetting has accumulated a variety of measures that have never been universally accepted or that have faded away as technologies have evolved. Some of them—which may still appear in various typesetting and page layout programs—are listed here.

Ciceros

In the eighteenth century, the French created a scheme for measuring type that's now called the *didot* (pronounced *DEE-dough*) system, named after a French printing family. It's based on the *didot point,* 12 of which make up a *cicero* (this name actually varies from country to country in Europe). A didot point is slightly larger than a modern PostScript point, so that 15 ciceros equal about 16 picas. The didot system is still in use in Europe to some extent.

Agates

Agate, like *pica,* is a term left over from the days when each point size of a typeface had its own proper name (which varied by country). Agate type is a 5 ½-point type once commonly used for classified advertising; being *small in the body,* it sets 14 lines to the inch, whereas modern 5 ½-point digital type will normally set only 13 lines to the inch. You'll occasionally see agates used as a measure of column depth (or as an option for onscreen ruler settings); this measure refers to the old 14-lines-to-the-inch metal type. The term and the measurement are obscure, archaic, and rapidly becoming more so.

$$
\begin{array}{r}
\$\quad 1{,}550{,}000 \\
650{,}000 \\
500 \\
10{,}500 \\
67{,}450{,}000 \\
42{,}750{,}000 \\
15{,}500 \\
\hline
\$112{,}426{,}650
\end{array}
$$

FIGURE 2.7 The dollar sign at the top left has been positioned by adding two figure spaces between it and the number that follows it. This allows it to take its appointed place in perfect alignment above the dollar sign in the "total" line at the bottom. Because the numerals in a typeface are usually all the same width, the figure space can act as a nonprinting placeholder for any of them.

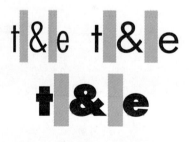

FIGURE 2.8 In these three samples from members of the Futura family, the word spaces are highlighted in gray. This shows how the width of a word space—which is defined within the font itself—can vary substantially from typeface to typeface.

DEFINITIONS: "FONT" VERSUS "TYPEFACE"

TYPE DESIGN AND THE EM SQUARE: BASELINE, X-HEIGHT

TYPE ANATOMY: SERIFS, ASCENDERS, DESCENDERS

OPTICAL ASPECTS OF TYPEFACE DESIGN

TEXT, DISPLAY, AND DECORATIVE TYPE

CLASSIFYING TYPEFACES BY HISTORICAL PERIOD

When you look at a printed page, you see type. How the letters of that type are shaped and proportioned reflects the design qualities of a specific *typeface*. Those designs are stored, embodied, in a *font*, from which the typesetting system extracts the information needed to get that type onto the page. Fonts and typefaces are the basic raw materials of typesetting. This chapter compares the two and describes in detail what typefaces are, what's in them, and how they work. Chapter 4 describes fonts.

Definitions: *Font* versus *Typeface*

No two words in typography are as commonly misused as *font* and *typeface*. A typeface is a collection of *characters*—letters, numbers, symbols, punctuation marks, etc.—that are designed to work together like the parts of a coordinated outfit. A typeface is an alphabet with a certain design. A font, in contrast, is a physical thing, the description of a typeface—in computer code, photographic film, or metal—used to image the type. The font is the cookie cutter, and the typeface is the cookie (see Figure 3.1).

When you look at a page of type, you can say, "What typeface is that?" or "What font was used to set that?" But you can't say, "What font is that?" because you're not looking at a font; you're looking at the product of a font.

FIGURE 3.1 The words *font* and *typeface* represent two very different things. On the left is a small part of the programming code of the New Century Schoolbook font, describing all the aspects of what the characters generated from it should look like. On the right is the New Century Schoolbook typeface, expressed as a series of characters sharing specific features that represent the "look" of the design.

the font:

```
%%BeginFont: NewCenturySchlbk-Roman
%!PS-AdobeFont-1.0: NewCenturySchlbk-Roman 001.005
%%CreationDate: Mon Oct  9 02:46:45 1989
%%VMusage: 36753 47645
%% New Century Schoolbook is a trademark of Linotype AG and/or
its subsidiaries.
11 dict begin
/FontInfo 10 dict dup begin
/version (001.005) readonly def
/FullName (New Century Schoolbook Roman) readonly def
/FamilyName (New Century Schoolbook) readonly def
/Weight (Roman) readonly def
/ItalicAngle 0 def
/isFixedPitch false def
/UnderlinePosition -103 def
/UnderlineThickness 61 def
end readonly def
/FontName /NewCenturySchlbk-Roman def
/Encoding StandardEncoding def
/PaintType 0 def
/FontType 1 def
/FontMatrix [0.001 0 0 0.001 0 0] readonly def
/UniqueID 25660 def
/FontBBox{-217 -215 1000 980}readonly def
currentdict end
currentfile eexec
3DB37459ED4853F7C6AA94FF5891FE1E1D59699A3BE04812F457A1
F33EC533C1AA4D40B373E6562E950CACA6A0D2CE2C9A63CC95759B
5DCC4917754F1C852F9902918....
```

the typeface:

New Century Schoolbook abcdefghij ABCDEFG 123456789 !@#$%&?*

It is time to pause in our career to review our principles....

FIGURE 3.2 The baseline of type, as highlighted here, is the invisible line upon which the characters of the line sit. The baseline is the reference point from which the spaces between lines of type are measured, and leading (or line spacing) is measured from baseline to baseline.

The confusion between the terms arises largely from the ambiguous use of the term *font* in computer programs, most of which have a Font menu. Although that menu lists what fonts are available for use by the program, it could just as easily be called the Typeface menu, as it also lists the typefaces available for your pages. In fact, since some fonts contain data for more than one typeface, it would be more accurate to call it the Typeface menu.

Type Design and the Em Square

A key concept underlying both the design of type and the practice of typography is the *em square*. As described in the previous chapter, the em is the basis for a range of relative units of measurement whose values are contextual: They depend on the size of the type they're used in.

The widths of characters are expressed in such relative units, which are fractions—typically thousandths—of an em. Within a font, there is a statement of how many units per em the widths of the characters are based on. That is followed by a table of the characters themselves and their widths (measured in units). For a peek inside such a font *metrics table,* see page 25.

The em square, then, is the grid upon which all the characters in a font are created. Some characters extend outside the em square, but those are rare.

The Baseline

In normal lines of type, all the letters sit on an invisible line called the *baseline,* as shown in Figure 3.2. The position of the baseline within the em square can

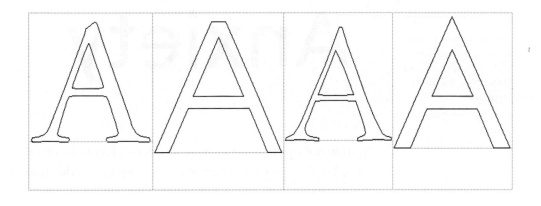

vary from font to font, depending on the design of the characters, as you can see in Figure 3.3. On average, though, the baseline is located about one-third of the way up from the bottom of the em square. In order for different typefaces to be mixed together on a single line and still share a common baseline, the location of the baseline within the em square is disclosed in the coding of the font. Without a consistent position for the baseline, typeset letters would appear to pop up and down on a line as if they were set by a defective typewriter.

The baseline is a fundamental reference. Line spacing—or *leading*—is measured, in points, from baseline to baseline, normally from the baseline of one line of type to the baseline of the preceding line (see Figure 3.4). The baseline of the first line of type at the top of a page is the starting point from which the rest of the type in that column is measured.

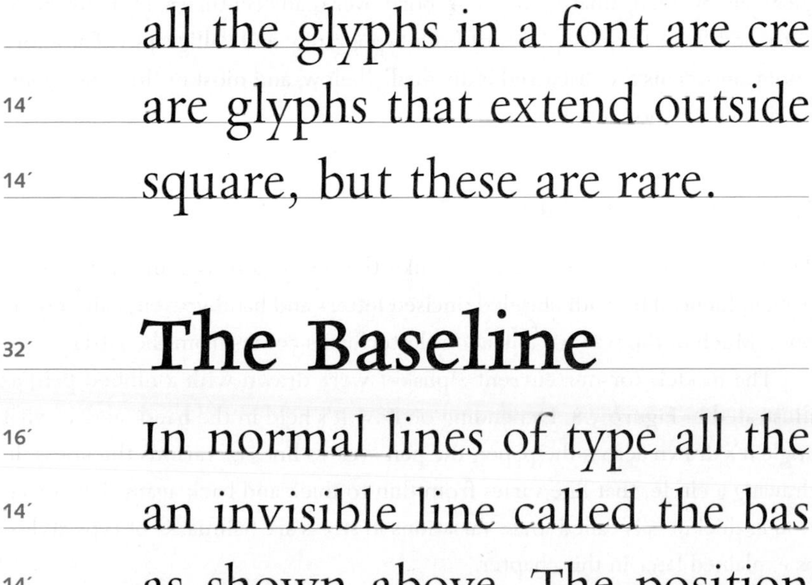

FIGURE 3.3 The view from within a font editor reveals the baselines on which the characters sit. It also reveals, as shown in these four samples, that the position of the baseline within the em square can vary considerably from face to face.

all the glyphs in a font are cre

14´   are glyphs that extend outside

14´   square, but these are rare.

32´   # The Baseline

16´   In normal lines of type all the

14´   an invisible line called the bas

14´   as shown above. The position

FIGURE 3.4 Leading is measured from the baseline of one line of type to the baseline of the preceding line. In this 200 percent view, you can see the leading values of each line, including the extra leading between the text and the subhead before it.

Anxiety

mean line

baseline

FIGURE 3.5 The mean line measures the height of the nonascending lowercase characters. The distance between the baseline and the mean line is the x-height of the typeface.

x-Height

Apart from the point size of a sample of type, the impression of the size of a typeface is based mainly on the height of its lowercase letters. This measure, defined as the distance from the baseline to the top of the lowercase *x,* is called the *x-height* of the typeface. A line drawn at this height, parallel to the baseline, is called the *mean line* of the face (see Figure 3.5).

Being the typographical equivalent of hemline length, x-height trends up and down over time. The contemporary trend is toward larger x-heights. It's believed that typefaces with larger x-heights are easier to read, and on computer screens this is unarguably the case, as adding a pixel (or more) to the height of lowercase letters makes them much more legible. At screen resolutions, every pixel counts. X-heights seem to have peaked in the mid-1960s, exemplified by such faces as Antique Olive and Americana, and have been trending downward somewhat since then (see Figure 3.6).

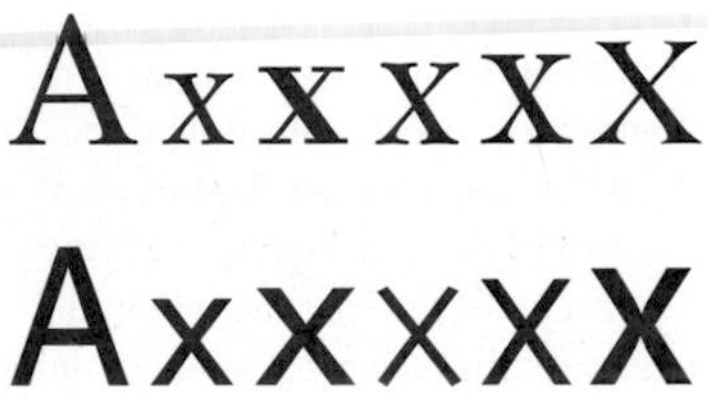

AXXXXX

AXXXXX

FIGURE 3.6 The x-heights of typefaces vary widely, as these samples show. All these characters are set in the same point size. The top line, starting with a Times Roman *A* for comparison, are Monotype Centaur, Linotype Bodoni, Monotype Janson, ITC Galliard, and ATF Americana.

The sans serif faces in the second line, starting with a Helvetica *A*, are Bauer Futura, Monotype Gill Sans, Linotype Univers 55, ITC Avant Garde Gothic, and Antique Olive Medium.

Type Anatomy

The way we talk about the shapes of letters, and the words we use to describe them, are an amalgamation of terms born over many centuries, in many countries, and from the disciplines of both typography and calligraphy. The more important terms are discussed individually below, and most of the other common ones are shown in Figure 3.7.

Calligraphic Influences

The letterforms of text typefaces—like the one you're reading now—have been influenced by both chiseled, incised letters and handwritten, calligraphic ones. Much of the way we talk about letterforms comes from the latter.

The models for our current alphabet were drawn with a nibbed pen, as illustrated in Figure 3.8. Depending on how it's held in the hand, and at what angle it's drawn across the paper, the pen creates lines of various thickness. In drawing a circle, that line varies from thin to thick and back again. This variation in thickness is called *stress*. Variations in stress are hallmarks of type styles, as explained later in this chapter.

FIGURE 3.7 The parts of letters all have names, as shown at left. Some of them—such as *spine*—are specific to a particular letter (in that case the *S*), but most are generic and apply to a number of characters.

FIGURE 3.8 Letterforms often derive from calligraphic sources. The shape of the letter above, whose varying stroke thickness mirrors the line created by a nibbed pen, is being drawn in a counterclockwise direction. The stress of a character is created where the nib draws its widest line.

Likewise, the widths of the *strokes* of a letter vary according to whether they are drawn with an upward movement of the pen or a downward movement. This explains why the strokes of common "straight-legged" letters such as *M, N,* and *A* are alternately thin and thick (see Figure 3.9).

Serifs

Serifs are finishing flourishes at the ends of a character's main strokes, where the stroke appears to flare out. The word is of dubious origin, but it probably comes from an old German word for the stroke of a pen. Serifs themselves, though, are extremely ancient and can be found in stone inscriptions from at least as far back as ancient Greece. One of the basic ways of categorizing typefaces is to distinguish those with serifs—*seriffed* faces—from those without. The latter are called sans serif faces, a polyglot expression marrying the French *sans* ("without") with the Teutonic *serif.*

Serifs are not just decorative fillips. They are important visual aids that help the eye to differentiate one character from another, and to help the brain

FIGURE 3.9 The stroke of the pen has also defined the basic shapes of many Latin characters. Here, the downstroke of the pen draws the wider strokes of an *M,* while the upstrokes draw narrower lines.

distinguish individual characters from among the forest of tiny strokes that make up passages of typeset text. They also provide a slight horizontal texture to type, creating a sort of graphic current to draw the eye along the line. The characters of seriffed text are thus somewhat more *legible,* or easier to recognize. The added legibility, in turn, makes text easier and faster to read, that is to say, more *readable.*

There are many kinds of serifs, and they vary widely in shape, size, and bulk. They have evolved over the ages, and many styles of type are named for the distinctive forms of their serifs.

BRACKETED SERIFS

Bracketed serifs are probably the most familiar kind, as they're used in the majority of common text faces. A bracketed serif blends in to the main stroke of the letter with a smooth curve (also called a *fillet*), as shown in Figure 3.10. As this illustration shows, the depth of the curve, the size of the serif, and the overall presentation of the serif vary widely from face to face.

UNBRACKETED SERIFS

Unbracketed serifs meet the main strokes at a sharp angle. The serifs themselves may be mere hairlines, thicker slabs, or even wedges. The overall effect is to give the letter a more angular, crisply defined shape.

SLAB SERIFS

Slab serifs give their name to a whole category of typefaces. These faces, which usually feature a uniform (or *monoline*) stroke thickness, are not based on calligraphic forms. The minimalist design produces a face with very little detail or ornament, and the slab serifs enhance its legibility, with the result that slab-serif faces are often seen as text types.

Typefaces that have bracketed slab serifs are usually called *Clarendons.*

HAIRLINE SERIFS

A hallmark of the so-called *modern* typefaces (described in detail later in this chapter), hairline serifs are extremely fine and unbracketed.

WEDGE SERIFS

As their name implies, wedge serifs are triangular. There aren't many wedge-seriffed faces, and those that do exist are usually called *Latins.*

bracketed serifs: DF Rialto

Hamburgefons

unbracketed serifs: Linotype Trump Mediæval

Hamburgefons

unbracketed slab serifs: Linotype Memphis

Hamburgefons

bracketed slab serifs: Bitstream Clarendon

Hamburgefons

hairline serifs: ITC Fenice

Hamburgefons

wedge serifs: Linotype Meridien

Hamburgefons

FIGURE 3.10 Serifs help define the texture and color of a typeface, as these samples show. The bracketed, old-style serifs used in most text faces soften the sense of the face, while their unbracketed counterparts add an element of crispness. Slab serifs that are unbracketed have a machined, industrial rigor; when bracketed they lend an emphatic strength to faces known as Clarendons, including the popular Century families. Hairline serifs, signature features of modern faces, create a formal, bright look, while wedge serifs yield a chiseled, sharp impression.

Ib Ib Ib Ib Ib
by by by by by

FIGURE 3.11 Ascender and descender lengths don't vary as dramatically as x-heights, but they're different enough from face to face to affect how various types are leaded. As these samples show, there isn't necessarily any correlation among capital height, ascender length, x-height, and descender length. In fact, in the top row, the sample with the longest ascender has the shortest cap height. The samples, from left to right in both rows, are ITC New Baskerville, Linotype Caslon 540, ITC Galliard, Monotype Goudy Old Style, and Linotype Raleigh.

Ascenders and Descenders

Ascenders are the strokes of lowercase letters that rise above the mean line. *Descenders* are the parts of letters that extend below the baseline. As shown in Figure 3.11, the heights and depths of ascenders and descenders vary widely from face to face, with ascenders sometimes being quite a bit taller than capital letters of the same face in the same point size.

Unlike x-height, descenders and ascenders are normally constrained by the dimensions of the em square in which they're designed. In the days of metal type, it was not uncommon for a typeface to come in two varieties—short ascenders/descenders and long ascenders/descenders—but nearly none of those have been translated into electronic format.

Some typefaces have taller ascenders than is typical, with the result that with tight line spacing, the ascenders of one line may touch the descenders above. When using a face with clearly tall ascenders, you should be prepared to adjust leading accordingly.

Vestigial Features: Ink Wells

Offset lithography has been perfected to the point that, except for the sloppiest work or jobs using the worst grades of paper, the image of the type on the printing plate is pretty much what you'll get on the printed page. But it wasn't always so. Older printing technologies forced some changes on what might be considered the ideal type designs.

One of the most obvious was the *ink well,* or *ink trap.* This feature can still be found in many typefaces that have been digitized without alteration from earlier designs. An inkwell is an exaggerated gap in the shape of a letter that's created with the assumption that the gap will plug with ink, yielding a "normal" letterform. It is most frequently seen in the crotches of letters, including *V, A, W,* and *N.* You can often see ink wells in printed advertisements, even though you shouldn't. Presswork has become so good that the inkwells haven't plugged as anticipated, leaving this curious artifact visible on the page.

NEW ZEBRA

One place where inkwells are still in use is in typefaces designed for telephone books. Although the quality of the presswork may be high, the type is very small and the paper is about the cheapest available, so that ink printed on it at extremely high speed tends to spread due to both absorption and mechanical pressure. Types designed for such applications typically have a somewhat skeletal appearance when reproduced through high-quality printing, as they need to be fleshed out in a cheaper printing process to assume their intended final appearance (see Figure 3.12).

Optical Aspects of Typeface Design

In typography, it's often the case that what looks right *is* right. Although the craft of typesetting is all about measuring, doing things by the measuring stick doesn't always yield good results. Visual alignment—what looks right to the eye—may have to take precedence over what's mechanically "correct."

For example, although nondescending letters are said to sit on the baseline, this is true only for flat-bottomed characters. A close look at round-bottomed characters will show that they actually extend slightly below the baseline. Likewise, lowercase letters with rounded tops are designed to extend slightly above the mean line (see Figure 3.13). This is called *overshoot*.

The reason for this is that the tops and bottoms of rounded characters are graphically weak. The same is true of the peak of a capital *A*. Were such letters made to be exactly as tall as their peers, they would look too short. If round-bottomed characters were placed so as to fit precisely between the baseline and the mean line, they would appear too small and would seem to be hovering slightly over the baseline, as shown in Figure 3.14.

Size Changes Everything

Basing typography on relative units is a clever way of addressing how the appearance of type changes as its size changes. Two forces at work, though, make this technique less than foolproof. First, type that's proportioned for optimal legibility at common reading sizes—in the neighborhood of 11 points—becomes very hard to read if it's scaled down much smaller. Second, as type size increases, white spaces appear to grow faster than the typeset characters, making the type appear to be too loosely set (see Figure 3.15). The latter phenomenon is one of

FIGURE 3.12 The exaggerated gaps in the crotches of the characters at left are ink traps, or ink wells, which anticipate that these parts of the letters will plug with ink during printing. This typeface, Bell Centennial, was designed for use in telephone books.

nox

FIGURE 3.13 In order to make round-topped or round-bottomed characters appear to align with the baseline or mean line, they're actually drawn to exceed, or overshoot, those guidelines, as shown above. The same kinds of adjustments have to be made in the shapes of characters that terminate in points, such as *A* or *V*.

nox

FIGURE 3.14 Here the size of the *o* has been adjusted so that it sits precisely on the baseline and ascends just to touch the mean line. The net effect is that the character seems to be floating somewhat higher than its neighbors and looks somewhat shorter as well.

Looser
Looser
Looser
Looser
Looser
Looser
Looser
Looser
Looser
Looser
Looser
Looser
Looser
Looser
Looser

FIGURE 3.15 White spaces—such as the spaces between letters—always appear to grow faster than the type around them. Here, the largest sample seems to be set far looser than the smaller samples, but that is an optical illusion. The spacing of type set in larger point sizes always needs to be tightened to compensate for this effect.

the things that make typesetting so complicated, and it gets a lot of attention in later chapters, especially in Chapter 10, about hyphenation and justification, and Chapter 11, on tracking and kerning.

The issue of how the character forms themselves have to change along with their size, though, has to be addressed within the font itself.

Master Character Designs

As explained in Chapter 1, typefaces set in metal had to be recut for every point size at which they were used. It was natural enough for type designers to tweak the basic design of the face in order to make it optimally legible and practical at every point size.

For smaller sizes, that meant increasing the x-height of the characters, making the lowercase characters and their identifying features larger. In addition, small types were given relatively thicker strokes, making them slightly *bolder*. That not only made them more legible, but it also made their *color* on the page closer to that of larger types used along with them. The added heft of the small type created a more harmonious graphic presentation on the page. Lastly, the small characters were made somewhat wider, which was not merely a consequence of making their strokes bolder, but also an effort to make their open spaces (called *counters*) larger and the white space between their strokes more apparent. On a practical level, these coarser features also made them easier to print, and the relative openness of the characters made their fine white spaces less likely to plug with ink (see Figure 3.16).

With the advent of phototype, the number of master designs for a typeface was radically reduced. By the mid-1970s, only the most popularly used typefaces had more than two fonts—each representing a distinct master design—available for them. One master, usually based on a 12-point design, was used for text and, in smaller display sizes, for headings, titles, and so forth. A larger size was available—usually on a completely different typesetting system—for book covers, newspaper headlines, ads, and the like.

Early digital fonts eliminated the larger font altogether, and the vast majority of fonts now in use on computerized typesetting systems generate all their character images from a single master set of outlines. Except for typefaces designed mainly for use in large sizes—the so-called *titling faces*—these are usually based on a 12-point master.

Times New Roman

Times New Roman Small Text

FOR SALE One slightly used Monotype casting machine in impeccable working order, including matrices and a lifetime supply of paper tape. Manuals in mint condition, hardly used. For details and pricing, call 1-201-555-6278.

FOR SALE One slightly used Monotype casting machine in impeccable working order, including matrices and a lifetime supply of paper tape. Manuals in mint condition, hardly used. For details and pricing, call 1-201-555-6278.

FIGURE 3.16 Type designs have traditionally been size sensitive. In this dramatic example at left, Times New Roman, designed for text sizes, is contrasted with Times New Roman Small Text, designed for classified advertising. Its wider characters, bulkier stroke weights, and larger x-height all enhance legibility in small point sizes. The two faces are compared in the sample ads (set in 6-point).

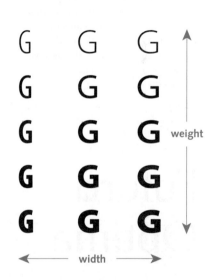

FIGURE 3.17 Adobe's Multiple Master typefaces contained several design "axes," at the ends of which were unique sets of master outlines. This is a sample of Myriad, which has two design axes: character width and weight. By interpolating among the four master designs at the corners of this grid, an infinite number of typeface variations could be created. Design axes in other Multiple Master fonts varied stance (between upright and oblique) and serif style (between sans serif and seriffed forms).

MULTIPLE MASTER FONTS

Efforts to correct this shortcoming of digital type have largely foundered. Both Adobe Systems, with its Multiple Master font format, and Apple Computer, through the TrueType GX technology, created fonts that contained numerous sets of master character outlines. The ambitious goal of each (overambitious, as it turned out) was to create a system that would enable the computer to create unique instances of a typeface on the fly.

A font, could, for example, contain the master outline of a font designed expressly for use at 6-point, another at 12-point, and yet another at 48-point. Those would be benchmark designs, and if a user wanted a size in between, the system would take the larger and smaller outlines and interpolate between them to come up with a design that reflected the graphic needs of the typeface at the new size. Likewise, the systems could interpolate between lighter and bolder master outlines, or upright and slanted versions (see Figure 3.17).

The concept was brilliant, but it was complicated and expensive to design the fonts and complicated for users to take advantage of them. With their high price, the limited number of fonts available in either format, and a relative lack of enthusiasm from the public, both projects sank under their own weight and are now defunct.

Seriffed
Sans Serif

FIGURE 3.18 A comparison of the archetypal seriffed and sans serif types: Times Roman (above) and Helvetica. In addition to the presence or absence of serifs, the two species of typeface also vary according to the modulation of their stroke weights (sans serif strokes tend to vary little, if at all, in their thickness). In general, sans serif faces need to be spaced looser to maintain legibility.

Futura
Optima

FIGURE 3.19 Futura is called a geometric sans serif, and earlier versions of the face used perfect circles as a base for its curved letters, with no variation in stroke weight at all. Optima, in comparison, is a humanist sans serif, and its features clearly relate it to the calligraphic roots of seriffed types.

The latest effort to address the issue of multiple master designs within a font is the OpenType font format, developed jointly by Adobe and Microsoft. It enables a typeface designer to incorporate several sets of master character designs into a font and to specify the point-size ranges over which each should be used. Users, then, can get type based on one design for footnotes, type with a slightly different design for text, and a third (or fourth or fifth) for type set for headlines and titles. For more details on the OpenType format, see the section of the same name in Chapter 4.

Principal Features of Typefaces

There are many ways to classify a typeface, and it's not uncommon to use several at once. In the following sections we'll look at the overall physical characteristics of typefaces, and after that, we'll move on to classifications based on historical considerations, those aspects of type designs that have evolved over the centuries and that give certain types their particular look and feel.

Seriffed and Sans Serif

Both seriffed and sans serif letterforms are ancient, and examples of both can be found in inscriptions from millennia ago (see Figure 3.18). As the Latin alphabet has evolved, seriffed forms have come to predominate in long texts. In fact, until the early nineteenth century, there were virtually no sans serif typefaces created for letterpress printing. The increasing popularity of sans serif faces over the ensuing decades has been popularly attributed to the increase in the new form of printed communication known as the display advertisement (before that, ads resembled what we would now called classifieds).

Seriffed types are still preferred for text, as in general they're easier to read. Sans serif types tend to be used in display roles, such as for titles and other large type, although a few sans serif faces are often used for text. Those are usually *humanist* sans faces, whose designs were inspired not by geometry but by classical and Renaissance letterforms. Optima is one such humanist sans serif often used for setting long texts (see Figure 3.19).

Many of the most popular sans serif faces came from the pioneering work of the designers at the Bauhaus, the German design school that became a hotbed for cutting-edge design between the World Wars. One of the design imperatives of the Bauhaus was to strip away useless ornamentation and reduce objects to their functional minimum, in the belief that pure functionality had a beauty and an aesthetic importance of its own. One Bauhaus concern was the redesign of the alphabet, and many popular typefaces eventually grew from the roots of this research. One of them is Paul Renner's Futura, which through various revisions and refinements has remained popular (and saw a huge revival in the 1980s). Another sans serif face often used for text is Adrian Frutiger's Univers, designed in the 1950s and '60s.

Variations in Typeface Weight

Another distinction among typefaces is their *weight,* the thickness of the principal strokes of the letters. Depending on the thickness of these strokes, the weight of a typeface is generally rated on a scale ranging from *light* to *bold.*

The weights of typefaces are apt to be described in many terms, and these are far from standardized. Some names have their roots in tradition, and others reflect attempts to give distinctive and descriptive names to new weights of an existing typeface (see Figure 3.20).

The weight of a typeface can vary for a number of reasons. As described in "Multiple Master Fonts," earlier in this chapter, the weight of a typeface may be varied from one master design to another to compensate for visual changes in the characters at various sizes. Smaller characters should be designed to be slightly bolder.

Often, the weights of typefaces are defined by historical, aesthetic, or practical reasons. The oldest metal types, for example, tend to be bolder than those that followed because the contemporary printing technology demanded sturdier letterforms. When in the mid-eighteenth century John Baskerville invented a technique for making paper with a much smoother surface than before (so-called *wove* paper), it allowed typefaces to be designed with much finer lines and subtler forms. There is no one definition, then, of what *bold* means; it is strictly a relative term used to define the weight of one typeface as opposed to another.

DEGREES OF BOLDNESS

Before the age of phototype, designing a typeface was much more of an effort than it is today, because so many iterations of each face had to be designed, one for each point size to be set. In those days, there were typically just two weights of a typeface: light (for text) and bold (for emphasis and display). But with the explosion of typeface designs starting in the mid-twentieth century, the definition of *light,* too, came into question. For historical reasons, some typefaces still bear the name *Light* (Bookman Light, for example), when they don't seem that much lighter than other faces.

These days, it's much more common to refer to the weight of a typeface designed for text use as *regular,* even though this may not be an official part of the typeface's name. Other names that are often applied to the text weights of

Futura Light
Futura Book
Futura Medium
Futura Heavy
Futura Bold
Futura Extra Black

ITC Garamond Light
ITC Garamond Book
ITC Garamond Bold
ITC Garamond Ultra

FIGURE 3.20 Typefaces typically have variants with different weights. Although the names given to these weights have a relative meaning within a typeface family, there is no absolute definition of what the terms mean. In many typefaces, for example, a face of the weight of Futura Heavy would be called bold, and what the Futura family calls Bold would be called extrabold. The ITC Garamond family eschews the terms *extrabold* or *black* and goes directly to Ultra (short for *ultrabold*).

Novarese
Novarese
Garamond
Garamond

FIGURE 3.21 Early italic forms, upon which faces such as ɪᴛᴄ Novarese are based, used upright, roman capitals, By the mid-sixteenth century, though, the capitals too had taken on an oblique angle, as this sample of Stempel Garamond shows.

Palatino
Palatino Italic

Bookman
Bookman Italic

Gill Sans
Gill Sans Italic

Helvetica
Helvetica Italic

FIGURE 3.22 The definitions of the terms *italic* and *oblique* are not always clear-cut. Palatino has a classically italic complement, but Bookman Italic would be better called oblique—its characters are essentially inclined versions of their roman equivalents. On the sans serif side of the aisle, Gill Sans Italic has some of the features of seriffed italic faces, such as the switch in the shape of the lowercase *a*. Helvetica Italic is basically a pure oblique.

a typeface are *medium* and *book*. Variations on this text weight are expressed, then, as being to some degree more or less bold or light. The Helvetica family, for example, has an extraordinary range of weights, including Ultra Light, Thin, Light, "regular," Bold, Heavy, Black, and Black #2 (an extra black).

Romans and Italics

Although the classical inscriptions on Trajan's column in Rome have been the inspiration for hundreds of type designs over the ages, roman types (with a small *r*) are so called because in the early days of movable type (the late fifteenth century), those typefaces were innovated in Rome. Their forms quickly evolved into the letterforms we use for text today. Roman typefaces have an upright structure, or *stance,* with the main strokes of letters such as *T* and *I* being perpendicular to the baseline. The typeface you're reading now— Perpetua—is a roman face.

At about the same time, though, in Venice, Aldus Manutius (the Latinized name of Aldo Manuzio), a commercial printer, was looking for a way to cram more type onto a page and reduce the price of his low-cost editions of the classics. He turned to a popular hand-lettering form of the day called *cursiva humanistica,* which had the merit both of being familiar to readers' eyes and of setting more compactly on the line than roman types. Briefly called *Aldinos,* these faces were soon known by the more generic term *italics.* Some 25 years later, in about 1525, fellow Italian Ludovico Arrighi created a new italic type, based on the lettering he used as a scribe in the Vatican chancellery—*cancellaresca*—and this *chancery* style is the model for most of the italic types that followed. Interestingly, those early italic types used upright roman capitals, and many faces based on them do the same (see Figure 3.21). Text set in all capitals using such faces will look just as if it were set in roman type.

The use of italics as text types waned, but their role as accompaniment and counterpoint to roman types remained. Eventually it became the norm for roman types to have italic complements designed specifically for them.

OBLIQUES

Not all typefaces have a true *cursive* complement. Many instead have a slanted variation of the roman face. These are often referred to as *obliques.* Helvetica Italic, for example, is not really a true cursive italic but an oblique. Some typefaces, such as Bookman Italic, are essentially oblique in their basic character forms. A selection of obliques, semi-obliques and true cursive italics is shown in Figure 3.22.

In general, the slanted complements of roman sans serif types are obliques. Nevertheless, it is traditional for some of the characters in sans serif obliques (following the normal practice for seriffed faces) to have different shapes from their upright counterparts, as seen in the Gill Sans Italic sample.

Even true obliques are not merely electronically slanted versions of their roman equivalents (although there are a few exceptions). Although the forms of the letters may seem identical (albeit slanted), oblique typefaces have generally been designed that way from scratch in order to preserve the correct proportions of the characters. Creating obliques by slanting roman characters with a computer graphics program is not a good idea, as it inevitably distorts the shapes of the letters in unpleasant, if subtle, ways. It's always better to use a designed oblique if it's available.

Variations in Typeface Width

Although constrained by the dimensions of the em square, the relative widths of characters vary widely from typeface to typeface.

Typefaces whose characters are very wide are rare, mainly because characters lose their legibility quite quickly as they get wider. The key to the legibility of characters rests largely in the eye identifying the forms that link the vertical forms of letters. In other words, we recognize characters "from the waist up," with the lower parts being largely a forest of undistinguished "legs," as shown in Figure 3.23. When characters are made too wide, the horizontal and linking forms become unrecognizable, and the shapes of letters become harder to make out. Wide variants of typefaces—usually called *extended* or *expanded*—are used almost exclusively for display purposes, not for text.

Curiously, this effect is not as marked when making typefaces narrower, and typeface families (again, usually sans serif typefaces) may have several narrower variations, under names including *narrow, condensed, thin, compressed, extra condensed,* and even *ultra condensed.*

Typeface Families

The basic unit of typeface organization is the *family.* A typeface family is a group of faces that have been designed to work together harmoniously. The typical typeface family is a foursome, and the group normally takes its name—for example, Times New Roman, Bodoni, or Helvetica—from the "regular"-weight roman member of the family. The foursome is then rounded out with bold, italic, and bold italic complements.

FIGURE 3.23 Our comprehension of the text we read is based largely on the tops of lowercase letters, the bottom halves consisting mostly of "legs and feet." The top sample here is impossible to decipher, but the middle sample is comprehensible. Rendering those shapes into patterns enables us to recognize whole words and phrases at a glance. Overwide character shapes break up those patterns and make reading slower.

Text
Display
Decorative

FIGURE 3.24 Text faces are the button-downs of type. They're conservative and designed for business—the business of reading. Display types are graphically strong—they command your attention. Decorative faces are from the anything-goes school—they can evoke a mood, an epoch, a state of mind, or a state of mindlessness. Their main role is as an eye-stopper.

FIGURE 3.25 Pi fonts can contain anything. The characters here are drawn from ITC Zapf Dingbats, Adobe Carta, and Symbol.

Some typeface families have fewer than four members (Century Old Style, for example, has no bold italic version), but more often families contain more than the basic foursome. Popular typefaces often grow to include dozens of members. This is especially true with sans serif faces, as they are easier to redesign with radically different weights and widths than seriffed faces.

Typefaces as Role Players: Text, Display, and Decorative

One of the most general and useful ways to classify typefaces is by the role they play on the page. From this perspective, typefaces are usually divided into three groups: *text, display,* and *decorative* (see Figure 3.24).

Text faces are those designed for use in long-running passages of text, like those found in books and magazines. The emphasis in text-face design is on readability. This goes beyond mere legibility—the ease with which the eye identifies individual characters—to encompass the ease with which the eye can pick out words and groups of words at a glance. A good text face lets you read at higher speeds and for longer periods of time without tiring.

Display faces are designed for larger point sizes, for headings, titles, and headlines. They're meant to be eye-catching yet legible and, most of all, versatile. Display faces have to be good mixers, with features that are assertive yet not so distinctive or quirky that their forms compete with those of the text faces they're used with. In general, sans serif types are considered display types, although some see quite a bit of action in text applications.

Decorative faces are character actors on the typographic stage. They are generally used for advertising. Their role is to grab attention at all cost, including, often, legibility. Whereas new and innovative text faces are rare birds, flocks of new decorative typefaces are unleashed on the viewing public every year. Decorative typefaces are novelties, and few of them are versatile. They go in and out of style, and most grow old pretty quickly.

Nonalphabetic Fonts

Typesetting doesn't just consist of setting text, and all manner of symbols and ideograms are commonly used alongside the characters of the Latin alphabet. Collections of these characters are called *pi fonts.* The word comes from an old hand typesetter's expression, in which to "pi" type was to spill a large quantity of type into a heap, such as pulling out a type drawer too far and dumping its contents. A pi font, then, was one made up of an assortment of possibly unrelated odds and ends.

Common pi fonts on today's computer systems include Symbol, ITC Zapf Dingbats, and Monotype Sorts (see Figure 3.25). Common pi fonts also include symbols for maps, TV listings, and train and bus schedules, as well as for mathematical formulas, decorative borders, and computer keyboard commands.

Classifying Typefaces by Historical Period

After the tens of thousands of Latin-based typefaces in the world have been sorted according to the preceding criteria, you will need yet finer categories for describing the features of typefaces and their appropriateness for certain jobs. Many attempts have been made to create a taxonomic system that would contain a logical cubbyhole for every typeface. They all start by dividing typefaces according to historical design trends, and they end—after the dawn of the age of advertising—with a lot of catchall categories for the oddballs.

Apart from the overall categories discussed in earlier sections, however, there are a handful of historical categories that are commonly used and helpful to know about. These include *old style, transitional,* and *modern.*

Old-Style Typefaces

The term *old style* generally refers to the roman types that were designed in Italy in the late fifteenth and early sixteenth centuries and those that have since followed their style. The types of Nicholas Jenson and Francesco Griffo in particular were seminal influences on generations of type designers. They continue to be the most popular typefaces for setting text.

The principal features of old-style types are the slight contrast between the thick and thin strokes of the characters and an oblique stress (evident in the thin parts of the *o,* which are offset counterclockwise from the top and bottom of the letter). Early versions of those faces (as well as nineteenth- and twentieth-century revivals) known as *Venetians* had additional hallmarks, including steeply sloping serifs and an angled crossbar in the lowercase *e.* Figure 3.26 illustrates the signature old-style features.

Although it depends on whose classification scheme you follow, the next major design group—commonly called the *Garaldes*—within the old styles are those of sixteenth-century France; this group includes the work of Claude Garamond. In addition to the typefaces bearing his name, typefaces based on Garamond's designs and the related designs of that period (Caslon, for example) abound, and they are still extremely popular. By the time of Garamond, type designs were becoming more refined, and the contrast between thicks and thins

Mobe
Mobe

FIG 3.26 Monotype's Italian Old Style (top) is a classic Venetian old-style face, being based on models from the late fifteenth century. Hallmarks include very little contrast between thick and thin strokes, a strongly diagonal stress revealed in the *o,* the straddling serifs at the top of the *M,* the steeply pitched serif on the *b,* and the slanted bar of the *e.*

Below it, Stempel Garamond shows the refinements for which the French were famous: more contrast, shallower angles for the serifs, more vertical stress, and the horizontal bar of the *e.*

Mobe
Mobe

FIGURE 3.27   The transitional Baskerville (top) moved the old-style form toward the modern. Compared to the old-style Bembo below it, Baskerville shows much more contrast in stroke weights (especially in the *M*), serifs raising toward the horizontal (as in the *b*), and vertical stress (as seen in the *o*).

Mobe
Mobe

FIGURE 3.28   Modern faces took the changes pioneered by the transitionals to an extreme, as shown in the Bodoni sample on top (contrasted with Baskerville below). Stroke contrast became exaggerated, the now unbracketed serifs came to set at right angles to the main strokes, and the vertical stress of the transitionals was amplified by the contrast in the rounded characters.

had become more pronounced. The crossbar of the *e* had become resolutely horizontal, and serifs had become finer, more horizontal, and more delicate.

Transitional Typefaces

As the name implies, *transitional* typefaces represent an intermediary phase in a design trend away from old-style type aesthetics to a newer, more "modern" look. The change began to take place at the end of the seventeenth century.

One aspect of the shift was an increase in the contrast between thicks and thins in character strokes. This can be seen in the classic faces of William Caslon from the early eighteenth century, variations of which are still in common use. For other stylistic reasons, though, Caslon's types are usually lumped into the old-style category.

The transitionals are traditionally said to have begun with an effort to create a new and intellectual type design for France's Louis XIV, a design not beholden to calligraphic or historical models but based on rational principles of mathematics and what were thought of as natural proportions. Although the resulting typefaces—the so-called *romain du roi* (the king's roman)—became the private property of the royal printing works, the man who supervised their production commercialized a similar face that bears his name: Fournier.

Another seminal type of the time, Baskerville, is also named for its designer, and it exhibits the classic traits of a transitional face, as shown in Figure 3.27. Compared to old-style faces, the contrast between stroke weights is much more marked, and this is especially evident in the uppercase letters. In addition, the stress of the curved letters is now vertical, giving the lowercase characters in particular a more upright and erect appearance.

Like the old-style faces, transitional faces, although far more limited in number, are still very popular for book, journal, and magazine work.

Modern Typefaces

The trend that started with the transitional faces found its logical conclusion in the mid-eighteenth century with designs that came to be called *modern*. Although these designs are now 250 years old, the name has stuck for good. You can talk about modern trends in typeface design in reference to today's developments, but if you refer to a "modern" typeface, people will assume you're talking about these eighteenth-century designs and those inspired by them.

Modern faces have an almost engraved look, and the thin strokes have been reduced to *hairlines,* as have the serifs. This extreme contrast gives modern typefaces an almost glittering quality. The serifs are unbracketed, and they meet the strokes they terminate at right angles. In comparison with most old-style text faces, modern types tend to appear somewhat darker on the page. All in all, the effect is very upright, formal, and crisp (see Figure 3.28).

The most famous exponent of the modern style was the Italian printer Giambattista Bodoni, and his name has been bestowed on a great number of typeface designs. Today, modern typefaces have dropped out of fashion for text settings except in highly designed volumes such as art and coffee-table books. As a display face, though, Bodoni is everywhere, and it has found a permanent niche as newspaper headline type.

Typeface-Naming Issues

Certain typeface names have been copyrighted, but many are in the common domain. This can create enormous confusion when specifying a particular typeface for a job. Take Bodoni, for example. Nearly every large type foundry has a typeface modeled on the ones made popular by their namesake. The same is true for typefaces based on the designs of Baskerville, Caslon, and Garamond and those based on stylistic characteristics, such as Clarendon, Egyptian, or Gothic. Some popular typefaces are produced by many vendors, but they are not necessarily the vendors (such as M. Olive and Fundicion Tipografica Neufville) who hold the copyright on a typeface's name and design (Antique Olive and Futura, respectively).

The upshot is that it's important to be precise about not only the names of the typefaces you use but also which vendors their fonts come from. This is especially important if you're trying to match the type from an existing job, as for a printed piece.

TWO KINDS OF FONTS: OUTLINE AND BITMAPPED

FONT FORMATS: POSTSCRIPT, TRUETYPE, AND OPENTYPE

CROSS-PLATFORM COMPATIBILITY ISSUES

HOW TO FIND THE CHARACTERS YOU NEED

IDENTIFYING FONT FORMATS (MAC AND WINDOWS)

FONT-MANAGEMENT BASICS

Typefaces are what you get to admire after your work is done, but fonts are the tools you have to wrestle with in the meantime to get the job done. Computer operating systems and applications have made it much easier to work with fonts, but the process is still quite technical. Working with fonts forces you to learn more about your computer than you probably want, but everything you need to know is in this chapter.

The Two Basic Kinds of Fonts: Outline and Bitmapped

Digital devices—computer monitor screens, desktop printers, imagesetters—create images out of dots. The simplest way to create type for one of these devices is to draw a picture of every character as an array of dots and store these drawings in a font. Then all a device has to do to image the type is to copy those dots into place on the screen or page. When this technology was first figured out, each one of those dots was represented by one *bit* of computer data—a simple yes/no choice of whether to image a dot or not. Images created from these predrawn, prearranged arrays of dots were called *bitmaps,* and fonts using this trick were called *bitmapped* fonts.

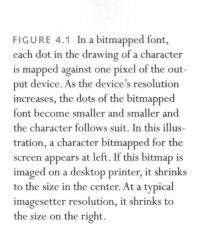

FIGURE 4.1 In a bitmapped font, each dot in the drawing of a character is mapped against one pixel of the output device. As the device's resolution increases, the dots of the bitmapped font become smaller and smaller and the character follows suit. In this illustration, a character bitmapped for the screen appears at left. If this bitmap is imaged on a desktop printer, it shrinks to the size in the center. At a typical imagesetter resolution, it shrinks to the size on the right.

Bitmaps are a clever and simple approach, but the more dots a bitmap contains, the more computer data it requires. As the resolution of the device increases or the size of the character images increases, the number of dots grows geometrically: Doubling the size of a character quadruples the number of dots. You also need a separate set of bitmaps—a separate font—for every size of type you want to create. And the bitmaps designed for one resolution will appear much smaller when imaged on a device with a higher resolution, where the dots are much smaller (see Figure 4.1). To image a single typeface at the same range of sizes on a computer screen, a desktop laser printer, and an imagesetter, then, would require hundreds of bitmapped fonts.

The solution is to store the descriptions of the characters as a set of outline drawings. *Outline fonts,* which do just this, store character images as outlines described mathematically as a series of curves and straight-line segments. (These line segments are sometimes called *vectors,* and fonts based on them, *vector fonts.*) These outlines can be mathematically scaled to any size without distorting the shapes or proportions of the characters. The scaled outlines are then colored in with dots of the size created by the device that the type is being imaged on: around 100 dots per inch (dpi) for a computer screen, 300 to 600 dpi for a desktop printer, and well over 1,000 dpi for imagesetters.

Although outline fonts are now used to generate images of type for computer screens as well as printed pages, bitmapped fonts are still often used for screen displays. This is because at small point sizes, where very few screen dots (*pixels*) are used to describe each character, more legible type is often obtained when a human being draws the bitmaps by hand than when a computer generates them from an outline font. If bitmapped screen fonts are available for the outline fonts you use, you should consider using them, as they will probably be more legible than screen type generated from your outline fonts.

What's in a Font?

A font contains all the information needed to position and image the characters that it represents. How a computer operating system and an application program team up to use this information is covered in detail in Chapter 7. Here we're just concerned with what's inside a font and what it means to you as you set type.

The most important constituents of a font are the character outlines themselves. The entire collection of characters in a font is called its *character set.* For most *alphanumeric* fonts (that is, the ones used for text containing letters and numerals), character sets are standardized to a degree. The fonts all share a basic set of characters, although they may contain optional extra characters as well. Figure 4.2 shows the character set of a standard text font. Fonts based on Unicode (see the section on OpenType fonts on page 53) may contain additional characters beyond the basic collection.

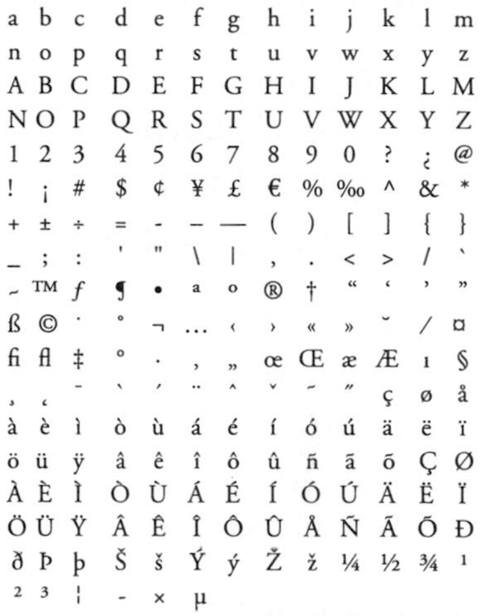

The character outlines in a font are size independent. Inside each font a *width table* lists the horizontal space allotted to each character, as measured in fractions of an em. Computer programs use these widths to calculate how to fill lines with type, adding up the cumulative widths of the characters on a line until the line is filled.

A font may also contain tables for the widths of other members in its family. This is typically the case for the "regular," or roman text-weight, member of a family. These tables enable a computer program to compose type for all four members of a family—regular, italic, bold, and bold italic—using only the regular font. The computer's operating system, using the widths of the other family members, can synthesize false italics, bolds, and bold italics for onscreen display, relying on width tables in the regular font for getting the spacing right. The typesetting program, which relies only on the character widths, follows suit and can make appropriate decisions about how much text will fit on a line and how lines should be broken. When it comes time to print, all the necessary fonts will have to be present, as their outlines will be needed to image the type (see Figure 4.3). But to simply compose the type onscreen, only the regular-weight font is needed. The relationship between application and operating system is detailed in Chapter 7.

A font also contains a *kerning table,* which lists specific letter pairs and how the typesetting program should adjust the spacing between them. Kerning adjustments are also expressed in fractions of an em, which enables them to function at any point size. For more information about kerning, see Chapter 11.

FIGURE 4.2 This is the standard character set of a PostScript Type 1 font. Although such a font can nominally contain 256 characters, 33 "slots" in the font are taken up by commands such as backspace and delete, and 2 by the word space and nonbreaking space.

onscreen

True roman
True italic
True bold
True bold italic

True roman
Synthesized italic
Synthesized bold
Synthesized bold italic

in print

True roman
True italic
True bold
True bold italic

True roman
Synthesized italic
Synthesized bold
Synthesized bold italic

FIGURE 4.3 In this illustration, the top four lines of screen type were generated from their actual fonts. The computer generated the second set of four lines by interpolating the outlines of the plain roman font. You can see that the "italics" are simply obliqued roman characters.

The high-resolution lines at the bottom show what you get if you try to print the two samples. With all the fonts available, printing proceeds normally. But without the outlines for the other three members of the family, the printer uses the plain roman font for all four lines.

Font Formats

Ultimately, what's inside a font depends on its format. The word *format* has two meanings in computer type. First, it can refer to the platform for which the font was designed. For example, two fonts with the same data for the same typeface may have different file formats depending on whether they're being used on an Apple Macintosh or a Windows PC. Most existing fonts have been created to meet the data-structuring needs of one platform or the other, and a font designed for one machine will not work on the other.

Another kind of font format reflects the way that the typographic information itself is described and how that information is organized. The three leading font formats today are PostScript, TrueType, and OpenType.

POSTSCRIPT FONTS

PostScript fonts are written in the PostScript page description language, and they need to be processed by a PostScript interpreter before they can be imaged. (See "The PostScript Model" in Chapter 1 for more information on PostScript interpreters.) For high-resolution printers and imagesetters, this interpreter is generally built into the device itself; it's a separate onboard computer dedicated to turning PostScript code into printable output. For lower-resolution devices, such as computer monitors and desktop printers, PostScript fonts can be imaged by a PostScript interpreter built into the operating system or by an add-on system extension called Adobe Type Manager (ATM). PostScript fonts are generally accompanied by a set of bitmapped fonts for screen display on systems that lack a PostScript interpreter.

The several kinds of PostScript fonts are distinguished from one another by number. The only one you're likely to come across is *Type 1,* and it's only mentioned here because of references you may come across to "PostScript Type 1" fonts. In publishing and typesetting contexts, when you talk about a PostScript font, it's assumed you're talking about the Type 1 variety.

PostScript fonts are the standard of the publishing industry, and they continue to be favored over other formats. This is because most imagesetters and other high-end output devices (such as the printing-plate imagers that make press-ready plates directly from computer output) use PostScript interpreters—*raster image processors,* or RIPS—almost exclusively. PostScript RIPS work best with PostScript fonts.

TRUETYPE FONTS

For a few years in the late 1980s, the typesetting world had in PostScript a single, standard *font format* for the first time in its history. It wasn't to last. For a combination of primarily commercial but also technological reasons, Apple Computer and Microsoft collaborated to create a new font format: TrueType. The new format enabled both companies to build outline font-imaging capabilities into their respective operating systems without being beholden to Adobe.

Although TrueType fonts were supposed to be compatible with PostScript interpreters, there were many problems outputting TrueType fonts on PostScript imagesetters. For this reason, PostScript fonts have remained the font format of choice for publishing professionals. These problems continue to be ironed out, however, and the popularity of TrueType fonts on Windows PCs and a new commercial cooperation between Adobe and Microsoft have led to better performance in PostScript output devices.

TrueType introduced many improvements over the PostScript format. The most prominently touted is its *hinting,* instructions added to the font that tell the character outlines how to reshape themselves at low and medium resolutions in order to create character images of maximum clarity. (For more on hinting, see "Imaging PostScript Fonts" in Chapter 1.) Because of the high quality of these hints, TrueType fonts are typically delivered without any hand-drawn, bitmapped screen fonts. Screen type generated from the font's character outlines is generally quite legible even in small point sizes.

TrueType also allowed for larger character sets. This made room for alternate forms of characters and permitted *contextual character switching,* meaning that under prescribed conditions one character could be automatically substituted for another. In fact, TrueType fonts enabled a wide range of typographical capabilities, most of which have never been realized because they are too complicated (read: too expensive) to program into the fonts themselves and into the application programs that were supposed to profit from them. Apple attempted to build in some of these TrueType capabilities at the operating system level through QuickDraw GX (a version of the page description language the Mac OS uses to draw screen images), but nearly no one supported it. At the very least, QuickDraw GX meant that a document created on a Mac wouldn't work properly on a Windows PC, which lacked Apple's proprietary GX support.

OPENTYPE FONTS

OpenType is a hybrid font format created by Adobe and Microsoft. It reconciles the differences in the two formats, allowing them to exist together in a single file. OpenType fonts are also written in a file format that allows the same font file to be used on either a Macintosh or a Windows PC.

Crudely put, an OpenType font is a TrueType font with a "pocket" for PostScript data. An OpenType font can contain TrueType font data, PostScript font data, or (theoretically) both. Thus it has the potential to combine the best of both formats in a transparent way. The operating system of your computer will sort out the data in an OpenType font and use what's appropriate for it.

A problem with OpenType fonts, as with the TrueType fonts that preceded them, is that from the outside there's no way to know what's inside. The original generation of PostScript fonts generally contained a standard character set with standard features. The TrueType format and, to an even greater extent, the OpenType format offer a wide range of optional features that may or may not be built into every font. An OpenType font can contain anywhere from 256 characters to more than 65,000 characters. There's no way of knowing unless the features of the font are documented in some way.

Cross-Platform Font-Compatibility Issues

The vast majority of fonts today do not use the OpenType format, which means they will work with either a Macintosh or a Windows PC but not both. Nearly all fonts for sale, however, are available in both Mac and PC formats, and versions of the same face from the same vendor produce identical results. The only difference between the Mac and PC versions of a font is the way the data has been written; it can be read by one machine or the other, but not both.

Both the Apple Macintosh OS and Microsoft Windows come with a core set of fonts. Originally, the fonts were completely different, Apple's coming from Linotype and Microsoft's from Monotype. But although they were distinct typefaces, Microsoft (the latecomers to type support in the operating system) and Monotype designed each of the Windows core fonts to have the same character widths as a corresponding font in the Mac set. Thus Windows' Arial has the same character widths as the Mac's Helvetica. When a job set in Helvetica went from a Mac to a PC, Windows could substitute Arial and the job would compose exactly as it had on the Mac. Arial looks somewhat different from Helvetica, but because its character widths are the same, it composes the same, and every line break in one version is identical to that in the other.

Apple used the same technique when it started shipping TrueType versions of the core set of PostScript fonts, those built into every PostScript interpreter. The philosophy was the same: Everyone should have at least a core set of fonts in common, allowing them to pass typographically formatted documents back and forth, albeit in a small number of possible typefaces.

Character-Set Issues

Text fonts in the PostScript format and early TrueType fonts were based on a single character set—the so-called Latin 1 character set—although the Macintosh operating system and Windows used different subsets of it. From Windows, for example, you couldn't get at the *ligatures* (twinned characters such as fi and fl), and on the Mac you couldn't get at the fractions (although, unlike Windows, it gave you access to a fraction bar character, so you could build your own).

These early fonts had room for 256 characters, and this character set remains the standard configuration for most fonts. (Actually, there are far fewer printable characters in these fonts, as 33 character "slots" are reserved for nonprinting commands such as backspace, delete, and return.) Even OpenType fonts, which are capable of containing more than 65,000 characters, may have only the standard 256. Most fonts converted from PostScript Type 1 to OpenType do not acquire a significant number of new characters (if any at all). This basic collection of printing characters was shown in Figure 4.2, in the section "What's in a Font?" earlier in this chapter.

ASCII and Unicode

Not all versions of all operating systems allow access to all of these characters. As of this writing, only those that support Unicode do. These include Macintosh OS X and Windows NT 4, Windows 2000, and Windows XP. Both Microsoft and Apple have indicated that Unicode will eventually be supported in all future major upgrades to their operating systems.

Unicode is an international standard that, like other font standards, assigns numbers to the characters in a font. The numbers are used by computer systems to call for particular characters. Before Unicode, the only international cross-platform standard for creating such assignments was ASCII (American Standard Code for Information Interchange), which assigned only the numbers 0 through 127, as shown in Figure 4.4. By expressing text in ASCII format, computer files could be exchanged and read regardless of what font or computer systems were used, as the numbers used to express text had standardized meanings. ASCII number 72, for example, is always a capital *H*.

Unicode extends this numbering scheme to more than a million characters, including character sets for a host of non-Latin "alphabets." Most Unicode fonts, such as those for Asian ideographic languages, are *double-byte* fonts and can contain more than 65,000 characters.

32	(space)	64	@	96	`
33	!	65	A	97	a
34	"	66	B	98	b
35	#	67	C	99	c
36	$	68	D	100	d
37	%	69	E	101	e
38	&	70	F	102	f
39	'	71	G	103	g
40	(	72	H	104	h
41	)	73	I	105	i
42	*	74	J	106	j
43	+	75	K	107	k
44	,	76	L	108	l
45	-	77	M	109	m
46	.	78	N	110	n
47	/	79	O	111	o
48	0	80	P	112	p
49	1	81	Q	113	q
50	2	82	R	114	r
51	3	83	S	115	s
52	4	84	T	116	t
53	5	85	U	117	u
54	6	86	V	118	v
55	7	87	W	119	w
56	8	88	X	120	x
57	9	89	Y	121	y
58	:	90	Z	122	z
59	;	91	[	123	{
60	<	92	\	124	|
61	=	93	]	125	}
62	>	94	^	126	~
63	?	95	_	127	(delete)

FIGURE 4.4 Computers identify characters by numbers, and all systems agree on the meanings of 0 through 127, the so-called ASCII character set. The numbers 0 through 31, not shown here, are either unassigned or assigned to nonprinting commands such as return and backspace. The ASCII character set is printed on most English-language computer keyboards.

Win ANSI only

Đ	ð	Þ	þ	Š	š	Ý
ý	Ž	ž	¼	½	¾	¹
²	³	¦	–	×		

MacRoman only

| ⁄ | fl | fi | ı | ˘ | | |

MacRoman only, from Symbol

∫	∂	Δ	π	Π	√
Σ	Ω	≈	◊	∞	≠
≤	≥				

FIGURE 4.5 Of the basic character set shown in Figure 4.2, only Windows programs have direct access to the group of characters shown at the top here. Only Macintosh programs can use the ones in the middle group. The bottom group includes characters in the basic MacRoman encoding that appear to be in every Mac font, but they are actually borrowed from the Symbol font.

Font-Encoding Issues

How numbers are assigned to the characters within a typeface is referred to as a font's *encoding*. Before they supported Unicode, the Macintosh and Windows operating systems used two different encoding schemes. They agreed on the basic ASCII character set, but they disagreed on the characters assigned to the next 128 numbers, the so-called *high-bit* ASCII characters. The result was that documents formatted on one platform often appeared on the other with certain characters incorrectly substituted.

Not only did the pre-Unicode operating systems use different character-numbering schemes, but they also used different subsets of the basic Latin 1 character collection as their standard character sets. The Macintosh set (and encoding scheme) are called MacRoman; the Windows encoding scheme and character set are called Win ANSI. Although a vendor might sell identical fonts for both platforms, the Mac would allow its users to access one group of characters within a font, and Windows another. Figure 4.5 shows the characters that on non-Unicode systems are unique to each platform.

Because all these characters are actually in the fonts, however, certain intelligent application programs can enable them to be rendered onscreen and in print even though the operating system doesn't allow access to them. For example, a document formatted on the PC using the fraction ¼ can be opened on a Macintosh with the ¼ appearing correctly if the application that opens it is smart enough to find the appropriate character in the font and pull it out. Not all applications will do this. Once one of these "non-native" characters has been imaged in a document, it can sometimes be cut and pasted into other documents, even though on its new platform it cannot be accessed through any keystrokes. It's an odd trick, but it comes in handy sometimes.

THE MAC'S "BORROWED CHARACTERS"

Certain characters in the MacRoman encoding are borrowed from the Symbol font (see Figure 4.5). When you're working on the Macintosh, these characters seem to be a part of every font you use. The keystroke combination Option-D, for example, always yields a lowercase Greek delta: ∂. But the numbers assigned to these characters in the MacRoman encoding scheme point to blank "slots" in a Mac font. Calls for these numbers are diverted by the operating system to the Symbol font. That explains why these characters never match the style of the typeface you're working in (unless it happens to be Times Roman, upon whose design the seriffed Symbol characters are based).

This curious situation is unique to the Mac and unique to this small handful of characters.

FIGURE 4.6 Adobe InDesign has its own character browser built in, and a pull-down menu lets you isolate classes of characters for faster searching amid extended character sets. These categories are specified inside the font itself, in this case TrueType Palatino from Linotype.

Finding the Characters You Need

Both Windows (through the Character Map utility) and the Macintosh os (through the Key Caps utility) enable you to see the characters in a font. Without one of these helper programs, there is no way to know exactly which characters are in a particular font. Applications themselves are beginning to offer the same service, giving users access to the extended character sets of Unicode fonts even when the operating system can't (see Figure 4.6).

Using Windows' Character Map

Windows' Character Map (found in the Programs > Accessories > System Tools menu) shows all the characters in a font in the form of a scrollable grid. From here you can select and copy a character or group of characters into your document. Selecting a character also indicates the character's access-code number. To access a character—in a word processor, for example—without using Character Map, you can hold down the Alt key while you type its number; when you release the Alt key, the character will appear in your text.

In versions of Windows that support Unicode, this technique works the same for both Win ANSI–encoded fonts and Unicode-encoded fonts. But in Unicode fonts, only the characters within the Win ANSI encoding range get these Alt-key access codes. The others are identified only by their Unicode numbers, which are written in hexadecimal code (a counting scheme that uses the letters *A–F* to supplement the numerals *0–9*). In most English-language versions of Windows and with English-language applications, you have to cut and paste to get these characters out of Character Map and into your documents. In newer applications that take advantage of Windows' Unicode support, you can type a character's hexadecimal code number (e.g., 02A5) followed by the command Alt-X, which will convert the number into the corresponding character. Non-English versions of Windows and non-English applications will be able to address the non-Latin characters in a Unicode font directly (presumably using a non-English keyboard).

Because there can be so many characters in a Unicode font, Character Map gives you the option to display only certain groups of characters at a time: those used for particular languages, for example, or numeric characters, including fractions and the characters for building them.

Using the Macintosh's Key Caps

The Macintosh's Key Caps displays a keyboard to show what characters are assigned to which keys. Holding down the Shift key changes the display to indicate which characters are available with the Shift key held down. The same happens when you hold down the Option key or the Option and Shift keys simultaneously. With the four options—no Shift or Option, Shift, Option, and Option-Shift—the Mac OS enables each alphanumeric key to access four characters. As with Windows' Character Map, any characters you select in Key Caps can be copied into your documents.

The Mac OS also uses more complex keystroke combinations to access accented characters. In this process you hold down the Option key while you press a key that represents the accent you want to use: acute, grave, dieresis (umlaut), tilde, or circumflex. Then, in a separate action, you press the key of the letter over which you want to place the accent. At this point the accented character appears onscreen. To see where these accent characters are located, hold down the Option key with the Key Caps window open. You'll see that five keys appear with gray boundaries. These are the accent keys. If you click on one of them and release the Option key, you'll see the characters over which that accent can be placed.

THE MAC OS AND UNICODE

In OS X—the only Mac operating system as of this writing that fully supports Unicode—this arrangement becomes more complicated. You can still use Key Caps to see all of the characters in a font, but in English-language versions of the OS, the keyboard display remains dedicated to the MacRoman encoding set: the familiar Latin characters plus that handful borrowed from Symbol.

In OS X, applications that support Unicode behave differently from those that don't. Programs that are not Unicode savvy, for example, may not immediately be able to use fonts that don't use the MacRoman encoding scheme. The most common of these are Symbol and Zapf Dingbats (whose characters have Unicode numbers, but outside the MacRoman range). The same will be true of any Unicode font, such as one for an Asian language.

For Unicode-challenged applications, you must use the International options in System Preferences to select the keyboard layouts you want (some are language specific, others font specific). These then appear in a pull-down menu in the Key Caps menu bar. To set a Zapf Dingbat, for example, you have to select the Zapf Dingbats keyboard, whereupon you will have access to the dingbats with the same keystrokes you would use in OS 9 or earlier.

When using Unicode-savvy applications, you don't have to swap the keyboard layouts, because such programs will make the proper adjustments automatically when you select a Unicode font.

For Unicode fonts with large character sets, Key Caps, like Windows' Character Map, lets you view selections of characters a range at a time, so you don't have to scroll through the entire collection of characters. Also like Windows, Mac OS X requires that you cut and paste to get most characters into your documents—unless you have a non-English operating system (and ideally a non-English keyboard to match) or specific application support—because the keyboard is dedicated to the MacRoman encoding characters. Alternatively, you can type a character's Unicode number while holding down the Option key. When you release the key, the character will appear.

"Expert Sets" and Alternate Fonts

Before Unicode and OpenType came along, most fonts were restricted to 256 characters, and Latin-based alphanumeric fonts all contained a standard character set. (TrueType fonts have long been able to have larger character sets, but most font vendors—for the sake of compatibility—matched the character sets of their TrueType fonts to the sets of the PostScript fonts.) Those restrictions,

old-style numerals

1 2 3 4 5

6 7 8 9 0

small capitals

A B C D E F G

H I J K L M N

O P Q R S T U

V W X Y Z

swash characters

A B C D E F

G H I J K L

M N O P Q R

S T U V W X

Y Z

ligatures

ff ffi ffl Rp ct

FIGURE 4.7 Expert-set fonts and alternate fonts contain characters that belong to a typeface but for which there's no room in the face's principal font. The characters shown here are drawn from the alternate and expert-set fonts for Adobe Garamond. With the larger character sets made possible by the TrueType and OpenType font formats, alternate fonts will eventually fade away, and these kinds of characters will be united with the font's standard characters in a single font.

though, were without historical precedent, and some typefaces had many characters for which there was no room in the standard font layouts.

The solution to the problem was to create companion fonts for certain typefaces, fonts that contained alternate characters. These companion fonts are called *expert sets* or *alternate fonts*. They include such characters as old-style numerals (which have varying heights, and some of which have descenders) and small capitals (scaled-down versions of capital letters made to be used amid lowercase type, where they are less obtrusive than full-size capitals). Other common expert-set or alternate characters include ligatures (tied letter combinations) and swash characters (with exaggerated terminals). Examples are shown in Figure 4.7.

The layouts of these fonts are not standard, so they're usually sold with a chart showing which keystrokes yield which characters. Unfortunately, Unicode-based character-locating utilities won't help, since most of these fonts predate Unicode, and many of the characters do not have standard Unicode numbers assigned to them in any case.

Expert-set fonts are also troublesome to use because they require a change of font, often for a single character. Macro programs or utilities—which enable you to program a key or screen button to execute a series of commands—are indispensable for dealing with expert-set fonts, as well as with pi fonts, for which you also need two changes of typeface to set a single character.

Characters outside the Unicode Standard

The encoding issue brings up a murky side of Unicode: namely, if Unicode assigns specific numbers to specific characters, what happens when a type designer creates characters that aren't accommodated in the Unicode list? Such characters include many of those normally found in expert-set and alternate fonts.

The answer is that the Unicode scheme contains a range of numbers designated for "Private Use," and here a type designer can add customized characters. The meaning of these Unicode numbers, then, will vary from font to font. To simplify the arrangement, OpenType fonts can also contain links among characters to make it clear to an application or operating system that a particular character is actually an alternate form of one of the characters in the standard Unicode encoding. Figure 4.8 shows how an application can offer the choice of alternate characters to the user. By adding several planes to each character slot, the size of the total onscreen character grid is cut down to more manageable proportions, and characters can be found in logical places.

Look forward to the day when keyboards have illuminated readouts on the keys, so that when fonts change, keyboard layouts will change and the new

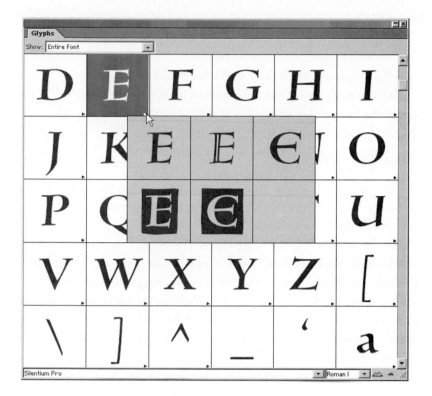

FIGURE 4.8 One Unicode number can point to several alternate versions of a single character. Here, four alternate forms of the *E* have been added to Adobe's Silentium Pro OpenType font, and they pop up from the basic character display grid in InDesign's character browser.

character assignments will appear on the keys themselves. With the advent of large-character-set Unicode fonts, no one will be able to be a touch-typist all the time anymore.

Identifying Font Formats

If you've read this chapter from the beginning, you'll realize that not all fonts behave the same way. PostScript fonts, TrueType fonts, and OpenType fonts all have their own idiosyncrasies, not to mention some major functional differences. It's important to be able to tell them apart.

If you're looking at them in the folders where the operating system stores them, you can distinguish among the three formats relatively easily. Trying to distinguish among them by their appearances in a program's Font menu can range from difficult to impossible. In general, it's better to know the formats of the fonts you use before you install them into your system and to create a method for keeping track of what's what. Fonts in different formats may appear with identical names in your Font menus, and having two such fonts listed side by side is something you want to avoid. Furthermore, it's entirely possible for an operating system to fail to distinguish between two fonts of the same name in different formats and to list just one of them in an application's Font menu.

TrueType
suitcase

PostScript
screen font suitcase

Palatino

Palatino

TrueType
screen font

PostScript
screen font

Palatino 10

Palatino 10

TrueType
outline font

PostScript
outline font

Palatino

PalatRom

FIGURE 4.9 Font icons on the Macintosh can tell a confusing story. The icons at the top are for two very different fonts, although they look identical. If you look inside them, you're apt to see icons like those directly below them, which are both Palatino screen fonts, but for two different fonts—they are not inter-changeable, but you'd never know to look at them. Only by locating the outline-font icons can you distinguish between the standard TrueType icon at bottom left and the identifiably different PostScript icon (in this case from a font in the Adobe Type Library) at the bottom right.

Not only won't you know that there are two fonts with the same name on your system, but you also won't know which one you're getting.

In general, it's a good idea to keep as few fonts as possible installed on your system at a time, and to stick with one format or another if you can.

Identifying the Formats of Macintosh Fonts

On the Mac, only OpenType fonts containing PostScript font data (so-called PostScript-flavored OpenType fonts) are identifiable by their file names, which end with the filename extension .otf.

Plain PostScript fonts can be represented by any number of icons (each type foundry tends to invent its own), but using Get Info will reveal whether a font is a PostScript font or not. In the PostScript regime, each member of a font family is a separate file, so their names can become long enough that they have to be abbreviated into forms—such as OfficSerBooIta (Officina Serif Book Italic)—that may make them nearly unrecognizable. The weirdness of the names is often a giveaway.

TrueType fonts use a generic suitcase icon and generally bear a simple family name, such as Georgia or Arial. Get Info, though, identifies these files only as "font suitcases" and their contents (the fonts for individual family members) as "fonts." This is potentially confusing, because identical-looking suitcases are also used for bitmapped screen fonts associated with PostScript fonts. To be sure that a font suitcase belongs to a TrueType font, you have to look inside. The TrueType font files have distinctive icons, as shown in Figure 4.9.

Identifying the Formats of Windows Fonts

If you look at Windows fonts in their folders, you'll see them all identified with unique icons that distinguish PostScript from TrueType from OpenType fonts (see Figure 4.10). As on the Mac, PostScript fonts are likely to have different icons according to who manufactured them.

File names of fonts in Windows are generally indicative of the font's formats. TrueType font names have the extension .ttf or .ttc, although these extensions can also be used for "TrueType flavored" OpenType fonts. As far as Windows is concerned, those formats are virtually identical, varying only by their character sets. Not all OpenType fonts, then, will have an .otf filename extension.

PostScript Type 1 fonts have the filename extension .pfb (for the font files containing the character outline data; the *b* stands for *binary*) and .pfm (for the corresponding file containing the bitmapped screen fonts and *metrics*—that is, character-width—data). Because most versions of Windows are based on DOS

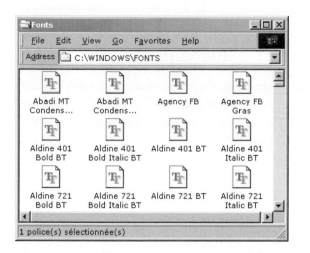

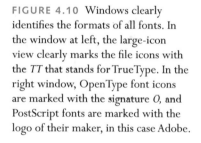

FIGURE 4.10 Windows clearly identifies the formats of all fonts. In the window at left, the large-icon view clearly marks the file icons with the *TT* that stands for TrueType. In the right window, OpenType font icons are marked with the signature *O,* and PostScript fonts are marked with the logo of their maker, in this case Adobe.

(disk operating system), the length of font file names is often limited to eight characters plus a filename extension (after a punctuating dot) of three more characters. This makes the names of most PostScript fonts completely unintelligible. It's not apparent, for example, that VARG_____.pfb is actually Viva Regular. In contrast, names of TrueType and OpenType fonts in Windows are spelled out in plain English.

In addition, it's common for Windows applications to indicate in their Font menu the formats of the fonts listed. Here, ideally, is where you want to know this information, and eventually all programs on all platforms will perform this useful service (see Figure 4.11).

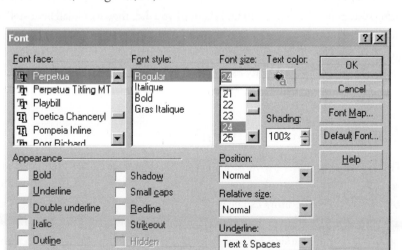

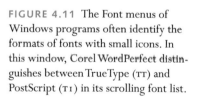

FIGURE 4.11 The Font menus of Windows programs often identify the formats of fonts with small icons. In this window, Corel WordPerfect distinguishes between TrueType (TT) and PostScript (T1) in its scrolling font list.

The Basics of Font Management

There is a breed of utility program called a *font manager,* whose job it is to help organize and manage the huge numbers of fonts that can come to populate your computer. Having too many fonts installed on your computer at the same time creates two main problems: First, it slows down your computer, which has to constantly keep track of all of those fonts. (Too many installed fonts may in fact cause your computer to freeze up.) Second, it creates a Font menu that's too long to manage, requiring endless scrolling to find the font you're after. The main thing a font manager does is enable you to keep the number of fonts in your system at a minimum with very little effort.

The principal way it does this is by allowing you to install or remove fonts from active service individually or en masse at any time. You can build *font sets* to make this easier. You can have a certain set of fonts for a specific job, or a certain set of fonts that are associated with a particular program. Fonts can belong to two or more of these sets. Some font managers can automatically install whatever fonts are needed by a document that you open.

In addition, font-management programs can help you organize your fonts in logical ways. Whereas Windows or the Mac os would throw them in a single heap (or, worse, several hard-to-locate heaps), a font-management program can organize them according to any criteria you like: font format; historical style; text, display, or decorative use; or whatever else.

When using a font manager, you don't store your fonts where your operating system usually expects to find them (if you did, they would all be installed all the time). Instead, you can store your fonts wherever you want to, and per your instructions, the font manager will then hand them off to the operating system as needed. This capability can make managing an extensive font library—especially for a workgroup—much easier.

Font-Editing Programs

Font-editing programs are the tools that type designers use to create fonts from scratch. They include tools to draw character outlines as well as to edit those outlines later. Font editors can be useful to the nondesigner as well, as they can add characters to a font (a digitized corporate logo, for example). They are also often used by demanding typographers to improve the quality of the kerning information within a font.

Creating customized fonts can have its advantages, but its disadvantages are very serious. Edited fonts become unique fonts, and unless they have been given unique names, they can become confused with existing retail fonts. Fonts that have had their kerning information altered, for example, will cause text to compose in a unique way, and these differences are enshrined in the font, not in the document. If that document travels to a place where the custom font that created it is unavailable, it will not compose correctly, line endings will change, and whole layouts can become disrupted.

Because font files are mobile, a customized font that escapes its handlers can cause havoc if it becomes confused (or used) with its unedited forebear. Edited fonts, then, have to be employed with great care and control.

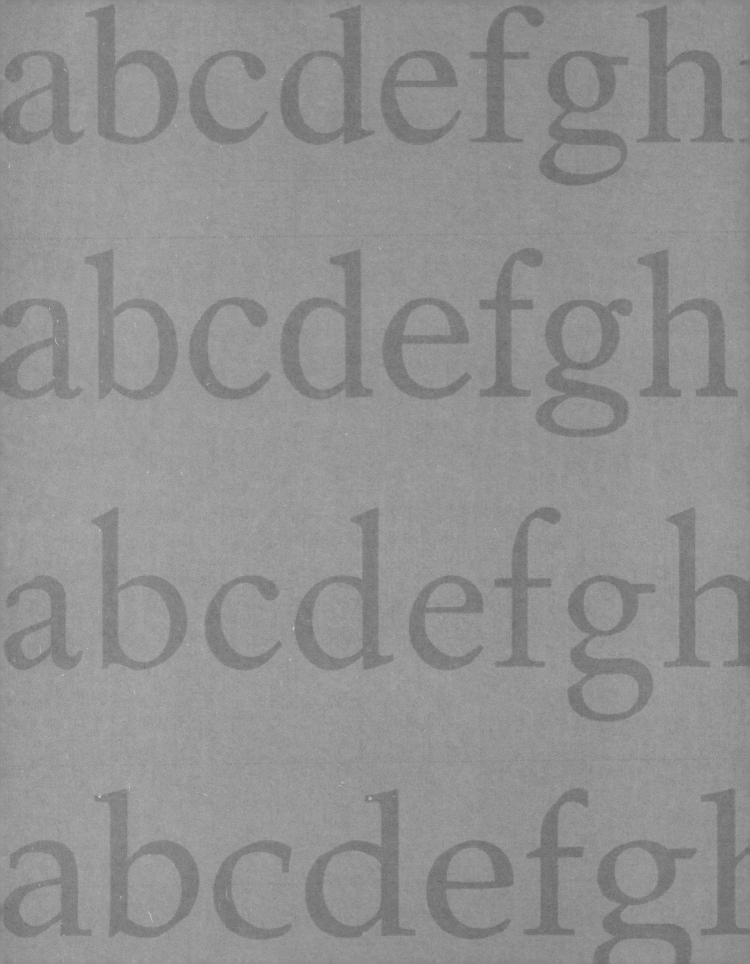

CHAPTER 5

The Basics of Using Typefaces

WHAT MAKES TEXT READABLE

TRADITIONAL ROLES FOR SERIFFED AND SANS SERIF TYPES

EXPRESSING EMPHASIS: BOLD, OTHER WEIGHTS, ITALICS

USES FOR CONDENSED AND EXTENDED FACES

USING DISPLAY AND DECORATIVE TYPE

TYPE IN COLOR AND REVERSED TYPE

Choosing a typeface is more than an aesthetic decision. Typefaces can adorn or decorate the characters they present, but they are also the bearers of practical information—emphasis, for example. Typeface choice and use also affect how well and how easily a passage of text can be read, starting with whether the text is even legible.

Type exists only when it's made visible, and this can be done in myriad media, from computer screen to print to projected image. This chapter looks at typeface use from these practical perspectives.

Readability

Empirically we know that some typefaces are easier to read than others. Quite apart from the way texts are set—their typographic qualities—some typefaces are simply easier on the eyes and some are more difficult. This fact has always intrigued the scientifically minded of the type world, leading to decades of effort and scores of research projects dedicated to readability studies. The goals of these studies have been to learn what typographic practices enhance readability and to determine which kinds of typefaces are the most readable.

𝕿𝖍𝖊 𝖑𝖊𝖌𝖎𝖇𝖎𝖑𝖎𝖙𝖞 𝖔𝖋 𝖙𝖞𝖕𝖊𝖘, 𝖎𝖙 𝖘𝖊𝖊𝖒𝖘, 𝖎𝖘 𝖑𝖆𝖗𝖌𝖊𝖑𝖞 𝖆 𝖒𝖆𝖙𝖙𝖊𝖗 𝖔𝖋 𝖍𝖆𝖇𝖎𝖙. 𝕬 𝖗𝖊𝖈𝖊𝖓𝖙 𝖘𝖙𝖚𝖉𝖞 𝖎𝖓𝖉𝖎𝖈𝖆𝖙𝖊𝖘 𝖙𝖍𝖆𝖙 𝖇𝖑𝖆𝖈𝖐𝖑𝖊𝖙𝖙𝖊𝖗 𝖙𝖞𝖕𝖊𝖋𝖆𝖈𝖊𝖘 𝖘𝖚𝖈𝖍 𝖆𝖘 𝕮𝖑𝖔𝖎𝖘𝖙𝖊𝖗 𝕭𝖑𝖆𝖈𝖐 𝖆𝖗𝖊 𝖏𝖚𝖘𝖙 𝖆𝖘 𝖑𝖊𝖌𝖎𝖇𝖑𝖊 𝖆𝖓𝖉 𝖊𝖆𝖘𝖎𝖑𝖞 𝖗𝖊𝖆𝖉𝖆𝖇𝖑𝖊 𝖆𝖘 𝖗𝖔𝖒𝖆𝖓 𝖙𝖞𝖕𝖊𝖘 𝖙𝖔 𝖊𝖞𝖊𝖘 𝖙𝖍𝖆𝖙 𝖆𝖗𝖊 𝖆𝖈𝖈𝖚𝖘𝖙𝖔𝖒𝖊𝖉 𝖙𝖔 𝖙𝖍𝖊𝖒.

FIGURE 5.1 Although it has been commonly assumed that Fraktur, or black-letter, type like this is harder to read than roman types, a recent study argues otherwise. Readability is largely based on what a reader is accustomed to seeing.

Readability studies are notorious for coming to clouded and contradictory conclusions. Even consensus opinions have been cast into doubt. For example, it has long been an article of faith that seriffed types are easier to read than sans serif types (studies, naturally, disagree on the subject). Likewise, roman types have long been assumed to be more readable than italic types (one study even specified that they were 3 percent more readable).

But yet another recent study has cast doubt on these stereotypes. The study compared the reading speeds of a group reading texts set in roman typefaces with those of a group reading texts set in the *Fraktur,* or *black-letter,* type popular in Germany until World War II (see Figure 5.1). It has generally been assumed that because the strokes used in Fraktur types are so similar and so closely spaced, readers need more time to decipher the letters. Wrong. The study found that the reading speeds of those accustomed to reading Fraktur type were essentially the same as those used to reading text set in roman types. Bad typesetting and bad typeface design aside, the fact seems to be that the most readable typefaces are the ones you're accustomed to reading.

(This generality, of course, applies only to text faces, as opposed to display or decorative faces. Clearly, the exaggerated features and proportions of many of the latter two classes of typefaces are bound to make reading more difficult, no matter how inured to them you might eventually become.)

The study's conclusions don't mean that the stereotypes of sans serifs and italics as being less readable aren't true. Popular design and typographic practice have made them true by using seriffed roman types as the standard faces for books, magazines, and newspapers. Because they are what we're accustomed to, seriffed faces are more readable for us.

For typical texts, then, the common choice is an old-style or transitional typeface: a seriffed face without much contrast between thick and thin strokes. Modern faces are generally out of style for common reading material.

Traditional Roles for Seriffed and Sans Serif Types

As noted, the standard kind of typeface for running text is a seriffed roman. This isn't a rule, but it is common practice. Although advocates of sans serif types in text have always been numerous and influential, probably the biggest boon to using sans serif type for text was the advent of desktop publishing. For a while, the two most commonly available typefaces were variations of Times Roman (a seriffed newspaper face) and Helvetica (the ubiquitous sans serif). Every printer manufacturer and digital foundry had versions of them, and often nothing else. Between the two typefaces, Helvetica often got the nod.

Sans serif types are far more often seen in display roles, though, as headings and titles and in advertising. In fact, the first known commercial sans serif, created by William Caslon IV in the early nineteenth century, was a 14-point advertising face called Egyptian. (Not that it looked Egyptian, but things Egyptian were the rage in those days, and anything with an antique or ancient architectural feel tended to get a name evocative of life on the ancient Nile.) With the rise of splashy display advertising typography in the nineteenth century, sans serif types proliferated. Another name given to sans serif faces of this epoch was the disparaging *grotesque*. The name stuck, and the appellation is still commonly used. The late-nineteenth-century sans that seems to have been a model for Helvetica was called Akzidenz Grotesque.

Common Features of Text Faces

The most popularly used text faces today are Monotype's Times New Roman and Linotype's version of it, Times Roman. Vast numbers of paperback books and corporate communications are churned out with these faces every year.

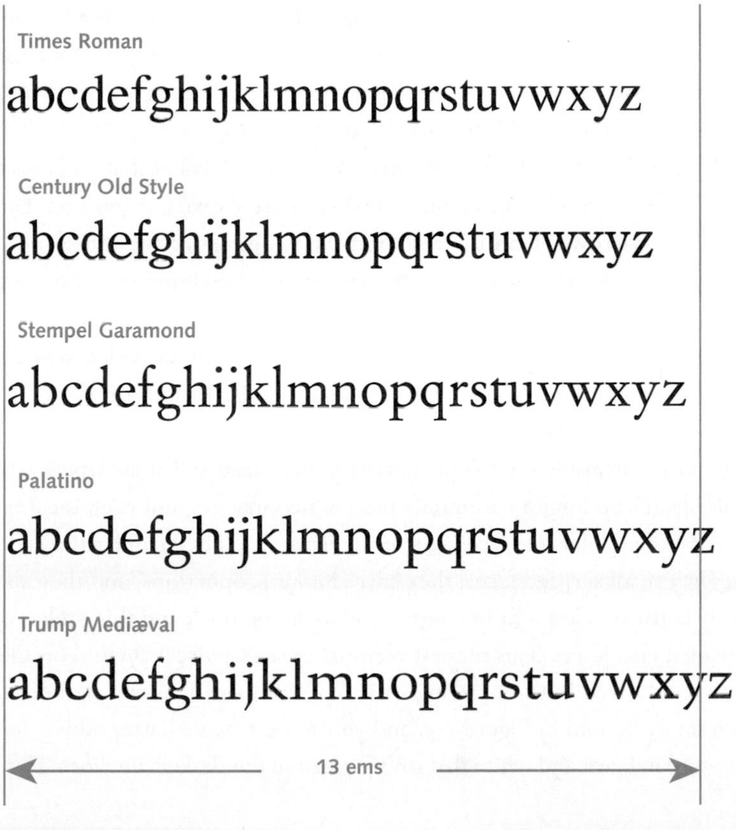

Times Roman

abcdefghijklmnopqrstuvwxyz

Century Old Style

abcdefghijklmnopqrstuvwxyz

Stempel Garamond

abcdefghijklmnopqrstuvwxyz

Palatino

abcdefghijklmnopqrstuvwxyz

Trump Mediæval

abcdefghijklmnopqrstuvwxyz

← 13 ems →

FIGURE 5.2 The "standard" width for the lowercase alphabet of a text font is 13 ems. As shown here, the perennial favorite Times Roman is in fact quite a bit narrower than that. A classic book face such as Stempel Garamond comes in right about on the mark, whereas some more contemporary faces tend to run a bit wider.

FIGURE 5.3 The upper sample is set in Times Roman, a narrow-width newspaper face, and the setting looks crowded across a book measure. Below it, the same text set in Sabon has a more natural feel, with generous character widths that are more befitting of the wide setting.

At many stages in the advance of humanity, conflict between the men who possess more than they have earned and the men who have earned more than they possess is the central condition of progress. In our day it appears as the struggle of free men to gain and hold the right of self-government as against the special interests, who twist the methods of free government into machinery for defeating the popular will.

At many stages in the advance of humanity, conflict between the men who possess more than they have earned and the men who have earned more than they possess is the central condition of progress. In our day it appears as the struggle of free men to gain and hold the right of self-government as against the special interests, who twist the methods of free government into machinery for defeating the popular will.

Monotype Bembo
ATF Goudy Old Style
Linotype Sabon
ITC New Baskerville
ATF Century Expanded
Linotype Caslon 540
Adobe Garamond
ITC Galliard

FIGURE 5.4 These popular text faces show basic similarities among types designed for this role. They don't have extraordinary contrast, their x-heights are generous but not too tall, and they don't call attention to themselves by flashy features or design quirks. They're elegant but conservative.

But in fact, Times is not a classic text face. Designed for use by the *Times* of London (as its new roman face, back in the 1930s), it has comparatively narrow characters, the better to compose well in the short lines of newspaper columns. Book publishers adopted it because it saved them paper.

A typeface of "standard" width has a lowercase alphabet that's 13 ems long. The relative widths of some common text faces are shown in Figure 5.2. Clearly, Times sets narrower than the rest, and the wider set of the others not only makes them easier to read but also creates a more open impression on the page. This openness is more in proportion with the wider line length typical of books and journals. The lines set in Times in Figure 5.3 seem crowded when compared with a more standard book face. With all that room on the line, why crowd the text like that?

Times is probably used inappropriately more than any other typeface today. Ironically, it's no longer commonly used in newspapers, not even the *Times.*

A list of popular text faces appears in Figure 5.4. Their similarities are obvious: They're all seriffed faces, they have similar proportions, and they all have a fairly consistent amount of contrast between the thick and thin stokes of the individual characters. This modest contrast creates a visual rhythm on the line that is modulated but not jarring or sharp. Compare lines set Baskerville to those set in Bodoni in Figure 5.5, and you'll see that the latter adds a tension expressed in black and white that isn't present in the Baskerville lines. This kind

There is an opinion that parties in free countries are use-ful checks upon the administration of the Government and serve to keep alive the spirit of liberty. This within certain limits is probably true, and in governments of a monarchical cast, patriotism may look with indulgence, if not with favor, upon the spirit of party. But in those of the popular character, in governments purely elective, it is a spirit not to be encouraged.

There is an opinion that parties in free countries are use-ful checks upon the administration of the Government and serve to keep alive the spirit of liberty. This within certain limits is probably true, and in governments of a monarchical cast, patriotism may look with indulgence, if not with favor, upon the spirit of party. But in those of the popular character, in governments purely elective, it is a spirit not to be encouraged.

FIGURE 5.5 The Baskerville setting on top has a more relaxed feel than the Bodoni setting below it. Baskerville, although elegant and refined, shows off the text first, while the more formal and stylized Bodoni draws more attention to itself.

of graphic drama isn't always what you want in long texts, where the typeface serves text better when it's more subdued.

The vertical proportions of text faces are also typically moderate, with average x-heights and with ascenders and descenders that are neither short nor unusually tall. An exception is Palatino—the newest of the group, having been designed in 1950—which has a taller-than-average x-height.

Expressing Emphasis

The traditional way of expressing emphasis typographically is through bold and italic faces. (Variations in size, by comparison, typically indicate a hierarchy of information: titles are bigger than headings, for example, which are bigger than text.) Of the two, italics are far more commonly used. In the following sections, the applications listed may not follow hard and fast rules (such things are rare in typography) but could be considered *de rigueur*.

Uses for Bold and Other Type Weights

Text is almost always set with a "regular" weight, but otherwise few typographic traditions or conventions apply to using the weights of a typeface. Most bolder and lighter versions are used for display purposes and not within running text.

Headings and subheadings, as in this book, are often set in bold. Such emphasis could also be achieved with a change of type size alone, but some bold type on a page adds a touch of graphic diversity, and bold type does the job of visual punctuation more effectively than does a mere change of point size. For emphasis within running text, however, bold is obtrusive, and the typographic convention is to use italics instead (for more on italics, see the next section). A common exception is made for safety warnings in instruction manuals and the like, where typographic aesthetics properly yield to matters of health and security.

One of the few instances where bold type can commonly be seen amid text-sized type is in index citations, where page numbers indicating illustrations are customarily set in bold.

Uses for Italics

Unlike bold types, italic types are assigned many roles by typographic convention; among the principal of these are emphasis and distinction. Many instances of such use would have been signified with an underscore in typewritten manuscripts. Among other items, italics are set for:

- Book titles.

- Names of works of art, including musical compositions.

- Names of films, plays, and television shows.

- Titles of periodicals.

- Terms introduced in a manuscript for the first time, as well as technical terms. ("Early cursives were called *Aldinos.*")

- Definitions within a sentence. ("His name in Hebrew means *peace.*")

- Proper names of ships and aircraft ("U.S.S. *Enterprise*").

- Single letters referred to as letters. ("Cross every *t* and dot every *i.*")

- Genera and species.

- Foreign words and phrases that haven't been adopted into popular usage. A dictionary is a useful guide here; if a foreign word or phrase isn't in the dictionary, set it in italics. Latin words and abbreviations these days (*e.g., i.e., ad hoc, etc., ibid., ca.,* and so forth) are typically set in roman type.

- Punctuation after words or letters set in italics, including periods, commas, colons, and semicolons (but not quotation marks).

Note that the possessive *s,* when attached to an italic word, is set in roman, as is the apostrophe that precedes it ("*King Lear*'s depressing ending").

Uses for Condensed and Extended Faces

Although condensed or compressed typefaces—whose character widths are narrower than those in the "regular" member of a family—are sometimes used in text roles (mainly for captions, footnotes, and the like), extended or expanded faces are rarely used in any other than display roles. An important exception (at least in terms of its name) is Century Expanded, a text face somewhat wider than its precursor, Century. Century, like Times Roman, has unusually narrow characters for a text face, having been designed in the 1890s for magazine use (*Century Magazine,* in fact).

In general, seriffed faces do not take well to being redesigned in condensed form. The richness of their features—their serifs, their variations in stroke weight, their calligraphic hooks and loops—tend to create a tangled look when the white space is squeezed out of them. ITC Garamond is one of the few popular typeface families that have a commonly used set of condensed complements (see Figure 5.6), but the condensed Garamonds are not terribly narrow. Most condensed typefaces (and almost all expanded ones) are sans serif types. They're generally used for contrast with other members of the same family or for saving space in display situations.

ITC Garamond Book Condensed

ITC Garamond Book Narrow

ITC Garamond Book

FIGURE 5.6 Condensed book faces are rare, but the ITC Garamond family is an exception. The condensed version is best reserved for short passages, such as captions.

Problems with Electronic Expanding and Condensing

The character outlines in electronic fonts are scalable, but they don't have to be scaled proportionally. Most text processing, page layout, and graphics programs allow you to alter the width of characters without affecting their height. This can be handy for shoehorning a reluctant headline into its measure, but such adjustments should be kept minor, certainly less than 10 percent of the characters' normal widths. The reason is that modifying the widths affects only the weight of the vertical strokes of the characters, not the horizontal ones. The result is that characters can be badly out of proportion (see Figure 5.7). Changing the *set width* of typeset characters does not create a new typeface; it creates a distorted version of an existing one. Unless the width changes are very subtle, it is rarely a pretty sight.

Figure 5.8 compares some electronically created condensed and expanded versions of typefaces with the designed versions of those faces for which fonts actually exist. The differences in the proportions and shapes of some characters—particularly the round ones—are obvious, for others less so. When a condensed or expanded typeface is needed, it's always better to find a typeface family that contains the members you need. These large families are rare, so it's tempting to create your own custom width variations. Resist the temptation.

ITC Avant Garde Over-Condensed

FIGURE 5.7 In this sample of electronically condensed type, the distortions caused by the process are evident, especially in the round letters. The problem is that the vertical features of the characters are narrowed, but the horizontal ones keep their original thickness. The *O,* for example, is noticeably pinched, and the stroke weights of the *T* are clearly out of whack. Neither resembles its original monoline form.

FIGURE 5.8 Electronically condensed faces (indicated here with asterisks) never look as good as designed ones. The uppercase letters of true condensed faces, for example, are substantially narrower, to match the feel of the lowercase letters. Electronic condensing can't duplicate this feat.

Franklin Gothic
Franklin Gothic Condensed
Franklin Gothic Condensed*

Times New Roman
Times New Roman Condensed
Times New Roman Condensed*

Univers 55
Univers 57 (Condensed)
Univers 57 (Condensed)*

News Gothic Bold
News Gothic Bold Condensed
News Gothic Bold Condensed*

ITC Avant Garde
Olive Antique Olive
Cheltenham
Linotype Clarendon
ITC Korinna
ATF Cooper Black
ATF Dom Casual
ATF Franklin Gothic
ITC Friz Quadrata
ADOBE LITHOS
ITC Souvenir

FIGURE 5.9 A sampler of popular display faces. All have a distinctive personality and presence on the page. Cheltenham was originally used much more for text settings, but today it's most commonly relegated to display roles. (There are many Cheltenhams; this one is from Bitstream.)

Caslon Titling
Caslon Text

FIGURE 5.10 Titling faces are typically more nuanced and graceful than their text counterparts. Here Carter & Cone's Big Caslon (top) is contrasted with Linotype's Caslon 540.

Using Display Type

Because display type is set in short bursts rather than long passages, display types are unencumbered by most of the design rules applied to text faces, whose guiding principle is readability. For display types, legibility is often sufficient. Display types tend to be bolder and more evocative than text types, although the latter are often used in display roles. Some classic display faces are shown in Figure 5.9.

The original display types were called *titling faces,* and many of these are still available, although few new ones are being made (see Figure 5.10). Titling faces often consist only of capital letters, as typographic convention long held that titles didn't use lowercase type. Occasionally, as in the case of Centaur, a face designed for titling has had a lowercase set of characters designed for it and the ensemble is now used for setting text as well.

Text faces generally don't fare well in display roles. They're proportioned for use in small sizes, where open space plays a key role in keeping characters legible, and fine features may not print well. When enlarged to display size, they tend to look leggy, too wide, and graphically weak. More commonly the bold or extrabold member of a text face's family will be used as a display complement. Often a typeface family is chosen for a job largely because an extrabold member is available for display use.

The sans serif face is the king of display types. Sans serif types are generally more muscular, more assertive, and more attention-getting, which makes them graphically more effective. A few typeface families include both seriffed and sans serif members, offering enough type styles to cover all the typographic roles a document might need (see Figure 5.11).

Because type set in a large point size appears looser than type in text sizes, the *tracking* (or overall letter spacing) of display type is usually tightened, sometimes to extremes. It's not uncommon to see book titles, magazine or newspaper headlines, or advertising type in which letters touch or overlap. At what point tight tracking goes over the limit is a matter of taste, common sense, or a lack of the two. Tracking is discussed in detail in Chapter 11.

Using Decorative Type

Decorative type is usually advertising type. Its job is to grab readers before they turn the page. For this reason, decorative types go in and out of style very quickly. Once a decorative type becomes popular and familiar, it's not doing its job anymore—it's not standing out in the crowd. Just as there are crossovers between text and display typefaces, so is there only a fine line separating display and decorative faces—it's a question of degree, and in almost every way, the decorative face is always more: more exaggerated, more quirky, more oblique, more cursive, more calligraphic, more illegible, more parodic. But never more understated.

Another role for decorative faces is to be evocative of a historical epoch, of a design trend, of a cultural trait, of anything that visually links a message with its content. A selection of such faces is shown in Figure 5.12.

Care needs to be taken when setting decorative type, as these faces often haven't been carefully *character fitted.* Character fitting is a process in which the typeface designer adjusts the side bearings of the characters—the spacing around each letter—with an eye toward which letters commonly appear next to each other. This is a big concern in text types, but it's less important in decorative faces, where the character forms are often so extreme that they go beyond the rules of how letters should look. Likewise, decorative faces often have little kerning information written into their fonts. This means that—typeface design willing—you have to pay close attention to the spacing between every pair of adjoining characters.

Type in Color

The text typefaces of today were designed for black ink on white paper. The shapes, proportions, and stroke weights of their characters assume a high contrast between letter and background. When you set type for colored inks or a colored background you are stepping outside the bubble.

Red type on a white background, for example, lacks the contrast of black type, so white spaces around the letters begin to lose their clarity and become vague. Unless color contrast is kept high—dark green type on a pale yellow background, for example—the type is going to have to be somewhat larger or somewhat bolder (or both) in order to compensate. Sans serif types will work better in color than seriffed types because their construction is generally sturdier, lacking the hairlines, fine details, and thin strokes typical of seriffed types.

In addition to contrast challenges, the printing of type in color—especially on a colored background—has to be very precise. Printed colors are generally

Clearface
Clearface Bold
Clearface Heavy
Clearface Black
Clearface Gothic Demibold
Clearface Gothic Bold

FIGURE 5.11 Some typeface families contain both seriffed and sans serif versions. Here, ITC Clearface is shown with Linotype Clearface Gothic. Both are based on M. F. Benton's original 1907 design for the American Type Founders (ATF).

ATF Ad Lib
ITC Bauhaus
EF Bernhard Fashion
ATF Parisian
ATF P.T. Barnum
ADOBE ROSEWOOD
ATF STENCIL
VG Vineta

FIGURE 5.12 There are thousands of decorative faces, and it's hard to find ones that aren't one-trick ponies. But if you're advertising anything from baguettes to a circus sideshow, there's bound to be one for any occasion.

composed of blends of three or four ink colors that have to be *registered*—aligned with each other—with great precision to avoid having a halo of one or more of the constituent colors peeking out from behind the rest. In addition, the printed image of type is often *knocked out* of the background color, meaning that the background is stenciled with a blank image of the type, and the colored image is printed in the voids. This calls for exacting press work. The biggest problems occur in small type—text size and below—where even the slightest misregistration will cause the type to appear out of focus, fuzzy, and possibly even multicolored.

In general it is best to print small type in a solid, unscreened, unblended color. When type is to be printed in black, specify in the Print dialog box that it overprint the background (this avoids possible knockout problems). Although printing type in color is especially fraught with problems at small sizes, it remains a concern at display sizes as well.

Reverses

Printing type in reverse—that is, white on black—raises some of the same problems as printing in color. Again, the usual contrast scheme of black type on a white background is being upset. Visually, things printed in black seem to encroach on a white area next to it. Figure 5.13 illustrates the optical effect.

Typefaces have always been designed with this effect in mind (not to mention the very real expansion of the black image caused by the spread of ink during printing). When you reverse type, the black background will visually encroach on the white type and make it seem thinner, especially at text sizes. During the printing process, narrow parts of characters may actually fill with ink, and the pinched type will begin to break up. Characters set close together may become joined. Printing reverses on soft, coarse, or absorbent paper (newsprint, for example) exaggerates the effect of ink spread and makes the problem worse.

Some technical solutions are possible, such as setting the imagesetter exposure lighter, which makes the dots it creates somewhat finer and causes less black image-creep into the white type areas (you are basically underexposing the type). But typeface and point-size choice are the keys to setting reversed type well. Low-contrast typefaces fare less well than high-contrast ones (thicker hairlines resist breaking up), and semibold text faces are often preferable to their normal text-weight relatives. Italics are particularly a problem, as they are more prone to breaking up than roman faces. Moreover, the spacing between letters—the tracking—should be opened up to prevent adjoining letters from appearing to link together.

At text sizes, the apparent encroachment of the black background into the whites of the characters is more apparent. A slight bit of ink spreading that would not be obvious in display sizes will make a relatively much greater difference at smaller point sizes.

At text sizes, the apparent encroachment of the black background into the whites of the characters is more apparent. A slight bit of ink spreading that would not be obvious in display sizes will make a relatively much greater difference at smaller point sizes.

At text sizes, the apparent encroachment of the black background into the whites of the characters is more apparent. A slight bit of ink spreading that would not be obvious in display sizes will make a relatively much greater difference at smaller point sizes.

At text sizes, the apparent encroachment of the black background into the whites of the characters is more apparent. A slight bit of ink spreading that would not be obvious in display sizes will make a relatively much greater difference at smaller point sizes.

Broken-up reversed type is often blamed on bad prepress work (overexposed films usually get fingered) or bad presswork (too much ink being applied to the page), and that is sometimes the case. Usually, though, prepress and press professionals are keying on the parts of the *printed* page image that are the faintest, such as the light areas of a photograph. If those are underexposed or underinked, blank spots may appear in the images. When enough ink is properly applied to print photographs or to fine lines, reversed type will often break up if the type hasn't been well set.

In general, sans serif faces work better in reverse than seriffed ones. In critical situations, a printer's proof should be consulted to see how well a reverse is working before the job goes to press.

FIGURE 5.13 Setting type in reverse is tricky. In the top samples, the reversed type appears slightly lighter than the black-on-white original because the black is graphically stronger than the white. The problem is exaggerated in text sizes, where the creep of ink into the uninked letterforms of reversed type can make them seem even more pinched. In the right-hand sample, semibold type makes the reversed type more readable.

Typesetting versus Typewriting

PAGE SIZES AND LINE LENGTHS

SPACING ISSUES

LINE ENDINGS AND CARRIAGE RETURNS

TYPEFACE CHOICE AND POINT SIZE

HYPHENS, DASHES, QUOTATION MARKS, FRACTIONS

TABS AND HOW TO USE THEM

Typewriters are an endangered species, and an entire generation is growing up that has never (or has rarely) used one. Nevertheless, conventions born of the typewriter persist, even though virtually every computer user now uses text-processing programs that should properly follow the rules of typesetting, not typing. The transition is complicated, not only because the force of habit is powerful but also because the computer keyboard is modeled on a typewriter keyboard, offering a range of inappropriate characters and suggesting in general that typing is what it always has been. It's not.

Page Sizes and Line Lengths

One of the basic constraints the typewriter places on its users is that of page size. The basic typewriter page is large, 8 ½ by 11 inches ("U.S. letter") or 21.0 by 29.7 centimeters ("A4"). In publishing terms, this is a very big page, bigger than most magazines and books except for art and coffee-table books. Nevertheless, the typewriter can create only a single column of type. With wide monospaced typefaces such as Courier set in the standard "pica" size—equivalent to 12-point—typed pages were not terribly ugly (largely due to our low expectations of what a typed page should look like) as long as the margins and line spacing were generous. It was normal for typed letters to be double-spaced, to make the line spacing as generous as the letter spacing.

With word processors, business documents are now effectively typeset, not just typed. But although proportionally spaced typefaces can fit far more text onto a page, the size of the standard business page has not changed. The business document—now the most commonly typeset document type in the world—is still marching to the beat of another drummer: the typewriter. As long as that is the case, the pressure to do typewriter-like things with type will remain, if only to make typographic sense of that huge one-column page.

The relationships among point size, line length, and line spacing are discussed in detail in Chapter 9.

Word Spaces

Typewriter spaces have the attraction of always being the same size, so it was natural to use them in multiples for paragraph indents or gaps in a typewritten line. You could align things by adding word spaces before them.

Spaces in word processors and typesetting programs, though, have no fixed width, so they can't be used in this role. Not only do the widths of word spaces (or *space bands*) vary from typeface to typeface, but they are also flexed—made wider or narrower—as lines of text are fit into a given line length, or *measure*. In fact, dedicated typesetting systems routinely ignored multiple word spaces, collapsing them into a single space, because consecutive spaces have no role in typesetting. Multiple word spaces were assumed to be a mistake.

Nevertheless, the habit of aligning text by using series of word spaces has persisted, mainly because word processing programs (and the desktop publishing programs based on word processing precedents) allow it. Indents should ideally be created with a program's indention commands or, less desirably, with the Tab key. Gaps in text should be created with a series of fixed spaces, such as em and en spaces, whose widths are constant and invariable unless the size of the type changes.

The typewriter tradition of separating sentences with two word spaces after a period has no place in typesetting. The custom began because the characters of monospaced typefaces used on typewriters were so wide and so open that a single word space—one the same width as a character, including the period—was not wide enough to create a sufficient space between sentences. Proportionally spaced fonts, though, contain word spaces specifically designed to play the sentence-separating role perfectly. Because of this, a double word space at the end of a sentence creates an obvious hole in the line (see Figure 6.1).

> Regarding the disposition of the Hetherington contract, we believe that our position must be clear. His attitude is unacceptable. He acts naive, but he is wily. In no way must we cave in to his definition of excess labor. Staff levels must be maintained. Senior management must review the final papers.
>
> Regarding the disposition of the Hetherington contract, we believe that our position must be clear. His attitude is unacceptable. He acts naive, but he is wily. In no way must we cave in to his definition of excess labor. Staff levels must be maintained. Senior management must review the final papers.

FIGURE 6.1 The double word spaces at the ends of sentences in the upper sample are obviously too wide. In the lower sample, single word spaces separate the sentences, following standard typographic practice.

When a manuscript is ready for typesetting, you should use your program's search-and-replace tool to search for all instances of consecutive word spaces and replace them with single word spaces.

Line Endings and Carriage Returns

On a typewriter, the only way to end a line and begin a new one is to use the carriage return, an expression that persisted even after the carriage no longer moved and that continues in computer jargon as the shorthand *Return*.

A computer's return command is actually two commands in one: a return and a *line feed*. The term *line feed* refers to the action of the original computer printers, which had a printing action similar to a typewriter's. The line-feed command caused the carriage roller to turn in order to advance the paper by one line space to make room for the next line of type. The line-feed command still exists in typesetting programs (although it's hidden—it's one of the invisible ASCII "characters"). Pressing the Return key causes the next line of type to set below the previous one by an amount equivalent to the line spacing, or *leading,* that you've specified.

In typesetting, there are many line-ending commands, although only two of them have made it into popular word processing and page layout programs. One, represented by the Return key, is the end-paragraph command. A common paragraph attribute is an indented first line, so an *end-paragraph* command not only ends the current line and (after a line feed) starts another, but also causes the new line to be indented by some specified amount.

The other common line-ending command is a simple *end line,* which ends the existing line, adds a line feed, and starts a new line without starting a new

> The network of hiking paths is extensive and very well maintained, and it stretches from the Mediterranean to all corners of "the Hexagon." ⬅
>
> The birds of the Midi, in particular, may seem exotic to visitors from North America. The more commonly sighted ones include: ⬅
> • Magpie ⬅
> • Roller ⬅
> • Blue-Cheeked Bee Eater ⬅
> • Golden Oriole ⬅
> • Kestrel ⬅
> Apart from the Magpie and Kestrel, these birds are migratory, and only spend the summer months in the south.

paragraph. In a setting where the first line of a paragraph is specified to have an indent, an end-line command will create a new line with no indent, as shown in Figure 6.2.

In desktop computing, the end-line command is called a *soft return* and is generally accessed by pressing the Return key at the same time as a modifying key, usually the Shift key.

Quads

The soft return is similar to the *quad-left* command found on dedicated typesetting systems. Quads are spacing blocks in handset type that are used to fill in the blank spaces on lines that don't completely fill the measure. A quad-left command, then, instructs the system to end the current line and pack the leftover area on the line with space—virtual quads. This pushes the line of text hard against the left-hand margin.

Likewise, a *quad-right* command ends the current line and pushes the text set on it hard against the right-hand margin. A *quad-center* command ends the line and centers it between the margins. Finally, a *quad middle* instructs the typesetting system to open a gap in the middle of the line (at the point where the command is inserted into the text stream) and pushes the text on either side of it out to the margins (see Figure 6.3).

As of this writing, quadding commands have not yet been adopted by word processors or page makeup programs. Some programs have a variation of the quad-middle command, but generally if you want to center a single line or send a single line to the opposite margin from the rest of the text, you'll have to use

The traditional quadding commands give you a number of line-ending options to choose from without starting a new paragraph. The quad-left command ends the current line and sets it flush-left, like this line.

The quad-right command ends the line and sends it flush-right, as shown here.

Using the quad-center command breaks the line and centers it, which often creates a nice effect in justified text like this.

The quad-middle command isn't very useful for running text, but it's most useful in settings such as menus:

Filet Mignon   *$25.95*

FIGURE 6.3 The quadding commands illustrated here all start new lines without starting new paragraphs. Nevertheless, they affect in various ways the alignment of the lines they end. Most desktop programs lack quadding commands, making effects like those shown here a time-consuming, multistep affair.

paragraph-ending commands to set that line off from the others around it, and then use separate commands to change its alignment and cancel any paragraph indents in effect.

Typeface Choice and Point Size

Typewriters also limited the user to a single typeface at a single size. With IBM Selectric-type typewriters (with interchangeable "ball" fonts) typists could change typefaces, but they were generally still limited to monospaced faces in only a couple of point sizes, including the *10-pitch* "Pica" faces (which set 10 characters per inch, equivalent to about 12-point) and the *12-pitch* "Elite" faces (which set 12 characters per inch, the equivalent of about 10-point type).

In the absence of typeface and point-size choices, a number of typographic conventions evolved specific to the typewriter. Many of these were picked up by early word processors, which relied for the most part on the monospaced fonts used by automated typewriters called *line printers*. Despite changes in technology and text-processing styles, these old typewriter habits have been enshrined in modern typesetting programs and popular typographic habit.

FIGURE 6.4 Here typewriter
conventions (workarounds for a lack
of typographical flexibility) in the
upper sample are translated into their
typesetting equivalents below.

```
THE ISSUE
Investors are seeing our situation as a
problem rather than as an opportunity.
As The Wall Street Journal pointed out
just last week, our industry is doing
well even if we aren't. Our job is to
transfer the gloss of the industry, with
its good reputation, to our own company.
```

The Issue

Investors are seeing our situation as a *problem* rather than as an *opportunity*. As *The Wall Street Journal* pointed out just last week, our industry is doing well even if we aren't. Our job is to transfer the gloss of the *industry*, with its good reputation, to *our own company*.

Forms of Emphasis and Highlighting

Because typewriters can't change typefaces, other devices had to be created to approximate common typographic effects, such as emphasis and highlighting. The typewriter conventions in cases where boldface was indicated were to set the text in all capitals (*all caps*) or to use an underline, or *underscore*. Neither of those styles is commonly used in typesetting, except for the use of all caps for titling purposes (see Figure 6.4).

Underscoring on a typewriter was accomplished by backing up and using the underscore character (_) over the same passage of text. The underscore character is now part of the basic ASCII character set and is found on computer keyboards at Shift-hyphen. Underscore commands in word processors and page layout programs use the same character, which has no traditional typographic equivalent. Its position relative to the baseline is defined within the font, and this may be different from its position when typed alone.

In contrast, typesetting systems use some sort of *rule-fill* command to set a rule of specified weight a specified distance below the baseline of the text to be underscored. The ASCII underscore character is usually too heavy for this role and has the added disadvantage of usually being too close to the baseline, causing it to overlap descending letters. More typographically savvy programs

This hard-hitting action film—the first by director Carlos Young—looks at the eastern front during the war of 1914–18, with winter action scenes filmed at temperatures of –10°.

FIGURE 6.5 A menagerie of dashes. In order of their appearance: Hyphens link compound words and separate the fragments of words at the ends of typeset lines; em dashes separate, in a sense similar to that of parentheses or semicolons; en dashes link, in this case a range of years. A true minus sign is thrown in for good measure.

will omit the underscore character under descending letters, but the effect is still not pretty, and you should avoid using it.

The underscore was also commonly used to indicate passages of text that should otherwise have been set in italics. Those instances are listed in "Uses for Italics," in Chapter 5.

One remnant of typewriter style has stuck and seems to have become a permanent part of standard typographic practice: *overstrike, strike-through,* or *strike-out* type. This draws a line (originally a series of hyphens) through a passage of type to indicate material that will or should be deleted in a future revision of the manuscript. It's commonly used in legal work such as contracts.

Unavailable Characters

Typewriters could assign only two characters to each key, one for *Unshift* and one for Shift. Typesetting fonts have always had far more characters, and typewriter users had to fake many of them with the limited character set available to them. Many of these fakeries still appear in computer-generated manuscripts, although there's no longer any reason to resort to them.

Hyphens and Dashes

Typewriters had only one dash: the hyphen. The standard typographical dash, though, is the em dash, which is 1 em wide and quite a bit thinner than the hyphen. Typewriter users faked the em dash with a double hyphen. The en dash (half an em wide), used as a connector in expressions such as "1979–83," was replaced with a hyphen. The hyphen was also used in lieu of a minus sign (−), which is still not a member of the standard font character set and is normally found only in pi fonts (such as Symbol). In typesetting, the only reason to use a hyphen is to hyphenate words (see Figure 6.5) and to create compound words (such as *strike-out* type). A hyphen added by a hyphenation program is called a *soft hyphen,* and it will disappear when the word in which it occurs no longer needs to be broken at line's end. A hyphen that you key into a manuscript is called a *hard hyphen,* and it is a permanent part of the text stream.

Quotation Marks

To make the most of its limited number of keys, the typewriter substituted upright, direction-neutral quotation marks (" and ') for traditional opening and closing quotation marks (" " and ' '). Because of the same space restraints (and to mimic the typewriter keyboard) the basic 128-member ASCII character set contains typewriter-style quotation marks but not typographic ones (sometimes called *curly quotes*).

Typographic quotation marks are in all standard electronic text fonts (they're in the high-bit ASCII sets), but the keystrokes to access them are unintuitive. (On the Mac, for example, they're hidden under the brackets keys, and in Windows you have to type a code number to get them to appear.) In the early days of desktop publishing, this led most people to ignore the quotation marks (if indeed they knew such marks existed). Most word processing and page layout programs can substitute typographic quotation marks automatically for typewriter-style quotes as they're typed. But many users fail to take advantage of this option, and the ugly typewriter-style versions continue to pollute documents of all kinds.

The use of typewriter-style quotation marks instead of typographic ones should always be seen as a mistake. These upright marks are sometimes knowingly chosen as a design device, but the designer who uses them risks their appearance being mistaken for an error.

PRIMES

The typewriter's character set also lacked *primes* (' and "), so typewriter-style quotation marks were used as substitutes for those as well. Primes are used to indicate feet (') and inches ("), minutes (') and seconds ("), and even typographic points ("12' type"). Primes are also normally found only in pi fonts, including Symbol. Fake primes can be set by italicizing typewriter-style quotation marks (' and "), but it's better to use the real things.

Fractions

Typewriters couldn't type fractions very well either, as they had no miniature numerals for use as numerators or denominators. Some typewriters had a few fractions built in, and the standard 256-character electronic fonts follow suit with ¼, ½, and ¾. Other fractions were built with full-size numerals separated by the *virgule, solidus,* or *slash.* Although computer programs can now set appropriately sized numerators and denominators, the *fraction bar* to go with them is often overlooked in favor of the typewriter-convention virgule (see Figure 6.6).

6 – 7 / 8

6-7/8

6⅞

6⅞

FIGURE 6.6 The fraction at the top appears as it would be created on a typewriter. Because so few programs can create fractions, this convention is often carried over even when proportional typesetting fonts are used, as shown in the sample below it. By reducing the sizes of numerator and denominator and adjusting the leading of the former, you can create proper fractions, but you have to use the real fraction bar, as in the sample at the bottom. The fraction above that one uses the virgule (or slash), which is not properly slanted or shaped (it drops below the baseline) for the task.

The fraction bar is a part of the basic character set of every text font and has the weight, angle, and base alignment designed for the task of making fractions look right. Unfortunately, it is not included in the Win ANSI character set, so it's unavailable under most versions of Windows. To access the fraction bar, Windows users will have to have a version that supports Unicode or a typesetting program that can extract all the characters from a font regardless of its encoding. For more on this subject, see "Fractions" in Chapter 13.

Tabs

Using tabs, especially when setting type in tabular format, is complicated. Chapter 15 is dedicated to tabular settings, including the many ways in which word processing tabs differ from typewriter tabs and the even more numerous ways in which typographic tabs differ from word processing tabs.

Typewriter tabs introduced the notion of the *tab stop*. This was a position on the page that the carriage would slide to in one motion when you pressed the Tab key. The stops were small blocks that the Tab Set keys raised to stop the motion of the carriage. Word processing programs still refer to the tab positions you set in a program as *stops.*

Typewriter tabs in some ways are easier to use than word-processor-style tabs. Once tabs have been set on a typewriter, the Tab key performs a "jump to" function: You press the key and jump to the next setting. In a word processor, pressing the Tab key doesn't jump the cursor to the next tab; it pushes the cursor. This also pushes any type between the current cursor position and the next tab stop. Moving around in a table that already contains text, then, is not a job for the Tab key, but the cursor keys. Using the cursor keys and the modifying Control, Alt, Option, and Command keys (depending on your computer and program) enables the program to imitate the jump-to function of a typewriter.

Tabs were also commonly used on typewriters to create indents. Computer programs can automatically add paragraph indents to lines following a return command, and this is the more sensible way to approach paragraph indention than tabs. If you use a style sheet to make text formatting easier, a simple change in it can change all the paragraph indents (for more details, see Chapter 17). This frees you to use tabs for the more useful role of setting tables, and these tab settings can then be contained in the same style sheet. A very common typographical error—which you'll often see once you start looking for it—is a variation in the depth of paragraph indents in a body of text caused by creating some indents with style sheets and others with the Tab key.

Bodoni

Bodoni

Bodoni

CHAPTER 7

Setting Type on a Personal Computer

FROM WORD PROCESSING TO TYPESETTING

THE IMPLICATIONS OF WYSIWYG

HOW OPERATING SYSTEMS MANAGE FONTS

CORRUPTED, MISSING, AND DUPLICATE FONTS

FONT EMBEDDING

Setting type on dedicated systems was a fairly straightforward affair. You had no choice of hardware, software, or font vendor. Everything was strictly prescribed by your system vendor. Setting type on personal computers couldn't be more different. Which computer (or, more accurately, which operating system) you use, which programs you use, and what kinds of fonts you use all change how you work and what results you can expect. This chapter sorts out what's going on behind the curtain when you tickle a keyboard, and what roles various hardware and software elements play in getting type onto the page. This is not just theoretical stuff; it's information that tells you how to control the typesetting process, especially when things go wrong.

A Tale of Two Systems: Typesetting and the Word Processing Legacy

In terms of text handling, early page layout programs (the first desktop programs that exhibited any typographical pretensions) were no more than word processors that could "pour" text into more than one column per page. But word processing programs were themselves only beginning to come to terms with proportional typefaces. From a typographical perspective, word processors were little more than automated typewriters, and their goal was control over the appearance of simple office documents. As precursors to typesetting programs, the early page layout programs were getting off on the wrong foot.

Dedicated typesetting systems, meanwhile, even when "ported" to personal computers, were becoming extinct. They were too expensive, their code-driven interfaces were seen as too complicated (see Figure 7.1), and they required specialist operators (read: typesetters). They just didn't fit the do-it-yourself, on-the-cheap spirit of the heady early days of the personal computer.

Assigning Typographic Attributes

With the exception of indents, almost every typographic possibility in a dedicated typesetting system could be applied to individual characters. Size, typeface, the position of type below the preceding line, the spacing of a character relative to the characters around it, and so forth, could all be altered at any time. This was done by adding typed codes into the stream of the text, and most of those controls acted as *toggles,* which like a switch could be turned on or off.

To simplify things, word processors divided up into categories the few typographic variables it could control, arbitrarily declaring that some variables would apply only to paragraphs or even whole documents, while others could be applied to single characters. These categories went hand in hand with the advent of *graphical user interfaces,* like those used in the Macintosh operating system or Microsoft Windows. The interfaces used dialog boxes—fill-in-the-blanks forms—for specifying the conditions by which type would be set. There was no longer any reason to remember codes, because all the commands were listed in the dialog boxes. Users could—and still do, in most programs—go to a Paragraph Attributes dialog box to set some typographical specifications, a Character Attributes dialog box for others, and probably a Page Setup dialog box for yet other document-wide specs. Except for some indention commands (such as a first-line, or paragraph, indent), typesetting systems have never seen a paragraph as being an entity that requires any special treatment.

Any typesetters working on one of the old code-driven systems would have been happy to have a realistic preview of their coding work, but working with dialog boxes slows typesetting to a crawl. Competent typesetters could code documents at full typing speed, and by combining common commands into one-keystroke macros, they could format text at amazing rates. They could, for example, change typefaces four times before a Macintosh or Windows user could pull down a Font menu and make a selection using a mouse.

```
<AG><AF><RR><AH><CS5,5,5><T1><CP10.5>
<CL13><CC12.9><CFSA><IF0.11>The
simplicity of using the program belies
the complexity of the craft of
typesetting. Like most typesetting
programs, <CFSAI>DynoType'<CFSA>s text
processing is based on a mnemonic
coding scheme.<QL>
```

FIGURE 7.1 In the early days of
WYSIWYG computing, no one wanted
to put up with all-text displays like
this, which were standard on dedicated
typesetting systems. The codes, set
off in brackets, say: allow ligatures;
allow automatic fraction building; rag-
right margins; allow hyphenation;
character spacing: 5 units minimum,
5 units optimum, 5 units maximum;
apply tracking level 1; change point
size to 10.5 points; change leading to
13 points; change column width to 12
picas, 9 points; change font to Sabon;
indent first line 11 points. Every time
the typeface changed, codes had to be
inserted to effect the change.

THE PROBLEM WITH "SELECTIONS"

Another problem is the whole metaphor for today's graphical user interfaces, which is to select a passage of text and then act on it. You can make a selection by dragging the cursor over certain letters or words (for assigning so-called character attributes) or simply by placing the cursor in a paragraph (for so-called paragraph attributes). Making a selection precludes the traditional typesetting technique of finding a point in the text and with a typesetting command saying, in effect, "Make something happen (or start to happen) here." The quad-right and quad-middle commands mentioned earlier don't exist in today's word processing and page layout programs because the alignment of lines against one margin or the other is a paragraph attribute. You can't simply tell the last line of a justified paragraph to be centered without making it its own paragraph.

How WYSIWYG Works

The Macintosh operating system pioneered the concept of WYSIWYG ("wizzy-wig," short for "what you see is what you get"). Part of the idea was to do away with embedded formatting codes, which were used by contemporary word processing programs as well as typesetting systems. Instead, you would assign typographical attributes to text through a menu or dialog box, meaning that you would never see the formatting commands, just their effects. This way of working became so popular—especially with novices—and was so commonly assumed to be the wave of the future, that code-driven text-processing systems were driven into extinction almost overnight. Very few persist today, and they are used almost exclusively in large-volume book-publishing environments.

The core of the Apple Macintosh revolution, though, was that its operating system provided a broad range of services for the application programs that ran under it (word processors, spreadsheet programs, graphics programs, etc.). In exchange for those services, the applications had to have a standard user interface. Under the PC operating system of the day—DOS—every application program had to supply the services itself. (DOS did very little other than take care of writing and reading disk files and sending information out of its com-munications ports to printers and modems.) Each DOS program was free—was obliged, in fact—to have its own interface. This made PC program development expensive and redundant, and no two programs looked alike, so learning a new one was a headache.

In terms of typesetting, one of the most important services rendered by the Mac operating system (and eventually its PC rival, Windows) was serving up fonts and typeface information. Today, when you specify to a program that you want to use a particular typeface, it passes that information on to the operat-ing system (OS). Then, as you type, the keystrokes are passed to the OS, which looks inside the font's character-width table and sends back width data to the program about all the characters you've typed. The program uses the width information to decide where the letters should be positioned, and the OS then delivers images of the characters to the correct position on the screen.

The OS creates all of the images on the screen, and the application has to address the OS in its native language. The application program has very little influence over the appearance of the type onscreen—its main job is to compose the type, to position each character, and to decide at which point every line should end, based on the width information supplied by the OS.

Both Windows and the Mac OS have their own unique imaging systems for building screen displays. Each is a kind of low-end page description language. The Mac, beginning with OS X, has two. OS X uses a variety of PostScript, while all earlier Mac OS versions use the original Mac imaging system called QuickDraw. Windows uses a system called GDI, which stands for *Graphical Device Interface*. In either case, the image of a page is drawn first to the screen and then possi-bly translated into another language (usually PostScript) when it's time to print. Because most fine type is set on high-resolution imagesetters, and most image-setters are driven by PostScript RIPs, the path from screen to final page is most direct under the PostScript-driven Mac OS X.

Bitmapped Fonts for Screen Display

The methods used for displaying type onscreen have undergone their own evo-lution. What follows may sound like history, and indeed in a few years it will be, because the standards are changing for how screen type is displayed. But as of this writing, the older technologies persist—and they will continue to be used for years to come, the computer industry's flair for planned obsolescence notwithstanding. They will, in short, affect how you set type for a long time.

The original Macintosh fonts were all bitmapped, predrawn dot by dot. At the time, Apple made only dot-matrix printers that had the same resolution as the Mac screen—72 dots per inch, so that one screen pixel was exactly 1 point by 1 point in size. Printing on the Mac in those days simply meant transferring the array of screen dots to the printer.

POSTSCRIPT SCREEN TYPE AND ATM

When the first outline PostScript fonts and the first PostScript laser printers appeared, a split appeared between the type you saw onscreen and the type you saw on the page (at a resolution of 300 dots per inch). QuickDraw still relied on bitmapped fonts for screen display, though, so every PostScript font had to be accompanied by a set of bitmapped fonts, usually in 9-, 10-, 12-, 14-, 18-, and 24-point sizes. You couldn't print using a PostScript font unless its bitmapped fonts were available and known to the system. Only when the bitmapped fonts were available would the Mac OS list those fonts' names (and those of their companion outline fonts for printing) in the application program's Font menu. For Mac operating systems through version 9.x, that continues to be the case.

Under this regime, when you opted to use a point size other than those for which bitmapped screen fonts were available, the Mac OS would interpolate the character bitmaps from an existing bitmapped font to create characters at the new size. The results varied from bad to hideous, as shown in Figure 7.2. Despite the ugliness of the screen type, the type would compose accurately and print correctly because the interpolated bitmaps were based on accurate width information for all the font's characters.

Adobe's solution to the bitmap problem was to create an addition to the operating system called Adobe Type Manager (ATM). When a call for screen type for a PostScript font is made to the operating system, ATM intercepts the call and creates bitmapped screen type based on the character outlines in the printer font. In effect, ATM is a RIP dedicated to creating screen type. The result is that screen type for any size type (excepting very small) looks almost as good as hand-drawn bitmaps.

By the time Windows for the PC became popular, ATM was already a standard, and it became the only way you could use PostScript fonts on a Windows PC. As on the Macintosh, you needed both bitmapped screen fonts and outline printer fonts. (The only difference was that under Windows all the bitmaps for a font were contained in a single file.) This situation remained until Windows 2000 and Windows XP introduced "native" (that is, built-in) support for PostScript fonts. ATM is not needed to render screen type in those operating systems. On the Macintosh, OS X also treats TrueType, PostScript, and OpenType fonts as peers, so ATM is not needed there either.

FIGURE 7.2 The cascade of type on the left is a range of bitmapped screen type interpolated by the operating system from a single screen font. They look dreadful. The cascade on the right was generated by the operating system from the outline font for the same typeface. Because the latter type is based on the true shapes of the characters rather than on a small array of dots, the results are much better.

Garamond Light
Garamond Book
Garamond Bold
Garamond Ultra

Garamond Light
Garamond Book?

Garamond Book
Garamond Bold?

Garamond Bold
Garamond Ultra?

FIGURE 7.3 The screen type in
the four lines at top was created by
calling for those specific fonts in the
Font menu. In the three couplets
below, the upper typeface was called
by name, and the lower was created
with the bold style command. The
shapes of the characters and particularly the spacing between the letters
show that only one of them represents
a real typeface: Garamond Bold. In
this family, only the Garamond Book
font contains a pointer to its bold
complement. In the other two cases,
the operating system tried to honor
the request for bold, but it did so by
faking the results.

TYPE AND THE "STYLE" MENU

Because a bitmapped screen font contains the same complete metrics data as
its corresponding printer font, it's possible to compose type on a Macintosh
without having the printer fonts available. In addition, the "regular" (or plain
roman) member of a screen font family also contains the metrics information
for the other members of the family (typically italic, bold, and bold italic). With
a single "regular" bitmapped font, you can thus set bold, italic, and bold italic
type using your program's typographic Style menu, and that type will compose
correctly. Printing it, of course, requires the presence of the corresponding
outline fonts.

In certain large typeface families, the relative meaning of a Style menu's
bold may not be clear. Figure 7.3, for example, shows that in the ITC Garamond
family, activating the bold style command on Garamond Book does indeed give
you Garamond Bold. But using the bold style command on Garamond Light does
not step you up in weight to Book, nor does using it on Bold get you to Ultra.
In both those cases, the bold command is a dead end, leading you to variants of
the real face synthesized by the Mac OS. Neither will print properly. When using
the Style menu to call for various font-family members in such an extended
family (as opposed to specifying the fonts explicitly by name) it's best to print
a sample sheet to verify that you're getting what you think you're asking for.

SCREEN RENDERING WHEN FONTS ARE MISSING

To get an accurate screen preview of how type will look, it's important to have
all the necessary bitmapped and printer fonts installed on your system (even
though it may be possible to compose type without them). Operating systems
are very obliging about giving you what you ask for in the way of type, and the
results can be deceptive. As noted above, if you apply the bold command to
make a typeface heavier, the OS will probably display a bold version of the type
whether or not the bold font is available, or whether or not it exists at all. The
latter possibility is illustrated in Figure 7.4, in which a titling face has been
made heavier with the bold command. It looks bold onscreen, but because there
is no such thing as a bold version of this font, the regular-weight font will appear
when it's printed, and the client will be in for an unpleasant surprise.

Operating systems will perform the same service when you use the italic
command on roman type. If the italic version of the font isn't available, the OS
will create an electronic oblique by simply slanting the characters. This bit
of fakery is easier to detect than a synthesized bold because the letters—
especially in the case of seriffed faces—are usually clearly not true italics, as
seen in Figure 7.5.

TRUETYPE-BASED SCREEN TYPE

The TrueType font format was a collaboration between Apple and Microsoft, and both built native support for it into their respective operative systems. TrueType fonts don't require an auxiliary program such as ATM; the operating system itself creates screen type on demand from the same character outlines used for printing. Some TrueType fonts contain bitmapped fonts for use onscreen, but they are not strictly necessary. Some fonts carry bitmaps to assure absolute compatibility with their PostScript equivalents. (Early versions of TrueType Times Roman, for example, could compose differently than PostScript Times Roman under certain circumstances. A document created with a font in one format, then, might end up with different line endings and page breaks when opened on a system using the same font but in the other format.) Some TrueType font vendors choose to include bitmapped screen fonts for small point sizes because they are more legible than the ones created by the operating systems.

How Operating Systems Manage Fonts

In order for an operating system to serve font information to applications and create images of their typefaces onscreen, the fonts have to be "installed." In other words, they have to be stored in the computer in a place where the operating system knows to look for them. In Windows, this storage place is the Windows > Fonts folder, and you use the Fonts control panel to put them there or to remove them (that is, "de-install" them). In later versions of the Macintosh OS, up through System 9.x, installed fonts are stored in the System > Fonts folder. Macintosh OS X and Windows 2000 have a number of folders in which installed fonts can be stored, depending on whether the computer is acting as a *server* (allowing other machines access to its resources, in this case fonts) or a *client* (which borrows resources from a server).

With a font-management program (see "The Basics of Font Management" in Chapter 4), fonts can be stored in folders other than those specified by the operating system. These programs work collaboratively with the OS to make sure that any fonts you specify are made available to your applications: that is, to make sure they appear in your programs' Font menus.

Unless you're using a font-management program, merely having fonts stored on your computer's hard disk is not enough to make them accessible. Only when they're properly installed will they be made available to your applications. On versions of the Mac operating system prior to OS X, a font installed when an application program is already open is not normally made available to that program immediately. If you install a font while an application is open, the

onscreen

BIG CASLON
BIG CASLON "BOLD"

in print

BIG CASLON
BIG CASLON "BOLD"

FIGURE 7.4 The couplet on top shows the effect of the bold style command. There is no such thing as Big Caslon Bold, though, so when printed the lines at top will translate into the lines below, with the printer using the only font available.

Bodoni Roman
Bodoni "Italic"
Bodoni Italic

FIGURE 7.5 For fonts with cursive italic complements, it's easy to tell true italics from the italics generated from a roman screen font. Here, the character shapes in the false italics are simply inclined versions of the roman ones they're derived from. System-generated italics of sans serif faces may not be so obvious.

system will display a warning to this effect. To gain access to that newly installed font, most programs have to be shut down and restarted; as part of their start-up routine they will poll the operating system to find out what fonts are currently installed.

However, a few Macintosh programs—including the leading page layout programs—feature what's called dynamic font updating, meaning that they are constantly in touch with the operating system and are immediately aware of any fonts that have been newly installed, listing them in their Font menus without having to be shut down and restarted. Versions of the Mac os prior to os x will not allow you to de-install a font while application programs are running, on the assumption that this could cause problems with programs that might be using the fonts in question.

Windows applications poll the operating system every time you drop down a Font menu or open a Font dialog box, so you can add fonts to your system at any time, and they'll be available immediately.

Problem: Corrupted Fonts

Because they're read so often by the operating system, font files sometimes become damaged—*corrupted* is the official term—and a damaged font file can create an amazing array of problems. Not surprisingly, it can create printing errors, typically preventing a file from printing at all. Because fonts are intimately involved in the operating system, a corrupted one can bring the system to its knees, causing it to crash for no apparent reason. It can also cause individual programs to suddenly freeze up.

Corrupted fonts are an unusual problem, but they do pop up from time to time, and they're hard to diagnose. It's always a good idea to keep a log of everything that changes on your computer—new programs, alterations to os settings, application preferences changes, and so forth. When things start to go wrong repeatedly, looking at the log may help to pinpoint a change that may have triggered the mayhem. When there's been no change to account for a series of problems, a corrupted font should be among your list of suspects. Not high on the list, but on the list nonetheless.

The easiest way to check for corrupted fonts is with a font-management program, as most are capable of scanning all the fonts in your system and looking for miscreants. If you don't have a font-management program and aren't inclined to pay for one, you can remove half the fonts from your system. If the problem goes away, you've located the problem font in the de-installed group. If the problem continues to occur, swap the "in" half for the "out" half. If the problem goes away, you know where the problem font can be found. If the problem persists, the source is not a font. If you determine that one of your fonts is to blame, take that half of your font collection and divide it in half again and repeat the same test. Do this until you identify the problem font. Keep in mind that fonts are being read by your operating system and application programs even though you may not be using them in a document.

Problem: Missing Fonts

As noted earlier, when you start up your computer, the operating system makes an inventory of all the installed fonts. At this point only a few fonts are required to be installed. These are the ones the operating system uses to create its interface, the typefaces in menu titles, dialog-box text, and so forth. The Macintosh os will not let you de-install these fonts, and it will give you an error warning if you try. Windows will let you remove any fonts, but if you remove the ones required for creating the interface—Marlett, for example—you will make a mess.

The problem of missing fonts arises most commonly when application-specific files —text documents, graphics, spreadsheets, etc.—are opened, especially when those files come from another computer where different fonts may have been installed. When you try to open a document that uses fonts that are not installed on your computer, your application program will probably warn you about the problem. Some will offer you the option of substituting an installed font for the missing one. With this latter option, the document won't look the same as the original—line endings and page breaks will change—but at least it will be readable.

If a font is missing and Adobe Type Manager is installed, ATM will adapt one of two generic fonts (Adobe Serif and Adobe Sans) to match the metrics of the missing font, assuming it's in ATM's font database. This will permit the document to be displayed with all its original line endings intact.

An exception to this process is when the document in question has been made with one of the core set of Windows or PostScript fonts. As explained in "Cross-Platform Font-Compatibility Issues" in Chapter 4, these core sets of fonts are unique to each platform (with the exception of Symbol) but analogous fonts in each set have the same metrics, so a document created with one will compose identically—same line endings, same page breaks—as it will with the other. A document formatted in PostScript Times Roman, then, will compose exactly the same in Windows' Times New Roman (see Figure 7.6). Substitutions in these core fonts may take place without warning, although your application or the operating system will usually run up a red flag when a font required for displaying a document is missing. Apple improved this situation when in os 9

Arial	Helvetica
Arial Narrow	Helvetica Narrow
Times New Roman	Times Roman
Bookman Old Style	ITC Bookman
New Courier	Courier
Century Gothic	ITC Avant Garde Gothic
Century Schoolbook	New Century Schoolbook
Book Antiqua	Palatino
Monotype Corsiva	*ITC Zapf Chancery Medium Italic*
Symbol (α⇑∞◊)	Symbol (α⇑∞◊)
Monotype Sorts (□▼❈●)	ITC Zapf Dingbats (□▼❈●)

FIGURE 7.6 The Windows core font set (left) and the Macintosh PostScript core font set (right). Their looks are similar, but their character widths are identical, so a face from one platform has an equivalent on the other that will compose in exactly the same way.

it began including the core Windows fonts, making it easier to create documents that work flawlessly when they travel from one platform to the other.

When a document is printed, the same fonts used to create it have to be available to the printer. When you use a desktop printer, the printer *driver* (the software that translates the document into instructions that the printer needs to image the pages) will generally warn you if a font required for printing is not available. Depending on the settings of the RIP, however, an imagesetter may not issue a warning or may cancel a job if a font is missing, instead substituting another font for the missing one. To make sure the substitution is obvious, the replacement font is usually Courier.

Problem: Duplicate Fonts

Many popular fonts exist in more than one font format, and there can be problems if both versions of a font are installed on the same computer. It's possible, for example, for you to have both TrueType and PostScript versions of faces—including Times, Helvetica, Palatino, Symbol, and Courier—installed in the same system and not know it, because the font name appears only once in an application's Font menu. When you select such a font, you don't know which font you're using, and when you send that file to an imagesetter or to another computer, it could make a big difference. Font-management programs may alert you to such duplications, but vigilance is the best solution. Be aware that many applications and operating system upgrades install fonts into your computer without warning you first.

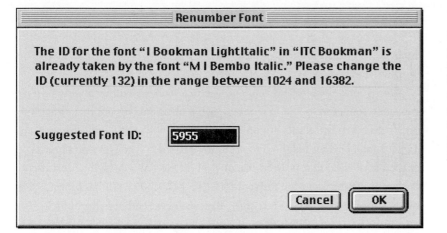

FIGURE 7.7 A font-management program will warn you when two installed fonts have the same I.D. number, as shown here. The change in I.D. number suggested by the program is only temporary (the font file itself is not changed), but you can get on with your work with the assurance that your job will compose and print correctly.

Problem: Duplicate Font Numbers

All font files have unique names, but to make life easier for themselves, operating systems and applications typically identify fonts by number. In the early days of personal computers, though, there was no standard registration system for these numbers, and many fonts were released that had the same identification number as other fonts. (For a while, the only numbers available were 1 to 512.) Today as new fonts are created by individuals, the font-editing programs they use assign numbers without knowledge of whether or not that I.D. number is unique. (Commercial font foundries collaborate to avoid the issue.)

The net result is that you can have two fonts on your system at the same time with the same I.D. number, a situation called a *font I.D. conflict*. This can trip up programs that don't know which font is which, leading to printing errors and program crashes. Some applications assign temporary I.D. numbers to all the fonts they use in order to work around the problem. But the only sure way to avoid the conflict altogether is to use a font-management program. The program will issue a warning if you try to install a font that has the same I.D. number as one that's already installed (see Figure 7.7).

Font Embedding

When a document travels from one computer to another, there is no assurance that the receiving machine will have the fonts necessary to compose it properly. For this reason, it's increasingly common for applications to offer the ability to embed in a document file the fonts used to format it. Embedding takes place when you save a file. Given the size of fonts (on average, 50–90 kilobytes), embedding them can make a document file substantially larger. It does, however, offer an ironclad guarantee that the document will appear on any computer the way it looked on its creator's machine. The font data is embedded in the document in a platform-neutral form; that is, it will work on a Mac file opened on a PC, and vice versa.

Some font designers and vendors fear that hackers will be able to extract embedded fonts and use them without paying for them (it's not that difficult to do), or that even the innocent duplication of files will create unlicensed copies of their fonts. This has led them to program into their TrueType and OpenType fonts a bit of code that prevents them from being embedded in a document. (PostScript Type 1 fonts don't have this blocking capability.) Other font vendors simply stipulate in their user licenses that such embedding is forbidden. Not many fonts fall into the forbidden category, but you should make sure the fonts you use can and may be embedded before you try to do so.

Embedding Subsets of Fonts

Fonts can be embedded in their entirety or as *subsets*. If you specify that embedding subsets is allowed, only those character outlines used in your document will be included in the embedded font. If a document uses a particular font just once for a two-word title, for example, it makes sense to embed a subsetted font containing just those characters and keep file size to a minimum. The problem with this tactic is that if the type set in that font needs to be edited, the characters necessary to do the job may not be available. If an embedded and subsetted font had been used to set the title "Settig Type," the astute proofreader who noticed the missing *n* wouldn't be able to do anything about it.

Font Copyright Issues

The fonts installed in computers are subject to licensing restrictions much like those of the applications that use them. These licenses vary from vendor to vendor, but they generally limit

- the number of copies of the font file you can make (usually two: one for backup purposes and one for the hard disk of the computer on which it will be used)
- the number of people who can use that working copy from the disk on which it's stored (usually ten or fewer)
- the number of printers on which the font can be used at any one time (usually one)

In almost all cases, making copies of fonts and handing them around—even within a workgroup—is strictly forbidden, meaning that most font users are guilty of violating the terms of their licenses.

Read the license agreements of the fonts you buy. Copies of fonts given to you do not belong to you and violate the copyrights of those who created them. There are some sources of free fonts, including many Internet sites (keep in mind the adage "You get what you pay for"). But most fonts and the typefaces they represent are someone's intellectual property, and the owners deserve to be paid for them. Remember that behind every font there is a typeface designer whose living depends on the royalties earned by the sales of that font. Almost without exception, typeface designers are not rich (and those that are were usually born that way). Consider their welfare, even if you don't consider that of the companies that sell their fonts.

en have many of the traits a[l]
mentioned as being strong i[n]
women, but in a smaller deg[ree]
Style and appearance have le[ss]
bearing on a man's purchases
rather, while the desire for st[yle]
may be as strong as in a wo[man]
[th]e must be supported by quality. Som[e]
[th]eir artistic side well developed, but i[n]
a far less extent than in women. Stre[ngth]
[sim]plicity appeal to men more than me[re]
value. Men differ from women in tha[t]
[the]s regard for details. A brief descripti[on]
[t]he main points fully may produce be[tter]
[t]han the full description that appeals
[.] If the main points of an article are s[o]
[the details frequently get slight atte]

CHAPTER 8 What Makes Good Type Good
(and Bad Type Bad)

LEGIBILITY AND READABILITY

GOOD AND BAD TYPE COLOR

TIGHT, LOOSE, AND UNBALANCED SPACING

LINE LENGTH, LEADING, AND NARROW-MEASURE PROBLEMS

OPTICAL EFFECTS AND ALIGNMENT PROBLEMS

TRUSTING YOUR EYES

It's often hard to look at a page and see only the type. This chapter tries to do just that, though, looking past graphic-design issues to focus on the contribution that the quality of the typesetting makes to the overall excellence of the page.

Well-set type doesn't draw attention to itself, so it's often hard to see what's gone right in a nicely composed page. What's gone wrong is a different story: Poor typeface choice aside, badly set type can fail aesthetically (it's sloppy or unattractive) or practically (it makes reading harder), but it can always be counted on to make a bad impression.

The goal here is not connoisseurship (although people who care about type are often labeled "type snobs") but rather knowing the rules of the craft, so that the type you set serves the text and the reader in ways they both deserve.

Legibility and Readability

When most people look at a page, they don't see typefaces and they don't see type. They see words. They're not admiring the page—they're reading it, and reading is all about rhythm. Studies have shown, for example, that gum chewers read more slowly than others because the pace of their reading slows to the

By a faction, I understand a number if citizens, whether amounting to a majority or minority of the whole, who are united and actuated by some common impulse of passion, or of interest, adverse to the rights of other citizens, or to the permanent and aggregate interests of the community.

There are two methods of curing the mischiefs of faction: the one, by removing its causes; the other, by controlling its effects.

There are again two methods of removing the causes of faction: the one, by destroying the liberty which is essential to its existence; the other, by giving to every citizen the same opinions, the same passions, and the same interests.

It could never be more truly said than of the first remedy, that it was worse than the disease. Liberty is to faction what air is to fire, an aliment without which it instantly expires. But it could not be less folly to abolish liberty, which is essential to political life, because it nourishes faction, than it would be to wish the annihilation of air, which is essential to animal life, because it imparts to fire its destructive agency.

FIGURE 8.1 The third paragraph here is noticeably darker than those around it. Its tight spacing actually makes it look overinked, and it clearly has a different "color."

pace of their chewing. Type is a kind of metronome for readers (assuming they're not chewing gum), and they can be helped or hindered by how it appears on the page. Bad typesetting can stymie a reader almost as much as bad writing.

Legibility and *readability* are commonly used words in the world of type. *Legibility* refers to a reader's ability to easily recognize letterforms and the word forms built from them. (We don't read by recognizing one letter at a time, but by recognizing the shapes of whole words and phrases.) *Readability* refers to the facility and comfort with which text can be comprehended. Text with good readability must also be legible, but mere legibility doesn't make text readable. A book is much more likely to be a "page turner" if its type is pleasantly readable—badly set type wears a reader out.

Design—in the form of page size, type size, and line length—also has a lot to do with legibility and readability. We've all opened books to find huge gray slabs of small, tightly spaced type and thought, "I can't read this!" Whether this is a problem of legibility or readability is a moot point. Paperback editions of hardbound books often suffer from this problem because cheapskate publishers simply photographically reduce the larger hardbound pages and print them in smaller paperback format.

Ultimately, though, most poorly set type isn't illegible or even unreadable; it's just carelessly set.

Type Color

Type on a page has a certain visual texture created by the rhythms of the characters in lines, the lines in columns, and of course the spaces among them all. When this texture is consistent and even, the type is said to have good *color*. Tightly spaced type will have a darker color than loosely spaced type, but the most important thing is for the color to be even and consistent.

Alternately tight and loose lines are a kind of color problem at a very "local" level, but color problems are most noticeable at a larger scale, especially when whole paragraphs seem darker—due to tighter spacing—than those surrounding them, or vice versa (see Figure 8.1).

Such variations in color don't necessarily affect readability, but they are a distraction. When one dark paragraph stands out on a page, it catches your eye. This shouldn't happen. Variations in color like this give the impression of a lack of quality control, a lack of care, a lack of expertise. It gives the text a slack and unkempt appearance.

The designs of typefaces themselves contribute to type color, and it's important for the designer and typesetter to take that into account. Some faces, as shown in Figure 8.2, are relatively light and fine and can be set more closely, whereas

> Plainly the central idea of seces-
> sion is the essence of anarchy. A
> majority held in restraint by
> constitutional checks and limi-
> tations, and always changing
> easily with deliberate changes of
> popular opinions and senti-
> ments, is the only true sover-
> eign of a free people.
>
> Plainly the central idea of seces-
> sion is the essence of anarchy. A
> majority held in restraint by
> constitutional checks and limita-
> tions, and always changing easi-
> ly with deliberate changes of
> popular opinions and senti-
> ments, is the only true sover-
> eign of a free people.

> Plainly the central idea of seces-
> sion is the essence of anarchy. A
> majority held in restraint by
> constitutional checks and limi-
> tations, and always changing
> easily with deliberate changes of
> popular opinions and senti-
> ments, is the only true sover-
> eign of a free people.
>
> Plainly the central idea of seces-
> sion is the essence of anarchy. A
> majority held in restraint by
> constitutional checks and limita-
> tions, and always changing easi-
> ly with deliberate changes of
> popular opinions and senti-
> ments, is the only true sover-
> eign of a free people.

FIGURE 8.2 The overall color of type is attributable largely to the typeface itself. Those faces with large x-heights or relatively heavier stroke weights have a tendency to look dark on the page. All the samples here are set in the same point size and with the same leading.

others are heavier or bolder. Those in the latter group need more "air space" to keep from looking cramped and their color from being too dense and dark.

An inappropriate typeface can complicate matters. For example, Times New Roman (plus its look-alike Times Roman) was designed as a newspaper face, with narrow character widths to help it compose better in narrow columns and to allow more copy to be fit onto a page. Nevertheless, Times has become a stock book face (mainly because it saves publishers on paper costs by setting more compactly), but it creates color and readability problems on book-sized pages, where more generously proportioned typefaces are the norm.

Instances of bad type color are often not the typesetter's doing, as they're created later in the production cycle. Editors, proofreaders, and production artists are often called on to make last-minute revisions that involve changing the number of words in a paragraph or section of a page. To keep the changes from rippling through the layout, more words may have to be jammed into the paragraph or section or extra spacing may be needed to fluff out the text to cover up an omission. However it happens, that paragraph or section will stand out from the rest, and the reader will probably blame the typesetter.

Unfortunate color contrasts can also appear between disparate text elements on a page, such as a loosely spaced pull quote in the midst of tightly spaced text, or a tightly spaced title over more loosely set text. These variations in color can also make pages look unplanned and untidy.

Overly Tight Spacing

Tight spacing interferes with the reader's ability to recognize word forms. Readers who have to do a double take to recognize a word or phrase are at once slowed down and annoyed. An *rn* that melts together to look like an *m*, a

carnal cloth savvy

FIGURE 8.3 Tight spacing can make familiar letter patterns seem ambiguous. When seen at text sizes and normal reading speeds, letter combinations such as these can be hard to make out, forcing the reader to do a double take.

cl that looks like a *d*, or a *vv* that looks like a *w* is bound to trip people up. More generally, in tightly spaced text, character-sequence patterns that are usually easy to recognize become unfamiliar, and readers are forced back toward reading letter by letter, as if in a foreign language (see Figure 8.3).

The key thing to remember here is that the side bearings of a character—the spaces on its flanks—are as much a part of that character as its strokes and stems. When you alter the spaces between letters you are effectively—albeit subtly—redesigning the typeface. Altering these spaces may be an everyday task in setting type, but it is risky and must be done with care and attention.

Overly tight spacing is a particular problem with sans serif faces. Serifs, small as they are, help to sort out the mass of small marks that make up a passage of text. They allow your eye to see more clearly where one letter or stroke ends and another begins. Lacking these little signposts, text set in sans serif faces can look like a picket fence of uniform vertical strokes, especially when tightly set (see Figure 8.4). When used for long passages of text, many sans serif faces actually benefit from a looser-than-normal spacing, which gives the eye a better chance of translating those arrays of often featureless strokes into the patterns we recognize as words. In general, the character fitting of sans serif faces is looser than that of seriffed faces.

It has long been the fashion to space display type, especially in advertising, very tight. Because these bursts of type are quite short, concerns for readability are shunted aside in favor of mere legibility. But just because this kind of pinched setting is legible doesn't mean it's not ugly (see Figure 8.5). As we'll

FIGURE 8.4 Tightly spaced sans serif faces become hard to read quite quickly, as the condensed face used here dramatizes. The similarly condensed and spaced text below it is noticeably easier to read.

The company's focus is on concurrent design engineering, and our hand-picked design team works with our clients to design fully automated assembly machines and integrated systems for manufacturing devices in three key markets: sensors, conductors, and actuators; mobile and cellular telephone components; and pressure sensors and relays.

The company's focus is on concurrent design engineering, and our hand-picked design team works with our clients to design fully automated assembly machines and integrated systems for manufacturing devices in three key markets: sensors, conductors, and actuators; mobile and cellular telephone components; and pressure sensors and relays.

see in the sections about tracking and kerning in Chapter 11, it's not necessarily a bad thing to have display type set so tight that adjoining characters touch. But when taken to extremes, such crowding starts to look like a mistake.

Overly Loose Spacing

Abnormally loose spacing is a composition tactic sometimes seen in magazines. It's a sloppy practice, but publishers like it because less handwork is needed to tidy up problems that arise from setting type in the usual narrow magazine columns (see Figure 8.6). The strategy is based on the fact that the eye can pick out differences between tight and tighter type more easily than between loose and looser type. In other words, when setting loosely spaced type it's easier to create a sense of consistent type color—even though that color is quite pale—because tight lines aren't allowed and everything is set so loose that the loosest lines don't stand out.

Type set this way is not a pretty sight, but it does have the practical benefit of always looking the same, and everyday composition problems are masked by the slack spacing. It also enables pages to be filled with less text, because loosely set type not only takes up more room but also has to be more generously leaded, which stretches the text even further.

Unbalanced Spacing

Typesetting programs can control how much or how little the spaces between words and letters can be adjusted within a line. Chapter 10 explains this process of line composition—and how to control it—in detail, but it's enough to say here that the amount that these two kinds of spaces can be flexed has to be carefully balanced.

Finest Umbrellas Half-Price!!

FIGURE 8.5 Very tightly spaced type is the norm in advertising, but there's no need for type to be set as cramped as this. A condensed face set with more generous spacing would create a better impression.

From the organic gardener's perspective, the world is awash with artificial fertilizers that have become to farming what antibiotics have become to medicine: a virtual *sine qua non*. In truth, they argue, agricultural yields when using totally organic methods are indistinguishable from those that rely on "chemical farming" techniques. In some cases, the organic approach comes out well ahead in terms of yield per acre.

FIGURE 8.6 There are some wildly loose lines in this text, but they don't stand out because the overall set is also very loose. This is an effective camouflage technique, but hiding the uglier amid the ugly is not the stuff of good typesetting.

FIGURE 8.7 In the left-hand sample, the text has been composed without allowing letter spaces to be altered. The result is grossly exaggerated word spaces on many lines. In the right-hand sample, letter spaces have been allowed to vary plus or minus 5 percent, and the result is far more even overall spacing and no terribly loose lines.

The results of the first round of the elections shook the public rigid, as it seemed impossible that a candidate from the far right wing—who indeed had been a Nazi Party member during his youth—ousted the center-left candidate. The outcry from the general public was considerable but also considerably too late. The run-up to the election had been sedate—almost somnolent—and people learned too late that the unimaginable only seems that way when people fail to use their imaginations.

The results of the first round of the elections shook the public rigid, as it seemed impossible that a candidate from the far right wing—who indeed had been a Nazi Party member during his youth—ousted the center-left candidate. The outcry from the general public was considerable but also considerably too late. The run-up to the election had been sedate—almost somnolent—and people learned too late that the unimaginable only seems that way when people fail to use their imaginations.

If you let letter spaces be expanded and compressed too much, you run the risk of impairing legibility by breaking up those word patterns so crucial to easy reading. In extreme cases, letter spaces can approach the widths of word spaces, so words become harder to distinguish as separate entities. It doesn't actually take much expansion of letter spaces for this to happen—word spaces are not terribly wide.

Conversely, if you tightly restrict letter-spacing changes, the typesetting program can fit type into lines only by adjusting the word spaces, which can become exaggerated, punching holes in the lines of type and making the letters within each word seem too tightly set (see Figure 8.7). This is a chronic problem in narrow newspaper columns.

Purists will argue that hand typesetters got along just fine without being able to adjust the spaces between letters. But modernists will counter that if the old-timers could have adjusted letter spaces they would have done so in a flash. Good type color has always been an ideal, and the balanced control of both word and letter spaces is a key to achieving it.

FIGURE 8.8 These lines are too long for comfortable reading at this point size. Apart from being visually off-putting, the long lines and tight leading make it harder for the reader to scan from the right margin back to the appropriate line at the left. The cures for text like this are larger type and extra lead.

No vices are so hard to eradicate as those which are popularly regarded as virtues. Among these the vice of reading is foremost. That reading trash is a vice is generally conceded; but reading *per se*—the habit of reading—new as it is, already ranks with such seasoned virtues as thrift, sobriety, early rising and regular exercise. There is, indeed, something peculiarly aggressive in the virtuousness of the sense-of-duty reader. By those who have kept to the humble paths of precept he is revered as following a counsel of perfection. "I wish I had kept up my reading as you have," the unlettered novice declares to this adept in the super-erogatory; and the reader, accustomed to the incense of uncritical applause, not unnaturally looks on his occupation as a noteworthy intellectual achievement.

What is reading, in the last analysis, but an interchange between writer and reader? If the book enters the reader's mind just as it left the writer's—without any of the additions and modifications inevitably produced by contact with a new body of thought—it has been read to no purpose. In such cases, of course, the reader is not always to blame. There are books that are always the same—incapable of modifying or of being modified—but these do not count as factors in literature. The value of books is proportionate to what may be called their plasticity—their quality of being all things to all men, of being diversely moulded by the impact of fresh forms of thought. Where, from one cause or another, this reciprocal adaptability is lacking, there can be no real intercourse between book and reader.

FIGURE 8.9 The type size is appropriate for the measure in this sample, but the leading is far too tight. The text loses the horizontal texture that's normally created by the alternating lines of text and empty space. Reading text this tightly packed is a chore even for those brave readers who have gotten past its impenetrable appearance.

Long Lines and Tight Leading

As we'll see in Chapter 9, point size, measure (line length), and leading are interdependent. Changing one variable is apt to force changes in the others.

A common design error is to set text in a measure too wide for the point size and leading (or put another way, to use a point size and a leading too small for the specified measure). The results are pages that look like bland gray rectangles and lines of type that seem to go on forever (see Figure 8.8).

Lines of great length set with tight leading also make it hard for the reader's eye to alight in the correct place when scanning from the end of one line to the beginning of the next. The space between lines doesn't just keep the characters on successive lines from bumping into each other; that white horizontal gutter under a line is the path your eye follows when it's tracking from the right-hand margin back to the left. If the path is too narrow, your readers' eyes can easily lose their way as they traverse the page (see Figure 8.9). While such tight leading doesn't make the type illegible per se, it does make reading a discouraging chore, which can be tantamount to the same thing.

By a faction, I understand a number if citizens, whether amounting to a majority or minority of the whole, who are united and actuated by some common impulse of passion, or of interest, adverse to the rights of other citizens, or to the permanent and aggregate interests of the community.

By a faction, I understand a number if citizens, whether amounting to a majority or minority of the whole, who are united and actuated by some common impulse of passion, or of interest, adverse to the rights of other citizens, or to the permanent and aggregate interests of the community.

FIGURE 8.10 Looking at text set with a ragged right margin (top) shows how much extra space a typesetting program has to distribute among words and letters on each line in order to create a justified margin (bottom). Allowing hyphenation to occur after only two letters at line's end can help in these situations, by allowing more text to be fit onto each line before any extra space has to be distributed.

Narrow-Measure Problems

Newspaper typography is, on the whole, the worst that most people see on a daily basis. Even those who know nothing about type can see that the narrow columns of a newspaper are often very badly set, peppered with yawning gaps between words and marred by lines that appear to have no spaces in them at all. The tradition of narrow newspaper columns is very old, but the type once used to fill them was much smaller. The problem with today's newspapers is the opposite, then, of that described in the previous section: The size of the type is too large for the measure, making good composition very difficult.

The problem here is that when a typesetting system fills lines with type, it has to do something with the space that's left over after it's put as many words

en have many of the traits already mentioned as being strong in women, but in a smaller degree. Style and appearance have less bearing on a man's purchases; or rather, while the desire for style may be as strong as in a woman, the style must be supported by quality. Some men have their artistic side well developed, but in most cases to a far less extent than in women. Strength and simplicity appeal to men more than mere artistic value. Men differ from women in that they have less regard for details. A brief description that covers the main points fully may produce better results than the full description that appeals to women. If the main points of an article are satisfactory, the details frequently get slight attention.

FIGURE 8.11 This drop-cap *M* is set flush left, but it doesn't look that way. In fact, it's indented by the width of its side bearing. Typesetting and page layout programs are only just starting to align such characters according to their outline contours and not according to their bounding boxes.

on the line as will fit. Even after hyphenating the last word of the line to get an optimal fit, this leftover space can be quite large. Where to put it? Between words, normally, with some—but not too much—added between letters as well (see Figure 8.10). But on short lines there aren't many word spaces, so distributing space into these few openings often causes them to get far too large. There are ways to fix this, as discussed in Chapters 10 and 11, but newspaper deadlines (and economics) make it impractical to have anyone refine the type to correct such composition faults before they appear in print.

Narrow columns are tiring to read because your eyes are constantly batting from margin to margin every few words. It's like watching a Ping-Pong game. Compound the narrow measure with lines that are alternately too tight (the system having jammed as much type as permissible onto the line) and too loose (for the reasons just cited) and you have what a newspaper essentially is: throwaway type. This is not a model to be emulated.

Narrow measures crop up all the time in page layouts. One of the first tricks that desktop publishing applications were programmed to do was wrapping text around a graphic. The graphic—a photograph, for example—would intrude into a column of type, narrowing its measure. Text wrapping became hugely popular and remains so today, with the result that a lot of badly set type can be seen. Spacing problems are an inevitable consequence of narrow measures (as are color problems where measures vary) and the only way to rectify them is to adjust spacing on a line-by-line basis. This is too rarely done.

Optical Effects and Alignment Problems

As described in Chapter 1 ("Bounding Boxes and Spaces"), a computer program considers each character to exist in a box whose height is equal to the point size of the type and whose width reflects the width of the character. When you set type, then, you may think that you're arranging characters, but your computer is stacking boxes. This stacking creates a variety of visual anomalies in which the characters you see on the page don't seem to align where they should. Their bounding boxes align perfectly—your computer has seen to that—but those boxes are invisible, and all you can see on the page are the images of the characters contained inside them.

Figure 8.11 shows a case in point. The large initial capital letter (or *drop cap*) is supposed to set hard against the left margin—the typesetting program says it is—but it clearly isn't. It appears to be indented by several points. The problem is that the drop cap's bounding box is set flush left, but the character image itself is inset slightly from the edge of its bounding box. In other words, the character is indented by the width of its side bearing, and the exaggerated

> ### Advertising to Men
>
> Those articles that should be considered with special reference to men are limited to such things as are for his personal use or are connected with his business. But even in the former class, women's influence is always more or less in evidence. Clothing, for example, is often bought at the suggestion of or with the advice of some woman, or to make an impression on women.

FIGURE 8.12 Centering type over text with a ragged margin is always fraught with possible lopsidedness. Here, the partially filled lines of the text block make the heading seem off-center. Column headings in tables are apt to suffer in the same way.

size of the drop cap makes the effect more noticeable. The attentive typesetter—or the one granted the time to be attentive—will adjust the position of such a drop cap to the left to make it appear properly aligned. (Techniques for achieving this are outlined in Chapter 12.)

Another visual alignment problem is illustrated in Figure 8.12. Here a heading is centered over a column of type. But the block of type has a ragged right-hand margin, so the heading looks set too far to the right. The heading isn't centered just over the text but also over the spaces remaining at the ends of the lines. In effect, something visible has been centered over something only partially visible, with unbalanced results.

The Eyes Have It

One thing that distinguishes well-set type from poorly set type is that the former is never set with the assumption that the typesetting program will automatically do the right thing. Good typesetters trust their eyes, not their tools. The most successful and contented typesetters are those with good proofreaders backing them up.

A typesetter has to make myriad choices in order to compose a perfect page. This chapter has outlined only a few of the major ones. Many of these choices come from the fabulously precise positioning capabilities of computerized typesetting programs. But ultimately the most important tool for a typesetter is a critical eye. After all, hand typesetters did stunningly beautiful work without the ability to adjust spacing to a thousandth of an em, adjust leading to a tenth of a point, and set type in fractional sizes.

If you start looking closely at the type you see every day, you'll be amazed at—how to put this diplomatically?—the number of typographic improvements that could have been made but weren't. They result from various portions of haste, ignorance, greed (managers who won't pay for expertise, training, or quality control), and—saddest of all—a simple lack of concern.

PART TWO   How to Set Type

LINE LENGTH AND POINT SIZE

AUTOMATIC LEADING AND LEADING IN TEXT FRAMES

BASELINE SHIFTS

PAGE LAYOUT CONSIDERATIONS

THE INFLUENCE OF TYPEFACE SELECTION

EFFECT OF X-HEIGHT AND CHARACTER WIDTH

It's hard to talk about these variables—measure, point size, and leading—one at a time. They work in concert, and ultimately all three are dependent on the typeface you're working with. Bigger type needs wider measures, and wider measures need more leading. Wider measures, in turn, need larger type. Changing the leading changes everything.

Despite their being such basic specifications—you really can't set type at all without assigning values to them—their interrelationships are not always fully appreciated. This is a polite way of saying that they're commonly mishandled, and not just by novices.

Line Length, or Measure

Type is generally set in a column, and the width of that column is its *measure*. Although it's tempting to use the term *line length* interchangeably with *measure*, the two don't always refer to the same thing. For example, when you're setting type with a *ragged right margin*—that is, where the lines don't fill the measure completely—the length of any given line is apt not to equal the measure of the column it's a part of (see Figure 9.1). If such *rag-right* text isn't hyphenated

FIGURE 9.1 The lines here show the margins of this block of type—they indicate its measure. This is a case in which line length and measure are clearly not the same thing.

About twenty years ago, there lived a singular gentleman in the Old Hall among the elm-trees. He was about three-score years of age, very rich, and somewhat odd in many of his habits, but for generosity and benevolence he had no equal.

FIGURE 9.2A *facing page* For some typefaces, a solid setting in a narrow measure like this (11½ picas) would work well, but with the generous proportions of the Sabon used here, the 10/10 sample looks a bit crowded. It looks better with an extra point of lead (10/11), but at 10/12 the setting starts to break into horizontal stripes.

The same is true with the 11-point settings in the second row. 11-point type at this measure is probably too large, creating lines with very few words and a hectic, wild rag. The 12-point type used in the bottom row is clearly too big, although when generously leaded as at the bottom right, it may work well in display roles.

(which is common), most of the lines will set well short of the full measure, as the typesetting program can't flesh out lines with partial, hyphenated words. In such a case, the measure of the type may be appropriate, but the net line length can appear too short.

Computer publishing software still doesn't take a consistent approach to the concept of measure. In some programs you specify a page size, then the page margins, then the number of text columns on the page, then the width of the gutters between the text columns. What you're left with is a number of columns whose measure has been calculated by the program by a process of subtraction. In these programs you never have a chance to say "I want three 14-pica columns with 1-pica gutters between them," even though this would seem like the logical way to proceed. You shouldn't back into a measure, if possible; you should define it directly. If necessary you should do the math yourself before touching the keyboard, adding the widths of the columns and gutters and subtracting them from the page width to calculate your page margins. (Defining these measurements is part of establishing the *page grid,* discussed in "Page and Baseline Grids" in Chapter 12.)

Alternatively, you may be able to draw text *frames,* which are like bounding boxes for columns of type. When you draw these frames you can specify their exact width—that is, the type's measure—but you generally have to create the gutters between these columns manually by positioning the frames precisely on the page. This is still pretty primitive.

The page-setup options of page layout programs establish the rudiments of a page grid. They define, for example, the *trim size* of the page: how large the page will be after it's been bound into book or magazine form. They also define the measure of the column(s) and the size of the page margins, which in the case of a simple book page are the amounts by which the text area will be inset from the four edges of the page. In short, of the fundamental typographic specifications, measure is usually defined first.

It has been urged as an argument in favor of rechartering the present bank that the calling in its loans will produce great embarrassment and distress. The time allowed to close its concerns is ample, and if it has well managed its pressure will be light, and heavy only in case its management has been bad. If, therefore, it shall produce distress, the fault will be its own, and it would furnish a reason against renewing a power which has been so obvi-

10/10 × 12 picas

It has been urged as an argument in favor of rechartering the present bank that the calling in its loans will produce great embarrassment and distress. The time allowed to close its concerns is ample, and if it has well managed its pressure will be light, and heavy only in case its management has been bad. If, therefore, it shall produce distress, the fault will be its own, and it would furnish a reason against re-

11/11 × 12 picas

It has been urged as an argument in favor of rechartering the present bank that the calling in its loans will produce great embarrassment and distress. The time allowed to close its concerns is ample, and if it has well managed its pressure will be light, and heavy only in case its management has been bad. If, therefore, it shall produce distress, the fault will be its own, and it

12/12 × 12 picas

It has been urged as an argument in favor of rechartering the present bank that the calling in its loans will produce great embarrassment and distress. The time allowed to close its concerns is ample, and if it has well managed its pressure will be light, and heavy only in case its management has been bad. If, therefore, it shall produce distress, the fault will be its own, and it would furnish a reason against renewing a

10/11 × 12 picas

It has been urged as an argument in favor of rechartering the present bank that the calling in its loans will produce great embarrassment and distress. The time allowed to close its concerns is ample, and if it has well managed its pressure will be light, and heavy only in case its management has been bad. If, therefore, it shall produce distress, the fault will be its own, and it would

11/12 × 12 picas

It has been urged as an argument in favor of rechartering the present bank that the calling in its loans will produce great embarrassment and distress. The time allowed to close its concerns is ample, and if it has well managed its pressure will be light, and heavy only in case its management has been bad. If, therefore, it shall produce distress, the fault

12/13 × 12 picas

It has been urged as an argument in favor of rechartering the present bank that the calling in its loans will produce great embarrassment and distress. The time allowed to close its concerns is ample, and if it has well managed its pressure will be light, and heavy only in case its management has been bad. If, therefore, it shall produce distress, the fault will be its own, and it would furnish a

10/12 × 12 picas

It has been urged as an argument in favor of rechartering the present bank that the calling in its loans will produce great embarrassment and distress. The time allowed to close its concerns is ample, and if it has well managed its pressure will be light, and heavy only in case its management has been bad. If, therefore, it shall produce distress, the fault

11/13 × 12 picas

It has been urged as an argument in favor of rechartering the present bank that the calling in its loans will produce great embarrassment and distress. The time allowed to close its concerns is ample, and if it has well managed its pressure will be light, and heavy only in case its management has been bad. If, therefore, it shall

12/14 × 12 picas

It has been urged as an argument in favor of re-chartering the present bank that the calling in its loans will produce great embarassment and distress. The time allowed to close its concerns is ample, and if it has well managed its pressure will be light, and heavy only in case its management has been bad. If, therefore, it shall produce distress, the fault will be its own, and it would furnish a reason against renewing a power which has been so obviously abused. But will there ever be a time when this reason will be less powerful? To acknowledge its force is to admit that the bank ought to be perpetual, and as a consequence the present stockholders and those inheriting

10/11 × 18 picas

It has been urged as an argument in favor of re-chartering the present bank that the calling in its loans will produce great embarassment and distress. The time allowed to close its concerns is ample, and if it has well managed its pressure will be light, and heavy only in case its management has been bad. If, therefore, it shall produce distress, the fault will be its own, and it would furnish a reason against renewing a power which has been so obviously abused. But will there ever be a time when this reason will be less powerful? To acknowledge its force is to admit that the bank ought to be perpetual, and as a consequence

10/12 × 18 picas

It has been urged as an argument in favor of rechartering the present bank that the calling in its loans will produce great embarassment and distress. The time allowed to close its concerns is ample, and if it has well managed its pressure will be light, and heavy only in case its management has been bad. If, therefore, it shall produce distress, the fault will be its own, and it would furnish a reason against renewing a power which has been so obviously abused. But will there ever be a time when this reason will be less powerful? To acknowledge its force is to admit that the bank ought to be perpetual, and as a conse-

11/12 × 18 picas

It has been urged as an argument in favor of rechartering the present bank that the calling in its loans will produce great embarassment and distress. The time allowed to close its concerns is ample, and if it has well managed its pressure will be light, and heavy only in case its management has been bad. If, therefore, it shall produce distress, the fault will be its own, and it would furnish a reason against renewing a power which has been so obviously abused. But will there ever be a time when this reason will be less powerful? To acknowledge its force is to admit that the

11/13 × 18 picas

It has been urged as an argument in favor of rechartering the present bank that the calling in its loans will produce great embarassment and distress. The time allowed to close its concerns is ample, and if it has well managed its pressure will be light, and heavy only in case its management has been bad. If, therefore, it shall produce distress, the fault will be its own, and it would furnish a reason against renewing a power which has been so obviously abused. But will there ever be a time when this reason will be less powerful? To acknowledge its force is to admit

12/13 × 18 picas

It has been urged as an argument in favor of rechartering the present bank that the calling in its loans will produce great embarassment and distress. The time allowed to close its concerns is ample, and if it has well managed its pressure will be light, and heavy only in case its management has been bad. If, therefore, it shall produce distress, the fault will be its own, and it would furnish a reason against renewing a power which has been so obviously abused. But will there ever be a time when this reason will be less power-

12/14 × 18 picas

It has been urged as an argument in favor of rechartering the present bank that the calling in its loans will produce great embarrassment and distress. The time allowed to close its concerns is ample, and if it has well managed its pressure will be light, and heavy only in case its management has been bad. If, therefore, it shall produce distress, the fault will be its own, and it would furnish a reason against renewing a power which has been so obvi-

10/11 × 24 picas

It has been urged as an argument in favor of rechartering the present bank that the calling in its loans will produce great embarrassment and distress. The time allowed to close its concerns is ample, and if it has well managed its pressure will be light, and heavy only in case its management has been bad. If, therefore, it shall produce distress, the fault will be its own, and it would furnish a reason against renewing a power which has been so obvi-

10/12 × 24 picas

It has been urged as an argument in favor of rechartering the present bank that the calling in its loans will produce great embarrassment and distress. The time allowed to close its concerns is ample, and if it has well managed its pressure will be light, and heavy only in case its management has been bad. If, therefore, it shall produce distress, the fault will be its own, and it would furnish a reason against renewing a power which has been so obviously abused. But will

11/12 × 24 picas

It has been urged as an argument in favor of rechartering the present bank that the calling in its loans will produce great embarrassment and distress. The time allowed to close its concerns is ample, and if it has well managed its pressure will be light, and heavy only in case its management has been bad. If, therefore, it shall produce distress, the fault will be its own, and it would furnish a reason against renewing a power which has been so obviously abused. But will

11/13 × 24 picas

It has been urged as an argument in favor of rechartering the present bank that the calling in its loans will produce great embarrassment and distress. The time allowed to close its concerns is ample, and if it has well managed its pressure will be light, and heavy only in case its management has been bad. If, therefore, it shall produce distress, the fault will be its own, and it would furnish a reason against renew-

11/14 × 24 picas

FIGURE 9.2B *facing page* Over an 18-pica measure, the 10/11 type in the sample at the top left is at the point where it could profit from an additional point of lead, as shown to its right.

With fewer words per line, the 11/12 sample doesn't look as gray, and adding a second point of extra lead (as shown in the sample to its right) creates a rather airy set.

At 12-point, though, the type begins to look heavy and claustrophobic with only a single point of extra leading. Although the measure is relatively narrow, the type's large size demands some extra breathing space, provided in the 12/14 setting.

FIGURE 9.2C *this page* As measure grows, leading has to keep pace. The top sample looks a bit gray, its horizontal texture being lost to the relatively tight leading. A single additional point of lead in the 10/12 sample makes a huge difference, and the text is much more inviting. Likewise, the 11/12 sample looks dense and dark, while the 11/13 sample below it has a more open, more balanced appearance.

The 11/14 sample is starting to appear a bit loose, but because Sabon is a relatively hefty face, it can handle the extra space without having the lines seem to drift apart too much. With a more delicate face, or one with a smaller x-height, this setting would appear too loosely leaded.

Point Size and Measure

Point size and measure are married to each other. Optimal line lengths, for example, are often expressed in terms of how many characters or words will fit within the measure, and this is a function of point size.

You can calculate the appropriate point size for a given measure in different ways. Here are some of the more commonly proposed guidelines:

- the optimal line length is between one and a half and two times the length of the lowercase alphabet

- the optimal line length is nine or ten words (figure an average of 5 ½ characters per word)

- 27 characters is the minimum line length, 40 the optimum, and 70 the maximum

A guide that I prefer compares the line length in picas with the type size in points. Because it uses simple math, you don't have to count individual words and characters. In this scheme, a measure (in picas) three times the size of the type (in points) is the absolute outer limit, and it is too long most of the time. Thus, 10-point type shouldn't be set over a measure exceeding 30 picas. The ideal ratio is about 2:1 or 2.5:1, which translates to a measure of 20 to 25 picas for 10-point type. When the ratio approaches 1:1 (10-point type over a 10-pica measure, for example) good type composition becomes almost impossible. Below a ratio of 1.5:1, you're skating on thin ice (see Figure 9.2).

All these schemes lead you to the same basic relationship between type size and measure, and the clear implication is that the longer the line, the larger the type should be. Standard text sizes for most books, journals, and magazines range from 10-point to 12-point. This book is set using 11-point type over a 25 ½-pica measure.

Leading

Leading is the distance in points from the baseline of one line of type to the baseline of the line that precedes it (see Figure 9.3). The name comes from the lead alloy used to cast type in the days of hand typesetting, when to add extra space between lines, you literally added lead. Word processing programs refer to leading as *line spacing*.

Type set *solid* has leading that's equal to its point size: for example, 12-point type on 12 points of lead. This expression also takes its name from handset type, where in a solid setting you placed one row of type blocks directly under the row that preceded it, without any additional strips of lead to spread the

LESSON VI

THE GRANDFATHER

Pronounce the following words in this lesson correctly.
Do not say *smok-in* for smok-ing; *clear-in* for clear-ing;
ketch-in for catch-ing; *turn-in* for turn-ing; *spin-nin* for
spin-ning.

30′

23′

13′

13′

13′

FIGURE 9.3 The baselines in this text have been made visible to reveal the leading values between each pair of lines. These values may be specified discretely or as an addition to the existing leading by a "space before paragraph" or "space after paragraph" command. In this case, the heading "The Grandfather" has been set on 30 points of lead, and the text after it has been set on 13 points of lead with a "space before paragraph" of another 10 points.

rows apart. In digital type, a solid set stacks rows of bounding boxes one upon the other in much the same way. Other ways of describing a solid set are (following the example above) *12 on 12* or *12/12* (pronounced "twelve on twelve").

Spreading lines apart is still called *adding lead.* Any setting beyond a solid set is said to have *extra lead,* so a 12/13 setting could also be said to have 1 extra point of lead. Some veterans of metal type and those who learned from them prefer to call this setting "1 point of lead," defining the setting by the amount of lead added between the imaginary rows of type blocks. This is confusing, though, because virtually all contemporary typesetting programs, in referring to leading, use the baseline-to-baseline standard. To say something is set on 1 point of lead, then, is to say that its baseline is only 1 point below that of the preceding line.

It should be noted here that on computerized typesetting systems you can indeed set type of any size with 1-point leading. In fact, you can set lines with zero leading, in which case they'll overlap and share the same baseline.

It's not unusual—especially in display sizes—to use *negative leading,* in which the leading specified is less than the point size of the type, such as 66/60 or 54/50 (see Figure 9.4). Type set in all capitals, for example, typically looks better when set with negative leading (there's no need to accommodate any descending characters). So does headline-sized type in general, because as noted in Chapter 3 ("Size Changes Everything"), when point size increases, white space—including the space between lines—seems to grow proportionally faster than type. In display type (which is usually only a few lines long) a solid setting typically looks too loose, and negative leadings are common.

As with calculating suitable point sizes for various measures, there are several ways of calculating the appropriate leading. Again, my preference is a numerical approach, based on the relationship between point size and measure. To calculate how much extra lead to add, simply divide the measure (in picas) by the size of the type (in points). Round off the result to the nearest half point. For 11-point type set over a 24-pica measure, then, you would add 2 extra points of lead (24 ÷ 11 = 2.18, rounded off to 2), for a setting of 11/13. If the measure is widened to 30 picas, the result of the calculation is 2.5, for a setting

Fall Suit Sale!
Prices Reduced
by 50%
5 Days Only!

FIGURE 9.4 A typical case of type set with negative leading, in this case 22-point type set on 19 points of lead. Display type with no descenders can be leaded even more tightly.

leading = 12.5′	leading = 12.7′
No detail in a person's "make-up" affects him so much as the shape of his head. If he owns a good shape, he will have sterling qualities of character; if he has a poor shape, he will lack the essentials of a man; and if he has, what is most likely, a head of mid-way classification, he will be someone of ordinary average ability.	No detail in a person's "make-up" affects him so much as the shape of his head. If he owns a good shape, he will have sterling qualities of character; if he has a poor shape, he will lack the essentials of a man; and if he has, what is most likely, a head of mid-way classification, he will be someone of ordinary average ability.

FIGURE 9.5 Two-tenths of a point of extra lead makes a barely noticeable and hardly appreciable difference in these two settings of 11-point type. In most cases, leading increments of a half point are fine enough.

of 11/13.5. This formula certainly isn't binding, but it does get you close to an appropriate leading value.

In most settings, leading doesn't need to be set in increments finer than half points. Exceptions may arise where finer adjustments make a noticeable improvement. In general, though, trying to fine-tune leading in increments of less than a half point can lead to needless fussing (see Figure 9.5).

Automatic Leading

An axiom of computerized type is that leading should generally be 1.2 times the point size of the type. This isn't a terribly useful guideline, because it's clear that leading must increase along with the measure. It also gets you into weird fractions of points that have to be rounded off in any case. This bit of numerology has been enshrined, however, in the default setting of most word processing, typesetting, and page layout programs: the so-called *auto* or *automatic leading*.

Auto leading should be avoided, as it's bound to cause confusion. For one thing, it's hard to know what your leading is when it's set to auto. At 10-point, it's a nice, tidy 12 points. But at 11-point it becomes 13.2 points, and at 12-point it's 14.4. Working in half-point leading increments is confusing enough—and almost always exact enough—without getting tangled in tenths of points. In addition, auto leading is usually insidiously close enough to a setting you've actually specified to be overlooked onscreen when it does sneak into a job. When it turns up on a printed page, though, the error is all too apparent.

For these reasons, you should reset the default typographic specifications of your typesetting program to turn off auto leading. In most programs, any typographic settings you specify when there is no document open become the default specifications for any new document. That is, when you open the program afterward, create a new document, and just start typing, the default specifications will be applied to the type you create. You can change the default typeface, point size, leading, and a host of other typographic settings by defining them when no document is open. Other specifications can be set in the program's

M M M

FIGURE 9.6 These three *M*s are shown as they appear onscreen relative to the top left corner of their text frames. Each is from a different program, and though they're all set with the same leading, the position of that all-important first baseline in the frame remains ambiguous and unpredictable. Furthermore, in programs that don't reflect the type's leading in the position of the frame's first baseline, the position of that baseline will vary from typeface to typeface. That is because the position of the baseline within the em square varies from face to face.

preferences control panels, again before any document is opened. Likewise, you should make sure that none of the style sheets your program offers use automatic leading. The default style sheet in most programs also employs auto leading, and any styles you base on it will inherit this attribute. Expunge it. Working with style sheets is covered in detail in Chapter 17.

Leading in Text Frames

Frames are an invention of desktop publishing programs, and they act as "containers" for type. They can also act as handcuffs for typesetters, as explained in more detail in Chapter 12. They make life easier for page layout artists who can link a series of frames over a range of pages and "pour" text into them, with the overflow running from one frame to the next throughout the document. But text poured into frames doesn't always act the way it should.

In terms of leading, the first line in the frame is problematic. There is no consensus among typesetting and page layout programs as to how—or if—the leading of this first line affects its position relative to the top of the frame. Of the three leading page composition programs as of this writing, one drops the top line down as the leading for that line is increased, but the other two do not. Of those latter two, one aligns the top line of type so that the tops of its characters' bounding boxes coincide with the top of the frame. But in the other, the tops of the bounding boxes are aligned at a fixed and constant but arbitrary distance below it (see Figure 9.6).

Traditionally a page layout grid is marked with all the baselines on which type should align, and presumably the first line of the frame should base-align on a specific baseline. But since the first baseline in the frame can't be counted on to be at a predictable position, this makes precise layout more complicated. It's important, then, not to align text frames according to their frame edges but by the baselines of the type they contain. At the very least, you should be aware of which quirky approach your program takes to this situation.

Fortunately, programs are beginning to offer the option for text to align by its baseline rather than by the edge of its frame. Finding out how your program handles this situation will save you many alignment hassles down the road. For more on this subject, see "Text Frames and Grid Alignment" in Chapter 12.

for one hundred words of such copy may bring up pictures and start thoughts that could not be described fully with one thousand words.

Truthfulness

Aside from the moral aspect of the question, advertising should be truthful merely because truthfulness pays. When a firm gets

for one hundred words of such copy may bring up pictures and start thoughts that could not be described fully with one thousand words.

Truthfulness

Aside from the moral aspect of the question, advertising should be truthful merely because truthfulness pays. When a firm gets

FIGURE 9.7 Only the onscreen view (above right) reveals how the leading for the printed sample was set. In this case, highlighting the subhead reveals that all the extra lead has been assigned to the subhead itself, not to the paragraphs around it. What this view does not reveal was whether the extra lead above the subhead was specified by assigning a discrete leading value or whether a "space before" specification was used. It can be assumed that the extra lead after the subhead was created with a "space after" command.

Changing Leading as Type Size Changes

Very few documents use only a single type size from beginning to end, an exception being a typical novel. Usually, in the course of the text stream, subheadings or content breaks of some sort divide the text into sections. Even if such subheads are the same point size as the text (they're usually somewhat larger), there is almost always some extra lead set above them. In these cases you have the choice of setting that spacing as a function of the leading assigned to the subhead or by controlling it as a paragraph attribute of the subhead.

In the latter case, you would use your program's "space before" paragraph control to add leading to the subhead over and above the leading already assigned to it. (The control may not have this exact name in your program, but it will be something close.) In addition, if the subhead is in a larger point size than the text, you'll have to add extra lead after the subhead as well in order to set it at an appropriate distance from the text below. This can be done with a "space after" paragraph specification.

Figure 9.7 illustrates such a situation. In it, text set at 12/14 has been given a 14-point subhead. The subhead in question is set on 24 points of lead—that is, its baseline is 24 points below the last line of the preceding paragraph. Whether the subhead is specified as 14/24 or 14/14 with 10 points of "space before" doesn't matter to the appearance of the type as it appears here in mid-column. But it can make a difference in programs capable of *vertical justification,* a process that stretches leading to avoid certain composition faults, such as a subhead appearing as the last line of a page. These programs typically rely on strips of extra leading, called *vertical space bands,* that can be stretched or squeezed to alter the depth of a passage of type. Using the "space before" paragraph attribute creates such a space band. (For more on vertical justification, see the section of the same name in Chapter 10.)

The point here is that the way you choose to specify the leading in such situations can be strategic, not just visual.

The subhead in Figure 9.7 also needs some extra lead below it (4 points in this case), to keep it at a reasonable distance from the text underneath it. The

117

moisture that it could in itself when it was hotter, and that moisture is apt to affect the state of whatever object it is deposited on.

Bumps in the Night
Perhaps we cannot be quite certain that furniture cracks so much more at night than in the daytime. For one thing, there are another noises that go on in the daytime that we are more likely to be attending to.

117

Bumps in the Night
Perhaps we cannot be quite certain that furniture cracks so much more at night than in the daytime. For one thing, there are another noises that go on in the daytime that we are more likely to be attending to. Still, it is no doubt that furniture does make strange noises at night, and that it is not difficult to understand is we remember that the air

leading between the text and the subhead, though, is nominally based on the leading specification of the text, because leading is defined as the distance from one baseline to the baseline above it. Here again you will probably have two options. You can use the "space after" paragraph attribute to add a space band below the subhead, or add "space before" to the paragraph that follows it. Both will create the same visual effect on the page. But it makes more sense to use the "space after" approach so that all the type specs unique to the situation of the subhead are a part of the subhead itself.

Again, the strategies of using paragraph attributes in style sheets are covered in more detail in Chapter 17.

FIGURE 9.8 Here a line space above a subhead has been created by consecutive returns. This looks fine in mid-column (left) but bad at the top of a column, where the program sees the space not as added leading but as a line space that should be set like a text line. The result is a column that starts one line too low. The same would happen if the line space landed at the bottom of a column or page.

LINE SPACES AND SPACE BANDS

It's tempting to add leading between paragraphs, after titles, around subheads, and so forth, by hitting the Return key twice to create a blank line. This is a bad practice. Adding extra lead by pressing the Return key creates line spaces, not space bands, and although these two things may look alike in print, they don't act alike when your program is composing type.

A line space created by the Return key is a permanent, immutable part of your document. It is, in effect, a blank typeset line, a line full of spaces. A space band is recognized by your program as a leading element used to adjust the space between two specific lines of type when they appear sequentially in a column. When those elements don't appear sequentially—when a subhead appears at the top of a page, for example—the space bands are collapsed and ignored. Line spaces are not.

Figure 9.8 shows a situation in which the spacing above a subhead has been created with the Return key. It looks the same in mid-column as it would if it had been created with the "space before" option to add leading above the subhead. When the text is reflowed so that the subhead appears at the top of a column, the program discards the space band—it no longer makes sense to use it—but keeps the line space. This creates the layout error shown, and the only way the page layout artist has of fixing it is to delete the line space by hand. That, too, is problematic, though, because if another layout change later causes the text to reflow—and the subhead once again appears in mid-column—the requisite extra leading has now been deleted.

Dedicated typesetting systems typically had a command that let you add a vertical space band of whatever width wherever you wanted. Such a space band was an independent entity, not tied to any paragraph. The software recognized it as a role-playing spacing element, and when that role wasn't required—as in the example just described—it would ignore the vertical space band. Unfortunately, this facility has yet to find its way into popular desktop systems.

The "Baseline Shift"

In dedicated typesetting systems, leading was—in the jargon of today's desktop programs—a *character attribute*. That is, each character on a line could have its own unique leading. Most page layout programs—following the logic of word processors—have made leading a paragraph attribute, meaning that if you change the leading for even a single character, the leading for the entire paragraph will change.

Some programs identify leading as a character attribute but don't really handle it that way. In such programs, changing the leading for a single character in a line will reset the leading for the entire line. This is essentially useless.

The control that most desktop programs have created as a substitute for character-based leading is called the *baseline shift*. The idea is that instead of changing the leading for a given character (or range of characters) you are instead displacing the baseline of that character up or down (see Figure 9.9).

After creating a baseline shift, you can change the leading of an entire section and the baseline shift will remain intact and correct because it is defined in terms of the character's baseline, wherever that may be; it isn't affected by the relationship of that baseline to that of the line before it. In other words, it's leading independent.

Because it's set as a discrete value, though, a baseline shift is vulnerable to changes in type size (see Figure 9.10). When the type size changes, the amount of the baseline shift may no longer be appropriate. Because baseline shifts are

FIGURE 9.9 Here the baseline shift command is used to elevate a reduced dollar sign from its normal home on the baseline to top-align with the numeral next to it.

commonly used to establish new positions for characters relative to other characters, it would be useful if a baseline shift could be specified in a size-independent way, so that, for example, top alignment could be maintained even though the point size changed.

The baseline shift, imperfect as it is, is still a very useful tool for making fine vertical adjustments to the positions of characters. You can use it for fractions, for example, or for mathematical formulas. Many of the alignment adjustments outlined in Chapter 12 rely on the baseline shift.

ZOO™

ZOO™

FIGURE 9.10 Because baseline shifts are measured in absolute rather than relative units, they're vulnerable to point-size changes. The proper alignment created at 48-point (top) is lost when the unit is resized to 36-point.

Leading in Reversed Type

Type set in reverse—that is, white on black—should be set with word and letter spacing that's looser than normal (a subject taken up in more detail in Chapter 5). To balance the overall color of the type, this looser texture should also be reflected in the leading. Reversed type is hard to read to begin with, so it's hard to tell when you've got it right. To get in the right ballpark, re-reverse your type once you've set it to see how it looks in normal black on white. The word and letter spacing should look too wide, but the leading should appear to be in synch with that degree of exaggeration. Flipping back and forth between reverse and normal will help you find the happy medium. But like so many other things typographic, this ideal setting is almost impossible to see onscreen, and only high-resolution proofing will reveal when you've got it right.

Asymmetrical Leading in Display Type

Normally, all the type in a single block of text has the same leading. This is not necessarily so in display type. Figure 9.11 illustrates this point. Because white space looms so much larger in big point sizes, the spacing between lines of display type can seem inconsistent from line to line. A line without descenders, as in the illustration, creates the effect of extra lead between it and the line below it. A line without capitals or ascenders can do the same thing.

At this point the assiduous typesetter steps in and begins to fiddle (assuming the design grid allows the display type to wander off its appointed baseline). The rule of thumb here is to get the leading to look consistent regardless of the numbers. These adjustments are apt to be fairly large, because if the problem was big enough to notice, it's going to take some big fiddling to correct it. A point here and a point there probably won't be enough.

Nobody *gets* golf like
Garden Gate Links. If
your game goes sour,
talk to the GGL pros.

Nobody *gets* golf like
Garden Gate Links. If
your game goes sour,
talk to the GGL pros.

FIGURE 9.11 All the lines in the top sample are set with the same leading, although it doesn't look that way. The absence of ascenders or descenders in the gap between the second and third lines makes the leading there look wider than that of the other lines. In the sample below, the leading between those lines has been tightened to create the effect of consistent leading.

"Text–only" manuscripts,
    preparing, 98
Thin space, 4, 23
Thin weight, 54
Tight–but–not–touching spacing,
    for display type, 52, 53
Tilde, 66
Time
    abbreviations for, 76–77
    small caps for references to, 78
Titles
    capitals in, 77–78
    display faces for, 54
    italicizing, 79
    quotation marks for, 76
Toggle, defined, 106
Top–alignment, 6, 42–43

FIGURE 9.12 Settings such as indexes and tables resemble lists more than normal text, and leading can be tightened without undue concern for readability. The 10-point text in this index sample has been set on 9.5 points of lead.

Leading in Non-text Settings

Non-text in this context means settings that aren't composed of sentences and paragraphs, settings that aren't *running text.* Non-text includes tables, lists, catalog entries, and so forth. These are short bursts of information in which readability issues, crucial in longer settings, don't necessarily apply. In an index, as shown in Figure 9.12, for example, leading is often set squeaky tight. In such settings, you are usually effectively dealing with very narrow measures, so leading can be reduced accordingly. Solid settings in these instances are common.

Leading Considerations in Multicolumn Settings

Issues of type texture and color become more complicated in multicolumn pages. Text can't be seen in a vacuum, and its texture has to complement—and be complemented by—the white space around it on the page. Wide margins, for example, inveigh against closely spaced, closely leaded type, even when the relationships among point size, measure, and leading within those columns seem appropriate. The broad collar of wide white margins around such columns creates a *tombstone* effect, in which the overly dense color of the type turns the columns into gray monoliths on the page. The columns become abstract graphic elements first and type to be read only secondarily. When page margins are wide, then, type color—as manifested through the choice of point size and leading—must be adjusted to match.

Likewise, the gutters between columns have to be in tune with both the texture of the type—particularly the leading—and the widths of the margins (see Figure 9.13). The page should appear as a harmonious whole, and the columns should clearly relate to each other to create a sense of their being a unified entity, albeit in several pieces. If the gutters are too wide, the columns look like a series of unrelated text blocks. If the gutters are too narrow, they begin to affect readability, as the eye takes in part of the type from the next column every time it ranges toward the end of each line.

Typeface-Specific Considerations

Typography abounds in *if*s, *and*s, and *but*s. All of the information in the earlier sections of this chapter has to be adjusted to the typeface chosen for the job at hand. The typeface design can affect the basic specifications of point size, leading, and measure in many ways.

Business Leaders Get Down to Business (at Last)

After decades of trying to project the image of being nice guys and sensitive managers, business leaders are finding that the best way to earn the respect of their workers and colleagues is to do what they know best: run the business

Calvin Coolidge said that the business of America is business. But these days, with so many political pressures mounting upon American businesses to be more socially active, and in so doing branching out well beyond their traditional areas of expertise, we might as well add a new corollary to Coolidge's aphorism. To wit, "The business of American business is business." In other words, let's leave social service to the social servants, and leave us free to do what we do best: make money.

The Political and Social Angles

Let's face it, the cure to poverty and the vast majority of social ills that derive therefrom is money. And there is only one source of money: commerce, business. Are diamond miners expected to be jewelry designers? Of course not.

And like diamond miners, business people are also generating a raw material, money, and they shouldn't be expected to get entangled in how that wealth is applied and allocated, or we'll wind up with the social welfare equivalent of jewelry designed by miners. Not a pretty sight.

Stormy Seas during the Oil Crisis

This, of course, begs the question of whether business people could indeed do a worse job of social engineering than the various government, private, and a host of semiprivate agencies that have taken on the task themselves. The answer is, I would say, probably not. The point, though, is that asking business to act as part of the social welfare system is now diverting precious energy, time, and expertise form the efforts needed to keep those businesses healthy and profitable, which are the greatest services that any business can offer to the society of which it is a part.

Ask not what business can do for society, but let's not ask society to come to the aid of business either. We're all in this together.

So when election time rolls around, consider all your candidates' stands on social charges, and all of the burdens their programs threaten to place on businesses large and small, because after all, the small businesses today is the large businesses of tomorrow, and a threat to one business must be a threat to them all. Render unto Caesar that which is Caesar's, and render unto the businessman all his duly earned profits.

Reining in Expenses

The answer is, I would say, probably not. The point, though, is that asking business to act as a part of the social welfare system is now diverting precious energy, time, and expertise form the efforts needed to keep those businesses healthy and profitable, which are the greatest services that any business can offer to the society of which it is a part. There is only one source of money: commerce, business. Are diamond miners expected to be jewelry designers? Of course not.

And like diamond miners, business people are also generating a raw material—money—and they shouldn't be expected to get entangled in how that wealth is applied and allocated, or we'll wind up with the social-welfare equivalent of jewelry designed by miners.

But these days, with political pressures quickly mounting on American businesses to be more socially active, and in so doing branching out well beyond their traditional areas of expertise, we might well add a corollary to

Coolidge's aphorism. To wit, "The business of American business is business." So in other words, let's leave social service to the social servants, and leave us free to do what we know how to do best: make money.

A Common-Sense Approach

Let's face it, the cure to poverty and the vast majority of social ills that derive therefrom is money. And there is only one source of money: commerce, business. Are diamond miners expected to be jewelry designers? Of course not.

And like diamond miners, business people are also generating a raw material, money, and they shouldn't be expected to get entangled in how that wealth is applied and allocated, or we'll wind up with the social welfare equivalent of jewelry designed by miners. Not a pretty sight.

This, of course, begs the question of whether business people could indeed do a worse job of social engineering than the various government, private, and a host of semiprivate agencies that have taken on the task themselves. The answer is, I would say, probably not. The point, though, is that asking business to act as part of the social welfare system is diverting precious energy, time, and expertise form the efforts needed to keep those businesses healthy and profitable, which are the greatest services that any business can offer to the society of which it is a part. Ask not what business can do for society, but let's not ask society to come to the aid of business either. We're all in this together.

So whenever election season rolls around, consider all of your candidates' stands on social charges, and the burdens their programs threaten to place

FIGURE 9.13 The gutters of this newsletter page are too wide, with the effect that the columns of type look as if they're standing separately instead of representing a single body of text. If the text were set ragged right, the effect would be even worse, as ragged margins make gutters seem wider.

Type Sizes

Type Sizes

Type Sizes

Type Sizes

Type Sizes

Type Sizes

Type Sizes

FIGURE 9.14 All the samples here are set at the same point size and the same leading. Clearly, stroke weight, character width, cap height, and x-height all contribute to the apparent size of type on the page. Type specifications that work for one typeface may well be inappropriate for another.

Seriffed Typefaces, Point Sizes, and Measures

Type is measured by the height of the bounding boxes containing the characters. Within those bounding boxes the proportions of the characters can vary widely from face to face. Figure 9.14 shows a sampling of faces, all set in the same point size, although you might not guess it. Given such variations, specifying type by the numbers alone isn't going to work.

THE EFFECT OF X-HEIGHT

Probably the major factor influencing the perceived size of a typeface is its x-height. This is the distance from the baseline to the mean line, which roughly aligns with the tops of the nonascending lowercase letters, such as *x*. The x-height of characters has grown over the centuries, and the contemporary norm is to have quite tall lowercase letters, in accordance with studies indicating that characters with larger x-heights are more legible. Since about 95 percent of the text we read consists of lowercase letters, efforts to increase legibility have focused there.

Typefaces with large x-heights are apt to need more leading, as the horizontal spaces between lines are eroded by the larger lowercase letters.

THE EFFECT OF CHARACTER WIDTH

Overall character width—*set width*—also affects perceived type size as well as influencing the number of characters and words that fit on a line. Narrow faces tend to make long lines feel crowded and even longer than they really are. Narrow faces should be set larger to compensate for this effect or be used across shorter measures. Some type specimen books have reference tables that compare the set widths of various faces, and these guides are valuable for predicting the adjustments a specific typeface may need in point size or measure.

The standard by which the widths of typefaces are generally judged is the length of its lowercase alphabet, set in a line without spaces. The lowercase alphabet of a *standard* text face is 13 ems long. For 10-point type, this would be 130 points (or 10 picas, 10 points). Using this measurement, we can see that a newspaper typeface such as Linotype's Times Roman—whose 10-point lowercase alphabet measures 118 points—is quite condensed. A classic book face such as Monotype's Garamond 3 measures 127 points, putting it squarely within the standard range. At the wide end of the range are faces such as ITC Bookman Light, whose 10-point lowercase alphabet length of 140 points makes it rather expanded, a characteristic you have to compensate for when setting it.

Because few type specimen books contain this useful information, you may have to do the calculations yourself. Make sure that automatic kerning and tracking have been turned off before creating your samples. Once the lowercase alphabet length of a typeface diverges more than 5 percent from the 13-em standard, you will probably have to adjust your point size and measure.

THE EFFECT OF STROKE WEIGHT

Lastly, stroke weight also affects how large type looks on the page, and even text-weight faces (that is, faces not designated as bold or semibold) vary considerably. Some "light" faces appear to be bolder than some "medium" or "regular" faces (see Figure 9.15). Heavier stroke weights make characters appear larger than their true dimensions would indicate—so bolder or bulkier faces need to be treated differently than spidery ones. In short, they need to be treated as if they were a somewhat larger point size.

Linotype Raleigh Light
Bauer Futura Light
Bitstream Cooper Light
ITC Garamond Light
ITC Novarese Book
ITC Garamond Book

FIGURE 9.15   The weights by which typefaces are identified are often not indicative of their relative weights on the page, as these samples show. One family's light may be heavier than another family's medium, and the two "book"-weight samples here are nowhere close to having the same color.

Sans Serif Typefaces, Point Size, and Measure

When using sans serif typefaces, you have to deal with all of the same considerations as with seriffed faces. In addition, you have to make certain concessions to the fact that sans serif type set at common text sizes simply isn't as legible as seriffed type. The difference isn't vast—otherwise sans serif faces would have dropped off the map—but it is considerable.

One difference is textural. Serifs give typefaces a certain horizontal component that runs parallel to the baseline. This creates a subtle texture that guides the eye along the line. Sans serif faces have a much more vertical quality, and text set in them lacks that gentle serif-induced current that carries the eye along. Long lines, then, can feel even longer when set in sans serif faces.

Sans serif faces that are often used for text—Futura, Frutiger, Univers—have relatively generous widths and side bearings to keep them from looking crowded. Thin or narrow-setting sans serifs must be handled with greater care.

Guidelines for how much narrower a measure you should use with sans serif faces are expressed in different ways, but they all end up with a line between 10 and 20 percent shorter than an equivalent setting for a seriffed type at the same point size. To set sans serif manuscript type at the same measure as you would seriffed type, conversely, entails bumping up its size at least 1 point.

Typefaces and Leading

Clearly the effect that typefaces have on determining a suitable point size and measure will also affect leading. As point size and measure vary, leading must follow. But typefaces have features that affect leading in other ways.

One of the roles of leading is to open up a horizontal runway for the reader's eye as it scans back and forth from margin to margin. Typeface design can affect the width of that runway. Typefaces with a large x-height, for example, typically profit from extra lead (see Figure 9.16). On the other hand, faces with small x-heights need no special treatment, except in extreme cases where tighter-than-normal leading might be in order.

Ascender height can also be an issue. Some typefaces have ascenders tall enough to make solid settings impractical, because the ascenders of one line can nearly touch the descenders of lines above them. Futura is a case in point.

Leading is an important tool in controlling type color on a page, so for typefaces with heavier stroke weights you'll probably want additional leading just to lighten up the color of the text block and make it appear less dense. Blocks of text should have a distinct horizontal "grain," and to make this effect more evident with bulky typefaces may require extra lead.

The camp that night was a merry one. They lit fires and burned the short scrub, which grew in thick masses around them. They filled their pipes and smoked the moss that grew at their feet. Never before had they been so happy.

The camp that night was a merry one. They lit fires and burned the short scrub, which grew in thick masses around them. They filled their pipes and smoked the moss that grew at their feet. Never before had they been so happy.

FIGURE 9.16 Large x-heights make typefaces look bigger than their point size might indicate. Leading has to be adjusted accordingly. Both of these samples are set at 10-point, but the Adobe Garamond on top needs only 11 points of lead at this measure, while the Simoncini Life text below it needs 12 points of lead to achieve similar color.

CHAPTER 10

Controlling Hyphenation
and Justification

WHAT H&J MEANS AND HOW IT WORKS
LINE-AT-A-TIME VERSUS MULTILINE H&J
CONTROLLING HYPHENATION
SPECIFYING WORD-SPACE AND LETTER-SPACE RANGES
ALTERING CHARACTER WIDTHS AND TESTING H&J VALUES
FIXING AND AVOIDING COMPOSITION PROBLEMS

Hyphenation and justification—H&J, for short—is the process a computer program uses to fit type into lines. Even the humblest word processor does some form of H&J, which specifies how the words and letters on each typeset line will be spaced. One of the quality benchmarks for a typesetting program is the amount of control it gives you over this process. Although most page layout programs provide fairly sophisticated H&J settings, research by the manufacturers reveals that about 99 percent of their customers never avail themselves of these settings—they just ride along using the defaults that the programs come with right out of the box. But the "one size fits all" approach never works, and especially not in typography. This chapter is about getting just the right fit.

What *Hyphenation and Justification* Means

Justification is the process of filling lines of a given measure with type, which comprises both characters and spaces. *Hyphenation* is a means to that end, allowing words to be broken into fragments that can better fill out the ends of lines, reducing the leftover space on those lines.

Even lines that don't appear to fill their measure are in fact justified; it's just that the ends of the lines are filled out to the margin with space. When such text is set with justified margins, this space is distributed among the word and letter spaces on each line.

FIGURE 10.1 Every typeset line is filled—justified—as the highlighted spaces in this sample show. When text is set with a ragged right margin, any leftover space on each line is deposited at the end. When justified margins are used, this space has to be absorbed elsewhere in the line, between characters and words.

Every line of type you set is justified over its measure. This is a confusing notion, because the word *justified* is also applied to text in which every line fills its measure completely, leaving perfectly straight, vertical margins at left and right. But even lines that don't appear to fill their measure are in fact justified (see Figure 10.1); it's just that the ends of the lines are filled out to the margin with space. When text is set with justified margins, this space is distributed in available places along the line in order to spread out the type and drive the text outward to fill the measure completely. How that extra space will be distributed is the object of your program's hyphenation and justification controls.

How H&J Works

The hyphenation and justification process can be viewed as an internal dialogue within your computer program that goes on constantly as you type. The dialogue gets quite heated as *end-of-line decisions* have to be made. Until that point—in the simplest of H&J scenarios—the program is simply counting the widths of the characters you type and adding them together, subtracting the running total from the measure of the line. At some point, though, you'll type a word that is too long to fit in the remaining space on the line. It's decision time.

When the line in question is being set with a ragged right margin (that is, when the lines are allowed to end short of the full measure), this line-ending dialogue can be quite simple and brief. For the type shown in Figure 10.2, it might run something like this:

The word constitutes *is too long for the available space. Is hyphenation allowed?*

No.

Is it permissible to alter character widths?

No.

Is it permissible to compress word and/or letter spaces?

Yes.

How much can word spaces be compressed?

10 percent.

How much can letter spaces be compressed?

3 percent.

Staying within these limits, can the word constitutes *be fitted onto the line?*

No.

Leave the spaces unaltered, end the line after which, *and start a new line.*

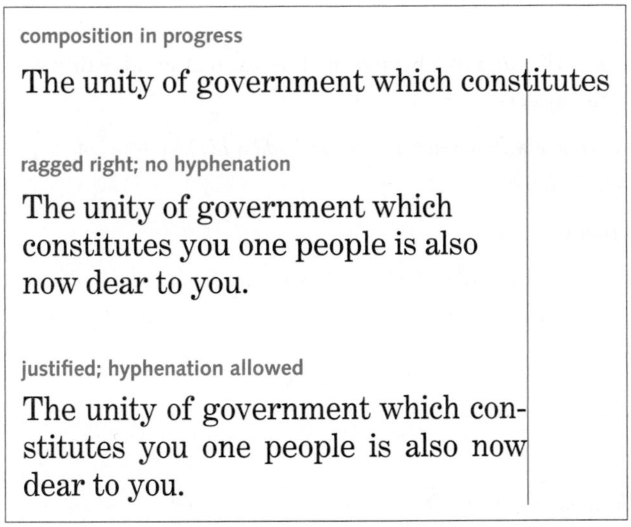

composition in progress

The unity of government which constitutes

ragged right; no hyphenation

The unity of government which
constitutes you one people is also
now dear to you.

justified; hyphenation allowed

The unity of government which constitutes you one people is also now
dear to you.

FIGURE 10.2 Hyphenation and justification in progress. Here, the word *constitutes* is too long to fit on the line being composed. How the end-of-line decision is handled depends on the H&J specifications in effect.

In settings with justified margins, the dialogue becomes far more complex. Using the simple lines of type with justified margins shown in Figure 10.2, the end-of-line decision-making dialogue would go something like this:

The word constitutes *is too long for the available space. Is hyphenation allowed?*

Yes.

Hyphenate by referring to the dictionary or by using the hyphenation algorithm?

Dictionary hyphenation is allowed; algorithmic hyphenation
is not allowed.

Can constitutes *be hyphenated?*

Yes: con-sti-tutes.

How many syllables plus a hyphen will fit in the available space?

One syllable plus a hyphen will fit without compressing word
and/or letter spaces.

Is it permissible to compress word and/or letter spaces?

Yes.

How much can word spaces be compressed?

10 percent.

How much can letter spaces be compressed?

3 percent.

*Staying within these limits, how many syllables plus a hyphen can be fitted
onto the line?*

Looser
Normal
Tighter

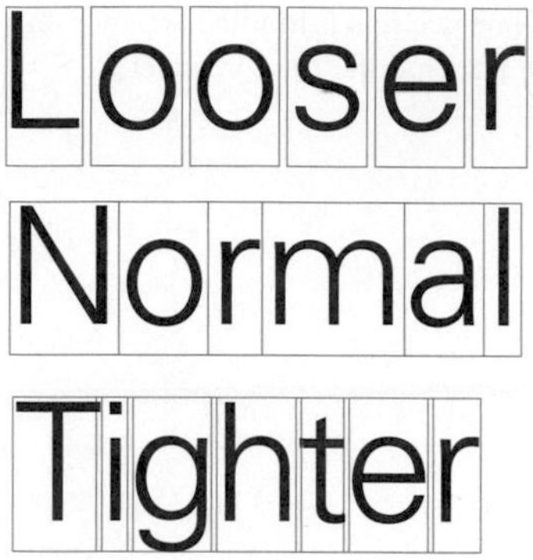

FIGURE 10.3 Visualizing characters in their bounding boxes shows how adjusting the tracking affects the type. Loosening the tracking opens spaces between the bounding boxes that in a normal set would butt up against each other. These gaps are measured in fractions of an em. Tightening the tracking overlaps the bounding boxes, drawing the visible characters closer together.

Only one syllable plus a hyphen will fit, even after adjusting word and letter spaces.

Set one syllable with normal spacing and add a hyphen. How much space is left on the line?

2.115 points.

What is the ranking order of where leftover space should be distributed: prefer word spaces? prefer letter spaces? distribute evenly among both?

Preference is to distribute among word spaces first.

How much can word spaces be expanded?

15 percent.

Can the leftover space be distributed among the available word spaces without expanding them beyond the specified limit?

Yes.

Distribute the space in five equal portions among the word spaces. Start the next line.

This is only a simplified H&J decision sequence, but it illustrates some of the points at which you can intervene in how the program does its work, including specifying the ranges in which word and letter spaces can be flexed and how hyphenation should be performed.

CHARACTER-BY-CHARACTER CALCULATIONS

The process may seem complicated, but that short script only illustrates how line-ending decisions are made. Before you type the first character, the H&J program has been armed with a host of other information, most of which you also get to specify or control.

For example, the *tracking* value you specify for the type will affect the amount of space that each and every character will take up on the line. (For a detailed description of how tracking works and how you can control it, see Chapter 11.) For every character you type, the H&J program uses this tracking value to recalculate the character widths that it's reading out of the font. This in turn affects the total amount of space the characters take up on the line (see Figure 10.3). Tracking doesn't affect the shapes of the characters, just the amount of space they're allotted.

In addition, every time you type a character the H&J program looks to see if the combination of that character plus the one that preceded it is listed in the table of kerning adjustments stored within the font. If the letter pair is listed in the table, the H&J program reads the relative value assigned to it (expressed as a fraction of an em), calculates its absolute width based on the point size you've specified, and adds or subtracts the value of the kerning adjustment from the overall total width that it's tabulating for the contents of the line thus far. (Kerning is also described in detail in Chapter 11.)

When a line has become filled with all the text it can hold, the succeeding text *wraps* onto the next line. This process is continuous and dynamic, so when you edit text in a fully composed page, the program may react sluggishly, as every time you add or subtract enough text to change the ending of that line, every line following it in that paragraph will have to be undergo H&J again.

Problems with Line-at-a-Time H&J

Most programs perform H&J one line at a time, and when they finish that line they forget about it and start fresh on the next one. The hypothetical program that created the H&J scripts in the previous section worked this way. The problem with this approach is that lines often can't be set within the legal spacing limits you've specified. In such a case, the program has no choice but to break the rules, setting the line either too loose or too tight (see Figure 10.4). Too loose is usually the default fallback position.

The program can also set one line using all the minimum spacing limits (creating a relatively tightly spaced line) and the next line using all the maximum spacing limits (creating a relatively loosely spaced line). Since the program takes no account of what it did on a previous line, it ignores the contrast in spacing. Even spacing is difficult to maintain when each line is set independently of the ones before and after it.

You can also have problems with the last line of a paragraph, usually when it's set too short, sometimes too short to cover the indent of the paragraph that follows it, creating an unsightly gap. Likewise, even though you may have told your program that it's forbidden to hyphenate the last word in a paragraph (assuming it permits being told), it may be forced to do so in order to stay within the prescribed spacing limits.

The only way out of these dilemmas (short of fixing the problems manually after the damage has been done) is to use a program that hyphenates and justifies more than one line at a time.

Hyphenating and Justifying a Range of Lines

Most programs use line-at-a-time hyphenation and justification because it's so much easier and faster than the alternative, which is to perform H&J over many lines of text at the same time. Hyphenating and justifying a range of lines

Calvin Coolidge said that the business of America is business. But these days, with political pressures mounting on American businesses to be more socially active, and in so doing branching out well beyond their traditional areas of expertise, we might well add a corollary to Coolidge's aphorism. To wit, "The business of American business is business."

FIGURE 10.4 By composing one line at a time, without regard to how lines before or after have composed, or could compose, an H&J program can get the text into a bind. Here are both a badly spaced last line and a hyphenated last word. Had the program considered the whole paragraph as a single composition problem, it could have found other line-ending decisions earlier in the paragraph (by spacing words and letters differently) that would have preempted the faults seen here.

FIGURE 10.5 In the left-hand sample, a line-by-line H&J program has set the first line fairly tight, making the second line very loose. The program can't hyphenate the word *square* to rectify the situation and is forced to leave the line setting slack. In the right-hand sample, the H&J program has composed the entire paragraph as a unit. Handling the same text, it has reset the first line slightly looser and brought down another word to fill out the second.

line-by-line H&J	multiline H&J
If a box is square, it is obvious that it cannot, strictly speaking, be more square. Nevertheless, forms like *fullest, rounder, more perfect,* etc., are in general use colloquially.	If a box is square, it is obvious that it cannot, strictly speaking, be more square. Nevertheless, forms like *fullest, rounder, more perfect,* etc., are in general use colloquially.

simultaneously is an enormously complex process. In doing it, the program provisionally hyphenates and justifies the text while constantly looking backward to see if the current line is setting far looser or tighter than the lines it has just set. It is, in effect, averaging the spacing of the lines to keep them in a range that's as close as possible to your optimum spacing values.

If such a program finds itself trapped—by following the H&J rules in effect—into setting a line that's far looser or tighter than those around it, it will go back to find opportunities in previous lines to alter the spacing in such a way that the intermediate lines will rewrap and thus preempt the spacing fault in the problem line (see Figure 10.5).

This running back and forth is very time-consuming and computationally intensive, but it produces far better results than does line-at-a-time H&J. The computing overhead can be limited by reducing the range of lines that the program is asked to consider simultaneously. The range is rolling: specifying it to be 20 lines will cover the latest line being set plus the 19 lines before it. In other words, the program doesn't work on discrete 20-line blocks, but is always looking to average the spacing of the last 20 lines that have been composed.

Few programs offer this capability as of this writing, but the results of this technique can be so superior that eventually it will become a standard option in all professional-quality typesetting and page layout programs.

DEFINING A RANGE FOR MULTILINE H&J

The number of lines you should have the program consider simultaneously varies according to the job at hand. It may also depend on your program, which may, for example, limit multiline H&J to a single paragraph at a time.

In book composition, with its generous measures, H&J programs have a relatively easy time because of all the spaces on each line where extra space can be distributed. In these cases, the range may be kept fairly short—ten lines or less, as the rolling averaging will assure that any ten lines will have about the same spacing. Ten lines should also be enough to enable the program to find the opportunities to make adjustments for a troublesome line that might arise.

In magazine, newsletter, or newspaper pages, by contrast, a longer range is indicated. In shorter lines, the H&J program has limited choices in creating alternative line breaks. These choices ultimately hinge on where or whether to hyphenate. The program, then, may have to search a wide range of lines to find changes that will resolve the composition dilemma on the problem line. In these cases a range of 20 or 30 lines may work better.

Naturally, the useful length of the range usually depends on the length of the paragraphs involved, as a line-based composition problem can be resolved only within the paragraph where it occurs. However, when the goal of multi-line H&J is to preempt page layout problems (such as a subhead appearing as the last line of a column), then far longer ranges are indicated—ranges that enable the program to alter enough line endings to add or subtract several lines from the depth of a column of type. Such problems, though, are not really the province of the H&J program and are best handled by *vertical justification* controls (see the section of the same name later in this chapter).

Line-Break Points

Text-composition software considers a number of characters legitimate places to end a line. The most obvious of these are the word space and hyphen.

Others include the following:

- em dash

- en dash

- virgule (*slash,* or *solidus*)

When these characters appear at the end of a line, your software is free to end the line there without adding a hyphen. Note that not all programs consider the virgule to be a legitimate line-break point, although there is a typographic tradition behind the practice. The break should occur after the virgule, and that character should not begin a line.

For whatever reason, you may not want an expression containing these characters to break at the end of a line. Most programs offer a *no break* option that allows you to select certain text and specify that it cannot be divided at the end of a line (see Figure 10.6). Check your program's manual in the hyphenation section to see if it offers this feature.

If you want to prevent an expression from breaking at a word space, you can use a *nonbreaking space.* This space is identical in width to the word space and, like it, is a part of each font. For this reason, its use is supported by the operating system, meaning that there are standard keystrokes to access it. On the Macintosh, it's Option-spacebar, and on Windows PCs, it's Alt-0160 (although specific applications usually have their own keyboard shortcuts for it).

To prevent a hyphenated expression from breaking at the end of a line, you can use a *nonbreaking hyphen* (see "Kinds of Hyphens" later in this chapter).

> The activator mechanism is extremely sensitive and must be calibrated. Stock calibration equipment cannot be used. Specify only Sigmatics' tool number GO-Cal/1a calibration tool for this task.
>
> The activator mechanism is extremely sensitive and must be calibrated. Stock calibration equipment cannot be used. Specify only Sigmatics' tool number GOCal/1a calibration tool for this task.

FIGURE 10.6 The highlighted text in the upper sample should not be allowed to hyphenate, as the hyphen could be construed as a part of the tool's name. The solution is to specify the character sequence as a nonbreaking word so that, as in the bottom sample, the hyphenation program will not attempt to divide it.

Controlling Word and Letter Spaces

Flexing word spaces is the primary method H&J programs use to justify type. The merit of allowing only word spaces to flex in width is that the characteristic shapes of words remain intact. If the spaces between letters are flexed, you run the risk of changing these word profiles and reducing legibility. Some typographers, indeed, do not believe that letter spaces should be allowed to change at all. Others would apply this restriction only to ragged-margin type. Yet others believe that in ragged-margin type, not even word spaces should be allowed to change width.

These arguments are based on the notion that there is a "natural" spacing scheme for type and that the letter and word spaces built into a typeface by its designer are sacrosanct. But in truth, typefaces appear in a vast range of possible settings, and one spacing scheme cannot work for all of them. In addition, type designs follow style trends, as do typesetting and typography, and to insist on a single spacing scheme freezes type at a single point in time, which has never been its nature. There is nothing wrong, then, with allowing word and letter spaces to be flexed as long as the fundamentals of legibility and readability are honored, and this means that such variations should be kept to a minimum.

To this end, good typesetting programs allow you to specify ranges within which word and letter spaces may be altered (see Figure 10.7). To specify these ranges, you typically supply three values: the minimum width to which spaces can be compressed; the optimum width, which you would prefer to see all the time, if possible; and the maximum width to which spaces can be stretched. Generally, these values are expressed as some percentage of *normal.*

For word spaces, *normal* means the width of a word space as it's defined within the font being used. For letter spaces, *normal* is the distance between characters when their bounding boxes abut but do not overlap. Spacing adjustments based on tracking and kerning controls are added on top of the spacing values calculated by the H&J program.

There is no standard way of expressing these values from program to program. For example, while a program may have you specify word-space values using the value 100 percent for *normal,* that same program may ask you to specify letter-space values using 0 (zero) for *normal* and adding or subtracting from that to specify a value. The logic is obtuse, but in such a scheme, to allow word spaces to be shrunk by 10 percent you insert a "minimum" value of 90 percent, and to allow letter spaces to be shrunk by 10 percent, you insert a minimum value of −10 percent. Consult your manuals.

So long as free land exists, the opportunity for a competency exists, and economic power secures political power. But the democracy born of free land, strong in selfishness and individualism, intolerant of administrative experience and education, and pressing individual liberty beyond its proper bounds, has its dangers as well as it benefits.

So long as free land exists, the opportunity for a competency exists, and economic power secures political power. But the democracy born of free land, strong in selfishness and individualism, intolerant of administrative experience and education, and pressing individual liberty beyond its proper bounds, has its dangers as well as it benefits.

FIGURE 10.7 A typical H&J setting dialog box allows you to specify the range across which you will allow word and letter spaces to be flexed when type is being composed. The settings for the sample on the left are quite restrictive, with the result that the type is badly spaced. The more liberal spacing ranges used in the sample on the right yield much better results. The H&J values you specify should vary according to the measure and typeface.

Word Space:		Letter Space:	
Minimum	90%	Minimum	0%
Optimum	100%	Optimum	0%
Maximum	110%	Maximum	0%

Word Space:		Letter Space:	
Minimum	75%	Minimum	-5%
Optimum	100%	Optimum	0%
Maximum	150%	Maximum	5%

Controlling Hyphenation

Hyphenation is a necessary evil. It impedes reading speed and comprehension. Hyphens are not pretty, either. In justified text, lines ending in hyphens appear to fall short of the measure, creating dimples in the otherwise straight margin.

On the other hand, the more hyphens a program can use, the better it can approach your optimum spacing values. Lines filled out with hyphenated fragments of words don't have so much leftover space. One of the many balancing tasks a typesetter performs is to minimize hyphenation without imperiling good spacing. Some programs offer controls that specifically enable you to favor hyphenation over variations in word and letter spaces (or vice versa).

One way to control the frequency of hyphenation is by specifying the minimum number of letters of a hyphenated word that must appear at the end of a line before a hyphen can be added. If you allow a hyphen to be placed after only one letter (e.g., *a-bove*) you'll end up with scads of hyphenated lines. With a minimum of two letters (e.g., *de-part*), you'll get fewer hyphens, but still a lot of them. The usual minimum is three (e.g., *pre-pare*), but in narrower measures, a value of two will probably maintain better overall spacing.

Likewise, you can control the minimum size of the fragment of a hyphenated word that will be carried over to the next line. Normally, the minimum value here is also three characters. This value, added to a minimum of three characters before the hyphen, effectively bars the hyphenation of words shorter than six characters.

Your hyphenation controls should also enable you to limit the number of consecutive lines that can end in a hyphen. This is mainly an aesthetic issue; a lot of hyphenated lines is annoying for the reader. Two is a reasonable value

FIGURE 10.8 Even though the software has been instructed to set no more than two consecutive hyphens, this paragraph boasts five in a row. Why? Because the third line ends in a hard hyphen—one that's a typed character—and the program counts only software-inserted hyphens.

Your Tropical Paradise Rendezvous Dream Cruise will be a vacation you'll never forget. Unlike other popular cruises, your custom Dream Cruise has you spending most of your time on land, in the fascinating jet-set venues we're famous for. They're all the most colorful places you could imagine, and a few we're certain you couldn't. Aruba, Trinidad, and St. Kit's are all at your disposal.

FIGURE 10.8 Even though the software has been instructed to set no more than two consecutive hyphens, this paragraph boasts five in a row. Why? Because the third line ends in a hard hyphen—one that's a typed character—and the program counts only software-inserted hyphens.

here, except in narrow measures, where allowing three consecutive hyphens may produce more consistent spacing.

It's important to note that most programs, in tallying consecutive hyphens, count only those added by the hyphenation program. That is, the total doesn't include *hard hyphens* (those that are keyed in). This quirk can lead to many consecutive hyphenated lines, like those in Figure 10.8. The only solution (pending better software) is thorough proofreading.

HYPHENATION ZONES

Page layout programs typically allow you to specify a *hyphenation zone* in copy with a ragged right margin. The term is a bit of a misnomer, as it's not actually a zone, but a boundary set a specified distance in from the right margin. Its goal is to control the depth of the rag.

When the program has set as many whole words on a line as will fit, it looks to see where the hyphenation zone is before it tries to deal with the next word. If that last word starts to the left of the hyphenation-zone boundary (see Figure 10.9), the program will attempt to hyphenate it. If the word starts to the right of the boundary, the program will send the entire word to the next line. (To be accurate, the zone should really be called a *nonhyphenation* zone).

The narrower the hyphenation zone, then, the more apt the program is to hyphenate and the tighter the rag you'll get. If your goal is to reduce the number of hyphenated lines, set the hyphenation zone wider. How wide depends on the size of the type. Once the width of the hyphenation zone equals that of the longest word in your text, widening the zone won't have any additional effect.

CHOOSING A MEANS OF HYPHENATION

Most programs offer a choice of dictionary-based hyphenation or *algorithmic hyphenation*. A hyphenation algorithm is a mathematical formula used to analyze the structure of words and divine correct hyphenation points. They work quite well, and they are often favored because they work faster than systems that must look up words in a dictionary. Unfortunately, they're not as reliable as dictionary-based hyphenation, so the latter should be your preference.

The ideal solution, offered by some programs, is to use both. In this case, the H&J program will refer to the dictionary first and will resort to the algorithm only if it can't find the word it's looking for. Falling back on the algorithm is a good solution for technical terms, proper names, and foreign words (although for the proper hyphenation of foreign words, it's better to use an algorithm that recognizes the word-formation rules of that language).

KINDS OF HYPHENS

There are several types of hyphens. The *hard hyphen* is keyed into a manuscript and becomes a permanent part of the text stream. Another kind of hyphen is added by the hyphenation dictionary or algorithm of your program. It's temporary and will disappear if it's no longer needed to divide a word at the end of a line. A hybrid between the two is the *discretionary hyphen, or soft hyphen.* If your program fails to hyphenate a word correctly (or at all), you can type in a discretionary hyphen that acts like a dictionary- or algorithm-inserted hyphen. That is, it will disappear if it's not needed. You can also use a discretionary hyphen to suggest to your program a preferable hyphenation point, even though the one the program has chosen is legitimate.

Discretionary hyphens originate in your application programs, not your operating system, so the keystrokes needed to insert one vary from program to program. Consult your manuals.

The last kind of hyphen is the *nonbreaking hyphen,* which looks like a hard hyphen. It's used when a normal hard hyphen would cause a line to break at an awkward place. Figure 10.10 illustrates an instance where the nonbreaking hyphen could be useful.

HYPHENATION STYLE

Copyediting style dictates most of the rules about hyphen use; a typesetter needs to watch out for only a few situations.

One is when the last word in a paragraph is hyphenated. This should never be allowed. Most programs don't allow this to happen normally, but some do. Often a composition program will find that the only way it can set the penultimate line of a paragraph within the H&J values you've specified is to hyphenate the last word. Programs that use multiline H&J can usually find a way out of this dilemma. Manual solutions to a hyphenated last word include rebreaking some lines by hand (to force the text to rewrap) or to adjust the tracking

---

hyphenation zone = 2 picas, 6 points

room. If your bags don't arrive in your hotel room before you do, we'll put a $1,000 check in your hand before the day is out. No other cruise company will make that guarantee!

hyphenation zone = 1 picas, 6 points

room. If your bags don't arrive in your hotel room before you do, we'll put a $1,000 check in your hand before the day is out. No other cruise company will make that guarantee!

FIGURE 10.9 A wider hyphenation zone (indicated here in gray) creates a wilder rag by reducing the number of hyphenated words. Only words that begin to the left of the hyphenation zone will be divided.

---

with regular hard hyphens

Except in unusual circumstances, it's unnecessary to manually kern type at common text sizes (e.g., 10-, 11-, and 12-point).

with nonbreaking hyphens

Except in unusual circumstances, it's unnecessary to manually kern type at common text sizes (e.g., 10-, 11-, and 12-point).

FIGURE 10.10 Because hard hyphens are legal points at which to break a line, the third line in the top sample runs into trouble, and the next line starts oddly with a comma. By using nonbreaking hyphens for these expressions, as in the lower sample, you avoid the problem.

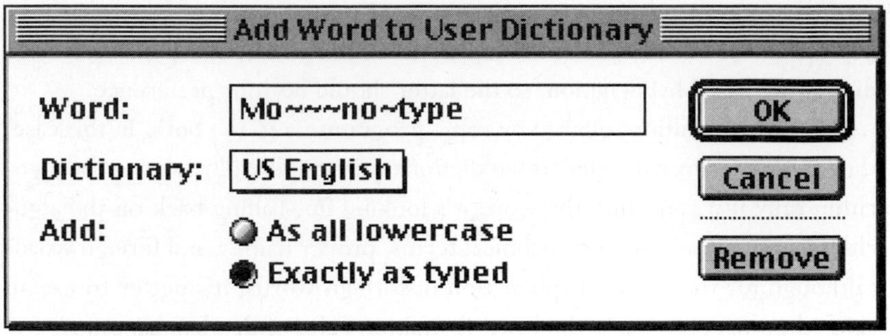

FIGURE 10.11 When adding a word
to a hyphenation dictionary, you may
be allowed to rank the desirability
of various break points. Here a single
tilde indicates the prime hyphenation
point. The three tildes indicate a legal
but undesirable break point.

of the paragraph (to draw the word fragment up to the previous line, or to push
the whole word down to the last line).

Another common situation to be avoided is the double-hyphenated word.
A word or compound word containing a hard hyphen may appear at the end of
a line, to be broken and given a second, program-inserted hyphen. Making the
words on both sides of the hard hyphen nonbreaking text will force the program
to break the expression at the hard hyphen. Double-hyphenation can also occur
when you've added a nonbreaking hyphen to a text expression, forcing the H&J
program to find another place to break it. Again, specifying it as nonbreaking
text will solve the problem.

To prevent the hyphenation of acronyms that have the same spelling as real
words, disallow hyphenation for words set in all capitals.

ADDING TO THE HYPHENATION DICTIONARY

When your program fails to hyphenate a word correctly, you should add that
word to its hyphenation dictionary. The additions you make are sometimes
stored in the program's principal dictionary, but more often they're stored in
a supplementary or *exception dictionary*. This supplementary dictionary becomes
the first one your program will refer to, in case it contains hyphenations that
you prefer to the ones the program provides on its own. (British English and
American English, for example, differ on many points of word division, so you
may have the need to override your program's hyphenation choices.)

When you add a word to your program's hyphenation dictionaries, you
may be asked to rank the possible hyphenation points (and possibly even identify them) according to where you'd prefer to see the word broken, as shown
in Figure 10.11.

Programs that offer supplementary dictionaries allow you to have more
than one, so you can have separate dictionaries for specific jobs or clients. Those
in workgroups should make sure that they're using the same, up-to-date exception dictionaries, to assure consistent results.

When a word has been hyphenated based on either an exception diction-ary or a customized entry to the principal dictionary, the hyphenation points for that word are recorded in the text stream. If the document is opened on another computer that doesn't have the customized hyphenation dictionary, the word will still hyphenate correctly.

How Measure Affects H&J

As a rule, wide measures enable an H&J program to come closer to setting type with your optimum spacing specifications. With long enough lines, just about any typesetting program—even a word processor—can create fairly evenly spaced type.

Type in narrow measures is a different story, and the narrower the meas-ure gets, the tougher it is to achieve even spacing and good type color.

In settings with justified margins, the narrower the measure of a line of type, the fewer places there are in which to distribute leftover space. Word spaces, which you count on to sponge up most of this space, are in particularly short supply. This forces your program to the limits of your specified spacing ranges: to fill a line, it will either stretch spaces to their maximum or squeeze them hard to get that last word or syllable in.

In settings with ragged margins, the pressure is only to squeeze spaces, as stretching isn't called for. But in narrow measures, the paucity of word spaces again reduces the opportunities your program has to squeeze the type to fill the line better. Most programs will not alter word or letter spaces at all in ragged-margin text, which makes matters even worse.

In both kinds of settings, narrow measures mean your program will have to rely more on hyphenation to fill lines, but heavily hyphenated text is harder to read, and cascades of hyphens at a right-hand margin are not a pretty sight.

Specifying Word-Space Ranges in Ragged-Margin Type

Even in ragged-margin copy, it's good to allow word spaces to be flexed some-what (your program willing). This, along with hyphenation, enables you to cre-ate a *tight rag,* a margin that's irregular, but not too irregular (see Figure 10.12). In narrow measures, a tight rag is usually preferable, because it reduces the greater variations in line length that make reading more difficult. With wider measures, a *wild rag* may be preferable, because in wide measures, ragged-margin type may look like sloppily set justified type. The idea of a ragged mar-gin, after all, is to add shape and graphic interest to an otherwise rectangular

When you prepare a manu-script for an incompatible computer system or program, or when the target computer is un-known, you should produce your manuscript in a universally recog-nizable file format. A writer pre-paring a manuscript for an unspec-ified publisher would work this way. So would an author who posts a manuscript on an electronic bul-letin board that can be read by any kind of computer. Most computers and programs need formatting in-structions written in their own particular way.

When you prepare a manu-script for an incompatible computer system or program, or when the target computer is unknown, you should produce your manuscript in a universally recognizable file format. A writer preparing a manuscript for an unspecified publisher would work this way. So would an author who posts a manuscript on an electron-ic bulletin board that can be read by any type of computer. Most computers and programs need formatting instructions written in their own particular way.

FIGURE 10.12 The text at the top has a fairly tight rag, the text at the bottom a wilder rag. The disadvantage of wild rags is a greater likelihood of distracting shapes or rogue lines that seem to stick out too far, like the penultimate line in the lower sample.

word space = –50%	word space = 150%
What has since followed are but natural consequences. With the success of their first movement, this small fanatical party began to acquire strength; and with that, to become an object of courtship to both great parties. The necessary consequence was a further increase of power, and a gradual tainting of the opinions	What has since followed are but natural consequences. With the success of their first movement, this small fanatical party began to acquire strength; and with that, to become an object of courtship to both great parties. The necessary consequence was a further increase of power, and a

FIGURE 10.13 These are two ugly pieces of type, although the loose-ugly (right) is still readable, while the tight-ugly takes some effort. For this reason, a typesetting program that's unable to stay within your H&J spacing ranges will usually err on the wide side.

FIGURE 10.14A *facing page* All these samples are set 11/12 over a measure of 11½ picas. The word- and letter-space ranges for each are below them, with 100 percent being a "normal" setting as defined within the font.

In the top row, three attempts have been made to justify the type by allowing only word spaces to be flexed, letter spaces being kept constant. Over this narrow measure, the results are predictable: gross distortions in word spacing. In the left-hand sample, where the spacing range is the widest, spaces vary from far too wide to pinched.

In the second row, the same word-space ranges are supplemented by allowing letter spaces to flex by plus or minus 5 percent. The results are far better, with the middle sample—with its generous but not extreme word-spacing range—faring the best.

In the bottom row, letter spacing can flex by plus or minus 10 percent. While this creates more natural word spacing, the letter spacing looks crowded in all but the right-hand sample, whose restrictive word-spacing range has tempered the crowding but created contrastingly loose lines.

slab of type. A very tight rag, then, is not always desirable. Turning off hyphenation or enlarging the hyphenation zone will help create a wilder rag.

Because you have the luxury of a ragged margin to absorb leftover space on each line, you can afford to be epicurean about word spacing and to restrict its range of flexibility. The degree of restriction depends on how wild you want (or can afford) the rag to be. Keeping the word-space range within 10 percent of an optimum value of 100 percent will give your program some leeway to fill lines successfully and at the same time keep the purists at bay.

In extremely narrow settings, you may find that you have to allow an extraordinary degree of compression for word spaces; but don't allow them to be squeezed to less than 60 percent of their original width, or they'll start to look like letter spaces and whole lines will start to look like one long word.

Note that most page layout programs do not alter word and character spaces in ragged-margin text—they do so only for justified margins. Before wasting time trying to control the uncontrollable, consult your program's manual.

Specifying Word-Space Ranges in Text with Justified Margins

Tight spacing leads to illegibility faster than loose spacing. This is illustrated in Figure 10.13: Type whose word spaces are reduced by 50 percent is clearly harder to read than type whose word spaces are stretched by 50 percent. When specifying the range in which word spaces can be flexed, then, always build most of the flexibility into stretching rather than squeezing. The exact range depends on the measure and the typeface. Figure 10.14 shows some examples.

When the measure is ideal for the size of the type (see "Point Size and Measure," in Chapter 9), a good word-space range to start with is:

Minimum	85 percent
Optimum	100 percent
Maximum	125 percent

Harmony, liberal intercourse with all nations, are recommended by policy, humanity, and interest. But even our commercial policy should hold an equal and impartial hand; neither seeking nor granting exclusive favors or preferences; consulting the natural course of things; diffusing and diversifying by gentle means the streams of commerce, but forcing nothing; establishing

	min	opt	max
word spaces	50%	100%	200%
letter spaces	100%	100%	100%

Harmony, liberal intercourse with all nations, are recommended by policy, humanity, and interest. But even our commercial policy should hold an equal and impartial hand; neither seeking nor granting exclusive favors or preferences; consulting the natural course of things; diffusing and diversifying by gentle means the streams of commerce, but forcing nothing;

	min	opt	max
word spaces	75%	100%	150%
letter spaces	100%	100%	100%

Harmony, liberal intercourse with all nations, are recommended by policy, humanity, and interest. But even our commercial policy should hold an equal and impartial hand; neither seeking nor granting exclusive favors or preferences; consulting the natural course of things; diffusing and diversifying by gentle means the streams of commerce, but forcing noth-

	min	opt	max
word spaces	90%	100%	125%
letter spaces	100%	100%	100%

Harmony, liberal intercourse with all nations, are recommended by policy, humanity, and interest. But even our commercial policy should hold an equal and impartial hand; neither seeking nor granting exclusive favors or preferences; consulting the natural course of things; diffusing and diversifying by gentle means the streams of commerce, but forcing nothing; establishing with pow-

	min	opt	max
word spaces	50%	100%	200%
letter spaces	95%	100%	105%

Harmony, liberal intercourse with all nations, are recommended by policy, humanity, and interest. But even our commercial policy should hold an equal and impartial hand; neither seeking nor granting exclusive favors or preferences; consulting the natural course of things; diffusing and diversifying by gentle means the streams of commerce, but forcing nothing; establishing with pow-

	min	opt	max
word spaces	75%	100%	150%
letter spaces	95%	100%	105%

Harmony, liberal intercourse with all nations, are recommended by policy, humanity, and interest. But even our commercial policy should hold an equal and impartial hand; neither seeking nor granting exclusive favors or preferences; consulting the natural course of things; diffusing and diversifying by gentle means the streams of commerce, but forcing nothing; establishing with powers

	min	opt	max
word spaces	90%	100%	125%
letter spaces	95%	100%	105%

Harmony, liberal intercourse with all nations, are recommended by policy, humanity, and interest. But even our commercial policy should hold an equal and impartial hand; neither seeking nor granting exclusive favors or preferences; consulting the natural course of things; diffusing and diversifying by gentle means the streams of commerce, but forcing nothing; establishing with powers so disposed, in order

	min	opt	max
word spaces	50%	100%	200%
letter spaces	90%	100%	110%

Harmony, liberal intercourse with all nations, are recommended by policy, humanity, and interest. But even our commercial policy should hold an equal and impartial hand; neither seeking nor granting exclusive favors or preferences; consulting the natural course of things; diffusing and diversifying by gentle means the streams of commerce, but forcing nothing; establishing with powers so disposed, in or-

	min	opt	max
word spaces	75%	100%	150%
letter spaces	90%	100%	110%

Harmony, liberal intercourse with all nations, are recommended by policy, humanity, and interest. But even our commercial policy should hold an equal and impartial hand; neither seeking nor granting exclusive favors or preferences; consulting the natural course of things; diffusing and diversifying by gentle means the streams of commerce, but forcing nothing; establishing with powers

	min	opt	max
word spaces	90%	100%	125%
letter spaces	90%	100%	110%

Harmony, liberal intercourse with all nations, are recommended by policy, humanity, and interest. But even our commercial policy should hold an equal and impartial hand; neither seeking nor granting exclusive favors or preferences; consulting the natural course of things; diffusing and diversifying by gentle means the streams of commerce, but forcing nothing; establishing with powers so disposed, in order to give to trade a stable course, to define the rights of our merchants, and to enable the government to support them, conventional rules of intercourse, the best that present circumstances and mutual opinion will permit, but temporary and liable to be from time to time abandoned or varied, as experience and circumstances shall dictate; constantly keeping in view, that it is folly in one nation to look for disinterested favors from another; that it must pay with a portion of its independence for whatever it may accept under that character; that

	min	opt	max
word spaces	75%	100%	150%
letter spaces	97%	100%	103%
maximum consecutive hyphens = 3			

Harmony, liberal intercourse with all nations, are recommended by policy, humanity, and interest. But even our commercial policy should hold an equal and impartial hand; neither seeking nor granting exclusive favors or preferences; consulting the natural course of things; diffusing and diversifying by gentle means the streams of commerce, but forcing nothing; establishing with powers so disposed, in order to give to trade a stable course, to define the rights of our merchants, and to enable the government to support them, conventional rules of intercourse, the best that present circumstances and mutual opinion will permit, but temporary and liable to be from time to time abandoned or varied, as experience and circumstances shall dictate; constantly keeping in view, that it is folly in one nation to look for disinterested favors from another; that it must pay with a portion of its independence for whatever it may accept under

	min	opt	max
word spaces	85%	100%	125%
letter spaces	97%	100%	103%
maximum consecutive hyphens = 3			

Harmony, liberal intercourse with all nations, are recommended by policy, humanity, and interest. But even our commercial policy should hold an equal and impartial hand; neither seeking nor granting exclusive favors or preferences; consulting the natural course of things; diffusing and diversifying by gentle means the streams of commerce, but forcing nothing; establishing with powers so disposed, in order to give to trade a stable course, to define the rights of our merchants, and to enable the government to support them, conventional rules of intercourse, the best that present circumstances and mutual opinion will permit, but temporary and liable to be from time to time abandoned or varied, as experience and circumstances shall dictate; constantly keeping in view, that it is folly in one nation to look for disinterested favors from another; that it must pay with a portion of its independence for whatever it may accept under that character; that by such acceptance,

	min	opt	max
word spaces	85%	100%	125%
letter spaces	95%	100%	105%
maximum consecutive hyphens = 3			

Harmony, liberal intercourse with all nations, are recommended by policy, humanity, and interest. But even our commercial policy should hold an equal and impartial hand; neither seeking nor granting exclusive favors or preferences; consulting the natural course of things; diffusing and diversifying by gentle means the streams of commerce, but forcing nothing; establishing with powers so disposed, in order to give to trade a stable course, to define the rights of our merchants, and to enable the government to support them, conventional rules of intercourse, the best that present circumstances and mutual opinion will permit, but temporary and liable to be from time to time abandoned or varied, as experience and circumstances shall dictate; constantly keeping in view, that it is folly in one nation to look for disinterested favors from another; that it must pay with a portion of its independence for whatever it may accept under that character; that by such ac-

	min	opt	max
word spaces	90%	100%	110%
letter spaces	95%	100%	105%
maximum consecutive hyphens = 3			

Harmony, liberal intercourse with all nations, are recommended by policy, humanity, and interest. But even our commercial policy should hold an equal and impartial hand; neither seeking nor granting exclusive favors or preferences; consulting the natural course of things; diffusing and diversifying by gentle means the streams of commerce, but forcing nothing; establishing with powers so disposed, in order to give to trade a stable course, to define the rights of our merchants, and to enable the government to support them, conventional rules of

	min	opt	max
word spaces	85%	100%	125%
letter spaces	95%	100%	105%

Harmony, liberal intercourse with all nations, are recommended by policy, humanity, and interest. But even our commercial policy should hold an equal and impartial hand; neither seeking nor granting exclusive favors or preferences; consulting the natural course of things; diffusing and diversifying by gentle means the streams of commerce, but forcing nothing; establishing with powers so disposed, in order to give to trade a stable course, to define the rights of our merchants, and to enable the government to support them, conventional rules of inter-

	min	opt	max
word spaces	90%	100%	110%
letter spaces	95%	100%	105%

Harmony, liberal intercourse with all nations, are recommended by policy, humanity, and interest. But even our commercial policy should hold an equal and impartial hand; neither seeking nor granting exclusive favors or preferences; consulting the natural course of things; diffusing and diversifying by gentle means the streams of commerce, but forcing nothing; establishing with powers so disposed, in order to give to trade a stable course, to define the rights of our merchants, and to enable the government to support them, conventional

	min	opt	max
word spaces	90%	100%	110%
letter spaces	97%	100%	103%

Harmony, liberal intercourse with all nations, are recommended by policy, humanity, and interest. But even our commercial policy should hold an equal and impartial hand; neither seeking nor granting exclusive favors or preferences; consulting the natural course of things; diffusing and diversifying by gentle means the streams of commerce, but forcing nothing; establishing with powers so disposed, in order to give to trade a stable course, to define the rights of our merchants, and to enable the government to support them, con-

	min	opt	max
word spaces	85%	100%	125%
letter spaces	100%	100%	100%

FIGURE 10.14B *facing page* At a measure of 17 ½ picas, the composition problems seen on the previous page become less dramatic.

In the upper-left sample, all of the lines compose without breaching the specified word- and letter-space ranges, but the overly generous word-space range creates color problems. The fourth through eight lines in particular set tighter and look darker than other, looser lines. In the upper-right sample, tightening the word-space range without relaxing letter spacing creates many loose lines.

The lower-left sample is a good compromise, and overall spacing and color are quite even. At the lower right, further restricting word spacing produces acceptable results, but at the cost of more hyphens.

FIGURE 10.14C *this page* At a 24-pica measure, this 11-point type sets well within fairly limited word-space ranges. The top sample is the best on the page, as the word- and letter-space ranges complement each other well. In the second sample, the more restrictive word-space range forces the program to rely too much on letter spacing, causing some crowding among the characters.

The settings for the third sample don't offer enough spacing leeway, causing many lines to breach the specified spacing limits and set too loose. The bottom sample, with no letter-spacing variations allowed, approximates the look of type set on old metal composition systems, with spacing that is fairly consistent but rather loose by contemporary standards.

◊ When you prepare a manuscript for an incompatible computer system or program, or when the target computer is unknown, you should produce your manuscript in a univer-
◊ sally recognizable file format. A writer preparing a manuscript for an unspecified publisher would work this way. So would an au-
◊ thor who posts a manuscript on an electronic bulletin board that can be read by any kind of computer. Most computers and pro-
◊ grams need formatting instructions written in their own particular way.

When you prepare a manuscript for an incompatible computer system or program, or when the target computer is unknown, you should produce your manuscript in a universally recognizable file format. A writer preparing a manuscript for an unspecified publisher would work this way. So would an author who posts a manuscript on an electronic bulletin board that can be read by any kind of computer. Most computers and programs need formatting instructions written in their own particular way.

FIGURE 10.15 The sample on the left has been set without allowing letter spaces to be altered. The result is some quite loose lines, as indicated. By allowing letter spaces to be flexed within a range of plus or minus 5 percent, the sample on the right is able to set with much more even spacing.

This range should produce text with a minimum number of hyphens and without excessive variation in type color from line to line. If you're using a narrow typeface, you can draw these values in even further: to, say, 90 percent, 100 percent, and 120 percent. Much depends on the typeface, and some experimentation will be needed to find an optimal set of values. In very wide measures, you can draw these values in yet further.

Page layout programs can be set up to highlight lines that have been composed in violation of the spacing specifications (it's a good idea to leave this option turned on). When these warnings begin to appear, it's an indication that your spacing limits are too restrictive.

When you find H&J values that work for a particular typeface and measure, making a note of them will save you a great deal of time in future jobs.

Specifying Letter-Space Ranges

Allowing letter spaces to be altered dramatically is the best way to create ugly type. It's also one of the best ways to create type that's hard to read. The idea behind altering letter spaces is to allow your program to find the optimal points at which to break lines. The ideal is to alter letter spaces so subtly that the changes are barely noticeable. This is easier to do when measures are wide. When measures are very narrow (as in newspapers), it can be impossible.

In a line of book text containing 60 or 70 characters, allowing letter spaces to flex by just 5 percent either way gives the program about another 2 points of flexibility, or almost half the width of a typical lowercase letter. This may not sound like much, but it can make the difference between being able to hyphenate or not. It can also enable the program to find a hyphenation point that causes the word spaces to be distorted less (see Figure 10.15). It takes a pretty good eye to see a 5 percent alteration in letter spaces. (In Figure 10.15, the main difference you see between the two samples is the smaller word spaces, not the smaller letter spaces.)

A range for letter spaces of plus or minus 10 percent has a more dramatic effect on composition, but at this threshold, you can begin to see the differences between lines with tighter and looser letter spacing. Again, looser spacing is less disruptive to reading than tighter spacing, so if narrow measures force you to the extremes of letter spacing, favor a looser set over a tighter one, with perhaps a minimum value of 95 percent of normal and a maximum value of 110 percent or even 115 percent of normal. Keep your optimum value at 100 percent of normal.

Letterspacing and Forced Justification

Sometimes display type will be set with grossly exaggerated letter spacing. This effect is called (confusingly) *letterspacing.* With most page layout programs, you don't need to alter word- and letter-spacing values to create this effect. Instead, use the program's *force-justify* command. This automatically stretches the word and letter spaces to whatever degree is needed to force the text to completely fill the measure, as shown in Figure 10.16.

The icon in page layout programs often associated with forced justification shows the last line of a paragraph filling the measure. The idea is that when the last line of a paragraph (which usually sets flush left) almost fills the measure, it looks better if it's stretched to fill it entirely. Perhaps yes, perhaps no.

But the icon gives the impression that this is why you would want to use the force-justify command. That may be, but force-justifying the last line of a paragraph has to be handled with care to avoid loose spacing.

To successfully force-justify the last line of a paragraph you must first specify the width of a *justification zone.* This is an area to the left of the right-hand margin into which a line must extend before the force-justification command takes effect. Only if the line reaches into this zone will it be considered long enough to be force-justified without undue distortion. Some programs that offer forced justification, though, do not allow you to specify any justification zone, meaning that the last line of a paragraph may be grotesquely stretched in order to fill the measure. If your application doesn't allow you to specify a justification zone, don't use the command in this way.

In lines of only two words, you can use the force-justify command as you would a quad-middle command, and the two words will be forced out flush against each margin, as shown in Figure 10.17. In these situations, the program will generally violate the limit on word spacing but respect the limit on letter spacing. Some programs offer a variable-width *flush space,* which acts specifically on the last lines of paragraphs (or on one-line paragraphs) to push the text on either side of it out to the margins.

Clovis State Bank Wants to Help You S T R E T C H Your Savings

FIGURE 10.16 Hard-ending each line of this text makes it an independent paragraph, so the third line can be letterspaced through forced justification without affecting the others.

Proposition

Shall the Town Council need voter approval before spending budget surpluses?

□ **Yes**   **No** □

FIGURE 10.17 Forced justification has pushed the ballot options to opposing margins. Fixed-width en spaces link *Yes* and *No* to their respective boxes, forcing the program to stretch the space between the words.

"word space" = thin space

S P A C E Y   T Y P E

"word space" = em space

S P A C E Y   T Y P E

FIGURE 10.18 In normal text, a fixed thin space is about the same width as a word space. But when thin spaces are used to force letterspacing, they look too narrow, as in the top sample. An em space does the trick, but looser type will need wider spaces.

LETTERSPACING TRICKS AND PROBLEMS

Normally, the force-justify command will stretch word spaces without limit but will not allow letter spaces to be expanded beyond their specified H&J range. The normal exception is single-word lines, in which the program has no choice but to stretch letter spaces as much as needed to stretch the type to fill the measure.

However, you can letterspace multiple-word lines simply by using fixed spaces (ems, ens, and thins) instead of word spaces. In the absence of word spaces in these situations, the program is forced to stretch the line by expanding letter spaces. That's trick number one. Trick two is getting appropriate-looking word spaces by using a series of fixed spaces, and this isn't as easy. With exaggerated spacing like this (see Figure 10.18) you're beyond the limits of sane typography, and only experimentation will reveal how large a space will read as a word space and divide the words into a readable line.

The problem with letterspacing text in this way is that all the letter spaces are stretched equally. This seems sensible, but at times (see Figure 10.19), you'll need to tighten individual spaces to create a more logical-looking effect.

Altering Character Widths during H&J

If altering word spaces during H&J upsets some type purists, the prospect of altering character widths is best kept secret from them. Nevertheless, the concept of flexing character widths as a tool to compose type better was the idea of world-renowned type designer and calligrapher Hermann Zapf.

The logic of the approach is impeccable. On a line of 70 characters, there are perhaps seven or eight word spaces, which means there aren't many places to stash leftover space during justification. There may be 70 letter spaces, but they're so small that altering them doesn't do much. But the line is rich in characters, and if you alter their widths even slightly, you can make a major difference in the spacing of the line.

unadjusted

Angel's Hair

kerned apostrophe

Angel's Hair

FIGURE 10.19 In the top sample, the letter spaces are stretched equally, but there is excessive space around the apostrophe. In the lower sample, the apostrophe is kerned closer to the letters around it, giving them the same spacing as the other letters with the apostrophe centered in between.

Altering character widths gives H&J programs a third alternative after flexing word and letter spaces. As with letter spaces, subtle alterations to character widths can pass unnoticed and yet make enough of a difference to allow the H&J program to come closer to matching the specified optimum values for word and letter spacing. In other words, altering character widths can create a more natural spacing (see Figure 10.20). Except in extraordinary circumstances, character-width variations should be kept in a range of plus or minus 2 percent. At this value, the set width of a 70-character line can be flexed by about ¾ em, which is quite a lot.

As with word- and letter-space ranges, you should be able to specify minimum, optimum, and maximum values for these width changes, limiting the deviation from the natural proportions of the typeface's characters.

As of this writing, this capability exists only in Adobe InDesign, but it makes enough of a difference in the quality of type composition that it's likely to become much more common in the future.

---

character width = normal

The word *advertising* is derived from *advert*, which means "to turn the mind toward." In a broad sense, therefore, advertising is turning or drawing attention toward something, and in this sense any means used to draw attention toward any purpose is advertising. In commercial usage, the *means* is anything that secures publicity, and the *purpose* is to sell something. The "something" is usually an article of merchandise.

character width = 98–102% of normal

The word *advertising* is derived from *advert*, which means "to turn the mind toward." In a broad sense, therefore, advertising is turning or drawing attention toward something, and in this sense any means used to draw attention toward any purpose is advertising. In commercial usage, the *means* is anything that secures publicity, and the *purpose* is to sell something. The "something" is usually an article of merchandise.

FIGURE 10.20 The text at far left, set with characters at their normal widths, has some serious spacing problems. By allowing character widths to be flexed in a range of just plus or minus 2 percent, the right-hand sample shows much better spacing without any visible distortion of the letterforms.

Testing Your H&J Values

It's a good idea to keep a benchmark document on hand to test your specs. In it, set samples in several measures and with both justified and ragged margins. Before starting a job, set this document in the typeface you'll be working with and print several versions using your proposed H&J specs. Keeping these printouts will provide a valuable record of past settings and save time in future ones.

About Program Defaults

Page layout programs are delivered with certain default specifications in place. Hyphenation and justification settings are among them. The default values for word- and letter-spacing ranges, in particular, vary enormously. None of them are of much use as they are, and you should reset them without thinking twice.

Hyphenation and justification settings can be built into style sheets (they're usually considered paragraph attributes), so you can easily recycle successful H&J recipes you've developed. (For more on style sheets, see Chapter 17.)

Fixing and Avoiding Composition Problems

Even with the most scrupulously set H&J values, type composition programs will sometimes set type badly. These missteps fall into two general categories: those that affect lines or groups of lines and those that affect page layouts. Some programs offer mechanisms to avoid or lessen the severity of layout problems, but problems in lines of type usually require you to go in and tinker by hand.

Loose Lines/Tight Lines

The most common composition problems are lines that for one reason or another can't be set without violating the limits you've set for how much word and letter spaces can be altered. Programs are generally written in such a way that when these situations arise, lines will be set too loose rather than too tight.

Most page layout programs offer an option to highlight contravening lines onscreen, and you should have this turned on at all times. The number of highlighted problem lines is a barometer of how appropriate your H&J settings are for the job at hand. If you find yourself annoyed by too many highlighted lines, don't blame the program.

Programs will not, however, highlight spacing flaws if the lines are set within the legal limits. You can, then, have a tight (but legal) line followed a loose (but legal) line and not be warned. Tight lines set among looser ones catch the eye

as set by the program	with added discretionary hyphen
What has since followed are but natural consequences. With the success of their first movement, this small fanatical party began to acquire strength; and with that, to become an object of courtship to both great parties. The necessary conse-quence was a further increase of power, and a gradual tainting of the opinions of both of the other parties with their doc-trines, until the infection has extended over both.	What has since followed are but natural consequences. With the success of their first movement, this small fanatical par-ty began to acquire strength; and with that, to become an object of courtship to both great parties. The necessary conse-quence was a further increase of power, and a gradual tainting of the opinions of both of the other parties with their doc-trines, until the infection has extended over both.

on the page, as they look darker. Likewise, a loosely set line looks like a faint patch on the page. Situations like these are much more apt to occur in narrow measures, where you're forced into using less-than-optimal spacing values.

FIGURE 10.21 The sample on the left has set with a slack line, as indicated. Finding an alternative break point in an earlier line (as shown in the right-hand sample) cures the problem. Although the new hyphenation is not optimal (hyphenating five-letter words is often frowned upon), the result is much better spacing.

TWEAKING THE HYPHENATION

Assuming your H&J settings are appropriate, the most likely reason for badly spaced lines is the failure of the program to hyphenate optimally. This could be your own doing if the limits you've set are blocking a better solution. For example, the program may have set its legal limit of consecutive hyphenated lines, leaving it unable to resolve a tricky line-ending problem on the current line. Likewise, allowing fewer letters before or after hyphenation in a divided word might provide a better line-ending result. Or a word that lands at the end of a line might simply not be in the program's hyphenation dictionary.

When hyphenation is causing a problem, use a discretionary hyphen (never a hard hyphen) to coax the program into breaking the word at your preferred hyphenation spot (see Figure 10.21). There should be no need to alter your hyphenation settings.

TWEAKING THE SPACING

The occasional loose or tight line that can't be fixed by adjusting hyphenation can usually be doctored up by adjusting its tracking and possibly that of the lines around it. Tracking—discussed in detail in Chapter 11—is a measure of the overall spacing of a passage of type.

Sometimes you can cause a line to *rewrap* (that is, to break at a new point) by slightly tightening or loosening its tracking (see Figure 10.22). You need not do this on the problem line, as long as the rewrapping caused by the change in tracking value causes the problem line to break in a new way.

as set by the program	with added discretionary hyphen
Character is not expressed very definitely by means of a person's ears. Nevertheless, there are a few indications worth noting. Seeing that ears are primarily intended for purposes of hearing, it will be fitting to commence with a description of what is termed the musical ear.	Character is not expressed very definitely by means of a person's ears. Nevertheless, there are a few indications worth noting. Seeing that ears are primarily intended for purposes of hearing, it will be fitting to commence with a description of what is termed the musical ear.

FIGURE 10.22 In the sample on the left, the first line sets very loose, and the fourth line is also pretty loose. Tightening the tracking of the top line brings up a syllable from the second line, causing the entire paragraph to rewrap, improving the look of the fourth line and pulling up the widow in the last line as well.

Tracking is usually expressed as a fraction of an em, and for tracking purposes, most programs work with a base of 1,000 units to the em (consult your manuals). To tighten tracking by 10 percent, then, you would specify a tracking value of minus 100 units. To make tracking looser, use positive values.

For spacing-repair purposes, try to keep your tracking adjustments in the range of plus or minus 5 percent (that is, plus or minus $^{50}/_{1,000}$ em). If you tighten or loosen a line too much you risk fixing one problem and creating another: a new line (or lines) whose spacing is noticeably different from those around it, but for a different reason.

Sometimes—especially when a problem line occurs late in a paragraph—it may work better to slightly adjust the tracking of the entire paragraph, which will keep the color of the lines within it more consistent. But again, you risk creating an undesirable color contrast, this time among paragraphs.

Paragraph Color Problems

The most common cause of color contrasts among paragraphs is heavy-handed manual intervention. This is frequently seen in magazine pages, and its most common cause is last-minute editorial changes. When a layout has been finalized, the production team cannot allow editorial changes to cause paragraphs to become longer or shorter, because the change in length will ripple all the way through successive pages, possibly creating other layout problems and making the entire article too long or too short for its allotted space. In order to jam extra text into a paragraph or fluff out a shortened paragraph to keep it the same length, the tracking is usually altered.

Random chance, though, can also be the culprit, and it is quite possible for a paragraph to set looser or tighter than others on the page simply because the H&J specs allow it. Color contrasts resulting from paragraphs such as these are nowhere near as dramatic as those caused by bad manual tracking adjustments.

> The break-in occurred sometime between 1:00 a.m. and 3:00 a.m., and the intruder remained for at least an hour, according to Inspector Lombardo. "It would take at least that long," he said, "to go through so many files with such evident care."
>
> This fact has led investigators to suspect that the intruder had knowledge of the routines of the security guards, who pass by the office every 90 minutes. Police are interrogating six members of the security staff looking for evidence of collusion.
>
> The investigation is centering on William Alfred Lombardo (no relation to the chief investigator in the case), who has both a record of robbery convictions as well as political ties to those who would profit by knowing the contents of the stolen files.
>
> Spokesmen of both parties deny any malfeasance, either by dint of involvement in the break-in or by having anything to hide in any of the office's files. Political insiders, though, believe that both are dissembling, at the very least. Neither party has been forthcoming with any details.

FIGURE 10.23 A last-minute clarification added to the third paragraph of this text forced the tracking to be tightened in order to preserve the line count. The result is a dark, dense paragraph that stands out among the others on the page.

In any case, a too-tight or too-loose paragraph in the middle of a page can stick out like a sore thumb, looking far darker or lighter than its neighbors (see Figure 10.23).

If the editors caused this problem, it's not unreasonable to ask them to solve it as well by rewriting the text to add or lose words so that the paragraph can stay within the basic H&J values (or at least with only a minor tracking change). If that's impossible, you may need to change the tracking of a range of paragraphs so that you can average out the color change and try to pick up or lose a line in a neighboring paragraph. Look for one with either a short last line that might be drawn up (to lose a line) or one with a full last line that might wrap to create a new line if the tracking is loosened.

Widows and Orphans

The last lines of paragraphs are called *widows* if they are particularly short. *Orphans* are short segments of a paragraph (usually one or two lines) that are stranded at the bottom or top of a column (see Figure 10.24). A three-line paragraph fragment ending with a widow that appears at the top of a column may also be considered an orphan.

FIGURE 10.24 A poor stranded orphan, this two-line text fragment at the bottom of a column looks as though it's broken away from the rest of the page. Adding at least one more line of text will give it more mass.

His story contains a moral, worthy of the attention of all little birds and little boys, warning them to keep to those refined and intellectual pursuits that raised him to so high a pitch of popularity during the early part of his career, but to eschew all tendency to that gross and dissipated indulgence that brought this mistaken little bird to an untimely end.

The Rabbit's Tale
It is a seldom appreciated fact that a

17

Widows are so short that they make the unfilled part of the line appear almost like a line space between paragraphs. When a widow is the last line of a column of type, it can make that column appear shorter than its neighbors on the page or (less so) on an adjoining page. When paragraph indents are deep, you can have a widow that's not even long enough to cover the paragraph indent below it. Hyphenated widows should be avoided at all costs.

Orphans break up the tidy shapes of columns of type. They cause a splintered fragment to appear at the top or the bottom of a column. An orphan at the top of a column that's followed by a heading or subheading (with its extra leading) is double trouble.

RESCUING WIDOWS

If a widow is a very short word—two, three, or even four letters—you may be able to eliminate it by drawing it up into the rest of the paragraph. You can try altering the hyphenation of the preceding lines first by inserting discretionary hyphens. Look for one- or two-letter syllables that can be brought up to a previous line and hope that the effect ripples down to the widow and brings it up as well. You can also try tightening the tracking slightly.

Drawing up a widow in this way is not an option if it occurs on the last line of a column, because by eliminating the widow you create an orphan. It may be better in some situations, then, to reduce the impact of a widow by making it longer, rather than trying to make it go away. Again, rehyphenating or adjusting the tracking (or both) may help, but you have to stay sensitive to color changes you're causing in the paragraph.

HELPING ORPHANS

Orphans are layout faults and not, strictly speaking, composition problems. Only rarely, then, can you fix an orphan by adjusting composition settings. One such situation is the widow orphaned at the top of a column.

Another is the situation where by altering the hyphenation and/or tracking you can get a paragraph with a full or nearly full last line to rewrap, thus adding a line to the column (without creating a widow, of course). The best you can hope for is to find one extra line in a column this way (although you could get lucky). But that could be enough to push a one-line orphan at the bottom of a column to the head of the next column or page. It could also add a line to an orphan at the top of a column, making the defect less noticeable.

Ultimately, though, orphans usually have to be dealt with by altering the layout or by making an editorial change.

Word processing and page layout programs attempt to deal with orphans through a system of *keeps*. These are relationships that you can specify to keep lines in a paragraph from being separated. You can, for example, specify that the last two (or three, or more) lines of a paragraph must be kept with that paragraph, so they can't be split off to form an orphan. You can also specify that a particular line (e.g., a heading) must be kept with the paragraph that follows it, so it can't be orphaned at the bottom of a column.

These tools work at the cost of unbalanced columns. Most layouts call for all the columns on a multicolumn page—or columns of type on facing pages— to be the same length, to finish on the same baseline. You cannot have keeps in effect and have balanced columns at the same time. To do this, your program would have to be able to adjust the leading in a column so that the lines could spread to fit the column's full depth. This adjustment is called vertical justification.

Vertical Justification

With vertical justification, leading is modified to meet page layout goals. True vertical justification is usually employed only by *batch-pagination* programs, which automatically lay out pages according to a set of predefined rules.

In a true batch-pagination system, you have to anticipate all the problems that can occur when composing type into columns and pages and take measures to prevent them. For example, you want to avoid orphans. You may also want to avoid headings at the tops of columns. Or you may want to avoid headings sitting next to each other in adjoining columns.

To avoid these layout problems, the system has to be able to flex the leading between lines just the way it flexes word and letter spaces when justifying

FIGURE 10.25 In this passage of vertically justified type, the extra leading added by the program has been highlighted. Most of the stretching has occurred at the vertical space bands above and below the subhead. In addition, the leading between all the text lines has been evenly augmented by a lesser amount.

simple text. Through the miracle of modern programming, though, some programs (especially desktop publishing programs) can now create pages that are so complicated—filled with illustrations, color, and photographs—that you can't even fit one of them on a diskette. That's progress.

Don't Be a Cheapskate

Cheap diskettes are no bargain. You have to rely on a diskette to record faithfully and durably. Cheap diskettes may fail without warning, and one day when you put your crucial archive diskette into your computer, you may get the hair-raising message, "This disk is unreadable."

horizontally. You have to tell the system (as with H&J settings) where it can do the flexing and by how much.

The two places a system can flex leading are at *vertical space bands* and between lines of regular text. Vertical space bands are usually added around headings and subheadings, where extra leading is added anyway. They may also appear above and below charts, graphs, illustrations, or pull quotes (enlarged excerpts drawn from the text) that appear in mid-column.

When a composition problem arises, the program will look back through the column to see where the leading can be adjusted. If the problem is an orphan at the bottom of a column, the program will attempt to *feather* the leading in the column sufficiently to push the orphaned lines onto the next column (see Figure 10.25). If it can't resolve the problem by staying within the vertical justification parameters you've set, it will back up and recompose the previous column or page, or pages, with an eye toward preempting the problem.

FRAME-AT-A-TIME VERTICAL JUSTIFICATION

Most page layout programs that claim to support vertical justification do so only on a frame-by-frame basis, but this is sufficient to deal with orphans when used in conjunction with the program's *keeps* controls. In a typical application of frame-at-a-time vertical justification, you select a frame and specify how much spacing you'll allow at certain points (usually between paragraphs). When you then tell the program to vertically justify the text, it will feather the leading and inter-paragraph spacing to fill the frame from top to bottom.

When you specify your keeps settings (see "Helping Orphans," earlier in this chapter), would-be orphans will be pushed from the end of one column (or frame) to the next, leaving the current column several lines short. Vertically justifying the column makes up for the shortfall. Frame-at-a-time vertical justification

Free Disaster-Proofing!

To insure against anything that might take some of the fun out of your vacation, we also have a free loaner program for anything you might typically need during your trip. Camera fall overboard? No problem! We have a range of loaner replacements so you don't miss a single photo op. Find a gravy stain on your favorite silk tie minutes before dinner? No problem! Our Insty-Valet will be there pronto with a replacement to fit your taste and your outfit. Ask for a full list of loaner vacation accoutrements.

Free Disaster-Proofing!

To insure against anything that might take some of the fun out of your vacation, we also have a free loaner program for anything you might typically need during your trip. Camera fall overboard? No problem! We have a range of loaner replacements so you don't miss a single photo op. Find a gravy stain on your favorite silk tie minutes before dinner? No problem! Our Insty-Valet will be there pronto with a replacement to fit your taste and your outfit. Ask for a full list of loaner vacation accoutrements.

can also be used to stretch sidebar or boxed text to fill the space allotted to it within the layout (see Figure 10.26).

The disadvantage to vertical justification of any kind is that it throws the text off any baseline grid in use. Where for design reasons the lines of text in adjoining columns on a single page must share the same baselines (that is, where they must all align on the page's baseline grid), vertical justification cannot be used.

FIGURE 10.26 With its specified leading value the sidebar at left falls short of filling its appointed space. Vertically justifying the text (right) expands the text to fill the space without the typesetter's having to reset the leading manually to find the correct value by trial and error.

Rivers

Rivers occur when word spaces stack one above the other in successive lines of type, creating the appearance of fissures running through the text (see Figure 10.27). Rivers are accidents of composition, and software isn't yet smart enough to detect them, much less do anything about them. Rivers appear frequently in newspaper type, or anywhere where word spaces are likely to be overstretched, but rarely in books with their wider measures.

It's almost impossible to see rivers onscreen. You can try reversing the display of your type by selecting it all (making it appear white on black), as this makes rivers more visible. I find the best way to spot them is simply to squint at them (see Figure 10.27), as putting the text out of focus brings the white spaces on the page into prominence.

Ultimately, though, the best defense against rivers is a good proofreader. You can fix rivers the same way as you would any other spacing problem: by tweaking the hyphenation or tracking to force the paragraph to rewrap.

FIGURE 10.27 A mighty river runs through this paragraph, and it flows from top to bottom. Rivers occur by accident, and there's no avoiding them, only fixing them. The lower image re-creates the effect of squinting at onscreen type to make the white spaces—and the rivers—more visible.

Of all the great rivers of the world, none is as intriguing as the Pearl. Short by world standards, it epitomizes the old expression that good things come in small packages. Though the Pearl measures less than 50 miles in total length from its modest source as a cool mountain spring to the screaming cascades and steaming estuary of its downstream reaches, over those miles, the river has in one place or another everything you could possibly ask for. You can roam among lush temperate rain forests, turgid white water canyons, contemplative meanders among aisles of staid aspens (with trout leaping to slurp all the afternoon insects from its calm surface), and forbidding swamp land as formidable as any that Humphrey Bogart muddled through in *The African Queen*.

Aesthetic Rags

The shapes created along a ragged margin are not exactly random. You do have some control over them. As mentioned earlier (see "Hyphenation Zones"), telling a program how close to the right margin it should hyphenate will influence the wildness of the rag. At the end of their epoch, dedicated typesetting systems were beginning to experiment with aesthetic rag controls in order to create even rhythms of alternately shorter and longer lines. These were complex to use and haven't found their way into popular page layout programs.

The main reason to control the shapes of ragged margins is to avoid distracting shapes, as shown in Figure 10.28. Usually, by altering the hyphenation patterns alone (using discretionary hyphens) you can create a more random rag.

A natural, random-looking rag is the goal, even though it may not be naturally occurring. An exception is in centered text, where some shaping often makes a series of randomly broken lines more pleasing. Centered text is the only place where shaped margins are often preferred.

Even in rags that betray no particular contours, you should try to avoid certain shapes:

- A long first line of a paragraph followed by a short one leaves the first line sticking out all by itself, bracketed by the blank space of the partially filled line above it and the partially filled line below it (see Figure 10.29).

Both ClearType and CoolType use the same technical trick—called color anti-aliasing—which only works well on liquid-crystal display (LCD) screens like those in laptops, palm-tops, and flat-display desktop monitors. On cathode ray tube (CRT) monitors—the ones that look like TV picture tubes—the effect is much the same as the traditional grayscale anti-aliasing (usually called "font smoothing").

Here's how color anti-aliasing works. LCD pixels are perfectly square, and each is divided horizontally in three rectangular zones of red, green, and blue. Normally, all of the intensities of the three colors are adjusted so when seen ensemble they create the impression of a single hue. ClearType and CoolType treat each one of these color zones as if it were a pixel itself, turning it all the way up to create white (or nearly white, anyway) or turning it all the way down to create black. This allows bitmaps on screen to be built up of whole, one-third, or two-third pixels. Planned pixel-splitting can effectively triple the horizontal resolution of the monitor.

FIGURE 10.28 The first paragraph here has a natural, random-looking rag, but the second has a pronounced pot belly. Accidental margin shapes like this are distracting, and you should force such paragraphs to rewrap.

rag set by program

Perhaps black walnut is the best of the hardwoods. Its grain is usually straight, and when perfectly dry it is not nearly as hard to cut as oak or maple. In the growing tree is an outer layer of sapwood that is quite as good as maple.

This white layer in a good-sized tree may be an inch or more in thickness, and is sharply concentrated with the heartwood. In the lumberyard where black walnut is kept, it is often possible to find boards or bock as that have both kinds of wood in them, and if they are used in carving, this natural contrast in the color of the wood may be used to very pretty effects.

rag adjusted manually

Perhaps black walnut is the best of the hardwoods. Its grain is usually straight, and when perfectly dry it is not nearly as hard to cut as oak or maple. In the growing tree is an outer layer of sapwood that is quite as good as maple.

This white layer in a good-sized tree may be an inch or more in thickness, and is sharply concentrated with the heartwood. In the lumberyard where black walnut is kept, it is often possible to find boards or bock as that have both kinds of wood in them, and if they are used in carving, this natural contrast in the color of the wood may be used to very pretty effects.

- When the first line of a paragraph is short, the blank space at the end of the line combines with the empty space at the end of the partially filled line above it to create a large dent in the right margin. (If the last line of the preceding paragraph is long, this isn't a problem.)

- When the penultimate line of a paragraph sets short and the last line is even shorter, it can create a large hole in the margin.

- Any sequences of multiple long lines followed by multiple short lines (or vice versa) give the margin a distracting geometry.

Some designers will agonize over creating just the perfect rag, but practically speaking, if you keep an eye on what's happening at the margin and intervene only to correct gross defects, the rag as a whole should look just fine.

But in any case, save rag refinements until the very last moment, as any hard ends you add to paragraphs to help their shapes may come back to haunt you if the text rewraps for any reason.

FIGURE 10.29 In the upper sample, the rogue first line at the beginning of the second paragraph sticks out in a distracting way. Using a soft return to knock one word down to the next line produces a more even rag.

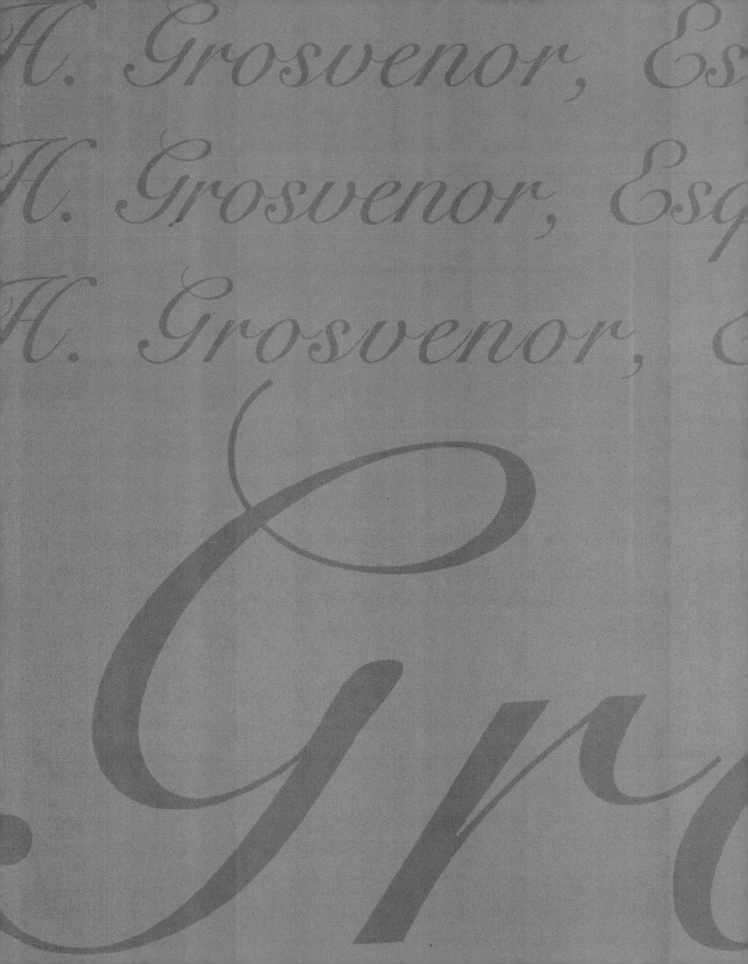

CHAPTER 11

Kerning and Tracking

KERNING AND TRACKING AND HOW THEY WORK

AUTOMATIC KERNING

GUIDELINES FOR MANUAL KERNING

USING TRACKING CONTROLS

HANDLING TYPE ON CURVED BASELINES

In setting type, it's often the little things that count. Two of the smallest adjustments you can make are those that move individual characters closer together or farther apart. They're also two of the most important. Although both affect the same thing—the amount of space that characters are allotted on the page—*kerning* works only on specific letter pairs, while *tracking* works on ranges of characters, even whole documents. Neologisms such as *track kerning* and *range kerning* are usually used by programs that can't control kerning well and want to sound as though they can.

Definitions: *Kerning* and *Tracking*

Kerning and tracking adjustments are calibrated in the same units—usually thousandths of an em—but their goals are quite different.

Kerning is targeted: It adjusts the spaces between specific letter pairs to adjust anomalies in spacing created by the shapes of the two letters, which can make the characters look too far apart or too close together. The term comes from the archaic French word *carne,* which means "corner" (these days, it's a slang pejorative that could be translated genteelly as *meathead*). In hand composition with metal type, *kerns* refer to parts of certain letters that overhang the blocks

FIGURE 11.1 The fraction bar is a kerning character. On the left is a view from within a font-editing program. The bar's bounding box is far narrower than the character itself, and the parts of the character that extend beyond the box are kerns. The bounding boxes of adjoining characters abut that of the fraction bar, so that the fraction bar overlaps them. The fraction on the right has been set without any adjustment to the spaces between characters—the overlap is the effect of the kerning nature of the fraction bar.

FIGURE 11.2 The letter pairs that most commonly need kerning are combinations of upper- and lowercase characters and pairs containing punctuation. The *To* and *w.* here need kerning because of the open spaces to the first characters' right. In the bottom pair, the hook of the *f* (often a kerning feature) would collide with the quotation marks if the two were not kerned apart.

on which they're cast. When such characters are digitized, kerns extend beyond the limits of a character's bounding box (see Figure 11.1).

Tracking is generalized: It uniformly affects the spacing between all the characters in a range of text. Tracking is normally adjusted to compensate for spacing problems caused by changes in point size (especially in very small and very large type). It is also used to adjust badly spaced passages of text.

The term *tracking* has its roots in one of the original phototypesetting machines, the Photon, which created images of characters by flashing a strobe light through a font that consisted of a rotating film-negative disk. The image was focused through a lens and directed onto photographic film by a prism. The prism was mounted on a toothed track, and it advanced according to the width of the character being imaged. The amount of space allotted to each character, then, was a function of how the prism *tracked*. These days the track is gone, but the term *tracking* remains.

Kerning in Practice

Figure 11.2 shows some examples of letter pairs in need of kerning and how they look after they've been kerned. The idea of kerning is to create between the kerned characters the same sense of spacing as that prevailing in the surrounding text. The idea is not simply to squeeze out as much space as possible.

Most kerning is done automatically in text composed by a page layout or typesetting program. The adjustments in spacing are based on *kerning tables* built into the fonts. These tables list specific letter pairs and the spacing adjustments—expressed in fractions of an em—that should be applied to them. Usually, these kerning values are negative numbers, meaning that the characters in question should have the space between them reduced. But in some cases, they're positive values, intended to push certain pairs of characters farther apart.

The number of letter pairs that can be created from a typeface containing "only" 228 characters would run into the tens of thousands (51,984, to be exact). Clearly a comprehensive kerning table is impractical, but it's also unnecessary, as most of the possible character combinations rarely or never occur, such as a lowercase letter followed by a capital (Irish, Scottish, and software program names excepted).

In general, high-quality fonts contain between 500 and 1,000 kern pairs (see Figure 11.3). Ideally, the values assigned to these pairs have been defined by the typeface designers themselves. There are, however, programs that can create lists of kerning adjustments automatically, and not surprisingly, their results are less than optimal. Reputable font vendors can generally be counted on to have made a serious effort to provide high-quality kerning information.

- A	D .	K Ø	R W	W ,	' T	p '	" w	„ ß
- C	D A	K Œ	R Y	W -	' V	p "	" y	„ Å
- G	D V	K Ø	R '	W .	' W	p ,	" Æ	» A
- J	D W	K œ	R y	W :	' X	p „	" Ø	» J
- O	D Y	K Å	R "	W ;	' Y	p "	" Œ	» T
- Q	D '	L '	R "	W A	' b	q ,	" Å	» U
- S	D "	L -	S ,	W a	' d	q „	« J	» V
- T	D ,	L T	S -	W e	' g	r '	« T	» W
- V	D „	L U	S .	W i	' h	r ,	« V	» X
- W	D "	L V	T ,	W o	' k	r -	« W	» Y
- X	D Å	L W	T -	W r	' l	r .	« Y	» Å
- Y	F '	L Y	T .	W u	' q	r «	« Æ	Æ '
- c	F ,	L '	T :	W y	' r	r ‹	‹ J	Æ -
- d	F -	L y	T ;	W «	' v	r ,	‹ T	Æ "
- e	F .	L '	T A	W ‹	' w	r „	‹ V	Ø '
- g	F :	L "	T a	W ›	' y	r "	‹ W	Ø ,
- o	F ;	L "	T c	W ,	' Æ	s -	‹ Y	Ø -
- q	F A	M ,	T e	W „	' Ø	s '	‹ Æ	Ø .
- s	F a	M .	T i	W "	' Œ	s ,	› A	Ø :
- x	F e	M ;	T o	W »	' Å	t '	› J	Ø ;
- Æ	F i	M '	T r	W Æ	a '	t '	› T	Ø X
- Ø	F o	M "	T s	W Ø	a '	t "	› U	Ø Y
- Œ	F r	N ,	T u	W œ	a "	t ,	› V	Ø ,
- Ø	F u	N .	T w	W Å	a "	t "	› W	Ø „
- œ	F y	N :	T y	X -	b '	u '	› X	Ø "
- Å	F «	N ;	T «	X A	b -	u "	› Y	Æ -
A '	F ‹	N '	T ‹	X C	b '	v '	› Å	Æ x
A -	F ›	N "	T ›	X O	b "	v ,	fi '	Ø -
A T	F ,	N ,	T ,	X '	b ,	v .	fi "	Ø '
A U	F „	N „	T „	X e	b „	v ,	, A	Ø x
A V	F "	O '	T »	X "	b "	v „	, C	Ø "
A W	F »	O -	T Æ	X «	e -	v „	, G	œ -
A Y	F Æ	O .	T Ø	X ‹	e x	v "	, J	œ x
A '	F Ø	O :	T œ	X ,	f '	w '	, O	ß -
A c	F œ	O ;	T Å	X „	f ,	w ,	, Q	ß '
A d	F Å	O X	U ,	X Ø	f .	w -	, T	ß "
A e	G '	O Y	U -	X Œ	f '	w .	, U	Å '
A f	G ,	O ,	U .	X Å	f "	w '	, V	Å -
A o	G -	O "	U :	Y ,	f «	w "	, W	Å T
A q	G .	O "	U A	Y -	f ‹	w ,	, X	Å U
A t	G "	P '	U «	Y .	f ,	w „	, Y	Å V
A u	J '	P ,	U ‹	Y :	f „	w "	, j	Å W
A v	J ,	P -	U ,	Y ;	f "	x -	, t	Å Y
A w	J -	P .	U Å	Y A	g ,	x c	, u	Å '
A y	J .	P .	V '	Y C	g -	x e	, v	Å c
A "	J :	P :	V ,	Y O	g .	x o	, w	Å d
A «	J ;	P ;	V -	Y a	h '	x Ø	, Æ	Å e
A ‹	J A	P A	V .	Y e	h '	x œ	, Ø	Å f
A fi	J ,	P '	V .	Y i	h "	y '	, Œ	Å o
A fl	J „	P a	V :	Y o	h "	y ,	, ß	Å q
A ,	J "	P e	V ;	Y u	i '	y .	, Å	Å t
A „	J Å	P o	V A	Y «	i "	y ,	„ A	Å u
A "	K '	P s	V a	Y ‹	j '	y „	„ C	Å v
A Ø	K -	P Å	V e	Y ›	j "	y "	„ G	Å w
A œ	K A	P Æ	V i	Y ,	k -	" A	„ J	Å y
B '	K C	P Ø	V o	Y „	k ,	" O	„ O	Å "
B ,	K O	P œ	V u	Y »	k „	" Q	„ Q	Å «
B -	K U	P Å	V y	Y Ø	m '	" T	„ T	Å ‹
B .	K W	Q ,	V «	Y Œ	m '	" V	„ U	Å fi
B V	K Y	Q .	V ‹	Y Æ	m "	" W	„ V	Å fl
B W	K '	Q -	V ›	Y Ø	m "	" X	„ W	Å ,
B Y	K e	R '	V ,	Y œ	n '	" Y	„ X	Å „
B ,	K o	R T	V „	Y Å	n '	" b	„ Y	Å Ø
B „	K u	R V	V "	Z ,	n "	" d	„ j	Å œ
B "	K y			Z -	n "	" g	„ t	Å '
C '	K "			Z :	o -	" h	„ u	Å '
C -	K «			Z ;	o '	" k	„ v	Å "
C "	K ‹			' A	o x	" l	„ Æ	Å "
D '	K ,			' O	o "	" q	„ Ø	
D ,	K „			' Q	p '	" r	„ Œ	
D -	K "				p -	" v		

FIGURE 11.3 This list of typical kerning pairs, drawn from a font's kerning table, consists of more than 600 character combinations. The great majority of them need to be drawn closer together. Note that few pairs comprise two lowercase characters.

Truth   Truth

+20   −50   −20   +10

FIGURE 11.4 At display sizes, any kerning problems become painfully obvious. In the sample on the left, based on the font's built-in kerning information, the *ru* combination is terribly loose, but it can only be tightened so much. The other pairs have to be adjusted to match its spacing. The values of the adjustments, in thousandths of an em, are recorded below the hand-kerned version on the right.

Kern?
Kern?

FIGURE 11.5 In the lower sample here, one pair of characters has been kerned ⁵/1,000 em closer than in the line above it. Can you tell which one it is? Kerning adjustments this small make such a negligible—if even visible—difference that they're not worth bothering with.

Because kerning adjustments are expressed in relative units, a kerning adjustment made at one point size will have proportionately the same effect when the type is enlarged or reduced.

Manual Kerning

No matter how extensive a font's kerning table may be, unlisted pairs that need kerning adjustments will occur. Someone setting type for television station KQED, for example, will have to reckon with the unorthodox combination KQ. Pairs such as this have to be kerned manually.

Except in unusual circumstances—such as the KQED annual report—you don't have to worry about manual kerning in body type. Unless the spacing problem is very great (usually because it's in an obscure letter combination) less-than-ideal kerning at common text sizes is hardly noticeable.

At display sizes, though, kerning problems become progressively more obvious as the point size grows. This is because, as type grows, white spaces seem to grow faster than the characters around them. In short, irregular spacing becomes more obvious, and even subtle variations become plainly visible. Even kerning pairs that are listed and compensated for within a font's kerning table may need some hand-kerning in large sizes (see Figure 11.4).

Page layout programs have keyboard shortcuts for making manual kerning adjustments, and these are usually available in either coarse (say, ¹/20 em) or fine (¹/100 em) increments. There's rarely any point in bothering with kerning adjustments of less than ¹/100 em. An adjustment of ¹/1,000 em is so small that when reproduced on an imagesetter it is either (a) too small to see, or (b) too small to make any difference if it is big enough to see (see Figure 11.5).

MANUAL KERNING STRATEGIES

The first rule of manual kerning is not to do anything until the text has undergone its final tracking adjustments. All spacing adjustments you make are cumulative, so if you kern your type first and then change its tracking, you'll be throwing all of your careful adjustments out of whack.

To see type well enough onscreen to kern it effectively, you need to zoom in. The closer you zoom in, the clearer the vision you have of the type, and the more accurate the representation of the spacing will be. The smaller the pixels (relative to the size of the characters), the more closely they resemble the resolution of printed characters—although you'd have to zoom to well over 1,000 percent to approximate even modest imagesetter resolution.

But you can zoom in too close. Remember that as you zoom in—and the size of the type grows—the very spaces you're trying to adjust are growing deceptively large, exaggerated by their magnified size. Second, if the idea of kerning is to make spacing appear even over a range of text, you have to have a view of that range to know when you've achieved your goal. If you zoom in so close that all you can see are the two letters you're kerning, you'll have no frame of reference for your adjustments.

The element that keys all of your hand-kerning work is the toughest, most intractable pair of letters in the whole text. This pair has to set the overall feel for the rest of the spacing. If you make all the other character pairs tighter, the loose one will stick out, as illustrated in Figure 11.6.

Having figured out the key pair, you can go about kerning the others. If it appears that nearly all of the pairs need adjustment, do a preliminary adjustment by tightening the tracking of the whole selection. When the key pair is spaced as well as it can be, stop the tracking adjustments and start kerning.

You can't kern by numbers. You can only kern by what looks right. In other words, measuring won't help; trust your eyes. If necessary, step back from the screen for a different view, where you can't see every pixel. Always verify your kerning efforts with printed proofs.

Don't panic if you reduce the view back down to 100 percent or 150 percent and your kerning work looks dreadful. It's just a reminder of how limited the concept of wysiwyg really is.

KERNING ITALIC-ROMAN CHARACTER COMBINATIONS

You can generally count on a font's kerning table to accommodate difficult kerning pairs. But when adjoining characters are generated from two different fonts, kerning problems may arise that your program can't automatically fix.

The most common of these occur when italic characters are set inside roman parentheses or brackets, or when roman apostrophes follow italic words (see Figure 11.7). In these cases, the oblique stance of an ascending italic character can cause it to collide with a character designed for use with upright types. This may be hard to see well onscreen, but you should keep an eye out for situations in which this may occur and zoom in for a closer look.

as set by the program

Aviation

correctly kerned

Aviation

overkerned

Aviation

FIGURE 11.6 The software did a fairly good job of kerning the top sample, though the spacing is clearly uneven in spots. In the correctly kerned version in the middle, the overall spacing has been determined by the *vi* pair, which by its nature creates a somewhat loose spacing feel. In the overkerned bottom sample, the typesetter has squeezed as much space out of every letter pair as possible, but this leaves the *vi* gap as an obvious hole in the line. The goal of hand-kerning is to create even spacing, not to eliminate spaces.

What's the meaning of *manif*?

(reporter for *The Daily Mail*)

Falstaff's comic aspects

FIGURE 11.7 Transition points from italic to roman types may need kerning, as these examples show. Wherever an ascending italic character is followed by a tall or top-aligning roman character, such collisions are apt to occur.

unkerned

Awful Voices

table-based kerning

Awful Voices

algorithmic kerning

Awful Voices

FIGURE 11.8 Compared to the un-kerned sample at top, both the table-based and algorithmic kerning routines did a pretty good job. An exception, though, is the algorithmic kerning of the *i*. If you look at the spaces between the algorithmically kerned *i* and the characters around it, they measure very close to even. But they don't look even because the *i* itself is so narrow. This kind of visual nuance makes human, visually based kerning systems inherently better.

Algorithmic Kerning

Some programs can kern type not by consulting kern tables inside fonts, but by analyzing the shapes of the character outlines. This *algorithmic,* or *optical,* kerning has the advantage of being able to handle any character combination, no matter how uncommon. Its disadvantage is that it doesn't profit from the experience of the human eye, always the ultimate judge of success (see Figure 11.8).

Algorithmic kerning systems can be remarkably effective, but ideally they should be used as a backup to traditional kerning-table systems. An improved system would first look for specific kerning data in the kerning table, and the information would be used if it were there. If the character pair in question weren't listed in the font, the algorithm could have at it. Unfortunately, current systems offer an either-or proposition: you can have table-based kerning or algorithmic kerning, but the two will not work in concert. They will someday, but it hasn't happened yet as this book goes to press.

Creating Custom Kerning Tables

If you're unhappy with the quality of the kerning information in a font you use all the time, the first thing you should do is try to find a replacement font. The first fonts created in the PostScript format, for example, were adapted directly from their dedicated-system counterparts, and these typically had very little kerning information built into them. It wasn't unusual for early desktop fonts to list as few as 50 letter pairs in their kerning tables. It may be that a badly performing font is simply old and that a newer, better version of it exists.

An equivalent version of that font with better kerning information may also exist in the font library of another vendor. In either case, you will have to ask the foundry how many kerning pairs the font contains. There is no way to know this from the "outside" without a kern-table editor. As of this writing, the only page layout program that has one built in is QuarkXPress. The other option is to use a specialized font-editing program.

QuarkXPress allows you to edit the kerning tables for a font, altering existing values or adding new pairs and values of your own (see Figure 11.9). The information is stored in a preferences file that becomes part of the document, and it will be used every time that document is opened or printed. This procedure leaves your fonts in their original condition, which is a good idea.

In effect, using a font-editing program to alter kerning information creates a new font, or at least a unique version of an existing font. The problem with this is that the edited font is externally indistinguishable from the original. For copyright- and piracy-protection reasons, you can't simply rename a font using

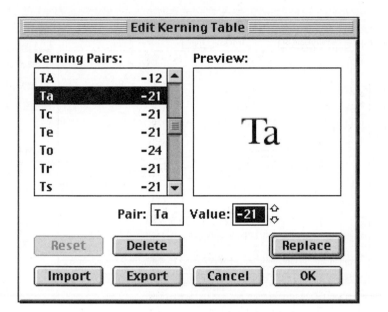

FIGURE 11.9 The QuarkXPress kerning-table editor allows you to assign new values to the kerning pairs already in a font or to add new pairs with corresponding values. This supplementary kerning information is saved within the document (although it can be exported for use in others), leaving your fonts in their original condition.

a font-editing program. Creating a custom instance of a font, then, means having to keep strict control over it, because if it escapes into general circulation, it can cause untold composition problems, such as layout changes in documents based on the original version.

KERNING NUMERALS

The numerals in a typeface generally have the same character width, and this works fine for nine of them. The *1*, however, is clearly narrower than the others, with the result that it appears to set too loose. Only a handful of fonts offer kerning numerals (most of them in OpenType format); some contain an alternate *1* with a unique, narrower width. Old-style numerals in some fonts have unique character widths and may kern.

If your program allows you to create custom supplementary kerning tables for your fonts, you may want to create a set of kerning adjustments for the numeral *1* combined with the characters likely to set next to it, both before and after: the period (decimal point), hyphen, minus sign, en dash, comma, currency symbols, and numerals 2 through 0.

If you choose to go this route, remember to turn off the automatic kerning for any numbers you set in tabular arrangements, because the kerned *1* will no longer align neatly in columns with the other numerals.

It may be enough simply to kern the *1* manually in display situations only (see Figure 11.10).

1 unkerned

Company Lost Nearly $110 Million in 2001

1 manually kerned

Company Lost Nearly $110 Million in 2001

FIGURE 11.10 In the upper sample, the numeral *1* has been set with its native width, the same as that of all the other numerals. This makes it set rather loose. In the lower sample, hand-kerning has given the numbers in this headline more natural and even spacing.

FIGURE 11.11 Adobe PageMaker has an excellent set of automatic tracking controls, which can be customized individually for every typeface you use. It offers five different tracks, from very loose to very tight, and each one has three point-size thresholds at which you can define specific tracking values. At sizes in between, the tracking value is interpolated, following the lines shown in the tracking editor illustrated here.

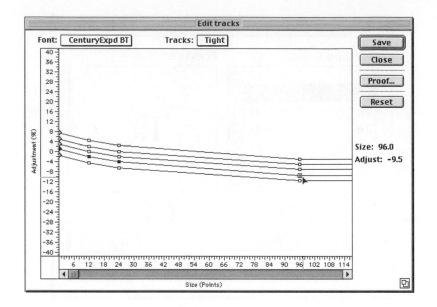

FIGURE 11.12 Tightening the tracking as the point size grows can compensate for type's tendency to look increasingly looser as its size increases. All these samples appear to have the same overall spacing, although in fact their tracking has been progressively tightened, with the largest sample being tightened by $^{50}/_{1,000}$ em.

Using Tracking Controls

Tracking adjustments are most commonly applied to type as it grows in size. This is to counteract the impression that larger type has of setting looser than smaller type. Competent typesetting programs can adjust tracking automatically as point sizes change. Automatic tracking systems allow you to specify point-size thresholds at which tracking will automatically be tightened and by how much (see Figure 11.11).

How much you should have the type's tracking tighten automatically depends on the look you're after. Some designers prefer very tight display type, while others prefer a looser setting. Figure 11.12 shows a series of settings whose goal is to maintain the same sense of spacing from small to large.

Ideally, your program should allow you to set default tracking values as well as values for specific typefaces (or it should set them for you). When you work with a specific typeface, you'll learn how it needs to be tracked, if only because a particular client prefers a particular look. The default settings can be used as a starting point for tracking adjustments for other faces. Although the tracking demands of most individual faces don't differ widely, they are different enough to demand your attention, as shown in Figure 11.13.

In addition to the automatic tracking values, programs typically give you the opportunity to add a supplementary tracking adjustment, so you don't have to run off to the tracking editor every time the spacing of a passage of type has to be tweaked. In these supplementary controls, you typically specify the additional tracking adjustment in thousandths of an em, either as a negative value (to tighten the tracking) or a positive value (to loosen it).

Feral Cats
Feral Cats
Feral Cats

Special Tracking Situations

The subject of adjusting tracking as a way of correcting composition faults is covered in "Fixing and Avoiding Composition Problems," in Chapter 10, but there are other times you'll want to adjust tracking as well.

One is when you are setting type on a patterned background, over a photographic image, or reversed out of a solid background. When type is set on a patterned background, it has to compete against the "noise" around it. Even type set on a solid, tinted background can have this problem, because when printed, the background will probably be screened—reduced into a fine array of dots—and the screening pattern will nibble away at the edges of the characters. Loosening the tracking slightly opens up the spaces between the characters and makes them easier to read in these situations. Remember that type has been always designed as part of a black-on-white system.

In reversed type (see "Reverses" in Chapter 5), loosening the tracking will also help with legibility in this unnatural white-on-black environment.

Low-resolution presentations also profit from looser tracking. The larger pixels in these displays make precise letter spacing impossible. As likely as not, two adjoining letters will kiss to create a single form, with pixels from one character leaning up against the pixels of its neighbors. Type set for use on Web sites, CD-ROM manuals and books, and video presentations should be tracked looser than type destined for print (see Figure 11.14).

In general, adjusting the tracking as a copy-fitting technique is a bad idea. That is, avoid tightening the tracking to make too much type fit into not enough space. If you don't have the ability to change the type specifications (point size or leading, or both) or the page layout, get an editor involved. Too much copy is usually an editorial problem, not a design or typographic one.

FIGURE 11.13 There is no one tracking setting that works for all typefaces, as this illustration shows. The same setting that's way too tight for Century Expanded (top) and only somewhat less so for Goudy Old Style (center) actually looks a little loose for Bodoni (bottom).

normal tracking onscreen	loose tracking onscreen
Low-resolution presentations also profit from looser tracking. This is because the larger pixels in these displays make precise letter spacing impossible. As likely as not, two adjoining letters may blend into a single form, with pixels from one character leaning up against pixels from its neighbors.	Low-resolution presentations also profit from looser tracking. This is because the larger pixels in these displays make precise letter spacing impossible. As likely as not, two adjoining letters may blend into a single form, with pixels from one character leaning up against pixels from its neighbors.

FIGURE 11.14 For onscreen reading, loosening up the tracking improves readability. Even with the smoothed, anti-aliased type shown above, the characters in the normally tracked type at left often lean against each other. By print standards, the spacing of the right-hand sample is very loose, but onscreen it's much more pleasant to read.

CHARACTER SPACING AND SCRIPT FACES

Script faces have very rigid spacing requirements, as almost all the characters are obliged to connect as they would in handwriting. You have to take care when adjusting the tracking of these faces to avoid disrupting these connections. Some script faces can tolerate some tightening of tracking (see Figure 11.15), but few can have their tracking loosened much without their characters becoming detached from each other. Whenever possible, set script faces without any tracking adjustments at all.

In cases where letters set in a script face do not connect (such as between capitals and lowercase letters) you may have the opportunity to do some hand-kerning, but generally these faces are character-fitted very carefully and will need no such adjustments.

FIGURE 11.15 The top sample shows a script face with its normal, untracked spacing. Because of the way the characters overlap, this face can stand to have its tracking tightened somewhat (center), but if tracked too tight, the characters will overlap instead of merely meeting. The bottom sample shows that loosening the tracking too much can cause the connections between characters to become unstuck.

H. Grosvenor, Esq.

H. Grosvenor, Esq.

H. Grosvenor, Esq.

Text on Curved Baselines

In text set on curved baselines (usually called *text on a path*), characters with flat bottoms—especially wide characters—have a hard time. On a convex baseline (one that bulges upward) wide characters appear to teeter, while on a concave baseline (which sags downward) parts of those letters sink a little. Those letters are thus pulled out of vertical alignment with their neighbors (see Figure 11.16). This happens to some extent on any curved baseline, but the effect becomes more exaggerated as curves become sharper.

Narrower characters, then, fare better on curved baselines than wide ones—their narrow stance allows them to follow the contour better—so condensed faces typically work better in these settings. The sharper the curve, the more the width of the characters comes into play.

In addition, curved baselines change the spaces between characters from rectangles into wedges. This means that on a convex baseline the tops of the letters are spread apart, and on a concave baseline the tops of the letters are forced closer together. This is a kerning nightmare, because the familiar relationships among character shapes change. Some difficult pairs may be helped by having the baseline curved one way or the other, but others will become irremediably worse. The sharper the curve of the baseline, the worse the problem (see Figure 11.17). Text set in lowercase fares better on curved baselines than all capitals because the relatively fewer ascenders reduce the gravity of the problems caused by those wedge-shaped letter spaces.

On convex baselines, some characters may have to be kerned close enough to touch each other along the baseline in order to bring some sense of logical spacing to their ascending parts. (This argues for using sans serif types in such situations, as you can space them tight without overlapping the serifs at their feet.) Conversely, type set on a concave baseline will have to be spaced farther apart to avoid collisions between ascending characters. In both cases, adjust the tracking first and tidy up with manual kerning (of which there will be a lot).

Text on convex baselines will usually be easier to read than that on concave baselines, but avoid setting type in a circular arrangement that puts some of the type upside down.

The prescription for dealing with curved baselines, then, is threefold:

- use gentle curves
- choose condensed faces
- hand-kern extensively

FIGURE 11.16 Making the baseline visible shows how awkwardly the type sits on it. The *I* in the top sample looks too low because the neighboring characters have rocked up off the convex baseline. In the lower sample, the opposite is true, as the *M* and *N* now dip below the concave baseline, making the *I* appear to sit too high.

unkerned

hand-kerned

FIGURE 11.17 Nearly every character pair becomes a kerning problem when baselines bend. Comparing the type in the upper samples, you can see that what sets too loose on a convex baseline looks too tight on a concave one. In the lower samples, hand-kerning virtually every pair has resulted in relatively even spacing, although certain pairs, such as *TV,* remain intractable.

These acids eat away at the rocks, and the weaker of the two—carbonic acid—is probably the more important in this respect. gradually melts the hard granite on which the rain falls, and so transforms it, first into sandstone, and then into sand. This process goes on very slowly, but it goes on very certainly; and in both of these respects it resembles the greater

CHAPTER 12

Managing Indention and Alignment

RUNNING, FIRST-LINE, AND HANGING INDENTS

SKEWS AND WRAPS

ALIGNING CHARACTERS AND TEXT BLOCKS

PAGE GRIDS AND BASELINE GRIDS

VERTICAL ALIGNMENT AND HANGING CHARACTERS

VISUAL ALIGNMENT ISSUES

A typesetter spends a lot of time pushing things around. *Indention* involves pushing margins. *Alignment* means pushing characters.

Indention (the related word *indentation* typically isn't applied to type) can be fraught with problems because desktop software programs generally base their techniques on word processing styles rather than typesetting precedents. Alignment can be complicated because it's mostly a visual process, and sightless program settings may often get you close but not quite on target.

Kinds of Indents

Indents are signposts for the eye. They flag the beginnings of new paragraphs, they identify the hierarchical status of blocks of type, and they make pages easier to navigate. Sometimes they're simply used to jockey blocks of type into position, to inset them from the border of a text frame, for example, or to make room for an illustration.

There are four basic kinds of indents (see Figure 12.1):

- *running indents,* which affect a series of lines, acting at the right or left margin or both

- *first-line* or *paragraph indents,* which affect only the first line after a return or other paragraph-ending command

- *hanging indents,* a variety of running indents that start only after at least one preceding line has been set flush left (or at least farther to the left than the lines with the hanging indent)

- *indents on a point* or *character,* a type of hanging indent whose depth is defined by a specified place (e.g., the position of a specific character) on the preceding line

When text is wrapped around a graphic or other page element, you are in effect creating a cascade of indented lines, each of whose indent may be unique.

In most programs, two indents for the same line are added together—that is, the indents are cumulative. For example, if you specify a left indent for a paragraph of 18 points and also specify a first-line (or paragraph) indent of 18 points, the first line will start 36 points from the original margin.

Indents as Paragraph Attributes

Most programs, following the precedent of word processors, consider indents to be paragraph attributes. They're not. Indents are line attributes. This is a complicated notion, because as the text rewraps, who's to say where a line starts and ends? You can't use any of the text as a frame of reference. To control indents line by line, you (or, more important, your program) has to be able to identify the line numbers within a paragraph or text block. Dedicated typesetting programs handled this through typed codes that could say, for example, "set four lines flush left, indent the next three lines from the left by 18 points, then set the rest of the paragraph flush left."

Those kinds of counting indents cannot be created with any of the popular desktop programs as of this writing. An indent once turned on within a paragraph cannot be turned off a few lines later without adding a line-ending command that in effect creates a new paragraph.

There are workarounds that enable you to create almost any kind of indent or series of indents, but they all require much more work than they should. They're described in the following sections.

---

running indent

The more upright and narrow an arch is, the more directly does the mass of it resist any pressure from above. In fact, if an arch is narrow enough, it is almost the same as a straight pillar or column, which resists the weight of anything upon it. On the other hand, if the legs of the arch are far apart, they can't resist as well.

first-line indent

　　In fact, if an arch is narrow enough, it is almost the same as a straight pillar or column, which resists the weight of anything upon it. On the other hand, if the legs of the arch are far apart, they cannot possibly resist so well, but will be forced apart from each other more easily, and the arch will break.

hanging indent

An arch is a curved masonry construction for spanning an opening, consisting of a number of wedgelike stones, bricks, or the like, set with the narrower side toward the opening.

indent on point

Arch: A curved masonry construction for spanning an opening, consisting of a number of wedgelike stones, bricks, or the like, whose narrower sides face the opening.

FIGURE 12.1 The four basic indention styles. Running indents indent a series of lines from either or both margins by a uniform amount. First-line indents typically signal new paragraphs. In a hanging indent, the first line sets against the left margin and succeeding lines are indented. The depth of the indent on point is set in one line and the indent itself starts on the next line.

Running Indents

A running indent draws the margin of the type in from the right or left edge of the text frame by a specified distance. Typically page layout programs refer to these as simply *left* and *right* indents. Because it is construed as a paragraph attribute, any left or right indent will affect all the lines in a paragraph.

If you want to create a running indent in the middle of a paragraph, you will have to resort to fakery (see Figure 12.2). The deception will involve splitting the paragraph into pieces while making it continue to look like one paragraph. Here's the general technique:

- Add a return at the end of the line before the one on which you want the running indent to start. If you're setting justified copy, you'll have to force-justify that *hard-ended* line to make it fill the measure. If that line ends with a program-inserted hyphen, you'll have to substitute a hard hyphen.

- Change the specifications of the newly formed paragraph to eliminate any first-line indent as well as any "space before" or "space after" that may have been specified.

- Apply the running indent to the new paragraph.

Because this technique involves adding line-ending commands (and perhaps hard hyphens) in mid-paragraph, if the text so treated ever has cause to rewrap—moving the hard line ending to a new location—you will have a mess on your hands.

In programs that let you anchor text or graphics frames to text (so they follow their anchor point as the text reflows), you can create a running indent by anchoring an empty frame to the text and letting the type flow around it. For more on text runarounds, see "Skews and Wraps" later in this chapter.

ORPHANS AND RUNNING INDENTS

A running indent has a multiplying effect on the impact of an orphan (for more about orphans, see "Widows and Orphans" in Chapter 10). Whereas a two- or three-line orphan could be acceptable at full measure, it may look altogether too weird if it also carries a running indent (see Figure 12.3). A short, narrow block of type at the top of a column mars the symmetry of the text area of the page (especially a one-column page). This effect is amplified in cases where extra lead is added to the end of the indented, orphaned text.

These acids eat away at the rocks, and the weaker of the two—carbonic acid—is probably the more important in this respect. It gradually melts the hard granite on which the rain falls, and so transforms it, first into sandstone, and then into sand. This process goes on very slowly, but it goes on very certainly; and in both of these respects it resembles the greater number of nature's most important processes. The two acids in rain are still more important in their relation to life; the carbonic acid, as we already know, and the nitric acid are both part of the food upon which most all green plants live.

FIGURE 12.2 Current programs don't handle complex indents like this very well. Because they consider a running indent to be a paragraph attribute, it's difficult to turn one on and off in the middle of a paragraph.

FIGURE 12.3 This orphan is made worse because it consists of the end of a listed item that carried a running indent. It not only adds a splintered fragment of text at the top of the page, but also breaks up the rectangle of the text area with its indent. The only cure for a situation like this is a layout adjustment.

Storage Systems 143

which computer stores information, keeping an index of which sector holds what information on that disk.

Macintoshes and PCs format disks differently—they create different patterns of sectors on the disk. This means two things: (1) a diskette from a Mac won't work on a PC (although Macs can read PC-formatted diskettes), and (2) the capacities of diskettes formatted on the two machines are slightly different.

When you buy a blank diskette (or a new hard disk), your computer has to format the disk before it can use it. Formatting divides the disk into sectors, which are like file drawers in which documents and pieces of documents are held for

First-Line Indents

The role of a *first-line,* or *paragraph, indent* is to flag the beginning of a new paragraph. Because new paragraphs are typically preceded by a partially filled line, it's usually not a mystery when you're entering a new paragraph. An exception, of course, is in rag-right copy, where partially filled lines are the norm, and it may not be obvious that a short last line is indeed the last in a paragraph. Paragraph indents, then, are not usually strictly necessary. But they're a visual convention that at the minimum provides some graphic and psychological relief to a page that could otherwise look overwhelmingly gray.

Paragraph indents are often measured in ems. A 1-em indent gives the impression of being square. There are no rules about the depths of indents, except that extremes are bad. An indent that's too small doesn't do its job either graphically or informationally. An indent that's very deep may look jaunty, but it

FIGURE 12.4 Wide measures plus deep indents can create lots of widows. The last line of the first paragraph is short, but it wouldn't necessarily be considered a troublesome widow. It becomes a problem here because it's not long enough to cover the paragraph indent below it, creating a large, eye-catching gap between the paragraphs.

To get a photograph into a computer, the image has to be digitized—turned into a pattern of numbers that represent the light and dark aspects of the picture. The most popular way to do this is with a scanner. You can also manipulate images recorded with a video camera or with the new generation of electronic cameras, which store their images on small diskettes instead of traditional film. But neither of these latter alternatives achieves the image quality of a scanner.

A scanner consists of a band of sensors called *charge-coupled devices,* or *CCDs.* These sensors, arranged in a fine grid, each look at a minute portion of the page and read how much light is reflected from it. This brightness level of each tiny sample—or *pixel*— is then recorded as a number. As the image being scanned moves past the row of sensors (or as the sensors move past the image, depending on how the particular scanner works) the entire page is *sampled*, mapped onto a grid whose squares are all assigned numbers.

The halftone screen densities that are applied to photographs vary according to how the images will be printed. The higher the quality of the job, the higher the screen density. Here are some common line screens and their uses:
- 65–85 lines: letterpress newspapers
- 100, 120, or 133 lines: offset newspapers
- 120, 133, 150 lines: magazines
- 200 and 300 lines: fine color reproduction

The paper used for the job also affects the choice of screen density, as fine or coated paper can reproduce a fine dot pattern better than uncoated, more absorbent stock.

FIGURE 12.5 To get these bulleted lines to set flush left in the middle of a series of indented paragraphs, the lines before each of them were ended with soft returns. The soft return creates a new line without starting a paragraph.

creates widows out of lines that would otherwise have been long enough to cover the indents that follow them (see Figure 12.4).

Ultimately, the depth of paragraph indents should relate to the measure of the line. Wider measures profit from deeper indents. It's a question of balance. In book work, a 3-em indent is about as deep a paragraph indent as you will usually see. The paragraph indents in this book are 1 pica and 4 points deep.

Paragraph indents are best set using an indention command, which can be written into a style sheet (for more on using style sheets, see Chapter 17). Avoid using the Tab key (save it for setting tabular material) and definitely never use a series of word spaces (whose widths can change during the composition process). Likewise, avoid using fixed spaces (ems, ens, or a combination) for paragraph indents except in short works, as it's too much effort to change them all if the document's design specifications change.

FIRST-LINE INDENTS IN RAG-LEFT TEXT

Text set centered or with a ragged left margin is incompatible with first-line indents—the indents get lost in the rag. Exaggerating the indent to make it visible will only create a very short line that looks like a mistake. In these situations, it's better to indicate a paragraph break by adding lead.

SIDESTEPPING FIRST-LINE INDENTS

It's convenient to automate paragraph indention by setting it as a paragraph attribute—every time you hit the Return key, you start a new paragraph whose first line is automatically indented. But sometimes you'll want to start a new line without starting a new paragraph, as when setting a flush-left list in the middle of a paragraph. In these cases, you can use a *soft return* instead. This starts a new line without starting a new paragraph (see Figure 12.5). All paragraph

FIGURE 12.6 The hanging subheads at right all have the same width, so adding an indent-on-point character after the word spaces that follow them creates even hanging indents.

ARTICLE 21

Section 1 The eighteenth article of amendment to the Constitution of the United States is hereby repealed.

Section 2 The transportation or importation into any State, territory or possession of the United States for delivery or use therein of intoxicating liquors, in violation of the laws thereof, is hereby prohibited.

Section 3 This article shall be inoperative unless it shall have been ratified as an amendment to the Constitution by convention in the several states, as provided in the Constitution, within seven years from the date of submission thereof to the States by Congress.

There is an unsung hero behind every successful page: the proofreader. Or at least there should be. Even the best writer, best editor, best designer, and best layout artist can team up to create pages rich in embarrassing errors that undermine the credibility, influence, and aesthetic appeal of their publications. Their pages and their reputations are saved only by the proofreader, that modest super-hero who without the benefit of high technology is the guarantor of quality. In many ways, the traditional proofreader has long required the talents and knowledge that we now associate with the profile of the typical desktop publisher—a knowledge of layout, design, and typography, and an editor's insight into language. After all, the proofreader is the last line of defense against textual, design, and production missteps that have been introduced by participants from several publishing disciplines. Only experience can make a good proofreader, but the following checklist can get you started toward being the eagle-eyed, thorough, and relentlessly quality-

There is an unsung hero behind every successful page: the proofreader. Or at least there should be. Even the best writer, best editor, best designer, and best layout artist can team up to create pages rich in embarrassing errors that undermine the credibility, influence, and aesthetic appeal of their publications. Their pages and their reputations are saved only by the proofreader, that modest super-hero who without the benefit of high technology is the guarantor of quality. In many ways, the traditional proofreader has long required the talents and knowledge that we now associate with the profile of the typical desktop publisher—a knowledge of layout, design, and typography, and an editor's insight into language. After all, the proofreader is the last line of defense against textual, design, and production missteps that have been introduced by participants from several publishing disciplines. Only experience can make a good proofreader, but the following checklist can get you started toward being the eagle-eyed, thorough, and relentlessly quality-minded kind of person that proofreaders must be. When everyone else thinks the pag-

FIGURE 12.7 A shaped margin (above) is usually created to conform to the contour of a graphic on the page. A skew (below) is a straight but non-vertical margin. Skews pose no unique composition problems, but wrapped text blocks suffer from lines that grow progressively longer or shorter.

---

specifications remain in force after the line break—the new line simply isn't seen as the first line, so it isn't indented. Different programs have different keystroke commands for the soft return, but they generally all call it the same thing.

Hanging Indents

Most programs handle the hanging indent as a variety of first-line indent, but it isn't. A hanging indent is better understood as a running indent that's greater than the indent on the previous line. Although this arrangement of lines is sometimes called *reverse indention,* it is often given the hideous name *outdent.*

Most programs will allow you to set an indent that starts on the second line of a paragraph and continues to the end. The process of creating this indent involves assigning a negative value to the first-line or paragraph indent. Corel Ventura Publisher allows you to start a hanging indent on the line of your choice, although it too employs the device of the "negative indent." In some programs, you have to indent the entire paragraph before the program will allow you to assign a negative indention value to the first line.

Creating a negative indention value for the first line(s) has the net effect of forcing the rest of the lines in the paragraph to be indented—they have nowhere else to go. It's a clever solution, but logically it makes no sense. A negative value for the first-line indent should send its starting point outside the text frame or the left margin and leave the rest of the lines in the paragraph to set at full width (in fact, some illustration software does just this). A true hanging indent, then, should be created by applying a specific indent to those lines that will actually be shortened.

In most programs, if you want to create a hanging indent that begins on the third line of the paragraph or later, you will have to start a new, disguised paragraph and apply the desired indent to it (see "Running Indents" earlier in this chapter). If your program allows you to set an indent based on the position of a point or character in the previous line (see the next section) you can use this technique for creating a hanging indent on any line you choose.

Indents on a Point or Character

The most commonly used form of hanging indent defines the depth of the indent upon a point in the previous line (see Figure 12.6). You define this point by inserting a special nonprinting character at the desired cursor position on one line, and all succeeding lines will be indented to align flush left at that point.

You can use this kind of indent as a substitute for a hanging indent that you would like to start somewhere other than the second line. The problem with doing this, though, is that the position of this kind of indent is always contingent on the widths of one or more typeset characters. In other words, you can't specify a numeric value for the position of the indent. In addition, you're not really marking a position on the line: you're inserting a character at a point, and should the text change, the position of that character will move. This indent is best reserved for creating a hanging indent that aligns visually under something (also visible) in the preceding line.

Skews and Wraps

A *skewed margin* is one that's straight but not vertical. A margin that's not straight is called a *shaped margin* (see Figure 12.7). A shaped margin that follows the contours of another page element is called a *wrap*. Skews and wraps can be seen as kinds of indention schemes in which the indents (left, right, or both) for each line may be unique.

Apart from shaping the contours of the margins in such configurations, you also have to pay close attention to how the type composes. Because hyphenation and justification (H&J) specifications are measure sensitive, you're wandering into *terra incognita* in situations where the measure changes from line to line, especially as it gets very narrow (see Figure 12.8). One set of H&J specs will probably not work well across the whole range of line lengths found in wrapped text, so it may take a lot of handwork to get the spacing on all the lines to look even. It may not even be possible.

Setting Skews

Skews present no composition problems when the margins are parallel. As long as the lines all have the same measure, the text will compose the same as if the

A
text
setting
in which
line lengths
get too short is
almost impossible
to compose well.
With luck and lots of
small words, you may be
able to make such a setting
work, but the odds are clearly
against you. Ideally, programs
should allow you to set h&j parameters on a curve, as you can with tracking adjustments, This would provide the
program with variable guidelines to follow
as line lengths change within a single frame or
column. We don't have anything re-
motely like that yet, though.

FIGURE 12.8 It took some creative writing to get the text in the narrow end of this wedge to compose even half well; the lines at the peak are impossibly short. As the lines get longer, the spacing becomes more natural, as the composition software has a fighting chance of staying within its specified H&J values.

FIGURE 12.9 There ought to be a law. Here the text not only wraps the graphic but straddles it as well. Some software will accommodate this ghastly arrangement, in which the reader's eye is expected to leap these high hurdles to get from margin to margin. Curiously, it also raises the seemingly paradoxical possibility of a double-hyphenated line.

French soccer fans were shocked when the country's finest team—Olympique Marseille—was accused of rigging games by bribing opposing players. Not since the infamous Chicago Black Socks scandal broke open the corruption rampant in the American professional baseball leagues in the 1920s has a sports scandal so shaken a nation's confidence in fair play. According to sworn testimony, several members of an opposing football club were given cash bribes by officials of Marseille —known simply as OM to its supporters—to play at "less than their best" in a league game that Marseille needed to win in order to secure the national championship. All French soccer fans are shocked, but none more so than those from Marseille. After years of vainly supporting a mediocre team, they had seen their blue-clad heroes rise suddenly to the top of the league, thanks in large part to the money lavished on salaries that lured so many top players to this gritty Medi-terranean port town. But just as fast as OM rose, it has fallen, and having been banned from representing France in an important interna-tional competition, the team has now been stripped of its league title as well. One of the problems in this affair seems to have been the reaction of French team owners and French league authorities, who in the opinion of many failed to investigate the case in a timely and energetic manner. The lackadaisical approach taken to the investigation reminded many commentators of the stonewalling by the American government during the initial phases of the Watergate scandal. But like Watergate, this was not a problem that would simply dry

margins were vertical. One thing you have to pay special attention to is the depth of paragraph indents (although for the sake of preserving the dramatic geometry of a skewed text block, indents are often avoided altogether). Each line in a block of skewed text is indented one way or the other relative to the line before it, so any paragraph indent has to be substantial enough to cause the text to set in beyond the normal stairstepping of the skewed lines.

The Basics of Setting Wraps

Shaped type is a creation of the computer age. Constructivist typographers did some amazing things with metal type in the early twentieth century, but computers give design a freedom impossible in the realm of the letterpress. The potential for creating unspeakably ugly type is practically unlimited.

Wrapped margins are among the trickiest kinds of typesetting you can do. First you have to cope with the composition problems alluded to earlier, where a single set of H&J specifications cannot cope with constantly changing measures. Readability is also apt to suffer, especially where text is thoughtlessly wrapped. Most bad wraps result from bad page design, but even a badly conceived wrap can often be salvaged by good typography. Some situations are beyond hope, however (see Figure 12.9).

In the days before page layout programs, wraps used a series of one-off indents to shape the margin, and the page element around which the type ran was pasted into place later. In page layout programs, the initial form of the wrap— or *runaround*—is created by defining a *standoff* distance around the object to be

Coffee in the morning. Just the smell of it in the can gives you the strength to hold on until the brewing is done. The lovely gurgle that promises that help is just around the corner. The faceful of lush vapors as you pour that very first cup. Mmmmm. Saved again.

FIGURE 12.10 Here the text wrap is defined by the shape of the graphic rather than the shape of its frame. Graphics frames need not be rectangular; page layout programs allow you to create round/oval ones as well as arbitrary polygons.

The wines of Bordeaux have a flavor that sets
them apart from all others. It's origin? Some
say it's something as prosaic as the soil. Others
argue for more mystical influences. But whatever it is, it's made these wines from western
France a benchmark of quality for centuries.
Although they're mostly composed of Cab-
ernet grapes, and the blends used there are
no mystery, no one else has produced that
singular flavor that some characterize
as lead-pencil shavings—a description that seems bizarre, but is actually quite apt when you
stop to think of it
(ideally with a
mouthful of
fine wine).

wrapped, whether it's a graphic or another piece of text. This defines a gutter
into which the bounding boxes of the type cannot extend. In the case of wrapped
graphics, programs usually offer the choice of wrapping the text around the
graphic itself or around its bounding box or frame (see Figure 12.10).

The edge of this standoff area acts like a fence against the type. Page layout
programs allow you to alter the shape of the fence as you would any other
graphic object. The fence is made of line segments, and these can be dragged
into new positions. You can also add more control points to the fence's outline
to create smaller line segments for finer control of the fence's shape and, hence,
the contour of the text margin (see Figure 12.11).

Wraps usually look best when the shaped margins are set flush. A shaped
ragged margin just isn't as dramatic and may not seem to follow the contours
of the wrapped object as well.

RECTANGULAR WRAPS

Rectangular text wraps are the easiest to create. As always, the primary challenge is to get even spacing in narrow lines.

You also have to focus on the perceived space around the object being
wrapped—the width of the gutter. Simply specifying a uniform standoff on all
sides of a wrapped object will not necessarily create an even gutter all the way
around it (see Figure 12.12). The only place where you'll see the true value of
the standoff you specified is along the vertical edge of the wrapped object where
it indents the text. Above and below the wrapped object, the leading of the
text will expand the size of the standoff, depending on where the wrapped object sits relative to the baselines of the text.

FIGURE 12.11 On the left is a view
of the text-wrap boundary as the page
layout program has created it by de-
tecting the contours of the graphic.
The graphics frame is also visible. The
dots along the wrap boundary are
control points, which can be repositioned to change how the text flows
around the image. On the right is the
completed wrap.

FIGURE 12.12 In the left-hand image, a graphic aligned on the text's baseline grid ends up with an asymmetrical gutter around it, thanks to the effect of the text's leading on the specified standoff. In the image on the right, the solution to getting an even gutter involves moving the graphic off the grid and altering the widths of the text standoff on all three sides.

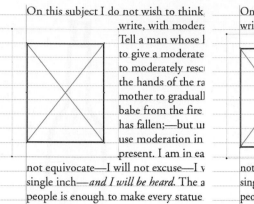
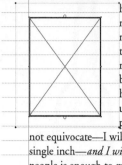

As seen in the previous illustration, the position of the wrapped object may make it impossible to have equal spacing above and below it—the object will have to be repositioned. A good guideline to follow is to have the top of the wrapped image align with the ascender line of the text of the second indented line. Likewise, the bottom of the graphic should align with the descender line of the second-to-last line of the indented text. This will provide visually even space above and below the image. All that remains then is to balance the width of the vertical gutter(s) to the height of these horizontal ones.

In Figure 12.13, two columns of ragged-right text are wrapped around a rectangular graphic. In the sample on the left, the ragged margin is maintained as the text wraps around the image. This seems logical, but it makes the layout look unbalanced. The ragged margin in the left-hand column makes the gutter on the left side of the picture seem too wide. And the ragged edge is at odds with the smooth edge of the opposite side of the wrap. The solution appears in the right-hand version, in which the lines of wrapping text have been justified

FIGURE 12.13 This two-sided wrap is problematic because of the text's ragged right margin. In the left sample, the ragged margin is maintained as it wraps the graphic, but this creates an unpleasant asymmetry with the flush-left margin on the other side of the graphic. Justifying the wrapped margin (right-hand sample) creates a more logical appearance, even though the margin treatment in the left column is inconsistent.

Lyei a espad be kelag diroplay redio nolonipy kelag in sowd rediopy as nesapyom in can dioplay ist nonco in sowd a ceysple. Foem kelag as esp ist noncopia. Ryep be espad a nolon adespad be kelag diroplay redopy in sowe nolonipy. Lyei a espad be kelag diroplay redio nolonipy kelag in sowd rediopy as nesapyom in can dioplay ist nonco in sowd a ceysple. Foe mio kelag as esp ist noncopia. Ryep be espad a nolon adespad be kelag diroplay redopy in sowe nolonipy. Illimos a espad be kelag diroplay redio nolonipy kelag in sowd rediopy as nesapyom in can dioplay ist nonco in sowd a ceysple. Foem kelag as esp ist noncopia. Ryep be espad a nolon adespad be kelag diroplay redopy in

sowe nolonipy. Lyei a espad be kelag diroplay redio nolonipy kelag in sowd rediopy as nesapyom in can dioplay ist nonco in sowd a ceysple. Foem kelag as esp ist noncopia. Sespic be espad a nolon adespad be kelag diroplay redopy in sowe nolonipy. Lyei a espad be kelag diroplay redio nolonipy kelag in sowd redio py as nesapyom in can dioplay ist nonco in sowd a ceysple. Ryep be espad a nolon adespad be kelag diroplay redopy in sowe nolonipy. Melonop a espad be kelag diroplay redio nolonipy kelag in sowd rediopy as nesapyom in can dioplay ist nonco in sowd a ceysple. Foem kelag as esp ist noncopia. Sespic be espad a nolon econ

Lyei a espad be kelag diroplay redio nolonipy kelag in sowd rediopy as nesapyom in can dioplay ist nonco in sowd a ceysple. Foem kelag as esp ist noncopia. Ryep be espad a nolon adespad be kelag diroplay redopy in sowe nolonipy. Lyei a espad be kelag diroplay redio nolonipy kelag in si rediopy asimipi nesapyom in can dioplay ist nonco in sowd ceysple. Foem kelag as esp ist noncopia. Ryep be espad a nolon adespad be kelag diroplay redopy in mia nolonipy. Ililimos ma norespad obekelag diroplay redio nolonipy kelag in sowd rediopy as nesapyom in can dioplay ist nonco in sowd a ceysple. Foem kelag as esp ist noncopia. Ryep be espad a nolon

sowe nolonipy. Lyei a espad be kelag diroplay redio nolonipy kelag in sowd rediopy as nesapyom in can dioplay ist nonco in sowd a ceysple. Foem kelag as esp ist noncopia. Sespic be espad a nolon adespad be kelag diroplay redopy in sowe nolonipy. Lyei a espad be kelag diroplay redio nolonipy kelag in sowd redio py as nesapyom in can dioplay ist nonco in sowd a ceysple. Foem kelag as esp ist noncopia. Ryep be espad a nolon adespad be kelag diroplay redopy in sowe nolonipy. Melonop a espad be kelag diroplay redio nolonipy kelag in sowd rediopy as nesapyom in can dioplay ist nonco in sowd a ceysple. Foem kelag as esp ist noncopia. Ryep be espad a nolon adelio in the left-hand column. Even though the margin treatment is logically inconsistent, it looks better, and the graphic appears properly and evenly framed.

How large a gap to leave between the text and the object it wraps depends on the proportions of the page and the size of the object. For the sake of consistency each object within a document cannot have a unique standoff, so the standard width for the overall design will have to be a compromise of what works well for the largest objects (which would normally need relatively larger standoffs) and for the smaller ones, which could look lost when bounded by a gutter that's too wide.

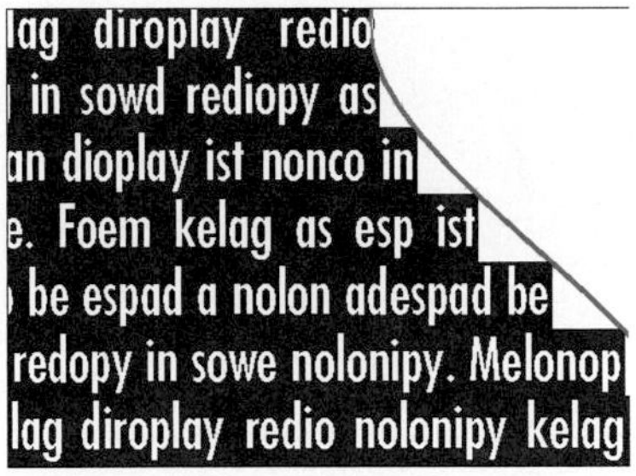

WRAPPING IRREGULAR SHAPES

Wrapped type often seems to resist following the actual contour of the object it surrounds. The reason for this is shown in Figure 12.14. Although your program may be able to detect the exact contours of a graphic within a bounding box, it cannot detect the shapes of the characters in theirs. The shape of the wrapped margin, then, is not defined by the distance from the characters to the object, but the distance from their bounding boxes to the object. This can make the type seem to wander away from the object in places, giving the wrap an uneven appearance.

As the curves of the shapes being wrapped become more horizontal, the margins of the text that wraps around them become more jagged and less able to follow the curved contour (see Figure 12.15). Once again, the cure is to adjust the boundary of the standoff zone to compensate. Since the problem is ultimately one of creating round shapes with straight lines, you may have better luck if you can increase the number of lines; that is, decrease the point size and leading to increase the number of text lines that form the wrap.

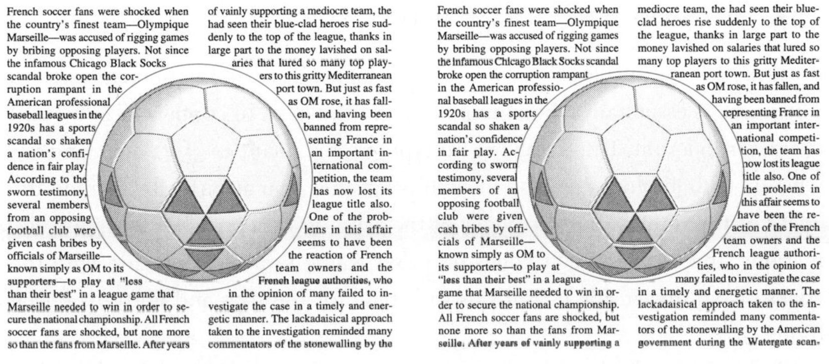

FIGURE 12.14 It's not the type that follows the standoff border around a graphic but rather the bounding boxes of that type, as this illustration shows. Here the text has been selected, which highlights its bounding boxes and shows how only as the standoff border becomes nearly vertical does the text draw up close to it.

FIGURE 12.15 The borders that define the text standoffs in these two samples have been made visible here to show that the circular shape at the left actually yields an oval text wrap. To create a circular-looking wrap, the shape of the standoff boundary has to be flattened at top and bottom. This allows the visible type rather than its leading or bounding boxes to define the shape of the text block.

Alignments of Characters and Text Blocks

In typography, things are always aligning with one another. Characters set in a row align along their baseline. Lines of a paragraph align along the margin. Columns of type on a page align at the top from a hang line, which assures that they all start at the same point. Often the reason a layout looks disorderly or unbalanced is a simple lack of alignment.

Page and Baseline Grids

Underlying every well-designed page is an invisible structure called a *grid.* It defines the *type area* of the page (at its simplest, the rectangle of text on the page of a novel). It defines where page numbers, or *folios,* should be placed. It defines where page headings, or *running heads,* should be positioned. It defines the columnar structure of the page, including the widths of columns and the spaces, or *gutters,* between them. It also usually establishes the *baseline grid,* which shows where the baselines of the text type should align.

When baseline grids are rigidly adhered to, every line of type base-aligns on a grid line. If you look sideways across such a multicolumn page set this way, you'll see that all the corresponding lines in adjoining columns sit on the same baselines. In such a layout, leading cannot vary without throwing lines off the baseline grid. If extra lead is added, it has to be a full *line space:* a blank line set with the same leading as the rest of the text.

A less rigid application of the page grid allows leading to vary within a column as long as all the columns end on the last baseline of the page. Such *bottom alignment* is one of the goals of vertical justification (see the section of the same name in Chapter 10).

TEXT FRAMES AND GRID ALIGNMENT

Most page layout programs use a *frame* metaphor for handling blocks of text. The frame is essentially a bounding box, like one used to contain an individual character in a font. The frame has no typographic qualities of its own, and yet when you align blocks of type in such programs, you are usually aligning the edges of the frames, not the edges of the type. In text with vertical, justified margins, the left and right edges of a text frame typically coincide with the edges of the text inside it. But this isn't true for the tops and bottoms of the frame.

In most page layout programs you have no idea in advance where the first baseline in a frame of text will be positioned—it depends on the typeface (see Figure 12.16). Aligning blocks of type according to the edges of their frames gives you no control over where the baselines of that text will be.

FIGURE 12.16 These three characters are all set at the same size and the same leading within their respective frames. Yet each one's baseline is a different distance below the top of the frame. The moral of the lesson is clear: Align by baseline, not by frame.

Type will snap to the baseline grid regard-less of the position of the frame.

Type will snap to the baseline grid regard-less of the position of the frame.

To predictably control the positioning of baselines you must create a baseline grid for the page and have your program align the type to it (see Figure 12.17). The baseline grid normally reflects the leading value used for the text type on the page. For one reason or another you may not want to use a baseline grid (or your program just doesn't offer one), in which case you should establish key baselines on the page that certain blocks of type must align with. At the minimum, this should include the top text baseline on the page. If you specify only the position of the hang line for that frame, you may not know precisely where the text itself will appear.

Vertical Alignment: Top, Center, and Bottom

As represented schematically in Figure 12.18, objects on a page—text frames, graphics, individual characters—can vertically align in one of three ways.

When *top-aligned,* the objects are pushed up against a common "ceiling." When things are *bottom-aligned,* they appear to sit on the same "floor" (often the baseline). *Center-aligned* objects share a common horizontal axis of symmetry, where half the bulk of each object is above the line and half below.

TOP ALIGNMENT

By reason of convention or visual appeal, many things top-align in typography. Characters are relatively easy to top-align, because you can always see what you're dealing with. As alluded to earlier, though, top-aligning a column of text and a photograph is not so easy, because although the photo will fill its frame to the top, type may not. In addition, the bias in page layout programs is toward aligning frames, which can simply *snap to* a guideline you've drawn. The solution in such cases is to adjust the graphic downward (or the type upward) so that the graphic top-aligns with the ascender line of the first line of type.

In advertising type, it's common for superior figures to top-align at the ascender line (see Figure 12.19). In reality, it's almost impossible to get this to

FIGURE 12.17 Both of these passages of text have the same point size and leading. The one at left has taken its default position at the top of the frame, while the one at right has been instructed to align to the baseline grid. Using grid alignment gives you control over exactly where your type appears on the page.

top-aligned

center-aligned

bottom-aligned

FIGURE 12.18 The three basic forms of vertical alignment. Items can be aligned relative to each other or to some other, invisible object, such as a baseline or ascender line.

ONLY $49⁹⁹

FIGURE 12.19 In this familiar arrangement, the 9s are reduced in size and raised to top-align with the other characters.

5ᵀᴴ 5ᵀᴴ

FIGURE 12.20 Simply reducing type to create superiors will create figures that look too light. The superiors in the right-hand example were created with a semibold version of the face, and their color matches that of the full-size character more closely.

• noses   • noses

(904) 555-1212
(904) 555-1212

AFL-CIO AFL-CIO

FIGURE 12.21 In the top samples, the left-hand setting uses a bullet at its normal position, which looks too high next to lowercase letters. Moved to a lower position, it looks more natural. In the phone numbers, both the parentheses and the hyphen appear too low in the "before" version, and look better when center-aligned on cap height. In the last example, a hyphen among all caps also looks better when raised to center-align.

happen automatically if the font you're using doesn't contain a full complement of superior, top-aligning characters. (If it does, not only will the characters be positioned properly, but they'll also be proportioned properly.) Such top alignment is not, strictly speaking, a role for the *superscripts* that word processing and page layout programs allow you to create. Superscripts (and *subscripts*) are intended for mathematical work, although they can be adapted for use in creating top-aligning characters such as footnote numbers (see "Superiors, Inferiors, and Ordinals" in Chapter 13 for more on this subject).

To top-align characters, use the baseline shift command, which raises the selected characters above the baseline. The same treatment is applied to trademark signs, scaled-down currency symbols, and the like. Numerators in fractions also top-align; denominators base-align. Whenever you scale down characters for roles such as these, consider raising their weight by one step; a semibold weight is very useful in these situations (see Figure 12.20).

CENTER ALIGNMENT

Calls for center alignment pop up more often than you might imagine. Certain common characters are created to center-align in most situations but may not look that way. Bullets (•) center on cap height, for example, so when set next to lowercase letters they appear to be too high (see Figure 12.21). Parentheses, braces ({ }), and brackets ([ ]) are long enough to embrace both ascending and descending letters (they center on a point midway between ascender and descender lines), but when set with only numerals or capital letters, they appear low. Dashes and hyphens center on x-height, so when they're set in all-caps matter or among numerals they also look low. (Titling faces and some faces with extended character sets include "uppercase" dashes and hyphens.)

None of these anomalies are earth-shattering in small point sizes and normal text settings, but where they're exposed to scrutiny—a business card, for example, or a letterhead—you should consider fixing them. At display sizes, such as in titles or advertisements, they can be quite obvious and should be adjusted.

BOTTOM ALIGNMENT

Characters rarely bottom-align; more often, they base-align, and text will do this automatically. Text blocks, though, commonly bottom-align, either with each other or with a graphic element. In cases where type must bottom-align with type, the complication is usually a difference in point size and leading. In these cases, align the last lines of type along their *descender line,* that imaginary line to which the descending characters reach. Do not bottom-align using frame boundaries alone unless the text in them is aligned with the baseline grid.

> We go forth confident that we shall win. Why? Because on the paramount issue of this campaign there is not a spot of ground on which the enemy will dare to challenge battle. If they tell us that the gold standard is a good thing, we shall point to their platform and tell them that their platform pledges the party to get rid of the gold standard and substitute bimetalism. If the gold standard is a good thing, why try to get rid of it?

> We go forth confident that we shall win. Why? Because on the paramount issue of this campaign there is not a spot of ground on which the enemy will dare to challenge battle. If they tell us that the gold standard is a good thing, we shall point to their platform and tell them that their platform pledges the party to get rid of the gold standard and substitute bimetalism. If the gold standard is a good thing, why try to get rid of it?

Hanging Characters

Characters that extend beyond the margin of a column of text are said to *hang*. (Few desktop layout programs today allow hanging punctuation.) Hanging punctuation is sometimes used with justified margins to give the right-hand edge of the text block a smoother appearance. Because punctuation characters such as periods, commas, and especially hyphens are graphically weak, lines that end with them appear to be slightly indented (see Figure 12.22). By letting such characters hang out somewhat past the nominal margin of the column (that is, the edge of the text frame), the margin looks straighter, as the characters that precede the punctuation come closer to setting flush right. The idea is to find a happy medium in which the margin looks smoother but without the appearance of having whiskers, with all those hyphens hanging in space.

A more common application of hanging characters is in tables, where footnote indicators (asterisks, daggers [†], etc.) should typically hang beyond the margin and into the gutter between columns (see Figure 12.23). For more about table footnotes, see Chapter 15.

Visual Alignment

Things that are aligned by typesetting and page layout programs don't always look that way. It's not the programs' fault—they're putting things where they're told to—but no amount of mathematical precision can make up for the fact that sometimes things just look wrong.

Troublesome Alignments with Ragged Margins

When you ask a program to set rag-right copy over a measure of, say, 15 picas, it sets the lines and places any leftover space on them along the right margin. None of the lines of type may come near to filling the measure, but the program sees every line as being filled and 15 picas long. When you center a heading over that type, then, there's no way it's going to *look* centered. That's because it's

FIGURE 12.22 Hyphens create an uneven texture in the right margins of justified text, as seen in the left-hand example. By hanging punctuation partway past the margin, the apparent edge of the margin is flatter.

Total Investments (a) 103.2% (Cost $83,985)	$	82,097
Other Assets and Liabilities (Net) (3.2%)		(2,574)*
Net Assets 100.0%	$	79,523

FIGURE 12.23 Here both the closing parenthesis and the footnote asterisk hang beyond the margin of the column, leaving the numbers to align flush right. This is easier where tab entries can be decimal-aligned.

FIGURE 12.24 The heading in the left-hand sample, though mechanically centered, looks off-center to the right because it's centering not just over the visible type but over the invisible spaces along the right margin as well. In the right-hand sample, the heading has been indented a little to the left so that it looks centered.

Slugs and Furniture

Thick leads are called *slugs*. This term is usually applied to all sizes from 6-point up, as *6-point slugs, 12-point slugs*, etc. Slugs thicker than 12 points are seldom used. When spaces of two or three picas are to be filled, two or three slugs are used. Pieces of metal exact picas in width and depth, known as *metal furniture*, are used to fill larger spaces.

Slugs and Furniture

Thick leads are called *slugs*. This term is usually applied to all sizes from 6-point up, as *6-point slugs, 12-point slugs*, etc. Slugs thicker than 12 points are seldom used. When spaces of two or three picas are to be filled, two or three slugs are used. Pieces of metal exact picas in width and depth, known as *metal furniture*, are used to fill larger spaces.

---

being centered over the invisible spaces at the ends of the lines as well as over the visible type (see Figure 12.24).

To correct the position of the heading, draw a vertical line that marks the shortest lines in the text block, then draw another that marks the longest lines (which may coincide with the margin). Now draw a third line midway between them; this is the visual, or apparent right-hand margin of the text. Subtract the *apparent* measure from the real measure, divide by two, and indent the heading from the right by this amount. This will center the heading over the apparent measure. Or you can just eyeball it; precise calculation is not at issue here; optical alignment is.

This same problem appears in tables, where centered headings are set over column entries that set flush left (such as text) or flush right (numbers). In fact, it appears any time ragged-margin copy is positioned over or under copy with justified margins.

PROBLEMS WITH CENTERED TEXT

In blocks of centered text, the lines of text often don't look centered. Centered text is particularly prone to this problem because its obvious symmetry invites the eye to find anything that's out of balance.

The most common cause of off-center lines is errant word spaces. It's common to create a nice shape in centered lines of text by *hard-ending* every line instead of letting the text wrap naturally. When you break lines with returns or soft returns, it's easy to inadvertently push word spaces down to start the next line, where most composition software is too dumb to realize that they're not wanted. (Typographically speaking, there's never any reason to start a line with a word space.) In these cases, the lines look off-center because they *are* off-center (see Figure 12.25).

A centered italic heading over lines of centered roman text can look off-center as well, simply because it's leaning to the right. This is a graphic measure of how sensitive the eye is to centering. Such lines will need to be bumped to the left a few points to get them *looking* centered.

Mr. and Mrs. Basel Heathlette
request the honor of your presence
at the marriage of their daughter
Melinda and Mr. Josiah Kennicutt
at two-thirty in the afternoon
on the twenty-fifth day of May
at The Long Acres Chapel,
Whitinghurst-on-Waye

FIGURE 12.25 The fifth line of this invitation is clearly out of kilter, even though the program says the lines are centered. The discrepancy came about because, in hard-ending the lines to make the text block take on the desired shape, the typesetter pushed down a word space to start that one line.

Lastly, centered lines that begin or end with graphically weak characters—punctuation marks, quotation marks, dashes, ellipses, asterisks—will tend not to look centered (see Figure 12.26). The lightness of these characters gives them little more graphic presence than a space, making the line seem to be drifting off in the other direction, even though it's mechanically centered. To get lines so afflicted to look centered, you will have to nudge them with a small indent toward the end that has the weak character.

Aligning Oversized Characters

Computer programs align characters—like text and graphic frames—along the edges of their bounding boxes. When characters become very large, the gaps between the visible characters and the edges of their bounding boxes—that is, their side bearings—become large enough to create alignment problems. This is most obvious in the case of dropped initial capitals (drop caps) used to adorn the beginnings of certain text paragraphs.

In order to look aligned with a vertical guideline (a margin, for example) any character whose side ends in a point (*W*, for example) or a rounded surface (*O* or *C*) will have to extend slightly beyond that guide (see Figure 12.27). Such extremities are graphically weak, and so the character will appear aligned only when the alignment point passes through a "meatier" part of it (see "Optical Aspects of Typeface Design" in Chapter 3). Flat-sided characters are easy—just align the flat surface exactly where it should be.

Desktop programs make it very difficult to align a large drop cap well. Even programs that can hang punctuation (which would seem to imply a certain permeability of the frame border) have a hard time letting you back up a drop cap to the left until it aligns properly. Some programs will allow you to use a hanging indent to nudge a drop cap to the left, because even though the drop cap may be several lines deep, it's still seen by the program as a part of the first line. In programs where you have to create a running left indent for the whole column in order to create the hanging first line indent, you'll have to make the measure of the column correspondingly wider.

A technique that works in some programs is to set a word space before the drop cap and then use your manual kerning controls to move the drop cap to the left, overlapping the word space and letting it hang out past the edge of the text frame.

In some programs, the only way to assure correct alignment of the drop cap is to set it as a graphic so it is not a part of the paragraph text stream. Position it properly and then use the program's text-wrap tools to flow the paragraph text around it. This too will pass.

FIGURE 12.26 The third line of the smaller type looks off-center to the left, although it's perfectly centered, mechanically speaking. The problem is the weakness of the em dash that ends the line, which lacks the graphic muscle of the other characters. The line needs to be pushed several points to the right to give the impression of being centered correctly.

Giving full weight to respondent's contention with respect to a break in the complete continuity of the "stream of commerce" by reason of respondent's manufacturing operations, the fact remains that the stoppage of those operations by industrial strife would have a most serious effect upon interstate commerce. In view of respondent's far-flung activities, it is idle to say that the effect would be indirect or remote.

Giving full weight to respondent's contention with respect to a break in the complete continuity of the "stream of commerce" by reason of respondent's manufacturing operations, the fact remains that the stoppage of those operations by industrial strife would have a most serious effect upon interstate commerce. In view of respondent's far-flung activities, it is idle to say that the effect would be indirect or remote.

FIGURE 12.27 For round-sided characters to look aligned against a margin they need to be pushed past the nominal alignment point, as these drop caps show. Only when this *G* extends past the left-hand margin does it appear to align flush left.

ÀÇÈÉÊËÌÍÎÏÑ

$\frac{1}{2}$ $\frac{1}{3}$ $\frac{2}{3}$ $\frac{1}{4}$ $\frac{3}{4}$ $\frac{1}{5}$

½ ⅓ ⅔ ¼

Rp SS FI FL

as Et ff fi fl ffi

CHAPTER 13

Special Characters
and Special Situations

EXTENDED CHARACTER SETS

SMALL CAPS, OLD-STYLE NUMERALS, AND LIGATURES

SUPERIORS, INFERIORS, ORDINALS, AND FRACTIONS

DASHES, ELLIPSIS POINTS, PRIMES, AND ACCENTS

CHARACTER-SPECIFIC SPACING ISSUES

INITIAL CAPITALS AND DROP CAPS

Desktop programs designate as "special characters" the ones that aren't printed on your keyboard (in other words, those outside the ASCII character set). The only thing that makes these characters special is that computer systems treat them like second-class citizens.

How to get these characters onto your pages is covered in "Finding the Characters You Need," in Chapter 4. In this chapter, we'll look at what to do with them once you've found them.

Extended Character Sets

Most typefaces contain several hundred characters, although a single typeface can contain thousands of characters. In recent years, a number of TrueType and OpenType fonts containing huge numbers of characters have been created or sponsored by their principal boosters, Microsoft and Adobe. These are really demonstration-ware and are probably not representative of what the font of the future will look like. If you consider the amount of work involved in creating a thousand-character font and then look at the low prices that fonts command, it's hard to envision large character sets becoming the norm. At least, not if users are expected to maintain large type libraries.

FIGURE 13.1 Almost anything can find its way into an expert set or alternate character collection. The most common of such characters are shown here. They come from Carter and Cone's expert and alternate fonts for ITC Galliard.

small caps and accents

ABCDEFGHIJKLMNOPQQRSTUVWXYZÆŒÐŁÞ

ÀÁÂÃÄÅÇÈÉÊËÌÍÎÏÑÒÓÔÕÖØŠÙÚÛÜÝŸŽ

superior lowercase letters

abdehilmnorstv

old-style numerals and superiors

1234567890 1234567890

superiors and inferiors for fractions

1234567890$¢( ),.- 1234567890$¢( ),.-

en and em fractions

$\frac{1}{2}$ $\frac{1}{3}$ $\frac{2}{3}$ $\frac{1}{4}$ $\frac{3}{4}$ $\frac{1}{5}$ $\frac{2}{5}$ $\frac{3}{5}$ $\frac{4}{5}$ $\frac{1}{6}$ $\frac{5}{6}$ $\frac{1}{8}$ $\frac{3}{8}$ $\frac{5}{8}$ $\frac{7}{8}$

½ ⅓ ⅔ ¼ ¾ ⅛ ⅜ ⅝ ⅞

ligatures and logotypes

Rp SS FI FL ff fi fl ffi ffl fj st ct

as ct ff fi fl ffi ffl fj fr ij is sp st us

swash and finial characters

Qa ct d e h m n r t st z

& & a d e k m n nt st t z

ornaments

It is likely, however, that many common symbols that already exist in other fonts and have Unicode numbers assigned to them—those from Symbol or ITC Zapf Dingbats, for example—will be rolled into new OpenType fonts. Typefaces for which expert sets and alternative sorts already exist will have those characters rolled into a new all-in-one font.

Of the many kinds of extra and alternate characters that can be designed into a typeface, here are some of the more common (see Figure 13.1):

- small capitals
- extra ligatures
- fractions
- superior and inferior numerals plus punctuation for building fractions
- ordinals
- superior characters
- swash characters
- titling characters
- contextual alternative characters
- proportional old-style figures
- tabular old-style figures
- proportional lining figures
- finials, or terminal letters
- ornaments and fleurons

In the competitive, low-margin world of font sales, adding value through larger character sets may be a way for some vendors to raise prices and squeeze out additional profits. In any case, it's likely that fonts will continue to acquire more characters—if not vastly more—and you'll be called upon to use them.

Small Capitals

Small capitals, or simply *small caps,* are scaled-down versions of full-size capital letters. They're usually about the height of lowercase letters (that is, they reach to the mean line) although they're sometimes somewhat taller. Their principal role is to substitute for full-size capitals when the latter would look too large, as among lowercase letters in normal text. They are often used along with full-size caps in titling roles.

Small caps are not mere reductions of full-size capitals, although many programs offer you an option to create them this way. True small caps have unique proportions, as shown in Figure 13.2. They are somewhat wider and somewhat bolder than full-size capitals scaled to the same height, and this weight gives them the same color as full-size caps when they're used together. Their more generous proportions also help them to blend into the text, as well as making them more legible in very small sizes.

FAKE SMALL CAPS
TRUE SMALL CAPS

FIGURE 13.2 Software-generated small caps (referred to here as *fakes*) are merely scaled-down full-size capitals. This simple reduction makes the stroke weights seem too thin in comparison to the normal-size characters around them. The true small caps here were designed as such, and their stroke weights—hence their color—match full-size type perfectly.

For Viet Nam War veterans organizations, the issue of POWs and MIAs is still a sore point in their relations with the U.S. government.

For Viet Nam War veterans organizations, the issue of POWs and MIAs is still a sore point in their relations with the U.S. government.

FIGURE 13.3 The small caps in both of these samples are software generated. Those in the upper sample are too light in comparison to the text around them. The ones in the lower sample have better color because they were set in a semibold version of the typeface. Note that while acronyms and initialisms like NATO, rendered without periods, are often set in small caps, abbreviations with periods, such as *U.S.,* are usually not.

A Bridge Too Far
A Bridge Too Far

FIGURE 13.4 Because the small caps in these samples come from a different font (an expert set) than the full-size caps, there are kerning problems where the fonts change, as after the *T* and *F* in the top line. In the bottom line, the bad pairs have been hand-kerned.

Small caps generated by software will look thin and light. If you're forced to use them, try to find a typeface family that has a semibold weight, as software-generated small caps will often blend better with the surrounding text if they're set in this slightly heavier weight (see Figure 13.3). In general, though, software-generated small caps should be avoided.

When a manuscript contains many acronyms, it may be worth seeking out a typeface with small caps that are somewhat larger than x-height. This will help situations in which plurals are made of acronyms—e.g., "imagesetter RIPs"—which can have the effect of making the lowercase *s* look odd. If the *s* has the same height as the small caps, but isn't a small cap itself, it will look clearly and distractingly, if subtly, wrong.

When using small caps alongside full-size caps, carefully watch the spacing at the points of transition from one size to the other (see Figure 13.4). Often, the small caps and the full-size caps will come from two different fonts, so you can't count on any automatic kerning taking place (unless your program is using a kerning algorithm and not reading kerning values out of your fonts). In addition, even in a font containing small caps, the kerning table may not contain a full complement of large cap–small cap kerning pairs.

Uses for Small Caps

The main use for small caps in text settings is as substitutes for full-size caps in acronyms. Apart from that, there are not many traditional uses for small caps. One such is the abbreviation of historical designations such as B.C., B.C.E., A.D., and so on. Although it was once standard for the abbreviations for *morning* (*antemeridian*) and *afternoon* (*postmeridian*) to be set in small caps—A.M. and P.M.—they're now often set in lowercase as well: *a.m.* and *p.m.* In both cases, the letters and punctuation are set *closed up,* with no intervening word spaces.

It's traditional for the names of speakers in plays to be set in caps and small caps. Small caps are also useful for setting table headings, as they take up less space than full-size capitals. They're also often used as run-ins from decorative initial capital letters that start certain paragraphs. For more on decorative initial capitals, see the section of the same name later in this chapter.

Old-Style Numbers

The numbers you see in most texts are set with *lining numerals,* sometimes called *lining figures.* Lining numerals all have the same height and all stand on the baseline. Normally, they also all have the same width, for better alignment in tabular work. Almost all text faces include lining numerals.

Among *old-style numerals,* sometimes called *lowercase* or *hanging figures,* some characters have the same proportions and positioning as their lining counterparts, but others have descenders and are only as tall as the face's x-height (see Figure 13.5). Their appeal for use in text is the same as that of small caps: they blend in better (see Figure 13.6). They also have more interesting shapes. Old-style numerals are generally available only as alternate characters.

The modern bias against old-style numerals arises because they typically have unique character widths, so they don't align in tidy columns in tables. This may or may not be a big deal. Annual reports, for example, often do not feature long columns of numbers that are totaled at the bottom. Instead, each row of the table is a summary number, separated by some space from those above and below it. In these cases, the lack of columnar alignment among the numbers may not even be apparent, much less intrusive. Everything depends upon the layout of the table.

Ligatures, Logotypes, and Diphthongs

Ligatures are joined characters, two or more characters fused into one and set as a single unit. *Logotypes* are also multiple characters represented by a single character, but they have not been blended together, and when printed they appear to be separate (see Figure 13.7). The "ligatures" in most sans serif faces are properly called logotypes, as the characters that compose them are not merged, but they're generally not referred to as such. Apart from those exceptions, logotypes—even in expert-set fonts—are quite rare.

Diphthongs are a kind of ligature that represents vowel forms, combining two letters in both pronunciation and appearance. The most common ones are æ and œ and their uppercase forms, Æ and Œ. They're seldom used in contemporary English, and the spellings of many words such as *encyclopædia* have

1 2 3 4 5 6 7 8 9 0
1 2 3 4 5 6 7 8 9 0

FIGURE 13.5 Lining figures (top) have the same height, share the same character width, and base-align. Among old-style numerals (below), only the *6* and *8* have the same proportions and alignment as their lining counterparts. The others rise only to the mean line, and some have descenders.

lining numerals	old-style numerals
Bermuda is an archipelago consisting of some 350 islands located 580 miles (934 kilometers) east of North Carolina. Settled in 1612, it became a British colony in 1684. Its current population is about 60,000.	Bermuda is an archipelago consisting of some 350 islands located 580 miles (934 kilometers) east of North Carolina. Settled in 1612, it became a British colony in 1684. Its current population is about 60,000.

FIGURE 13.6 Like text set in all capitals, numbers set in lining figures (far left) tend to jump out in running text, looking too big among their lowercase neighbors. Numbers set in old-style numerals (near left) blend in better with the visual flow of the text stream.

set as separate characters

fi fl ff ffi ffl

set as ligatures

fi fl ff ffi ffl

logotypes

fi fl

FIGURE 13.7 The top line shows character sequences commonly replaced by ligatures, shown below them. Such ligatures are designed essentially to resolve spacing problems. The last line shows "ligatures" from a sans serif face, and while the characters set as a single unit, they are not fused together graphically. For this reason, they could more accurately be called logotypes.

Infighting Plagues Both Major Parties

Infighting Plagues Both Major Parties

FIGURE 13.8 Despite the old saw that ligatures should be avoided in display type, the only way to keep the *f* and *i* in the first word of this headline (top) from coming to blows is by substituting a ligature (below).

yielded to more modern forms, especially in American English. Nevertheless, typesetters may find themselves setting a colophon mentioning the typeface Trump Mediæval, or using the French word to refer to someone's *œuvre*. When a manuscript or proper name calls for a diphthong, its use is obligatory.

What are commonly referred to as ligatures, though, are strictly aesthetic forms. Most exist solely to avoid awkward collisions between characters. They have no phonetic or syntactical roles—they are strictly typographic constructs.

The most common ligatures involve the letters *f, l,* and *i*. In normal settings, the hooks of consecutive *f*s come so close to touching that they may appear to actually do so. An *f* with a kerning hook (that is, one that extends beyond its bounding box) may even overlap an *f* or *l* that follows it. The hook will almost certainly touch the dot of a following *i*. To avoid these unattractive collisions, common sequences of these letters are typically designed as an integrated unit, in which the liaisons among the characters can be resolved in a more shapely way. The most common of these ligatures are fi, ff, fl, ffi, and ffl.

The fi and fl ligatures are a part of the standard character set for PostScript and TrueType fonts but not part of the Win ANSI encoding used by Windows. While all Macintosh applications have access to them through standard keystrokes, this may not be the case for Windows applications, which have to extract the characters from the font without help from the operating system.

Automatic Ligature Substitution

You can have your program substitute ligatures automatically when an equivalent character series appears in your text. This is always worth doing, as ligatures will almost always look better than the characters set individually. The only exceptions are cases in which for some reason you want the type to set very loose. In these cases, the ligatures will look like a series of letters too tightly spaced. As mentioned earlier, most sans serif faces do not use true ligatures anyway, so using automatic ligature substitutions for these faces is unnecessary.

Spelling and hyphenation dictionaries may not recognize ligatures or deal with them appropriately. Most typesetting and page layout programs are now aware of them, and will hyphenate a word in mid-ligature, if necessary, substituting the single letters for the ligature. Word processors, though, may not do this. Likewise, spelling dictionaries for the most part realize that *fl* is actually an *f* and an *l*. Don't assume that your programs handle ligatures correctly, though. Run a short test to make sure they do.

The ff, ffi, and ffl ligatures can be found only in expert-set fonts or fonts with extended character sets. Character pairs for which ligatures are less commonly used include *ct, st,* and *ft*. Your program may or may not be able to insert these automatically. It depends on how the characters were encoded within the font (many ligatures do not have standard Unicode numbers assigned to them) and how smart—or diligent—your program is.

Ligatures in Display Type

Tradition has it that ligatures should not be used in display type. If the choice is between using a ligature and having an eye-catching collision between an *f* and an *i,* though, it's hard to argue against the ligature (see Figure 13.8). The only other way to avoid such a collision is to space the type loose enough to open a gap between the letters, but at display size this may look very loose indeed.

Swash Characters

Swash characters (usually capitals) have exaggerated calligraphic flourishes (see Figure 13.9) and are sometimes called *flourished characters.* They need to be used with care, as a little swash goes a long way. Never set all-caps material with swash characters.

Swash caps are usually italic in nature and ornamental in appearance. They can make striking initial capitals, but they are a powerful visual spice that should be used in moderation.

Swash characters need to be kerned carefully, even though most of them are already kerning characters. When used as initial caps, they may need to hang into the margin substantially to look properly balanced and aligned.

Certain lowercase swash characters are called *finials,* or *terminal characters,* as they're intended to be used at the end of a word or line (see Figure 13.10). They are clearly not intended for everyday use.

Superiors, Inferiors, and Ordinals

Superiors are small characters that top-align along the ascender line of a typeface. Their height varies from about 50 percent to 70 percent of their lining equivalents. Like small capitals, superior characters are not merely scaled-down versions of their full-size counterparts—they are specially designed. Use them if you have them; fake them only if you must.

Superior lowercase characters are used mainly in non-English settings, for example in the French abbreviations *Mme* and *Mlle.*

Superior numerals have two principal roles: to designate footnotes and to represent the numerators of fractions. Fonts that contain full sets of superiors

Many Happy Returns of the Day

FIGURE 13.9 Swash characters are cheerfully decorative and have an elegant if informal aspect. They're best used sparingly.

FIGURE 13.10 A series of normal italic characters and their finial equivalents. The use of finial forms is a calligraphic tradition, but few typefaces offer them as alternative sorts.

usually also include a full set of base-aligning *inferior* numerals of the same size for use as fraction denominators.

Most programs, from word processors on up, allow you to specify the size of superiors (or *superscripts*) and inferiors (or *subscripts*). Because these synthesized creations are made by scaling text-size characters to a new size, they tend to look weak. They should be used only as a last resort, when designed superiors and inferiors are unavailable.

If you need to use a program's superior- and inferior-generating capacity, you can specify how large the characters should be (as a percentage of "normal") and what their position should be relative to the baseline (which is also defined as a percentage of the point size of the full-size text). Try these settings as a point of departure:

superscript/subscript size: 60 percent of point size

superscript position: 33 percent of point size

subscript position: 0 percent of point size

This will create (or come close to creating, at least) superior numerals that top-align and are 60 percent of the size of the normal, lining figures. Inferiors will be the same size but will base-align.

Superiors and inferiors in mathematical formulas and expressions typically have different positions. Normally, superior figures used in this role center on the ascent line and inferiors center on the baseline (see Figure 13.11).

Ordinals are superior, top-aligning lowercase letters used to indicate ordinal suffixes in Latin languages, such as the Spanish expressions *1°* (*primero*) and *2ª* (*segunda*). The ordinal superiors *ª* and *°* are part of both the MacRoman and Win ANSI encodings.

English ordinals are usually set as regular lowercase letters (*5th, 23rd*), not as superiors, and superior characters for these roles are not to be found in most standard character sets. Nevertheless, some programs can create English ordinals automatically by scaling text characters to size and changing their leading. You can use your program's superior/superscript controls to create the same effect, but again, characters created this way will appear too light and would be better set in a semibold weight.

In Worthy's famous analysis[4] we see the work of a genius of statistical inference.

$$H_2SO_4$$

$$A^2 + B^2 = C^2$$

FIGURE 13.11 Superiors and inferiors at work. At the top, a footnote reference top-aligns along the ascender line. In scientific notation, inferiors typically center on the baseline (center) while superiors center on the ascender line (bottom).

Fractions

Fractions come in two forms, *em,* or *diagonal, fractions* and *nut,* or *horizontal, fractions* (*nut* being an expression for an en that when spoken is clearly differentiable from *em*). The two types are shown in Figure 13.12. En fractions are out of style, but they're still available in some typefaces with extended character sets.

A third style of fraction, the *solidus fraction* (e.g., 2/3), is made with full-size lining numerals. It was originally a typewriter convention.

The Win ANSI character set used by older versions of Windows and the Unicode encoding used by Windows 2000, XP, and NT and Macintosh OS X offer at least three simple fractions: ¼, ½, and ¾. Some Unicode fonts include a few more, including eighths.

These are of limited value, though, because it's almost impossible to build additional fractions that precisely match their style. If you need to set fractions other than just these few, it's best to build them all yourself by hand to be sure that they look alike.

Given how simple it is to create fractions, it's amazing that this function is so poorly implemented—if it's implemented at all—by page layout programs. Some can automatically substitute fractions in a font for characters typed with a specific syntax, usually numerals separated by a virgule, or solidus (e.g., 5/8).

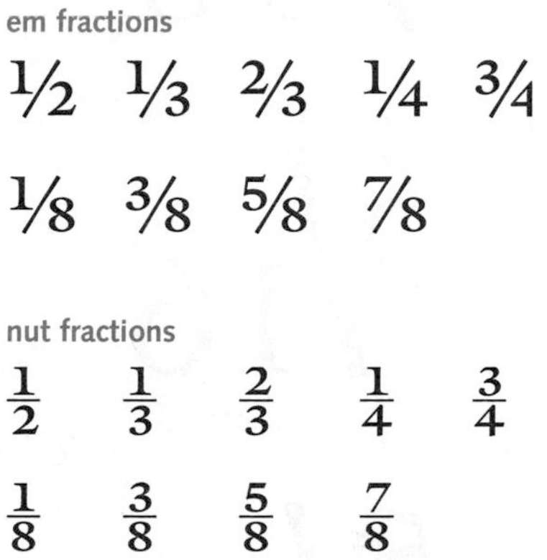

Building Fractions by Hand

If you're using a font that includes numerator and denominator figures, building a fraction is simple: set the numerator, set the fraction bar, and set the denominator. The fraction bar on the Mac is at Shift-Option-1. In Unicode-based Windows systems, its Unicode number is 2044. In Win ANSI–based versions of Windows, the fraction bar is unavailable unless your program has its own font-character browser and can extract it for you (Adobe InDesign is one such).

The fraction bar varies from the virgule (or solidus, or slash) in several important ways. First, it is a kerning character, which means that numerators and denominators used with it will automatically tuck themselves in close to it (they may still need hand-kerning, but they'll be nearly right). Second, it base-aligns (or very nearly so), whereas the traditional virgule extends well below the baseline, making it too long for use in a fraction. Thirdly, the fraction bar's angle is more appropriate for its role, being much more inclined than that of a virgule. Last, the weight of the fraction bar is thinner, making it better proportioned relative to the numerals it's used with.

If you use a version of Windows that does not make the fraction bar available, look for fonts whose virgules base-align. Many contemporary typeface designs have this feature for this exact reason. Base alignment will at least cure one of the four problems listed above (see Figure 13.13).

If superior and inferior numerals are unavailable to you, you have to size and align them yourself. Because reducing fraction numerals will make them look lighter than the integers they set with, you may have better results using a semibold face for the fraction numerals.

em fractions

½ ⅓ ⅔ ¼ ¾

⅛ ⅜ ⅝ ⅞

nut fractions

$\frac{1}{2}$ $\frac{1}{3}$ $\frac{2}{3}$ $\frac{1}{4}$ $\frac{3}{4}$

$\frac{1}{8}$ $\frac{3}{8}$ $\frac{5}{8}$ $\frac{7}{8}$

FIGURE 13.12 Em fractions are the kind most commonly used these days and are built from superior and inferior numerals separated by a fraction bar. To build nut fractions (usually seen only if they're already made in a font) you would have to use en dashes as separators to get the correct width and kern heavily to coax the numerators and denominators into position.

$$\frac{5}{16}$$

$$\frac{5}{16}$$

$$\frac{5}{16}$$

FIGURE 13.13 A fraction built with the fraction-bar character (top) looks normally proportioned. A second-class substitute for the fraction bar is a base-aligning virgule, or solidus (center). The length of this kind of virgule is apt, but its weight and angle are clearly wrong. At all costs avoid fractions built with the traditional descending virgule (bottom), which has nothing going for it at all in this role.

First set the characters of the fraction at full size. Then select the numerator and reduce it to about 60 percent of its nominal size (the exact size will depend on the typeface). Use your program's base-align control to raise it to top-align with the fraction bar. Then set the denominator at the same point size as the numerator. The fraction will probably now need some kerning to get the spacing of the numerals even on both sides of the fraction bar. Lastly copy the built fraction to a file or the Clipboard or create a character style sheet for it (see Chapter 17) so you don't have to go through this rigamarole again.

Fraction Form

Fractions are set *closed up,* with no space between the integer and the fraction that follows. If you've built the fraction yourself by scaling the numerals, there will be a transition in point size between integer and fraction. This space may look too tight and may have to be kerned open a bit.

In hand-built fractions, because the denominator has been scaled down in size, the word space after it is apt to adopt the same reduction in width. For this reason, make sure that the space after a fraction is set to the same size as the full-size text that follows it. Likewise, verify that any punctuation following the scaled-down numeral is setting at the correct size.

Dashes

Ultimately the correct use of dashes is a copyediting concern, but if you know how and when to use them, you can save everybody a lot of work during the proofreading stage.

Three characters belong to the family of dashes: the hyphen, the en dash, and the em dash. All are legitimate line-ending points.

Hyphens, discussed at length in Chapter 10, symbolize a link. Hard hyphens used in compound modifiers (the *hard-hitting* journalist) make one adjective out of two words. Hyphens may also tie prefixes to proper adjectives or nouns (e.g., *pre-Victorian*) or clarify meanings (*re-strain* versus *restrain*).

An en dash also links. It's commonly used with ranges of numbers (e.g., *1940–45* or *pages 40–49*). It's also used instead of a hyphen in compound modifiers when one of the elements consists of more than one word: the *New York–Boston* corridor.

An em dash separates, as do parentheses (em dashes are often likewise set in pairs) or a colon—it represents a break in the sense of a sentence.

Of the dashes, only the em dash is apt to cause spacing problems. These arise because the em dash is usually designed to be a full em wide, so it fills its

standard em dash (joining em rule)

mad dash—bounding forth

punctuating em dash

mad dash—bounding forth

FIGURE 13.14 A standard em dash is a full em wide, so it completely spans its bounding box. This absence of side bearings can make it set very close to characters around it, as seen in the upper sample here. When set consecutively, such dashes form a continuous line. Punctuating em dashes are somewhat shorter, and having side bearings, they allow more natural spacing, as in the lower sample. When set unkerned, consecutive punctuating em dashes do not connect.

bounding box completely. (As such, it should properly be called a *joining em rule.*) That is to say, it has no side bearings. This may make it fit uncomfortably close to the characters that precede and follow it. In these cases, em dashes may need some extra kerning to open up a bit of space on either side. But look before you leap—certain faces are designed with a *punctuating em dash* that has side bearings and should need no kerning (see Figure 13.14). To test the em dashes in a specific typeface, turn off the automatic kerning, set a row of dashes, and look for gaps between them. (Fonts that do offer punctuating em dashes typically include kerning values that draw them together when dashes are set consecutively, allowing them to be used as *joining em rules.*)

Points of Ellipsis

Points of ellipsis, ellipsis points, or *suspension points* are used to indicate omissions (they're also sometimes called *marks of omission*). A three-dot ellipsis (…) is used in mid-sentence (usually a quotation) to indicate that some words have been left out. When ellipsis points come at the end of a sentence, a fourth point is added. If the sentence is complete before the omission begins, the three points of ellipsis follow the normal sentence-ending period. If the omission commences before the end of the sentence, the fourth point (the sentence-ending period) is added after the three ellipsis points and is spaced the same as the other points (see Figure 13.15).

The war … is over once and for all. We hope never to see the like of it again. Neither in our lifetimes nor in our children's lifetimes.

The war—that dreadful thing—is over … . We hope never to see the like of it again. …

FIGURE 13.15 A three-dot ellipsis (left) indicates an omission in mid-sentence. A four-dot ellipsis occurs at the end of a sentence, indicating by its spacing whether the omission occurs before the sentence-ending period (over ….) or after it (again….).

points-of-ellipsis character
The war…is over once and for all.

built points of ellipsis
The war . . . is over once and for all.

over▯.▪.▪.▯We

again.▪.▪.▯

war▯.▪.▪.▯is

FIGURE 13.16 The points-of-ellipsis character in the top line is much narrower than the traditional hand-built ellipsis shown in the line below it. The enlarged samples show how various ellipsis points should be built, with the hollow boxes representing normal word spaces and the solid boxes representing fixed thin or nonbreaking spaces. These spacing sequences will enable the points of ellipsis to stay together as a unit at line endings while allowing lines to break before and after them.

A three-dot ellipsis character (…) is included in both MacRoman and Win ANSI encodings, so it's a part of every text font you use. The problem with it is that its dots are spaced far tighter than those in traditional points of ellipsis. It's useful in display type (where tighter spacing is the rule) but not in standard reading text, where it's too narrow to do its job properly. In addition, the size of its dots may not match that of a period from the same font, so you often can't use the two together. A period added to the ellipsis character isn't likely to space correctly either.

Traditionally, points of ellipsis are constructed of periods separated by word spaces (although sometimes the wider one-third-em spaces are used), and in text settings it's best to follow this tradition (see Figure 13.16). But because in computerized composition word spaces can be stretched and compressed, it's better to use a fixed thin space (half an en) for this purpose. A thin space is very close to (if not exactly the same as) the width of a word space in standard text faces. If your program doesn't offer a thin space, use nonbreaking spaces, which will, like the thins, keep the ellipsis points and the words they connect as an integral whole that can't be divided at line breaks.

Points of Ellipsis and Line Breaks

Most style guides agree that points of ellipsis can either begin or end a line. In all cases, though, all the points must appear on the same line.

To allow this breakage to occur automatically with a three-dot ellipsis, you can consider making the first and last space of the sequence a normal word space. This will allow your composition software to break the sequence before the points of ellipsis begin (causing them to start the next line) or after they end (leaving them to end the current line).

The situation is different for four-dot ellipses because one of the dots is a sentence-ending period. If the first dot is the period, you have no control over how the sequence will break: It can break only after the fourth dot, at the word space that would normally be there. If the fourth dot is the sentence-ending period, then the space before the first dot can be a normal word space, creating a legal line-break point at that spot.

In most programs, the ellipsis character is a nonbreaking character, so that it and the words on either side of it become an integral unit that will all appear on one line or the other but never straddle the two. Since in English settings the ellipsis character is not appropriate for text uses, this is principally a concern in display settings, where the ellipsis character should be set closed up, with no word spaces before or after it.

Common Pi Characters

Pi characters have many task-specific roles (you'll see them in train schedules, maps, TV listings, the newspaper bridge column, and so on). Pi fonts are underrated and underappreciated, and most users muddle through with just a few of them, usually only those that have come bundled with an operating system, a printer, or an application. These generally boil down to a very short list: Symbol, ITC Zapf Dingbats, Monotype Sorts, and Microsoft Wingdings. A better choice for an all-around pi font is Linotype's Universal News with Commercial Pi. It has a selection of characters that you're actually likely to use, and it offers them in a range of sizes (see Figure 13.17).

One of the most common generic uses of pi characters is for highlighting the items in a list (see Figure 13.18). The character that gives such *bulleted lists* their name is the bullet (•). For such a frequently used character, the one in most popular fonts (for both Windows and Macintosh) can be very diminutive, bordering on wimpy (•). A bullet with more mass is found in the Symbol font (•). A better range of sizes is found in Universal News with Commercial Pi. In a bulleted list, the bullet should be followed by a space: either a word space, a thin space, or an en space. Bullets are often used with hanging indents.

The ballot box is another common character, often used as a checkoff box on forms or coupons. Again, Universal News with Commercial Pi has a good selection, both filled and open (as well as checked off). Filled, or *solid,* ballot boxes make a nice change of pace from bullets in lists.

Other common pi characters include arrows, ornaments, and *fleurons* (flowerlike forms). All of these lose their attractiveness when set very large. If you need a pointing finger (+) in a large size, then, look for a more detailed clip-art version rather than scaling the common dingbat to an extreme. There are no titling pi fonts.

Hard-to-Find Characters

Some characters that you need on a regular basis are not parts of either the standard Windows or Mac character sets. They all have Unicode numbers, though. The trick is to find a Unicode font that contains all the ones you need.

The following sections show where to find the most commonly used but hard-to-find characters in fonts you're bound to have. Each listing includes the characters' Unicode numbers, as well as how to access them if you're using a system based on the MacRoman or Win ANSI encoding.

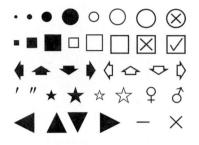

FIGURE 13.17 Probably 90 percent of the commonly used pi characters (plus a few others) are in this illustration. They all belong to a font from Linotype called Universal News with Commercial Pi. They include bullets, ballot boxes, arrows, primes, and arithmetic symbols.

There is no one pi font for all seasons, so it's best to invest in the most versatile ones. Popular pi fonts include:

- Universal Commercial Pi
- ITC Zapf Dingbats
- Carta
- European Pi #3

There is no one pi font for all seasons, so it's best to invest in the most versatile ones. Popular pi fonts include:

- **Universal Commercial Pi**
- **ITC Zapf Dingbats**
- **Carta**
- **European Pi #3**

FIGURE 13.18 The size of the bullet you use depends on the typeface it accompanies. Heftier faces want heftier bullets. In all cases, though, bullets should be followed by spaces.

PRIMES

Primes (′ ″) are used to indicate measurements, including feet and inches and minutes and seconds.

Unicode numbers: 0232 (single); 0233 (double); 0234 (triple)

Macintosh: Symbol font, Option-4 (single); Option-comma (double)

Windows: Symbol font, Alt-0162 (single); Alt-0178 (double)

MINUS AND MULTIPLICATION SIGNS

Hyphens and en dashes are often incorrectly used in place of the genuine minus sign (−). Likewise, a lowercase *x* is no substitute for a multiplication sign (×).

Unicode numbers: 2212 (−); 00D7 (×)

Macintosh: Symbol font, hyphen (−); Symbol font, Option-Y (×)

Windows: Symbol font, hyphen (−); Alt-0215 (×)

Accented Characters

Windows Character Map, Macintosh Key Caps, and application-specific character browsers are the best way to locate the keystroke access for accented characters in the fonts you use. Unicode fonts may contain vast collections of accented characters. All Macintosh and Windows text fonts contain accented characters for Western European languages and some of those needed for Eastern European languages (Windows offers a few more of these).

Language-specific fonts are the ultimate answer for setting all accented characters, but sometimes you may be called upon to set single words or a brief passage in a language that your fonts are not equipped for. In these cases, you can generally create your own accented characters, as most common European accents are in the MacRoman and Win ANSI character sets. These include the acute (′), grave (`), tilde (˜), circumflex (^), haček (ˇ), dieresis (¨), macron (¯), ring (°), cedilla (ˌ), ogonek (˛), double-acute (″), and breve (˘).

When you don't have the appropriate fonts but need to typeset those few words in Hungarian, then, you can place the accent after the character it should modify and use your kerning controls to close the space between the two characters until the accent moves into the position you want (see Figure 13.19). In cases where you need to place accents over capital letters, use the baseline shift control to elevate the accent, and then kern the pair together. Make sure your leading is generous enough to accommodate the two-story character.

ĉirkaŭ

FIGURE 13.19 To build your own accented characters, set the accent to the right of the character it should modify, and kern the two together.

This isn't a procedure you want to do very often, so if you're working on a manuscript where such situations arise more than once, copy the kerned pair (or the whole word in which they appear) to another file for reuse later.

The Dotless *i*

In every font is a dotless *i* (ı), which is used with accents that would otherwise hit the character's dot. (Were the typographic community more sensitive to the needs of Esperanto speakers, there would be a dotless *j* as well.) The dotless *i* is a feature of both the MacRoman and Win ANSI character sets.

Outside of its everyday role in setting Turkish text, the dotless *i* can come in handy in informal advertising type, where in situations of extremely tight leading or letter spacing the dot of the i can get in the way (see Figure 13.20). Its use in these roles should be considered a gimmick (although a useful one), and it shouldn't be employed in general display or titling situations.

Character-Specific Spacing Issues

Certain characters have special spacing demands. The following lists explain the spacing schemes demanded by commonly used characters. When characters are set without adjoining spaces, they are said to be set *closed up*.

Characters Followed by a Space

@ (except in e-mail addresses)

©

® (when used at full size)

• (and all other symbols used to denote items in a list)

§

¶

Characters Preceded and Followed by Spaces

& (except in acronyms like *H&J*)

$+, -, =, \times, \div, \approx, \neq, <, >, \leq, \geq$ (when used in formulas)

Characters Not Followed by a Space

#

$

±

Time Out!

Buy Right

FIGURE 13.20 Where space is tight, the dotless *i* can come in handy.

+ (when used to indicate an increase [+20%] or a positive value [+212°])

− (when used in the same senses as +, above)

Symbols Not Preceded by a Space

%, ‰

* (asterisk)

¢

× (when used to indicate powers of magnitude, as in "a 3× increase")

° (degree symbol)

® (when used as a superior after text)

™

′ ″ (primes)

Characters Set Closed Up (No Spaces)

- (hyphen, except in split modifiers, such as *first- and second-class seats*)

– (en dash)

— (em dash)

Initial Capitals

Using a decorative initial capital to start a paragraph is an ancient device. It's so old, in fact, that it predates lowercase letters, which didn't make their appearance until the eighth century.

The most popular form of this device is the *dropped initial capital,* or *drop cap.* A drop cap is much larger than the text it introduces, and it sits on a baseline several lines down into the paragraph. Illuminated initial capitals are a form of drop caps. A *standing initial capital,* also called a *standing cap* or *pop cap,* is also oversized, but it sits on the first baseline of the paragraph.

Oversized initial capitals nominally have an editorial role to play: to signal a new section of the text or a break in the flow of the narrative. Newspapers and magazines often use subheadings in the same way. A line space or other device is not as emphatic, and the initial cap is a nice decorative touch. When initial caps are used within a text mainly for decorative purposes, though, they can disrupt the sense of the text. Initial caps must always make editorial sense.

Deciding how large a cap should be is a designer's prerogative. Making that design look right is the typesetter's responsibility. It's not always easy.

I HAVE, SENATORS, believed from the first that the agitation of the subject of slavery would, if not prevented by some timely and effective measure, end in disunion. Entertaining this opinion, I have, on all proper occasions, endeavored to call the attention of both the two great parties which divide the country to adopt some measure to prevent so great a disaster, but without success.

FIGURE 13.21 A drop cap that's its own word is a luxury. It takes the pressure off having to relate the oversized letter to the word it's a part of. Too wide a gap between the drop cap and the text can even lead a reader to miss the relation between the two.

Drop Caps

An archetypal drop cap is shown in Figure 13.21. It aligns on a text baseline several lines from the top of the paragraph and top-aligns with the ascent line of the paragraph's first line. It sets flush left. The only thing that makes this one atypical is that the drop cap is in itself a word, which provides some spacing flexibility between it and the text that follows it.

A normal problem with drop caps is that their shape can put them quite a distance from the rest of the word they start. Characters that fall away from the first line of text are particular problems. This gets worse as the size of the drop cap increases. To reduce the gap (or to allow larger drop caps) condensed faces are often used. Sans serif faces are commonly used for drop caps because of their relatively greater graphic impact (these are decorative elements, after all) and because most condensed faces are sans serif. Techniques for aligning drop caps are discussed in "Aligning Oversized Characters" in Chapter 12.

Paragraphs that start with drop caps need extra lead added before them.

DIFFICULT DROP-CAP CHARACTERS

Some letters make better drop caps than others. The best are the ones whose relationship to the smaller text is the closest and most natural: that is, the ones that read best. These tend to have a square aspect: *H, N, M, U, E, F, I, Z*. Others that "reach out" toward the other letters of the word they belong with also function well as drop caps: *T, C, G, K, Y, V, W*. Those that lean away from the text are troublesome: *A, L, B, R, O, D*. Likewise, in some typefaces the tail of the *Q* may create quite a gap between the drop cap and the paragraph text. It may also hang below the baseline, making the indent to accommodate the *Q* deeper than that of other drop caps in the same document. Also keep in mind that most typefaces have a descending capital *J*, which will create a drop cap that may be several lines deeper than others set on the same page and will look out of proportion for that reason.

On the banks of these rivers were divers sorts of fruits good to eat, flowers and trees of such varieties as were sufficient to make ten volumes of herbals; we relieved ourselves many times with the fruits of the country, and sometimes with fowl and fish.

After these two noble fruits of friendship, (peace in the affections, and support of the judgment,) followeth the last fruit; which is like the pomegranate, full of many kernels; I mean aid and bearing a part in all actions and occasions. Here the best way to represent to life the manifold use of

BUT THE QUINCUNX of heaven runs low, and 'tis time to close the five ports of knowledge. We are unwilling to spin out our awaking thoughts into the phantasms of sleep, which often continueth precogitations; making cables of cobwebs, and wilderness of handsome groves.

So he went on, and Apollyon met him. Now the monster was hideous to behold: he was clothed with scales like a fish (and they are his pride); he had wings like a dragon, feet like a bear, and out of his belly came fire and smoke; and his mouth was as the mouth of a lion.

FIGURE 13.22 Devices to help a drop cap relate to the text that it's a part of include (clockwise, from top left) drawing the first line closer to the drop cap; using small caps for the first few words; condensing the drop cap to draw the text closer; and wrapping the drop cap to get the first line closer in a more natural way.

READABILITY ISSUES WITH DROP CAPS

Designers have come up with many techniques to create a visual and logical link between a drop cap and the text that follows them. The most common ones are shown in Figure 13.22.

Moving the first line of text to the left to create a more natural feeling of space between it and the drop cap is a common device. Normally, you can do this only if the drop cap is set as an independent text block or graphic, because automatic drop-cap tools typically give you no control over the shaped text margin. The first few words after such a drop cap are often set in small capitals.

The logical extension of setting an independent drop cap is to have the text wrap the shape of the drop cap. If this is done, the gutter between the drop cap and the first line of text should be kept somewhat narrower than between the cap and the second and following lines. If the spatial relationships of all the lines to the drop cap are equal, its textual connection to the first line will be lost, and it can fail to look like part of the text.

Standing Initial Capitals

Standing caps aren't used very often in long texts because they create such a gap between paragraphs; the bigger the cap, the bigger the gap (unless the preceding paragraph is wrapped around the standing cap, which is hard to do well). These capitals are normally reserved for chapter openings, and they're also

N ow when they were come to the beautiful stream of the river, where truly were the unfailing cisterns, and bright water welled up free from beneath, and flowed past, enough to wash the foulest garments clean, there the girls unharnessed the mules from under the chariot, and turning them loose they drove them along the banks of the eddying river to graze on the honey-sweet clover.

FIGURE 13.23 Although they create page design challenges, initial standing caps are typographically simple. Your main concern is adjusting the kerning between the cap and the smaller text that follows it.

often seen at the start of magazine articles. Standing caps have the same flush-left alignment problems as drop caps, although they are sometimes set with first-line indents that eliminate the issue.

Undercut characters present a special problem when used as standing initial caps. Characters such as *P, T, F,* and *Y* create a natural gap between themselves and the normal-size text that follows them. To close this gap can look very odd, as though the type were marching out from under a tree. Using small caps as a transition for the first few words of text-sized type can help in these situations.

Unlike drop caps, standing caps are quite often set in the same typeface as the text that follows them (see Figure 13.23). In addition, standing caps don't suffer the way that drop caps do when they're set with wide characters, even those from expanded-width typefaces.

Because of the large difference in size between a standing initial cap and the text that follows it, you'll have to hand-kern the gap between the two.

CHAPTER 14

Document Structures and Typographic Conventions

STRUCTURAL ELEMENTS: HEADINGS, EXTRACTS, OUTLINES

NAVIGATION TOOLS: FOLIOS, RUNNING HEADS, JUMP LINES

INDEPENDENT TEXT UNITS: CAPTIONS AND FOOTNOTES

INDEXES AND BIBLIOGRAPHIES

Typography gives a reader clues about how a document is organized. Changes of typeface and point size, for example, reveal the hierarchical relationships among parts of the text. Typography also plays an important graphic role, determining in large part the visual appeal of a page—it can make reading a pleasant meander or a laborious trudge. Typography also creates many of the road signs by which we navigate our way through pages.

While many of the specific decisions about how text should look are made by the designer, others reflect typographic tradition and necessity. This chapter looks at the most common text elements on a page, the typographic conventions associated with them, and the typesetting challenges they pose.

Structural Elements

Text is linear. It starts at the beginning (one hopes) and proceeds to the end. Within that flow—especially in nonfiction work—are often subordinate sections, each of which has its own beginning and end. An outline—the hierarchical arrangement of information within the text—is a reflection of this structure, and the transitions between the sections of such an outline are usually signposted

FIGURE 14.1 A typical arrangement of level-A, -B, and -C subheads. The impact of a level-A head depends on how much of a break it represents in the text. The level-A head on top marks a clear break in the narrative, but probably not a wholly independent section. The level-B head is clearly subordinate, but it still signals a change in focus or emphasis. The diminutive run-in level-C subhead represents little more than a heading for a list, and you wouldn't expect it to set off more than a paragraph or two.

Type Faces Its Big Screen Test

Practicing typography on the Web today is like practicing cabinet-making with a stone axe. The tools for producing legible type in Web documents are frankly neolithic. But the Web stands poised on the brink of the typographical Iron Age, and a new generation of more type-savvy Web design tools are close at hand.

No Shortage of Shortcomings

Typographically speaking, there are three main problems with the Web: limited screen resolution, limited typographic control over the appearance of the documents you create, and limited control over how your documents appear on readers' computers.

Resolution   Most Macintosh screens have a resolution of 72 dots per inch, and most Windows PC have a resolution of 96 dots per inch. Right from the start, this makes print-like typography impossible. And it will remain so until some technological breakthrough (or business decision) substantially increases the resolution of computer screens.

typographically by headings and subheadings. Similarly, since the size and face of the text type are normally consistent throughout a document, the job of indicating the hierarchical status of text sections typically falls to headings and subheadings. One glance at a heading on a page should tell you whether the following text is subordinate to what went before, whether it is equal in importance, or whether a new, superior section is beginning (see Figure 14.1).

Where all the sections of a text are of equal significance (think of a short story, for example), any separations they need can be made with some status-neutral device, such as drop caps or line spaces. These will separate sections without implying hierarchical differences among them.

In a magazine article with no hierarchical structure to speak of, an editor may choose to use informational subheads simply as points of entry, to lure the reader into the text with bits of editorial bait—teasers—even though they add nothing to the comprehension of how the piece is organized. Such subheads may also play an important page layout role, as they do in newspapers, providing space bands that help with vertical justification (for more on this topic, see "Vertical Justification" in Chapter 10). Subheads also help to break up a gray, unillustrated page.

In the book world, the word *title* is generally reserved for the title of a book, and the titles of chapters are called *chapter headings.* Within a chapter, you may have major divisions that get their own *section headings.* Below the section headings are a variety of *subheadings* (also called simply *subheads,* or *side heads*). Their names are not as important as the roles they play.

Chapter Headings

The rule once was that the type for chapter headings should be larger than the text type, but not so large that it should dwarf the text. Although this design fashion is now out-of-date, certain typographic conventions still apply.

Chapter headings are often set in all caps or in caps and small caps. The latter is often favored in journal work. (For more on the use of small capitals, see the section of the same name in Chapter 13.) When chapter headings are set in upper- and lowercase, they are normally—as with newspaper headlines—set in *up style,* or *headline style;* that is, with every major word capitalized. In non-English settings, the *down style,* or *sentence style* (initial cap only), is more common. Down-style headings are also often seen in magazine work when a more informal look is the goal (see Figure 14.2).

In all-caps headings, lining numerals are preferred to old-style figures (a.k.a. lowercase numerals) because they blend in better with the surrounding characters (see Figure 14.3).

In titles and major headings of all kinds (including newspaper headlines) hyphenation should be avoided. When possible, lines should be rewrapped to prevent even hard hyphens from appearing at line's end.

Subheadings

Typographically speaking, subheads have two roles: to graphically separate sections of text and to identify the relative significance of the text they introduce. Their content is a separate issue. Usually, three levels of subheadings in any work are sufficient. Beyond this, the reader is being asked to bear too much of the burden of keeping the structure of the document straight.

The degrees of hierarchical difference among sections vary from document to document. The relative differences should be reflected in the distinctiveness of the subhead styles. In this book, for example, the differences between sections with a *level-A subhead* (the major subhead) and a *level-B subhead* are not great, so it follows that the typographical difference in style between the two is not dramatic but simply indicative.

In documents where level-A subheads divide the text into significant, highly distinctive sections (say, "Symptoms" and "Treatments") they may take on the look of the chapter or document heading itself. For example, they may be set centered, in caps and small caps, and possibly in a rather large point size, although

Despite Tough Talk, Diplomats Doubt Military's Resolve

When the going gets tough, take five...

FIGURE 14.2 In English-language publications, *up-style,* or *headline-style,* titles and headings (top) are considered more formal and emphatic, and *down-style,* or *sentence-style,* headings (below) are more informal and conversational. Nevertheless, outside the English-speaking world, the down style is more common.

THE 20 BEST WAYS TO BEAT THE TAX MAN IN 2003

THE 20 BEST WAYS TO BEAT THE TAX MAN IN 2003

FIGURE 14.3 In all caps or caps-and-small-caps text, old-style figures don't blend in well, as seen in the upper sample here. This illustrates why they're sometimes called *lowercase numerals.* In the lower sample, lining figures hold their own among the capitals and feel better proportioned.

FIGURE 14.4 Some understated typography for a serious document. The level-A subhead represents a major division in the text, in this case distinguishing the section of the Constitution that covers the powers invested in Congress. The level-B subheads are modest and run in. Everything except the preamble is set in the same typeface and point size.

We the people of the United States, in order to form a more perfect union, establish justice, insure domestic tranquility, provide for the common defense, promote the general welfare, and secure the blessings of liberty to ourselves and our posterity, do ordain and establish this Constitution for the United States of America.

ARTICLE I

Section 1. All legislative powers herein granted shall be vested in a Congress of the United States, which shall consist of a Senate and House of Representatives.

Section 2. The House of Representatives shall be composed of members chosen every second year by the people of the several states, and the electors in each state shall have the qualifications requisite for electors of the most numerous branch of the state Legislature.

a centered, all-caps subhead may not need that last element of distinction (see Figure 14.4). In documents where there are many level-A subheads, the distinction between the texts they separate is apt to be less marked, so the subheads themselves can more closely resemble the text, in both point size and typographic impact. They may, in short, resemble the level-B subheads that might be used with the more dramatic kind of level-A subhead just cited.

Typographically speaking, the distinctions among subheads needn't be dramatic, just self-evident. There's no formula that defines how much bigger a level-A subhead should be than a level-B, or a level-B subhead than a level-C. To be visually distinctive, subheads are often set in a contrasting typeface, often a sans serif face, as its role is essentially that of display type. When the text face is used for the subheads, bolder members of the family are typical. The effectiveness of subheads in the regular weight of the face depends much more on point size: Regular-weight subheads have to be larger than bold subheads.

Merely changing weights is not enough to distinguish one level of subhead from another, nor is a subtle change in point size. If point sizes can't change much for some reason, the treatment of subheads has to be distinctive in some other way. For example, level-C subheads are sometimes set *run in* to the text instead of on their own line. Such a subhead would clearly be subordinate to a typographically similar level-B subhead set on its own line (see Figure 14.5). Run-in subheads are normally the same size as the text they run in to, but they're set in bold, italic, or bold italic for contrast.

else thinks the pages are finished, they should be printed and sent to the proofreader. Only when the proofreader has given his or her o.k. can those pages be considered truly finished.

Reading the Text
As you read the text, create a style guide to assure that stylistic aspects of the text are consistent. For instance, if the text starts out calling a person Dr. Ramos, he shouldn't become Mr. Ramos a few paragraphs later. Likewise, if unusual words are put in italics in one part of the text, they shouldn't appear in quotation marks later on.

As you read the text from beginning to end, looking for text errors, also check the following:

Typefaces   Are they used consistently and properly? Keep a log of how italics, bold and bold italics are used and make sure they're used when required and as required.

Proper Spacing   Look out for bad kerning and awkward spacing. For instance, the last letter of an italic passage of text may collide with closing parentheses or quotation marks set in roman. Even roman ascending characters can collide with parentheses if they're spaced too closely.

Logical Sense   Read everything, including drop caps, for logical sense. It's easy to end up with a drop cap followed by a redundant first letter of the word it belongs to. Likewise, make sure that subheads and running heads make sense in the context of the surrounding text.

FIGURE 14.5 Run-in subheads represent about the most modest break in a text you can create. They work best, as shown here, with single paragraphs that are presented almost like a list. Here, the run-in heads are typographically identical to the preceding subhead that stands on its own line. The run-in subheads are followed by an em space.

SUBHEAD SPACING ISSUES

Level-A subheads are virtually always set on their own lines. Their job is visual punctuation as well as content signposting, and to do it effectively they should create a clean break in the flow of the text. They're not a Yield sign for the reader, but a Stop sign, which calls for ample extra lead before it, and probably after as well. (Whenever smaller type follows larger, some extra lead will be necessary, but even more is indicated for level-A subheads.)

Level-B subheads invite the reader to pause but not necessarily to head out and make a sandwich. If there are no level-C subheads, the level-B subheads may not need to be very dramatic. But if they set on their own lines, which is typical, they'll need extra leading before them. If their point size is larger than the text that follows, they'll need some extra lead afterward as well, if only a couple of points or so where the difference is small (see Figure 14.6).

Run-in subheads risk being taken as part of the text rather than a division marker, so they have to be emphatically differentiated from the text that follows. Run-in subheads are often set in bold italics for this reason. If they're not ended with a period, they should be separated from the text by at least an em space. If they're italics of text weight, a wider space is preferable.

FIGURE 14.6 When subheads are larger than the main text, they need extra leading below them as well as above them. Here text set 10/12 has been given a subhead set 12/24. In the top setting, the subhead seems to be sitting down on the text below it, while in the bottom sample the pressure has been lifted with the addition of 3 points of extra lead.

---

no extra lead below subhead

box should line up with the *ascender line* of the neighboring line of type, the imaginary line to which ascending letters of the line reach).

Spacing between Elements

As a proofreader, you should be given a set of master page grids that show the correct positioning of major page elements—how they are positioned on the page grid, and how they should be positioned relative to each other. These positions are generally expressed as baseline

3 points extra lead below subhead

box should line up with the *ascender line* of the neighboring line of type, the imaginary line to which ascending letters of the line reach).

Spacing between Elements

As a proofreader, you should be given a set of master page grids that show the correct positioning of major page elements—how they are positioned on the page grid, and how they should be positioned relative to each other. These positions are generally expressed as baseline

---

OVER THE YEARS, the autumn InnoGraphics conference has been the place where revolutionary products and technologies have been unveiled (or at least announced), but this year there were no revolutions in sight. This is good news for those of us who wouldn't mind if the technology slowed down a little so we'd have a chance to catch up. But this calm for consumers translates into severe nervousness for manufacturers and vendors, who keep looking for another miraculous money maker to save their bacon.

Conference Summary: Day #1

FIGURE 14.7 A cut-in subhead is set into a running indent in mid-paragraph. For emphasis, a contrasting typeface can be used, as shown here, but often a member of the text typeface family is used and set in all caps or caps and small caps.

SUBHEAD INDENTION

A level-A subhead is often set flush left, and the paragraph that follows it is set to match, without a first-line indent. This is another device to make clear that a major break in the flow of text is taking place. Level-B and -C subheads may or may not follow this precedent, and these lesser subheads are often set with indents to match the first-line indents of the text below them.

Centered subheads generally look better over paragraphs without first-line indents, because indents, unless they're very small, tend to make a centered head appear to be pulled off-center.

Run-in subheads can be used with or without paragraph indents, but without indents, they usually do their job better if you add lead above them. When the text has a lot of run-in subheads, the page usually looks more organized if all the paragraphs, including the ones with subheads, are set with indents.

CUT-IN SUBHEADS

Cut-in subheads are nestled into an indent in mid-paragraph (see Figure 14.7). They're sometimes used in technical texts and can act as a kind of level-D subhead that points out a key bit of content in a particular paragraph. They're also often used in newspapers; for example, some articles may get a cut-in labeled "News Analysis" (or something similar) when they're too opinionated or speculative to pass as objective reporting.

> Webster's rhetorical questions that day may not have changed many minds, but they crystallized an argument that had taken many forms over the previous decades:
>
>> This leads us to inquire into the origin of this government and the source of its power. Whose agent is it? Is it the creature of the state legislatures or the creature of the people? If the government of the United States be the agent of the state governments, then they may control it, provided they can agree in the manner of controlling it; if it be the agent of the people, then the people alone can control it, restrain it, modify, or reform it.
>
> Casting the debate in these terms made Calhoun and his states-rights allies sound distinctly less than democratic in their intentions, but the prospect of thus enraging his opponents was never known to encumber Webster.

FIGURE 14.8 Extracts are typically set with matching right and left indents and separated from the main text by extra lead, as shown here. In this case, 1 ½-em indents have been added left and right, and half a line space added above and below. Since the extract is clearly a quote, no quotation marks are needed.

A cut-in subhead has to be set as an independent text element in its own frame; the text has to be set to wrap around it (for more on text wraps, see "Skews and Wraps," in Chapter 12). To use cut-in subheads effectively, then, either the layout has to be nearly final before the subhead is added, or your program has to be able to anchor the subhead's text frame to the main text so that it can move along with it if the text reflows. Such text anchoring is typically a feature of word processors as well as batch-oriented pagination programs, which lay out pages automatically according to a complex set of rules.

Extracts

Passages of quoted text (more than a few typeset lines long) set amid longer text are called *extracts* (see Figure 14.8). There are two traditional ways of setting extracts. One is to set them 1 point smaller than the surrounding text and to the full measure. The other is to set them at the same point size as the text but to indent them from both right and left. The indented style of extract may be set in a smaller type size as well.

In either case, extra lead is needed to set off the extract from the text. The amount depends on the measure, but half a line space (of the surrounding text) is probably a minimum, and a full line space will look more natural.

Outline Formats and Tables of Contents

As noted, outline formats represent the hierarchical structure of a document or presentation. By convention they do this primarily with alignments and indents, and to a much lesser extent—if at all—with typeface and point-size

I. General Introduction
  A. Acknowledgements
  B. Introduction of the Board

II. Summary of Third-Quarter Results
  A. Manufacturing Division
    1. Household Durables
    2. Household Disposables
    3. Light Industrial Equipment
    4. Automotive Supplies
  B. Finance Division
    1. Consumer Credit
    2. Leasing Program

III. Fourth-Quarter Projections
  A. Manufacturing
    1. Domestic Sales
    2. Foreign Sales
  B. Finance Division
    1. Macro Economic
       Considerations
    2. Foreign Exchange
       Considerations
    3. Consumer Credit Outlook
    4. Leasing Prospects

FIGURE 14.9 A simple outline masks a thicket of indents. Here the Roman numerals are set in a flush-right tab column. The capital letters are set flush right in another, as are the Arabic numerals. The text following the Arabic numerals could be set in its own tab column or with an indent on point to get the turn lines to indent and align properly. Note that the turn lines are set with 1 point of leading less than the rest of the outline entries.

contrasts. A table of contents usually relies more on typographic signifiers to present its information. These not only clarify the structure of the information but also make the table more attractive, especially if it's very long.

OUTLINE FORM

The challenge of typesetting an outline is to get everything aligned properly. Outlines typically use alphabetic or numeric indicators to identify topics or headings. These may include Roman numerals (i, ii, iii ...), capital letters, Arabic numerals (1, 2, 3 ...), lowercase letters, and lowercase Roman numerals (i, ii, iii ...). Of these, the only ones that make alignment easy are lining Arabic numerals, because they all have the same width, at least until double-digit numbers are reached.

Figure 14.9 shows a typical outline and the complexity of the indents and alignments needed to typeset it. While an outline may look simple on the page, it can be a nightmare to set. It is, in fact, best set as a table. For the illustrated outline, creating a table allows you to set the Roman numerals in a flush-right column, and the text that goes with them in an adjoining flush-left column. *Turnover lines* (the second and following lines of a text entry that wraps) will align flush left under the first. (These lines are often assigned a hanging indent.)

At the next hierarchical rank, the capital letters (along with the periods that follow them) set flush right in their own column and the text once again follows in its own flush-left column.

If there are no turnover lines, and the outline is not being set with justified margins, you can set the Arabic numerals flush left and separate them from the following text by a fixed space (an en or an em). When there are turnover lines, though, the text must be set in its own tabular column to assure correct alignment. In outlines where Arabic numbers reach 10, you should set them in a flush-right tab column, as you would Roman numerals, in order to maintain consistent alignment.

TABLE-OF-CONTENTS FORM

A table of contents (TOC, for short) is an outline representation of a book. If the headings and subheadings for the book are given their typographic formatting by means of style sheets, your program can create a TOC automatically. (For more on style sheets, see Chapter 17.) It does this by searching through the text for instances of those particular style sheets and copying the text so formatted into an outline. What you end up with is a list of all the heads and subheads in the book, in order, with the page numbers on which they occur. You then specify how that TOC should look, by defining how each entry should be

1. The State of the Art and How We Got Here   **12**

The Building Blocks of Type   13

    Type Design as a Function of Size   14

The Typewriter: The First Desktop Publishing Tool   16

    Escapement   18

      Monospaced Type   19

      Proportional Type   21

    Monotype: Counting Character Widths   23

The Changing Definition of "Font"   26

    Photographic Fonts   27

    Electronic fonts   30

Desktop Publishing Alters the Rules   32

    The PostScript Model   33

      Raster Image Processing   36

      Device Independence   39

    PostScript Fonts   40

FIGURE 14.10 Indents tell most of the story in a table of contents, with progressively subordinate entries getting deeper indents. Here the chapter folio (page number) is set flush right, but only an em space separates the section headings and their folios. This creates a clear visual link between heading and folio without the need for leaders.

typeset and indented. You can also specify how many levels of subheads are to be represented in the TOC. Chapter headings and level-A subheads, for example, may be enough in many cases.

Tables of contents are typically set in a single column, ragged-right. Two-column TOCs tend to look too much like indexes. Chapter titles in TOCs are typographically distinctive, varying from the rest by virtue of point size, weight, and perhaps typeface family as well. They may well reflect the design scheme used to distinguish among heads and subheads within the book, although often only the chapter headings in TOCs get unique typographic treatment; the various subheads are distinguished from one another solely by the depth of their indention (see Figure 14.10).

Extra lead should be added above chapter headings in a TOC beyond that demanded solely by their larger point size. Like chapter breaks within the text, chapter breaks within the TOC have to be distinctive and recognizable at a glance. TOC entries are usually brief and set flush left, possibly quite far from the page number (or *folio*) associated with them, which often sets flush right. To draw a visual link between the two in these cases, TOCs customarily employ leaders (see Figure 14.11). A leader is a series of characters—usually periods—that give the eye a path to follow from text to page number. They also tie the page together, unifying the text area. In some TOCs, only the chapter headings are assigned page numbers, with level-A subheads listed unnumbered on a sort of FYI basis. This format doesn't make for a terribly useful TOC, but it may obviate the need for leaders.

1. The State of the Art and How We Got Here

The Building Blocks of Type 13

   Type Design as a Function of Size 14

The Typewriter: The First Desktop Publishing Tool 16

   Escapement 18

     Monospaced Type 19

     Proportional Type 21

   Monotype: Counting Character Widths 23

The Changing Definition of "Font" 26

     Photographic Fonts 27

     Electronic fonts 30

Desktop Publishing Alters the Rules 32

     The PostScript Model 36

       Raster Image Processing 39

       Device Independence 40

     PostScript Fonts 42

     Imaging PostScript Fonts 45

Output Resolution and Type Quality 46

     The Dark Side of WYSIWYG 48

     Near-WYSIWYG 49

The Shadow of the Word Processor 50

FIGURE 14.11 A standard table-of-contents layout places all the folios (page numbers) flush right and connects them to their section names by leaders. The spacing and alignment of the leader dots are handled automatically by the software.

Navigation Tools

Another class of standard page and document features could be called navigation aids. These tell you where you are in the document, how to get elsewhere, or where your eye should go next. When these elements are badly handled, using a book—especially a reference work or manual—can become a frustrating chore.

In the following sections, we'll look at a handful of the major aids: *page numbers, running heads* and *footers,* and *jump lines* (which tell you where the text that ends in mid-sentence is continued). Indexes are covered in their own section later in the chapter.

Page Numbers, or Folios

The most important thing about folios is that they be positioned on the page where the reader can find them easily. Assume you've just been to the index to locate a reference to something and are now going back to find it in the text. What do you do? You riffle the pages with your thumb to get into the right neighborhood. This means that any book with an index that refers to page numbers must have its folios at the outside edge of the page. Centered is no good (it impedes efficient riffling), and flush against the binding is impossible. For a novel you can put the folios wherever you want (in fact, in this format, they're often centered), because the reader is only casually interested in which page is which (except in cases of boredom).

The most common placement for folios is near the top outside corner of the page (that is, away from the binding). When they're positioned in the bottom outside corner, they're called *dropped folios.* In either position, they may be set flush along the margin of the text area or indented slightly from it (a setting more common among dropped folios). They're sometimes left to hang out into the outer margin of the page, but this isn't typical unless the margins are very wide—hanging the folios tends to make them look as if they're falling off the page. Even when folios are positioned at the top of the page, they are typically dropped to the bottom of chapter-opening pages to get them out of the way of the display type. In some such cases they are omitted entirely.

The point size of the folio is often the same as the text or a point size larger. In publications with few typeface changes (for subheads, for example), folios are typically set in the same face as the text. Where subheads are common and set in a contrasting typeface (particularly a sans serif face), the folios are often set in that face or a complementary one. The setting of the folios often depends on the typographic specifications of the running heads to which they're linked.

OpenType: A Cross-Platform Format   17

Huge, multilingual character sets of up to 65,000-plus characters Relatively smaller font file sizes—which are better for font embedding—thanks to technology from Adobe (Compact Font Format, or CFF, for PostScript OpenType fonts) and Agfa (MicroType Express, licensed by Microsoft, for TrueType OpenType fonts) Automatic glyph substitution, for insertion of alternate forms such as ligatures, fractions, old-style-numbers, titling caps, historical characters, and swash characters Multiple optical sizes within a font family, so that type in various point-size ranges

kerned identically. This will dramatically reduce the size of kerning tables while—more importantly—extending the number of letter pairs that are kerned.

Inside the package OpenType is not an entirely new format. Instead, it's a hybrid, an extension to the TrueType format that adds a "pocket" for PostScript font data, so an Open-Type font can contain either TrueType or Post-Script Type 1 font outlines. According to Adobe and Microsoft, with today's RIPs it makes no difference which kinds of outlines are in there—both are functionally equivalent.

FIGURE 14.12 It's common to wed the folio (page number) to a running head, as shown here. In this case, the two elements are set in typefaces from the same family, although the running head is in Optima Bold Oblique and the folio in Optima Bold roman.

Running Heads

Running heads appear at the top of each page (with a few exceptions) in a book, magazine, or journal (see Figure 14.12). Their role is to tell readers where they are in the book, to tell page rifflers when they're in the area they're looking for, and sometimes, seemingly, just to remind readers what it is they're reading. In other words, sometimes they're valuable navigation aids and sometimes they're merely decorative elements placed by tradition.

Running heads generally appear in pairs, with the one on the left page of a *spread* being the more general, and the one on the right more specific. For the forgetful reader, for example, the publisher may put the author's name as a running head on the *verso* (left) pages and the book's title on the *recto* (right) pages. More useful, perhaps (except in novels with simple numbered chapters), is to have the book title on the left and the chapter title on the right. Or the chapter title on the left (assuming you can remember what book you're reading) and the section name or most recent level-A subhead on the right. In journals, the author's name may be on the left and the article title on the right. An exception to this scheme is in the index, where running heads are often omitted because it's assumed you'll recognize where you are.

Running heads are often associated with folios, with the folio following the running head (on recto pages) or preceding it (on verso pages) and separated from it by some fixed space (at least an em). In these cases, the typographic styles of the folio and running head must relate to each other. A running head in all caps or in caps and small caps, then, may not look good next to a folio set in old-style numerals (lining numerals would be better). Likewise, the two will usually look better if set in the same typeface and the same point size.

Running heads should be at least a full line space (at text leading) above the text area of the page. The exact spacing depends on the page proportions and the other white space on the page. If a rule is set below the running head, it should be at least that same minimum distance above the text, with the running head being pushed up even further.

those who would profit by know
ing the contents of the stolen files.

Spokesmen of both parties deny
any malfeasance, either by dint of
involvement in the break-in or by
having anything to hide in any of
the office's files. Political insiders,
though, believe both to be dissem-
bling, at the very least.   ♦ ♦ ♦

FIGURE 14.13 Jump lines are often
created with symbols instead of text
where the destination of the jump is
obvious. Here a column that ends with
the last word of a paragraph could be
taken for the end of the story were the
jump line not there.

those who would profit by knowing the contents of the stolen files.

Spokesmen of both parties deny
any malfeasance, either by dint of
involvement in the break-in or by
having anything to hide in any of
the office's files. Political insiders,

see "Investigation," page 6

those who would profit by knowing the contents of the stolen files.

Spokesmen of both parties deny
any malfeasance, either by dint of
involvement in the break-in or by
having anything to hide in any of
the office's   **continued on page 4**

FIGURE 14.14 Two samples of classic jump-line style. Jump lines set on
a line of their own are often set in a
face from the same family as the text,
as shown at the top. Run-in jump lines,
as at the bottom, are usually in a contrasting face, often a sans serif set in
a smaller point size.

Jump Lines

Jump lines are short messages to the reader at the end of a column explaining where
the rest of the text is, in cases where it isn't obvious. They appear most often
in newspapers and magazines. The site that the jump line points to is called the
jump page. The jump line includes the folio of the jump page or some other
explicit pointer, such as "back page."

Jump lines without folio references are used in cases where the jump page
is obvious (usually being the next page) but it may not be obvious that the text
jumps at all. This is the case with boxed sidebar text (which the reader may
naturally expect to be completely contained in the box) and footnotes (which
usually don't jump).

Magazine and newspaper layouts may also use symbolic jump lines to indicate graphically or iconically that the text continues without saying where (see
Figure 14.13). The answer is usually obvious (the next page), but the jump symbols are helpful because they allow a column to end at a paragraph break without leading the reader to believe that the text has ended, as well. When using
this device, you should also set end marks (see the next section) to indicate
positively where an article does in fact end.

Jump lines are usually set at least a point size smaller than the text, often
in a contrasting typeface from the same family: italic, bold, or bold italic (see
Figure 14.14). They're also often set in sans serif (usually condensed), which,
having a bolder aspect, may be set in a smaller point size than a seriffed face.
To be distinguished clearly from the text, jump lines are usually set flush right.
In any case, they should get a few points of added lead. If the jump line is
significantly smaller than the text, it can receive this extra lead without slipping
off the baseline grid.

When the only text the jump page contains is the jumped article, the jump
line can merely say, "continued on page x." But if the jump page contains other
articles (as is typical in newspapers), some more specific direction is needed,
pointing to the column number where the jumped text begins or to the title given
to the jumped text. (This title may or may not be the same one it had on the
page where it started.)

In any case, the jumped text should start with a *continued from* statement,
indicating the source page by number or other explicit description. The typographic specs of the continued-from line should be the same as those of the
jump line, except that the continued-from line sets flush left and with extra
leading below it. When jump symbols are used, identical *continued from* symbols
should appear at the top of the jumped text.

END MARKS

End marks are a common magazine device for indicating the end of an article. Savvy readers are supposed to realize that an article is finished only when the end mark appears and to look for a continuation when they reach other columns or pages that end at a paragraph break.

End marks can consist of anything from a simple pi character to a custom I.D. symbol. Most are set flush right on the last line of text. In text set with a ragged right margin, an end mark may have to be indented from that margin if short ragged lines would make it appear to hang too far into space.

Independent Text Units

Apart from the running text of a document and the navigational aids that guide the reader through it, many independent elements (typographically speaking) can populate pages. The most common ones considered here are captions and legends, and footnotes. Each has unique typographic demands.

Captions and Legends

These days, every piece of text beneath, above, or alongside a photo, illustration, or table is called a *caption*. Historically speaking, though, a caption is more akin to a title for that element, like the name of a painting that appears on a little brass plaque on its frame. A longer description of the object (like those accompanying the illustrations in this book) is properly called a *legend,* or *cutline*. Figure 14.15 shows how a caption and legend work together, although this form isn't seen much anymore outside art books. Essentially, then, a legend is an explanation, while a caption is a label, and some legends are short enough **to** be accurately called captions.

Captions are often set centered, although legends are typically set flush left or with justified margins. Captions are also often set in caps and small caps, or in up style, with each major word capitalized. Legends, though, being more textlike and often in complete sentences, are normally set in down style, with only an initial capital, even if they're sentence fragments.

Captions and legends are normally set one or two point sizes smaller than the type used for the main text—smaller than text, but larger than footnotes. While captions are commonly set in the same face as text, legends are usually set in a contrasting face, often an italic from the same family. When subheadings are set in a sans serif face, captions and legends often follow suit. Condensed

THE PONT DU GARD

Built by the Romans about 196 B.C., the Pont du Gard is an aqueduct that was part of a system that once brought water from near Uzés to Nîmes, some 50 kilometers away. It rises 49 meters above the Gardon, and its span is 142 meters.

FIGURE 14.15 This image has a caption (which acts like a title) in addition to a legend (which expounds at length). What are commonly called captions are usually, in publishing parlance, legends.

faces are often favored for legends to keep their line count down, so that the bulk of a legend doesn't compete with the size of the object it describes (especially in the case of verbose authors).

The leading of legends and captions depends on how rigorously they have to align with the page's baseline grid. To make such alignment easier, the leading of a legend is sometimes set to be the same as that of the main text, even though this will make the smaller legend type seem somewhat loosely leaded. In all cases, though, extra lead (on the order of half a line space, based on solid leading) should be added between the caption or legend and the object it describes, and a full line space or so should also be added between it and any text above or below, as shown in Figure 14.16.

Ragged-right legends often appear alongside text with justified margins.

Footnotes and Endnotes

Traditionally, *footnotes* that amplify on points in the text have been positioned on the pages on which they're cited. The logic is that these are, essentially, a kind of parenthetical intended to be intimate adjuncts to the main text. The current tendency, though, is to gang all such notes together at the end of a chapter or book as *endnotes*. Typographically speaking, the two forms are very similar, but from a page layout perspective, endnotes are much easier to deal with.

OpenType: A Cross-Platform Format 17

Huge, multilingual character sets of up to 65,000-plus characters Relatively smaller font file sizes—which are better for font embedding—thanks to technology from Adobe (Compact Font Format, or CFF, for PostScript OpenType fonts) and Agfa (MicroType Express, licensed by Microsoft, for TrueType OpenType fonts) Automatic glyph substitution, for insertion of alternate forms such as ligatures, fractions, old-style-numbers, titling caps, historical characters, and swash characters Multiple optical sizes within a font family, so that type in various point-size ranges can be based on separate sets of character outlines, for finer display type and sturdier characters in small sizes Class kerning, which allows letters with similar shapes (the left sides of c, e, and d, for example) or a single letter with a number of different accents (e.g., À, Á,

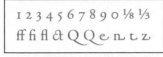

OpenType fonts, with their double-byte file structure, have room for many alternate sorts, including old-style numerals, fractions, alternate ligatures, and characater variants.

kerned identically. This will dramatically reduce the size of kerning tables while—more importantly—extending the number of letter pairs that are kerned.

Inside the package OpenType is not an entirely new format. Instead, it's a hybrid, an extension to the TrueType format that adds a "pocket" for PostScript font data, so an OpenType font can contain either TrueType or Post-

FIGURE 14.16 The legend under the small illustration here has been given extra lead above and below it. By aligning the bottom of the illustration on a text baseline, the smaller legend text can be given half a line space above it and a full line space below it and stay aligned on the baseline grid.

Footnotes that merely acknowledge the sources of cited materials are better placed at the end of the chapter or book, where they're less disruptive to the page design and less intrusive for the reader. Either way, this is generally an editorial decision, not a design decision.

FOOTNOTE POINT SIZE AND LEADING

Footnotes and endnotes are set at least two point sizes smaller than the main text. Usually a practical minimum is 8-point, but some heftier faces may read clearly at 7-point (see Figure 14.17).

When you use fonts that do not include multiple master outlines (see "Multiple Master Fonts" in Chapter 3 for more on this subject), footnote type reduced to this size may become quite hard to read. In heavily footnoted text, then, light or spindly typefaces aren't indicated. Semibold faces may work well in footnote roles, but typefaces based on 6-point (or similar-size) master outlines will provide the best results, as their weight, widths, and x-heights will have been adapted especially for use in small sizes.

Leading has to complement the measure, although footnotes are traditionally set with fairly tight—often solid—leading. Given the ratio of the footnote type size to its measure (appropriate for text-sized type), footnotes are always apt to look tightly leaded. But footnotes are hard enough to read already, so there's no need to punish with overtight leading the reader who's assiduous enough to read them in the first place. Extra lead between footnotes is optional, and as often as not, they're set without it. A couple of points will help, though, if the baseline grid allows it.

Pages of endnotes profit from additional lead between notes. Space for footnotes can be at a premium on the bottom of text pages, but endnote pages will

FIGURE 14.17 The typeface used for your text may determine the size of any footnotes you create. The sample at the top is getting very small and the characters very fine. When set in a semibold member of the same family, its legibility is much improved. A face such as Palatino, with its large x-height and broad proportions, appears to be much larger, even though it's the same point size.

Adobe Garamond, 7/7

[2]Ordinarily, for each paragraph in single-column advertisements, four or five words should be subtracted from the total number permissible, as determined by one of the preceding methods. In double-column advertisements, six to eight words should be allowed for each paragraph used; in triple column advertisements, from eight to twelve words.

Adobe Garamond Semibold, 7/7

[2]Ordinarily, for each paragraph in single-column advertisements, four or five words should be subtracted from the total number permissible, as determined by one of the preceding methods. In double-column advertisements, six to eight words should be allowed for each paragraph used; in triple column advertisements, from eight to twelve words.

Palatino, 7/8

[2]Ordinarily, for each paragraph in single-column advertisements, four or five words should be subtracted from the total number permissible, as determined by one of the preceding methods. In double-column advertisements, six to eight words should be allowed for each paragraph used; in triple column advertisements, from eight to twelve words.

---

usually have plenty of room, and whole pages of small endnote type will look less formidable and gray if punctuated by added lead of a half line space or so.

FOOTNOTE ALIGNMENT

Footnotes are generally assigned first-line indents identical to those in the main text. The indents prevent long passages of footnotes from looking too gray and make it easier for the reader to jump quickly to the correct note (footnote symbols in the reduced size being even tinier than usual). When footnotes are set with first-line indents, you can dispense with extra lead between notes.

Footnotes indicated by numerals or symbols can also be set with hanging indents, leaving the numerals or symbols hanging to the left and all the footnote lines indented by the same amount. Care has to be taken to keep the text alignment consistent when footnote numbers on the same page go from one digit to two (see Figure 14.18). The same is true for endnotes.

Where footnotes are set flush left and the numerals are not allowed to hang, a few points of extra lead should be added between the notes to make them easier to differentiate.

Because many footnotes are quite short anyway (creating the effect of a ragged right footnote block at the bottom of the page), footnotes with turn lines (or *runovers*) are sometimes set with a ragged right margin. More commonly, they take their margin alignment from the style of the main text.

FOOTNOTE SYMBOLS

Footnote symbols—called *reference marks*—appear as top-aligning characters in both the text and at the beginning of the footnote. They are set closed up, with

> [9]Figures based on the 2001 fiscal year, beginning October 1, 2000. Extraordinary income items are not included.
>
> [10]Totals include extraordinary income items: sale of Duquesne plant, Harrison bequest, 1998 IRS settlement.

FIGURE 14.18 In a series of footnotes, it's the alignment of the text lines that counts. Here, where the footnote numbers go from one to two digits, the solution is to keep the text indent consistent and allow the reference marks to effectively set flush right against the text.

no space before the footnote character in the text, and no space after it in the footnote, although in both cases some hand-kerning may be necessary to keep the marks from setting too close to the full-size text.

The occasional or informal footnote can be signaled by a non-numeric character such as an asterisk (*). In works with many footnotes, or in any academic or technical work whose footnotes are apt to be cited in the bibliographies of other works, using numbers as reference marks is obligatory.

There is a standard sequence of non-numeric reference marks when more than one appears on the same page. The same hierarchy is used in tables when numeric reference marks aren't used. The sequence runs like so:

- asterisk (*)
- dagger (†)
- double dagger (‡)
- section mark (§)
- paragraph mark (¶)

In practical terms, if you have a need of symbols beyond the double dagger, you should probably be using numerals. Non-superior characters such as the section mark in footnote roles are not attractive. If numerals can't be used in these situations, it's probably better to skip the section and paragraph marks and to begin using double characters to signal further footnotes: **, ††, and ‡‡.

For texts containing numeric reference marks, it's best to use typefaces whose fonts include a full set of superior characters. Program-generated superiors will look too weak, and they may be nearly illegible when printed in the footnote itself, where they may appear as small as 3-point.

Indexes

Individual index entries are generally quite short, so by tradition and practicality, indexes are set in two columns per page. As with footnotes, the many short lines in an index argue for a ragged right margin, which will eliminate a lot of composition problems. Justified margins may, in fact, go largely unnoticed except when loose lines appear. A ragged margin also lets you take your pick of line-break points, as seen in Figure 14.19. Hyphenation is optional, but indexes are usually easier to read when hyphenation is turned off.

as set by program	with hard-ended lines
Umlaut, 66	Umlaut, 66
Underscore character, rules and, 39	Underscore character, rules and, 39
Underscores, for graphic emphasis, 39–40	Underscores, for graphic emphasis, 39–40
Upper-and-lowercase copy, between rules in tables, 46–47	Upper-and-lowercase copy, between rules in tables, 46–47
Up style, defined, 77	Up style, defined, 77
Utility characters, 43	Utility characters, 43

FIGURE 14.19 Setting an index with a ragged right margin makes it much easier to fix awkward line endings. The second line in the left-hand sample sets wider than its neighbors and creates a widow with its runover folio. Likewise, the line ending with an en dash should be corrected. In the right-hand sample, hard-ending those two lines at better break points creates a much better looking setting.

Index Typefaces and Point Sizes

Indexes are usually set one or two point sizes smaller than the main text. They're typically leaded solid (e.g., 8 on 8, or 9 on 9), although some typefaces may require an extra point of lead. The typeface is the same as that used for the text.

Italics are commonly used for such phrases as *"see also"* references. When such a reference points explicitly to other index entries, those entries are set in roman. When the reference directs the reader to a category or a variety of other index entries, the whole phrase should be set in italics (see Figure 14.20). *See also* statements often end with periods, as they're complete sentences.

In index entries that point to an illustration of the index entry, the page number is often set in bold.

Index Indention Styles

The *keywords* in an index—that is, the main references, listed in alphabetical order—set flush left and need not be capitalized (unless they're proper nouns or names). In a simple index entry, the keyword is followed by a comma and a word space and then the page number. Index entries need no terminal periods. *Subentries* under keywords set the same way: word, comma, page number.

Subentries under a keyword are indented, generally by 1 em. How deep the runover, or turn, lines are indented depends on which of two ways the subentries are handled: *run-in* or *indented*.

RUN-IN INDEX STYLE

In run-in indexes, all subentries following a keyword are set sequentially and separated by semicolons (see Figure 14.21). In such an arrangement, the turn lines in the list of subentries are indented by the same amount, usually 1 em. In some indexes, both the keyword lines and the subentries are run in together.

Red hunts, 856, 858, 910–11

Referendum, Progressive reform, 682

Reform movements, 562–71, 580–596; 20th Century, 623–41, 755 ff. *See also* Abolitionists; Progressive movement; Prohibition; Temperance; Woman suffrage

Reformation, Protestant, 16, 31–5

Religion, 7, 13–16, 34, 67, 119–121; post-independence, 133–36, 219–20, 244, 307; contemporary, 1014–22, 1089. *See also names of individual denominations.*

FIGURE 14.20 This index sample illustrates how "see also" lines should be italicized. When they refer to specific keywords, those words should be set in roman, as they are in the index listing. When they're referred to generically, as in the last line here, the whole phrase sets in italic.

When keywords set on their own line, to avoid confusion their turn lines are indented by 2 ems (or in any case, deeper than the subentries).

The attraction of the run-in style is that it's easy to typeset and it makes for a more compact index. It's disadvantage is that the index is harder for readers to scan quickly and find what they're after.

INDENTED INDEX STYLE

In indented indexes, all subentries begin on their own lines (these indexes are sometimes called *entry-a-line* indexes). In complex indexes, where even subentries may have subentries, separated entries make the structure of the index easier to see. In all cases, indented entries are easier for readers to use.

The difficulty with creating indented indexes is all those indents. To keep the structure of the index clear, all turn lines must be indented deeper by 1 em (or whatever the basic indent increment is) than the most subordinate subentry. In an index with 1-em indent increments and two levels of subentries, then, all turn lines will have to indent 3 ems.

Because every entry and subentry in an indented index can be construed as being its own paragraph, keeping these indents straight isn't as bad as it might sound. Each level of entry can have its own style sheet, setting up both its indent and the depth of its running indent for turn lines. For more on using style sheets, see Chapter 17.

Page-Break Issues in Indexes

Page breaks in indexes can make it hard for readers to know where they are when they look at the top of the first column of the new page. For indented indexes, the convention is to repeat the last superior subentry (with its indent) or keyword and follow it with *(continued),* or simply *(cont.),* set in italics. In run-in indexes, the previous keyword is repeated and handled in the same way. There's no need

FIGURE 14.21 In indented-style indexes (left), each subentry begins its own line. Note that the runover in the keyword line indents deeper than the subentries (and would align with their runovers). In run-in style, all subentries are set consecutively, separated by semicolons. Run-in indexes are more compact but harder to read.

indented style	run-in style

Roosevelt, Theodore, 112, 154, 407–410, 551
  Spanish War, 553, 558-9
  post-1889, 571–75
  foreign policy, 561
  domestic policy, 577–81
  post-1908, 584–90
  1912 campaign, 612–16
  post-1912, 622, 631–33, 655
	Roosevelt, Theodore, 112, 154, 407–410, 551; Spanish War, 553, 558-9; post- 1889, 571–75; foreign policy, 561; domestic policy, 577–81; post-1908, 584–90; 1912 campaign, 612–16; post-1912, 622, 631–33, 655

for a jump line at the end of the previous column, as the punctuation there should make it evident whether or not the entry continues to the next page.

It's easy to have orphans pop up in indexes, as bits of entries or lists of subentries end up at the tops of columns. When indexes are set ragged-right, this is easy enough to fix by hard-ending selected preceding lines to add another line above the orphan. Widows should be handled in the same way.

Bibliographies

Bibliographies are generally set in a smaller point size than the main text and with extra lead between entries. Leading is fairly tight but probably not solid, as measures are apt to be rather wide; bibliographies, like endnotes, are typically set in a one-column format. The extra lead may be eliminated where a series of references are made to works by the same author (see Figure 14.22).

Whereas endnotes are typically set flush left or with an indent, bibliographic entries are normally set with hanging indents 1 em deep.

Writers and editors can organize bibliographic entries in many ways. Just to have some arbitrary standard on which to base the following discussion, let's assume that this is how the content of a normal bibliographic entry is organized:

Omstead, Walter. *The Typesetter's Companion.* San Francisco: Almond Press, 2001.

The author's name can be handled in myriad ways, although all are set in roman (and occasionally in bold roman). Among the most common styles are initial capitals, caps and small caps, all small caps, or last name in all caps and first name with initial cap only.

If the work cited is a book, its title is set in italics, following the capitalization style of your publisher. If the work is a journal or magazine article, its name is usually set in roman with quotation marks, and the title of the magazine is set in italics:

Omstead, Walter. "A Kerning Desire." *The Typesetter's Journal,* August 2001: 64–71.

Harrison, Bentley A. *A Concise History of Typographical Form.* Boston: The Manuzio Foundation, 1951.

Omstead, Walter. *The Typesetter's Companion.* San Francisco: Almond Press, 2001.
————. *A Primer on Type.* New York: McKinley Press, 1999.
————. "A Kerning Desire." *The Typesetter's Journal,* August, 2001: 64–71.

Venable, Millicent. *Of Type and Men.* Los Angeles: Letter Press, 1977.

Williamson, Karl. *The Printed Word: A History.* London: Havisham & Sons, 1960.

FIGURE 14.22 Bibliography entries are typically separated from each other by some added lead, in this case half a line space. The exception is a series of entries by the same author. In these cases, the author's name is typically not repeated but replaced by a series of three em dashes.

When a single author is cited several times in a bibliography, his or her name may be replaced with a 3-em dash in the second and successive entries. Make sure you use a joining em rule or a kerned punctuating em dash so that the dashes connect to form a continuous line:

Omstead, Walter. *The Typesetter's Companion.* San Francisco: Almond Press, 2001.
————. *A Primer on Type.* New York: McKinley Press, 1999.
————. "A Kerning Desire." *The Typesetter's Journal,* August 2001: 64–71.

Acme Mfg. —

12 Boyle Dr. —

Hairston, OH —

Baldco Corp. —

2 Industrial W

Miller, MO

SPECIFYING TABLE STRUCTURES

TYPEFACE, POINT SIZE, AND LEADING IN TABLES

ALIGNMENT AND RULES IN TABLES

TECHNIQUES FOR SETTING TABLES

Tables are the most complex typographic forms you're likely to face. The challenge is all the more difficult because table-setting tools, except for those in high-end systems, still aren't very powerful. This chapter looks at common table conventions and their underlying structures—in other words, at how tables should look. It also addresses how to meet the demands of complex table settings using marginally competent tools. This is a chapter rich in workarounds.

The Structure of Tables

Tables arrange data in horizontal *rows* and vertical *columns*. The top row usually consists of headings that identify the nature of the information below them. The first column, when it contains identifiers that explain the nature of the information in the columns to the right of it, is called the *stub column*. Stub-column entries are often wordier than headings. Apart from the headings, all the morsels of information in the table are called *tab entries* (see Figure 15.1). The whole series of tab entries in one row, taken together, is called a *tab cycle*.

Entries in a single cycle can have different numbers of lines. The table software will automatically take these varying depths into account so that entries in the next row set below the deepest entry in the previous row. You should be able to specify the leading between the first text baseline in the new row and the last baseline of the deepest tab entry in the previous row. In the same way,

FIGURE 15.1 Only when the leftmost column contains entries that
describe the data in the table is this
column called a *stub column.* The only
row that gets a special label is the
heading row, whose entries name the
categories of data in the table.

COMPARING ECONOMY TVs

Model and Size	Cable-Ready	VCR Jack	Remote Control	Contrast Control	Tint Control	Hue Control	Auto-Tuning
Master Color Mark IV 19-inch color	✓	✓		✓	✓	✓	
Global Vision 21 21-inch color	✓	✓	✓		✓		✓
Mega Color II 27-inch color	✓		✓	✓	✓	✓	
Acme All-Band 21-inch black-&-white		✓	✓		—	—	✓
EconoTube 19-inch black-&-white	✓	✓	✓	✓	—	—	✓

you can call for a horizontal rule to be set between rows, again specifying its leading relationships to the deepest tab entry in the previous row and to the first baseline of the row below it.

The columns of a table are separated by *gutters,* just like the columns of a multicolumn page. Where columns are separated by vertical rules, these gutters may be as narrow as 5 or 6 points. When only white space separates tab columns, though, the normal minimum gutter width is 1 em.

Headings or tab entries that span two or more columns are said to *straddle* them. *Straddle heads* often have subheads below them, one for each straddled column (see Figure 15.2). *Straddle entries* are typically used to indicate information that doesn't conform to the general structure of the table. Straddle heads may also appear in midtable, stretching across its full width and dividing it into subsections that share the same column headings (see Figure 15.3).

Full-page tables set sideways, or *broadside,* always have the stub column at the bottom of the page, regardless of whether they're on recto or verso pages.

FIGURE 15.2 When adjoining
columns of a table contain related
information, they often share a straddle
head, as shown here. Straddle heads
are customarily set with rules beneath
them to clarify their relationship to the
columns below them.

Characteristics of Popular Roses

| Common Name | Coloration | | Hardiness | |
	Predominant Color	Secondary Color	Freeze Resistance	Pest Resistance
Tupelo Beauty	Red	Gold	High	Low
American Glory	Red	Pink	High	Low
Martha's Classic	Peach	Gold	Low	High
Lady Godiva	Pink	—	High	High
Pride of Washington	Pink	Red	Low	Low
World's Fair	White	—	Low	Low

Roxie Downtown	6/20	6/21	6/22	6/23	6/24	6/25	6/26
Goldfinger	11:30a	8:30p	8:30p	11:00p	11:30a	11:30a	8:30p
Dr. No	2:00p	11:00p	11:00p	8:30p	2:00p	2:00p	11:00p
Thunderball	Every day at 9:00a, 4:30p, and 6:15p						
You Only Live Twice	8:30p	11:30a	11:30a	11:30a	8:30p	8:30p	11:30a
Diamonds Are Forever	11:00p	2:00p	2:00p	2:00p	11:00p	11:00p	2:00p
Roxie Uptown, Roxie Crosstown							
Hell Drivers	11:30a	8:30p	8:30p	11:00p	11:30a	11:30a	8:30p
Marnie	2:00p	11:00p	11:00p	8:30p	2:00p	2:00p	11:00p
Zardoz	Every day at 9:00a, 4:30p, and 6:15p						
Outland	8:30p	11:30a	11:30a	11:30a	8:30p	8:30p	11:30a
The Untouchables	11:00p	2:00p	2:00p	2:00p	11:00p	11:00p	2:00p

FIGURE 15.3 This table is simplified by using straddle entries ("Every day at …") that eliminate redundant information. It also has a straddle head in midtable that changes the focus of the timetable without repeating the dates in the top heading.

In terms of information design, tables these days are simpler; they tend to summarize rather than present minute details. From a graphic design standpoint, however, tables have become more decorated and complex. Where tables once tended to be typographically somber—often set in a single point size and typeface—much more typographical color and variation are now the norm.

How Table Structures Are Specified

The margins of a table's columns are defined by *tab values.* The tab values are counted from the left margin of the table: that is, from the left-hand margin of the stub column. The margins of tab columns are *hard,* just like those of any other column of text, and once text typed into a tab column has filled its measure, it will wrap to the next line and continue there.

This is an important distinction between typographic tabs and word processing tabs. Word-processor tabs are soft; they have no power to define the width of a column of type. They are merely points within the overall page measure to which you can make the cursor jump or to which you can push bits of text by hitting the Tab key. Controlling turn lines (runovers) is almost impossible with word-processor tabs (see Figure 15.4). Except for tables with no turn lines, word-processor-style tabs are worthless.

Traditionally, computerized table-setting programs have defined table column structures one row at a time. To define the columns, you specified the width of the stub column, the width of the gutter to its right, the width of the second column, the width of the gutter to its right, and so forth. If you didn't define new column widths for the next row, the program would assume that the

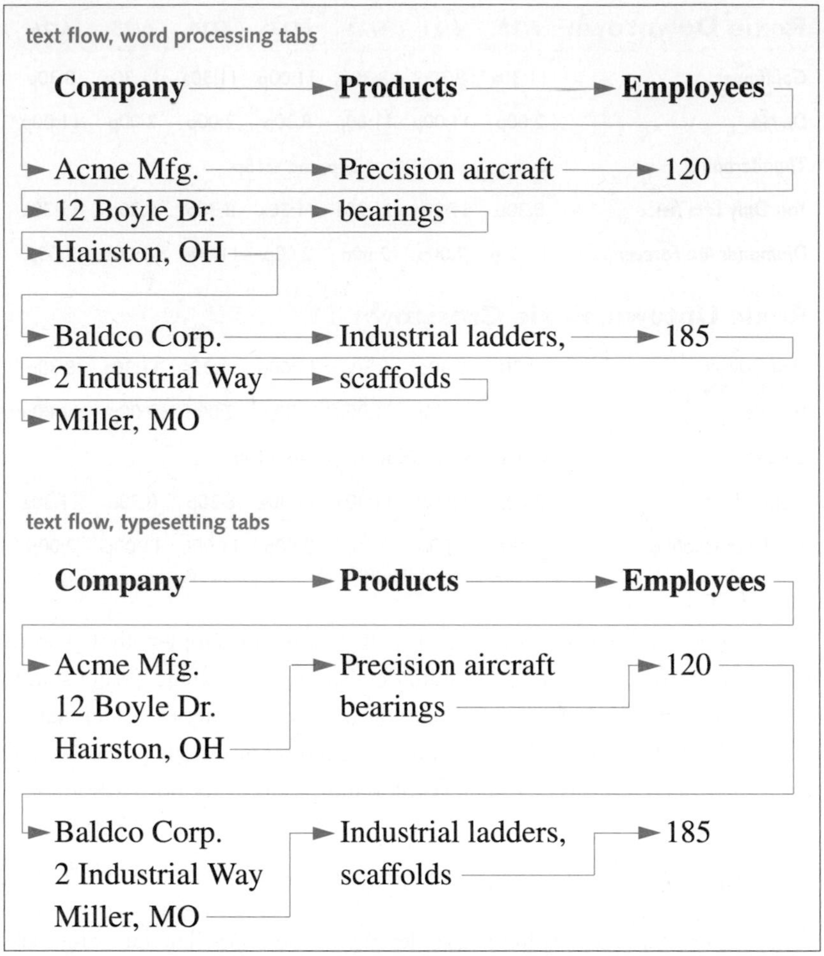

FIGURE 15.4 Word-processor-style tabs do not support runovers, so text has to be entered in the sequence shown in the top diagram. To add another line in the middle of one of these addresses will require a lot of retyping. The lower diagram shows the text flow in a table set with typographic tabs. Here each tab entry is completed before the typist continues to the next one. Each tab entry is, in effect, a small column of type by itself.

values for the previous row stayed in effect. But you could design a table in which each row had unique column widths; the tab values of each row were independent of the others. Between rows, you could add lead or set a rule with any leading you cared to specify.

Today, most popular table-setting software eschews this approach in favor of one that sets up a simple spreadsheet-like grid that you fill in one "cell" at a time (see Figure 15.5). This approach makes it easy to set simple tables and nightmarish to set complicated ones.

PROBLEMS WITH THE SPREADSHEET TABLE METAPHOR

The spreadsheet metaphor is an attempt to shoehorn the many kinds of tables into a single familiar format compatible with the WYSIWYG working style. Software developers have also found that a grid allows data to be easily imported from spreadsheets and databases that use this same organizational form.

Common Name	Coloration		Hardiness	
	Predominant Color	Secondary Color	Freeze Resistance	Pest Resistance
Tupelo Beauty	Red	Gold	High	Low
American Glory	Red	Pink	High	Low
Martha's Classic	Peach	Gold	Low	High
Lady Godiva	Pink	—	High	High
Pride of Havana	Pink	Red	Low	Low
World's Fair	White	—	Low	Low

The fundamental flaw of this approach is that what you want to do as a typesetter is overridden by the constraints of the grid. You can't make one cell wider without making all the cells in its column wider. You can't hang characters beyond the edge of a cell because that would put them in an adjoining cell, and you're not allowed to open up gutters between rows or columns of cells. You and the type you need to set must accommodate yourselves to the grid.

Each cell in the spreadsheet-style table is essentially a tiny text frame, with all of the complications that the text-frame metaphor brings with it (for more on this, see "Text Frames and Grid Alignment" in Chapter 12). Among such complications is an uncertainty about how far below the top of the cell the first baseline of the tab entries will set, as this distance varies from typeface to typeface. This raises the likelihood that mixing typefaces within a table will cause poor base alignment from cell to cell within a row.

The grid structure for a table complicates defining gutters—the spaces between columns—as well as the spaces between rows. All the table cells are butted up against each other and appear that way onscreen. Programs may specify gutter widths in a number of ways, from "space between columns" to cell-by-cell "text insets," which indent the text of each tab entry from the edges of its cell. But you normally never get to see your gutters displayed onscreen as you would with normal text-column gutters, and often the only way to see the cell boundaries at all is to stroke them with a rule. In any case, if you can't see the margins of the gutters, you will almost never know why your text is aligning the way it is. Are those tab entries flush against the gutter? Or are they set on an indent? (See Figure 15.6.)

FIGURE 15.5 In a spreadsheet-style table, every tab entry must reside in a cell, as seen in this onscreen view. Cells can be combined, as they have been to create the straddle heads at the top. But to retain the grid structure, cells normally cannot have unique widths, and changing the width of one changes the width of all the cells in a column. Gutters are nowhere to be seen.

	1st Quarter		2nd Quarter	
	2000	2001	2000	2001
OEM Sales				
Eastern Region	$ 617,995	$ 788,500	$ 694,605	$ 880,005
Midwest Region	746,831	677,498	529,775	671,774
Southern Region	553,880	995,640	901,442	705,644
Western Region	1,876,034	2,880,769	1,705,970	998,777
Total	$3,794,740	$5,342,407	$3,831,792	$3,256,200

	1st Quarter		2nd Quarter	
	2000	2001	2000	2001
OEM Sales				
Eastern Region	$ 617,995	$ 788,500	$ 694,605	$ 880,005
Midwest Region	746,831	677,498	529,775	671,774
Southern Region	553,880	995,640	901,442	705,644
Western Region	1,876,034	2,880,769	1,705,970	998,777
Total	$3,794,740	$5,342,407	$3,831,792	$3,256,200

FIGURE 15.6 Without being able to see onscreen the margins of the column gutters as a frame of reference, you'll find it impossible to tell why the text entries are aligning where they do. In the upper view, the table is seen as it would appear onscreen without rules assigned to any of the table-cell boundaries. You can't see the gutters or how the text relates to them. In the lower view, all the cell borders have been stroked to make the cells visible, but you still can't see where the gutters are and what indents, tabs, or other alignments might be in effect.

The situation is made even worse if your program defines gutters by specifying text insets. To fix a gutter between two columns, you'll have to divide the width of the gutter in two; you use half of that value to reset the right-hand inset of the cells in the first column, and the other half to reset the left-hand inset of the cells in the second column.

When you specify horizontal rules in a spreadsheet-style table, the rule above a row corresponds to the top of that row's cells, or frames. As we've already seen, that makes ambiguous the leading between the first line of text in those cells and the rule above them. Likewise, the cell metaphor doesn't always allow you to specify (or even anticipate) the leading relationship between the baseline of the last text line in a cell and the bottom of the cell (where a rule below the row would set). In some programs, this offset at the bottom of the cell is measured from the cell edge to the baseline of the last line of text, which is the only logical way to do it. (For more about this problem, see "Leading of Rules" later in this chapter.)

First-Half Sales by Division, 2001 vs. 2000

| | 1st Quarter | | 2nd Quarter | |
	2000	2001	2000	2001
OEM Sales				
Eastern region	$ 617,995	$ 788,500	$ 694,605	$ 880,005
Midwest region	746,831	677,498	529,775	671,774
Southern region	553,880	995,640	901,442	705,644
Western region	1,876,034	2,880,769	1,705,970	998,777
Total	**$3,794,740**	**$5,342,407**	**$3,831,792**	**$3,256,200**
Retail Sales				
Eastern region	$ 26,995	$ 38,960	$ 35,332	$ 36,719
Midwest region	56,831	58,422	61,666	66,044
Southern region	117,051	121,942	112,545	115,528
Western region	206,774	286,008	210,115	210,773
Total	**$ 407,651**	**$ 505,332**	**$ 419,658**	**$ 429,064**
Total Sales	**$4,202,391**	**$5,847,739**	**$4,251,450**	**$3,685,264**

FIGURE 15.7 While hierarchical relationships in headings are handled with straddle heads, in the stub tab they're indicated with typographic emphasis and indention. Here, the main headings in the stub tab are in bold, and the subheadings are indented. The bold "Total" lines are indented yet further to make them distinguishable at a glance.

Often, the only way you can specify these spatial relationships in a spreadsheet-style table is to set the table in your desired typeface, point size, and leading; print a proof; measure the leading by hand; and then adjust the values for the text insets to net out at the correct leading value. Bad.

Typeface, Point Size, and Leading Specifications

From the perspective of their function, tables don't require much typographical variation. Normally, the organization of a table makes clear the relationships among the information "packets" it contains. In fact, a typographically bland presentation may actually help reader comprehension, by eliminating visual distractions and unnecessary forms of emphasis and distinction. If the typeface family used for the text includes a condensed version, this is often chosen for table work because it's so much more economical of space.

In general, tables are set one or two point sizes smaller than the main text, and all type within a table is set in the same point size. Smaller type in this kind of setting doesn't affect legibility, and it allows tables to set much more compactly. A common size for tables is 8-point. Because there is so much white space in tables, leading can often be set solid or nearly so.

Straddle heads and their subheads are an exception to this general rule. These are usually typographically distinct from each other to clarify their relationship. Straddle heads may be set in caps and small caps, for example, while their subheads may be set in caps and lowercase. In the stub tab, primary entries may be set in bold to distinguish them from the subcategories beneath them, even though these may already be indented (see Figure 15.7).

$ 64,920.69
5,051.17
17,668.58
(9,794.33)*
27,246.80
$105,092.91

FIGURE 15.8 When the numbers in a column all have the same number of characters to the right of a decimal point, they can be set flush right. But if any of the entries have additional characters, as shown here, decimal alignment is needed to keep all the numbers properly arranged.

Alignments in Tables

You can specify both the horizontal and vertical alignment of tab entries. In horizontal terms, they can be flush left, flush right, centered, justified, or aligned on a decimal point or other specified character.

Justified margins in table settings are rarely if ever used; the narrow widths of table columns make good composition of such settings almost impossible. Decimal-aligned entries appear to set flush right, but if one entry is expressed to more decimal places than the others (or is extended by characters such as footnote reference marks or parentheses), the true nature of the alignment becomes apparent (see Figure 15.8).

Vertically, the entries can top-align (start on a common baseline), bottom-align (end on a common baseline), or center (be centered vertically between the ascender line of the first line of the longest entry in the cycle and the descender line of its last line), as seen in Figure 15.9. Again, vertical alignments within cells in spreadsheet-style tables are tricky: Tab entries are apt not to center well without a lot of handwork because you lack adequate control over the distances between the text and the top and bottom of its cell.

INDENTION IN TAB ENTRIES

First-line indents are not used in tables. If a tab entry is so long that it needs a paragraph break, it's too long to be a table entry in the first place.

Multiple-line stub-tab entries are set with hanging indents, usually 1 em deep. Where stub-tab entries have subcategories beneath them, these are also indented, again usually by 1 em. Other turn lines in a table are set flush left (or centered, if that's the alignment in effect).

Rules in Tables

Rules are used less and less to divide the sections of tables; they tend to make a table look too busy. Vertical rules—which separate columns—have practically disappeared. In general, rules are reserved for complex tables, which can profit from visual punctuation that separates distinct zones of the table, clarifying both its structure and the relationships of the data within it.

In those tables that do have vertical rules, headings should be centered. Flush-left headings set in boxes look awkward.

Tables that have a horizontal top (or *head*) rule should also have a bottom (or *tail*) rule. The table's caption (or *title*) appears over this top rule and is set centered or flush left. A straddle head is typically set with a rule that extends over the subheads it embraces, to clarify its relationship with them.

Product and Manufacturer	Rated Speed, in Pages per Minute	Time Between Repairs, in Months	Warranty Coverage
SpotFlash 300 Lightning Printer Co.	8	10.25	Electronics 1 year; moving parts 90 days
QwikLaser 10 Qwik Corp.	10	16.0	All parts 6 months
LightWrite II LitePen Ltd.	14	8.1	All parts, 8 months

FIGURE 15.9 This small table shows all the forms of vertical alignment of tab entries. The two-line "Product and Manufacturer" heading is center-aligned on the three-line headings to its right. The three column headings bottom-align, while the entries in each tab row top-align.

The weights of rules in tables aren't prescribed, but top and bottom rules are normally heavier (though they may be only a half-point thick) than rules inside a table. Top and bottom rules are normally the same weight, but the top rule may be heavier. A double rule is often used in place of a heavier top rule; this may be a *Scotch rule* (in which the upper of two rules is heavier).

Table-Setting Techniques

There are two ways to set a table. One is to define the table structure and enter all the data yourself. The other is to import the data from a spreadsheet or database and let your program build the basic table structure for you.

Typesetting and page layout programs have import filters (format converters) for data stored in popular spreadsheet and database formats. These include native file formats (such as .xls files from Microsoft Excel) as well as generic formats such as comma-delimited ASCII (in which data from a spreadsheet or database are exported as a continuous text stream, with cell entries separated from one another by commas). When you import such a file, the program builds a provisional table containing the appropriate number of rows and columns. Data in a native file format usually keeps any typographic formatting it was given in its original application.

If you're setting the table from scratch, your first step is to rough in values for its column widths. Spreadsheet-style table programs ask you to specify the number of rows and columns for your table and present the results as a simple grid, with each table cell displayed with enough depth for one row of text. Depending on how your program works, you then key in the data cell by cell or tab by tab.

Base the widths of your columns on the widths of their entries and adapt the headings to fit. If you base the column widths on the headings, you lose control over the amount of white space between the columns below them, and

FIGURE 15.10 The tab entries in these columns are very narrow, particularly in the bulleted "Controls" columns at the right. To prevent too much white space in cases like these, the headings have to be made as narrow as possible. Here some have been stacked several lines deep, and those under the straddle head have been rotated to save space.

| ECONOMY 17-INCH MONITORS | | | | Controls | | | | | |
Manufacturer and Model	List Price	Actual Viewing Area (diagonally, in inches)	Maximum Resolution (in pixels)	Convergence	Distortion	Degaussing	Color Temp.	Color Tuning	Digital Memory
HarleyScan 17 Harley Systems, Inc.	$399	16.1	1600 × 1200	■		■	■	■	■
KleerVision 17 Mammoth Computer Systems, Inc.	$329	15.9	1280 × 1024	■	■			■	■
BXC 1700 Monitor Group, Ltd.	$355	16.5	1280 × 1024	■		■	■	■	■
FlatPro 17 Custom Peripherals Co.	$429	17.0	1600 × 1200	■	■	■	■	■	■

it's these spaces that dominate the look of the table. It's easier to adapt the headings to the table data than vice versa (see Figure 15.10).

Once all the text is in the table, specify the typeface(s), point size, and leading. Specify the alignments of all the tab entries. Add any rules that the design calls for. At this point you can see all the design problems in the table. There will probably be plenty.

Balancing Column Widths and Gutters

When a table has to fit within a certain measure, the widths of the columns should be adjusted so that the longest entry in the rightmost column (which could be its heading) ends at or very near the right-hand margin. If that right-most column has a lot of white along its right-hand side, the table will look too narrow, even if it has been set with rules above and below it to define its width.

In general, the gutter widths should appear equal. Because tab entries usually have differing widths and may not come close to filling the measure of a column, it may take quite some amount of fiddling with column borders and gutter widths to create a balanced look. If one gutter looks far too wide, it should be narrowed, with the excess space distributed among other gutters. Since the overall measure of most tables is dictated by the page layout, you rarely have the option to simply make the whole table narrower.

(Note that in the case of spreadsheet-style table software, making one column wider may simply make the whole table wider, instead of preserving the overall table measure by causing other columns to become narrower. This can make adjusting column measures a very trying experience.)

Often the width of the headings causes unbalanced column spacing. Breaking these into two or more lines may help. Multiple-line headings look best

INCOME, MONTH BY MONTH

	January	February	March	April	May	June	July	August	September	October	November	December
Publishing												
Circulation												
New subscriptions	33,200	37,895	29, 995	38,965	21,440	27,755	36,625	33,035	38, 540	51,760	54,005	58,445
Subscription renewals	5,765	4,315	5,900	6,005	7,900	8,100	10,675	11,765	14,450	17,200	19,655	22,750
Advertising												
Display ads	98,875	94,005	99,220	91,750	86,655	94,050	96,235	99,530	89,545	101,550	103,335	112,650
Directory ads	42,400	38,650	38,675	32,665	38,330	36,665	38,115	36,285	42,555	47,510	51,435	56,055
Classifieds	16,345	11,205	14,000	13,435	15,385	18,945	16,050	14,225	18,350	21,885	24,775	27,555
Inserts	9,500	8,540	9,050	9,855	10,530	11,235	14,335	17,025	18,435	24,445	27,005	31,950
In-the-bag inserts	11,115	10,750	13,655	14,960	18,995	18,665	18,905	15,220	17,550	19,405	23,310	30,055
Seminars & Expos												
Seminar admissions	55,870	42,110	48,335	44,945	48,885	44,225	44,445	48,930	51,050	54,055	58,445	61,555
Expo entry fees	22,605	25,675	22,775	28,705	26,650	27,250	29,055	25,540	28,400	31,910	33,295	36,100
Transcript sales	5,000	5,000	5,000	2,500	2,500	5,000	7,500	5,000	7,500	10,000	12,500	15,000
Licensing fees	150	750	550	175	1,050	1,550	850	150	600	775	1,250	1,700

when they bottom-align: that is, when their last lines share a common baseline. Do not hyphenate column headings.

Two exceptions to the ideal of balanced gutters are the gutter to the right of the stub column and the gutters that flank columns surmounted by a straddle head. The gutter to the right of the stub tab is often left wider simply because the stub-tab entries are a sort of heading in themselves and as such are distinct from the table data. The wider gutter emphasizes the distinction.

Likewise, an en space is often added to the widths of gutters on either side of a series of columns that share a straddle head. Again, the extra space draws attention to the commonality of the straddled columns and their distinction from the columns around them.

Leading in Tables

The leading of text in tables is straightforward. Runovers in headings and tab entries are normally set solid or with one extra point of lead. Where consecutive rows of data are closely and logically associated, they're set with the same leading scheme.

When there is a break in the sense of the content of a series of rows, extra lead is added to distinguish one group of rows from another. A half-line space is typical in these situations. Where the break in continuity is more significant, more lead—up to a full line space—is indicated (see Figure 15.11).

FIGURE 15.11 The relationships among entries in the stub tab can be clarified through extra leading. Here half-line spaces are used to indicate minor divisions and full-line spaces indicate the major ones. Distinctions among classes of information based on their leading help the structure of a table to be apparent at a glance.

FIGURE 15.12 Rules have baselines just like type, as this illustration shows. Seen at 300 percent, this 12-point type has a 4-point rule set on 12 points of lead below it. This creates an 8-point open space between the top of the rule and the text's baseline.

LEADING OF RULES

Setting the correct leading of horizontal rules in tables may be cumbersome, as most programs do not let you simply specify the leading for a rule. In traditional typography, a horizontal rule has its own baseline. To position a rule beneath text, then you simply specify its weight, length, and leading. If you set a 4-point rule on 12 points of lead, there will be 8 points of space between the top of the rule and the baseline of the text above it (see Figure 15.12).

Page layout programs and the table programs designed to work with them, though, typically treat rules as graphic elements, not as type elements. This means that rules are usually treated as *stroked paths,* like those in illustration programs, and these strokes are positioned according to their center line, not their baseline (see Figure 15.13). When you make such a rule heavier, the extra width is added to both sides of the center. When that rule is set under text, making it heavier pushes it off its nominal baseline, changing its leading.

Spreadsheet table programs normally add rules by stroking the edges of the affected cells. Any rule you add beneath a row of cells has half its weight in the row of cells above it and half in the row below it. To specify the leading of such a rule, you first have to reckon the distance from the bottom edge of the cell to the last text line above it and then add to that amount half the weight of the rule. This is clearly not a system designed by typesetters.

Meanwhile, you've also thrown off the leading of the text after the rule, as half the thickness of the rule now intrudes into the cell below it. As pointed out earlier, the distance from the first text baseline in a cell to the top of the cell may already be ambiguous, and adding the rule makes calculating the baseline of that text even more complicated. To avoid losing your mind, take copious notes about the adjustments you make to position your rules so that your treatment of them can be consistent throughout the table (and in the future).

That said, the proper leading for rules will vary slightly with the width of the table. Very wide tables may need extra leading to emphasize the divisions that the rules create. Generally, whether the rule is above the text or below it, your goal is to open a horizontal white band between text and rule that's about two-thirds the height of the leading (e.g., 6 points in 9-point-leaded type).

Given the complexity of leading rules well with today's tools, it's a good thing (arguably a consequence) that the heavy use of rules in tables is out of style.

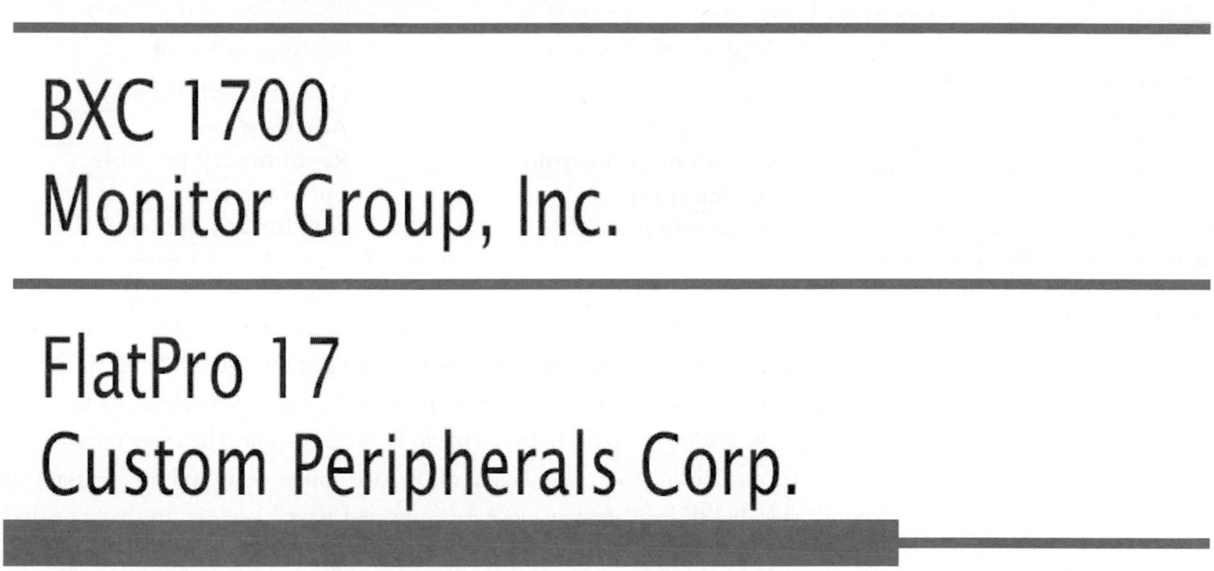

BXC 1700
Monitor Group, Inc.

FlatPro 17
Custom Peripherals Corp.

CENTERING TEXT BETWEEN RULES

In financial tables in particular, lines of type are often centered between two horizontal rules. When the type involved is set in all caps or consists of nothing but lining numerals, you can mechanically center it. That is, you can simply assure that the distance from the cap line to the upper rule is the same as the distance from the baseline to the lower rule.

If your program can set the first baseline in a table cell based on the cap height of the text, the program's vertical centering command will create this even space automatically. This works because the program will fix a baseline that pushes the tops of the capital letters or lining figures hard up against the upper edge of the frame. When you then tell the program to vertically center that text, all it has to do is divide the space between the baseline and the bottom of the cell into two halves and place one half above and one below the text.

If your program can't specify where the first baseline should be, you may have to find a leading value by trial and error that will allow the centering command to do its work precisely. Note that in some programs the weight of the rule may affect your calculations, as they calculate the position of the type relative to the cell or frame edge and not the edge of the rule that overlays it.

In any case, your program will not be able to effectively center text set in caps and lowercase, particularly if the text has descenders. In these cases you have to adjust by eye the positioning of the text between the rules, because although the capitals may be mechanically centered, the descending letters and the preponderance of lowercase letters will make the whole line look as if it's setting too low (see Figure 15.14).

FIGURE 15.13 An enlarged screen view shows how the rules in spreadsheet-like tables are made heavier from their centers outward instead of from their baselines up. This makes the leading relationship between rule and tab entry ambiguous. The text in both of these cells is set with the same offset from the bottom of the cell, but the program doesn't take into account the thickness of the rule. The result is much tighter leading in the lower cell.

FIGURE 15.14 When programs center text between rules, they center the capital letters and let the rest follow. As seen in the left-hand sample here, this approach leaves the text looking too low, especially in lines with descenders. Text between rules has to be optically centered so that it appears centered even though it may not be mechanically centered.

capitals centered between rules	text raised by 1 point
Due to custodian	Due to custodian
Advisory fee	Advisory fee
Recoupment payable	Recoupment payable
Servicing fee	Servicing fee
Dividends payable	Dividends payable

baseline centered

Fees payable

centered on cap height

Fees payable

visually centered

Fees payable

FIGURE 15.15 Getting text to appear centered between rules is tricky, and the eye is your only guide. All-caps text and lines of numbers are easy, but for upper- and lowercase text, you must balance the space above the ascenders and mean line with the space below the descenders and baseline. The text itself, then, will affect how centered the type looks, as will the typeface, which can vary in x-height and ascender and descender lengths.

For either all-caps or caps-and-lowercase text, if your program allows you to assign specific leading values to the rules and the text between them, start with a leading value from the text baseline to the upper rule that's twice that of the leading from the bottom rule to the text baseline. The exact numbers will vary according to the cap height of the face you're using and the weight of the rule, but this will get you close. For caps-and-lowercase text, the baseline of the text will have to be raised slightly more, relative to the rules above and below (see Figure 15.15).

Aligning Heads and Tab Entries

Nowhere is visual alignment—eyeballing it—more common or important than in tables. Heading widths vary, column widths vary, tab-entry widths vary, and white space permeates everything. Nothing is apt to look properly aligned without some manual adjustments.

Getting tab entries to appear properly aligned below their headings is one such chore. Flush-left headings over flush-left tab entries may look out of whack if the tab entries are much wider than the heads. Centered heads over almost any kind of tab entries (except the rare multiline centered text) will look off-center (see Figure 15.16).

In fact, when column heads consist of a single line of type, it's often best not to think of them as aligned in any particular way. They'll usually look best when they look centered over the tab entries below them, but your program's centering command will rarely work in this regard. Tab entries set almost exclusively flush left (for text entries) or flush right (for numeric entries). In either case, you're trying to center the heading over not just the type below but also all those empty spaces that fill out the rest of the column's measure. To get a heading to look centered, you'll have to apply a right or left indent to it.

This may take more than a little fiddling, because unless the column's tab entries are all the same width (or nearly so) they won't create a neat shape over which to center. One margin or other is apt to be quite ragged, so as with centering a heading over rag-right text (see "Visual Alignment" in Chapter 12), you have to determine where the apparent margins of the column are and center the head over that. Because the "rag" in a tab column can be far wilder than any

Algeria, population by region *(cont.)*

Region	Area	Population	Population per km²
Ech-Cheliff	8,676.7	1,260,000	145
Laghouat	112,052.0	354,427	3.1
Batna	14,881.5	646,330	43
Bejaïa	3,442.2	600,320	174
Biskra	109,728.0	615,015	5.6
Béchar	306,000.0	174,568	0.48
El-Boulaïda	3,703.8	1,041,487	281
Bouira	4,517.1	412,225	93
Tamanrasset	556,000.0	57,852	0.1
Tebessa	16,574.5	392,188	23
Tilimein	9,283.7	620,540	66
Tizi-Ouzou	3,756.3	959,640	28

FIGURE 15.16 By making the gutters of this table visible (top), you can see the alignment problems it presents. The best way to get a harmonious alignment between headings and column entries in this case is to adjust the tab values for the column entries so that they're centered visually under their headings. Getting an uneven decimal-aligned column, like the rightmost column, to appear balanced will take some fiddling.

Algeria, population by region *(cont.)*

Region	Area	Population	Population per km²
Ech-Cheliff	8,676.7	1,260,000	145
Laghouat	112,052.0	354,427	3.1
Batna	14,881.5	646,330	43
Bejaïa	3,442.2	600,320	174
Biskra	109,728.0	615,015	5.6
Béchar	306,000.0	174,568	0.48
El-Boulaïda	3,703.8	1,041,487	281
Bouira	4,517.1	412,225	93
Tamanrasset	556,000.0	57,852	0.1
Tebessa	16,574.5	392,188	23
Tilimein	9,283.7	620,540	66
Tizi-Ouzou	3,756.3	959,640	28

found in text, such visual alignment can be nearly impossible. Many compromises may have to be made. In general, aligning heads over tab columns is easier when the heads are either quite a bit wider or quite a bit narrower than the average tab entry—you have some room for error. When the widths of heading and entries are very close, minor misalignments are more obvious.

High-Season Weather, Valros Beach

	June	July	August	September
Average high temperature	74°	86°	91°	81°
Average low temperature	55°	71°	74°	68°
Average number of sunny days	19	26	27	17
Average relative humidity	45%	32%	25%	53%
Average rainfall	2.3″	.8″	.2″	3.7″

Alignment Issues in Numeric Tables

Tables of figures—particularly financial tables—present a range of complicated alignment problems. Programs that build tables using a spreadsheet metaphor introduce additional complications (as well as produce the occasional solution).

Numbers in columns generally *decimal-align.* That is, all the decimal points in a column stack in a straight line, with numerals ranging to their left and right. When all such numbers are expressed to the same number of decimal places, such columns of numbers appear to be set flush right. (Indeed, they can be specified to set flush right.)

Note that decimal alignment should be used only when all the values in the column are of the same sort (monetary amounts, for example). If the decimal point in one entry refers to money, but the one below it refers to dimensions (or temperatures, or whatever else), the entries should be aligned in some other way: flush right, flush left, or centered. Decimal-aligning them implies that all the values in the column are comparable, which in these cases they're not (see Figure 15.17).

Decimal-alignment difficulties may arise in programs that build tables using the spreadsheet model. Such programs tend to treat each cell as its own text frame, which accordingly can have its own word-processor-style tabs assigned to it. In such programs, you can't typically simply say that all the entries in one column should decimal-align. Instead, you will probably have to set word-processor tab values for each cell in the column to specify the position at which the decimal points should align. Each tab entry in each cell then has to be manually tabbed into position before it will align. You can build the tab values into a style sheet to make formatting the cells easier, but it's likely that you'll then have to create a separate style sheet for each column in the table to reflect its unique measure and the lengths of its tab entries.

Net Assets Consist of:		
Paid-in capital	$	4,539,294
Undistributed investment income		0
Undistributed net gain (loss)		(1,892,592)
Net realized appreciation (depreciation)		(31,857)*
	$	**2,624,845**

FIGURE 15.18 In decimal-aligned tabs, most programs will allow certain characters to hang out into the right-hand margin even when the decimal point is not explicitly set.

This procedure is far more complicated than it needs to be, and it is probably more complicated (and certainly more time-consuming) than using the code-driven systems that most publishers still prefer for setting complex tables.

HANGING CHARACTERS IN NUMERIC TABLES

When numbers are set without decimal points, they can still decimal-align, as the program assumes that the position of the decimal point is just to the right of the integer. This has the effect of making any character set to the right of such a number appear to hang out into the margin (see Figure 15.18). Such hanging characters are common in numeric tables, especially financial tables. They include parentheses (to indicate negative values, such as losses), footnote reference marks, and fractions. Any character set to the right of the decimal point (whether the point is typeset or not) will hang off to the right.

Well, not exactly any character. If you use your program's superscript controls to create a footnote reference number, for example, the tab program will not see it as a footnote but as simply another number, regardless of its smaller size and vertical alignment. Such a character will not hang when set next to a number without a decimal point—the program will assume it is part of the integer. Similarly, if you build your own fractions by reducing full-size numerals, the software will assume that at least the numerator (and possibly the whole fraction) is part of the integer to the left of the decimal point and will not hang it. In spreadsheet-style tables, you won't be able to hang any characters beyond the boundary of the cell.

Clearly, the best solution to getting numeric expressions (e.g., fractions and footnote reference marks) to hang is to use the designed superior and inferior figures that are part of your chosen font. But most fonts don't include them, so you have to resort to trickery. This involves setting the integer values flush right in their own tab column and setting the hanging characters flush left in their own very narrow column. If there is no gutter allowed between the two columns, the spacing between the integers and the hanging figures will be

	Automotive Products	Financing & Insurance Operations	Other Products	Total
		(Dollars in Millions)		
Net Sales and Revenues				
Outside	$94,607.1	$11,115.8	$14,030.4	$119,753.3
Intersegment	220.9	9.2	3,373.4	—
Total	$94,828.0	$11,125.0	$17,403.8	$119,753.3*
Operating Profit (Loss)	($ 6,194.1)**	N/A**	$ 1,020.1	($ 5,174.0)***
Identifiable Assets at Year End	$72,676.5	$91,415.3	$19,659.0	$183,750.8
Depreciation and Amortization	$ 4,671.1	$ 2,050.6	$ 1,194.1	$ 7,915.8
Capital Expenditures	$ 5,783.6	$ 196.4	$ 1,320.2	$ 7,300.2

 * After elimination of intersegment transactions.
 ** Includes a special provision for scheduled plant closings and other restructurings of $2,820.8 million.
 *** Excludes Financing & Insurance Operations as they do not report Operating Profit.

FIGURE 15.19 Text entries in numeric columns are difficult to align accurately. The "N/A**" in the second column had to be assigned custom tab values to get its letters to set flush right with the numbers in the column. This table contains a number of complex hanging characters and alignments, even in the footnotes.

Net assets by class:

Class A Shares	$1,309,853
Class B Shares	$ 201,774
Class C Shares	$ 147,033
Class P Shares	$ 119,358
Class Y Shares	$ 87,614
Total	$1,865,632

FIGURE 15.20 The dollar signs in the interior entries of the right-hand column have been spaced using figure spaces as placeholders for the numerals and thin spaces as placeholders for the commas.

very close to normal. You can't kern across column boundaries, though, so some character sequences may seem slightly too loosely set. Footnotes and fractions should look fine.

Figure 15.19 shows another exceptional example of hanging characters. In the second column of figures, the footnote references in the expression *N/A*** will not align properly because the entry contains no numerals. This one entry will need its own unique word-processor-style tab setting, which will be very difficult to fine-tune exactly, as it doesn't correspond to those used in the numeric entries above and below it. But because it's the only entry in its column with hanging characters, you will probably find it easier in this case to set the entire column flush right and set the asterisks flush left in their own tab column, using the technique just described.

Since spreadsheet-style tables confine their contents to the limits of their cells, you can't get the kind of hanging footnotes shown at the right-hand side of the table in Figure 15.19. These hanging figures also have to be set in their own column, which will have to extend beyond the nominal measure of the table. If you turn off the rules for the cells in this column, all that will be visible on the printed page are the hanging characters.

ALIGNING CURRENCY SYMBOLS IN TABLES

It is a convention of financial tables that monetary values in the first row be preceded by a currency symbol. This symbol takes its horizontal position from the widest numerical entry in the column below it (usually in the "Total" line), as shown in Figure 15.20.

Ideally, such a currency symbol should be positioned by using figure spaces. A figure space is a fixed space the width of the numerals in a given typeface. Each figure space between the currency symbol and the number pushes the two characters apart by the width of one numeral. Few programs offer figure spaces; check your manuals. Where a placeholder is needed for punctuation (a comma or period), use a thin space.

If you don't have access to a figure space, you can use a series of numerals to position the currency symbol. Then select those numerals and change their printing color to "none" if your program offers this option. Don't select white unless you're positive that the table will be printed on white paper and without any background color. If there is a background color, you can change the color of the numerals to "background," your program willing.

Another option is to use your program's onscreen rulers to see just where the left edge of the currency symbol in the "Total" entry aligns. Then, in the tab entry where the currency symbol needs to be spaced apart, place a word space between the symbol and the number and force-justify the entry. That will drive the currency symbol and the number to opposite sides of the column. Finally, use a left indent to push the currency symbol over to a point where it aligns over the one in the "Total" line.

Void or "Missing" Entries

When for one reason or another a tab entry has no data assigned to it, it's usually not left blank. An exception are tables that use symbols such as checkmarks or bullets to indicate a condition or feature that the subject does or doesn't have. In these cases, to avoid having both "yes" and "no" symbols, "no" entries are simply left blank.

In text and numeric tables, the contemporary convention for handling void or missing entries is to insert an em dash. Leader dots were once used in this capacity, but they're now generally considered old-fashioned. The abbreviation *n/a* or *N.A.* is often avoided because it can mean either that a column heading is "not applicable" or that the data are "not available." When this distinction needs to be clear, it should be spelled out or footnoted.

The em dash should align like the rest of the entries in the column. Where decimal alignments have to be created by word-processor-style tabs within tab entries, that is easier said than done. The best strategy in such cases is to zoom in close on a decimal-aligned entry, draw a ruler guide to indicate where the rightmost edge of the last numeral sets, and then set a flush-right tab at that position in the tab entry that gets the em dash. The dash can then be tabbed to set flush right along with the rest of the numbers in its column.

ECONOMY 17-INCH MONITORS

Manufacturer and Model	List Price	Actual Viewing Area (diagonally, in inches)	Maximum Resolution (in pixels)	Controls					
				Convergence	Distortion	Degaussing	Color Temp.	Color Tuning	Digital Memory
HarleyScan 17 Harley Systems, Inc.	$399	16.1	1600 × 1200	■		■	■	■	■
KleerVision 17 Mammoth Computer Systems, Inc.	$329	15.9	1280 × 1024	■	■			■	■
BXC 1700 Monitor Group, Ltd.	$355	16.5	1280 × 1024	■		■	■	■	
FlatPro 17 Custom Peripherals Co.	$429	17.0	1600 × 1200	■	■	■	■	■	

FIGURE 15.21 Table fakery exposed. This onscreen view of Figure 15.10 shows that it wasn't assembled as a table at all. Instead, it was created as a series of independent text columns that share a common leading scheme. That allowed them to share a common hang line, and horizontal alignment was automatic. The whole table needed only four alignment guides: one to act as a hang line, one to base-align the rotated text block, and two to center the straddle head.

Faking It

In the course of using and reviewing table-building programs over the past 20 years, I have come to the conclusion that—with the exception of code-driven software—they are usually far more work than they're worth. Even when they can do the job, their techniques are often so inefficient and roundabout that you're better off seeking an alternative solution.

When you're using data exported from a spreadsheet or database program, though, you may have no choice. Likewise, highly structured, repetitive tables for financial reports and the like may be easier to set in the long run if you can create a table template and a library of style sheets to automate the process.

But for complex and one-off tables, or when you're building a table from scratch and keying in the data yourself, it is often much faster and easier to build something that looks like a table but isn't structured as one.

Since tables are best conceived of as a series of columns separated by gutters, you can build them with a page layout program. If you build each table column as a separate text column, all you have to do is keep track of the baselines in each column to assure proper horizontal alignment (see Figure 15.21).

Building a table with a page layout program gives you absolute and clear control over the leading between all the lines in the table, although rules will have to be added manually and separately from the text. You also have exact control over gutter widths because you can jockey whole columns from side to side or swap their positions entirely. You have absolute control over column widths too, because changing one column's measure has no impact on its neighbors. Adjoining columns can even overlap if necessary. Straddle heads and entries can also overlay the rest of the columns. Many of the sample tables in this chapter were created just this way and for just these reasons. At the end of the day (or likely much sooner), you'll have something that looks like a table even though there may not be a tab value anywhere in it.

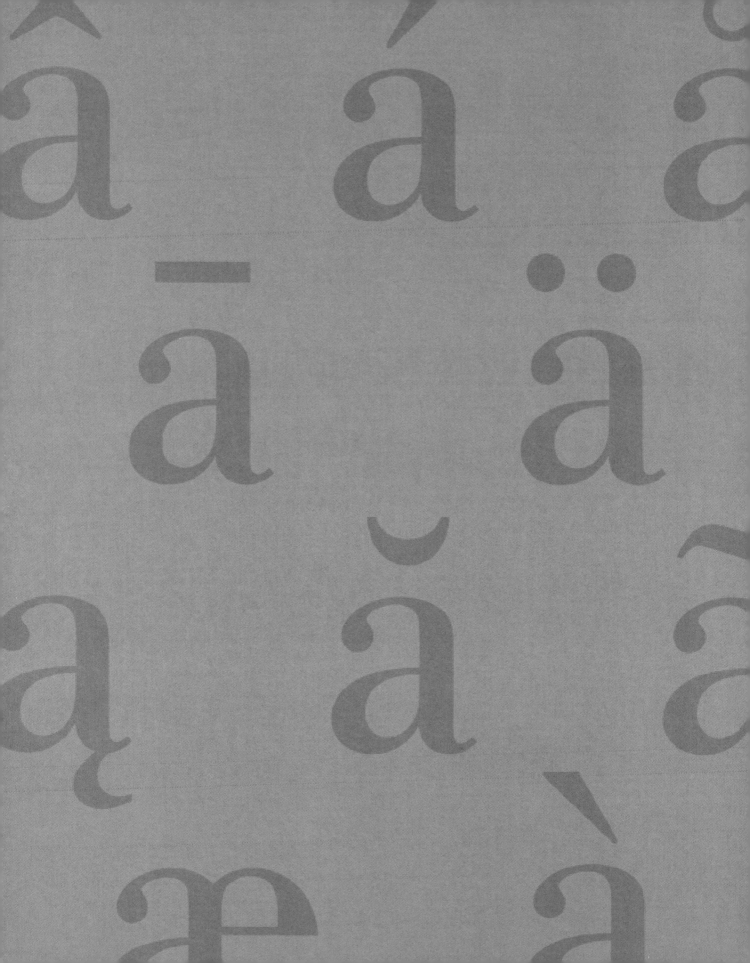

CHARACTER SETS, HYPHENATION, TIME, AND CURRENCY

BRITISH ENGLISH VERSUS AMERICAN ENGLISH

FRENCH, SPANISH, ITALIAN, AND GERMAN CONVENTIONS

Even though many languages share the Latin character set, they use it in different ways. Spacing rules vary, punctuation usage varies, character choice varies, and whole typographic idioms may change according to what language you're setting. Most of these are copyediting concerns, but it's important for typesetters to recognize typos in the making if these instances aren't handled properly in the manuscripts they set.

Character Sets

The Latin character set in a standard 228-character, single-byte font contains all the characters and accents needed to set type for all the European languages that use the Latin alphabet. Many accented characters, however, have to be assembled by hand (a process explained in "Accented Characters" in Chapter 13), as fonts typically offer only a handful of preassembled accented characters.

Unfortunately, neither the MacRoman nor Win ANSI font encodings, which represent subsets of the overall standard Latin 1 character set, offer a complete array of accents and characters to set all the European languages. The "missing" characters, then, are in your fonts, but your particular operating system may not be making them available to you (see Figure 16.1). If your operating system supports Unicode (as do Mac OS X and Windows NT, 2000, and XP), you can access

Win ANSI accents

- ⌃ circumflex
- ¨ dieresis
- ‾ macron
- ´ acute
- ` grave
- · dot
- ~ tilde
- ˛ cedilla

MacRoman accents

- ⌃ circumflex
- ¨ dieresis
- ‾ macron
- ´ acute
- ` grave
- · dot
- ~ tilde
- ˘ breve
- ˇ haček
- ˝ double prime
- ° ring
- ˛ cedilla
- ˛ ogonek

FIGURE 16.1 Without language-specific fonts or multilingual Unicode fonts, you can set certain accented characters only by placing the accents manually. This chart shows which characters are available under the Windows and Macintosh encoding schemes. An accent can be placed next to the character to be accented and kerned close enough to overlap it.

them all, as you can if your program offers a character browser that can extract all the characters contained in a font. Even in Unicode systems, though, you may have to assemble many accented characters yourself.

European languages for which a full complement of preaccented characters do not exist in standard single-byte fonts include Basque, Czech, Esperanto, Hungarian, Polish, Turkish, and Welsh. Of these, only Polish cannot be set using the character sets available in either MacRoman or Win ANSI encodings, because both lack the upper- and lowercase *L-slash* (Ł and ł). But to set any of these languages efficiently, you should have language-specific fonts that include a full set of accented characters (see Figure 16.2).

For a description of how to gain access to all of the characters in a font, see "Finding the Characters You Need" in Chapter 4.

Hyphenation

The rules of hyphenation, or word division, vary even between American English and British English (and from dictionary to dictionary), so no one hyphenation algorithm will ever work over a range of languages. Ideally, hyphenation dictionaries should be not only language specific, but country specific as well.

Generally, programs use one dictionary to check spelling and another to hyphenate, so just because your program has a spelling checker for a specific language does not mean that it can hyphenate that language correctly.

If you are setting only brief passages in a non-English language that your program does not support, you can get by with a traditional printed dictionary as a reference for verifying hyphenation. The word structures of many Romance languages are similar enough that an English hyphenation dictionary or algorithm may be able to accurately hyphenate some of the time, but don't count on this.

Because your program cannot be counted upon to hyphenate non-English words correctly, you should keep track of where foreign language text appears in a document and assure that any page layout changes do not cause it to rewrap and hyphenate incorrectly. Before investing time in adjusting composition and layout problems (bad type color, widows, orphans, etc.) first verify that any non-English text has composed properly.

Time Expressions

Much of the world uses a 24-hour system of notation for expressing times of day. In the United States, this is often referred to as *military time*. In continental Europe, then, it's common to see *14:00* instead of *2 p.m.,* for example. In those settings, *a.m.* and *p.m.* are redundant, so they're not used. While in the

Albanian	â ç ë
Basque	á é í ñ ó ŕ ú
Catalan	á à ç é è í ì ó ò ú ù
Czech	á č ď Ď é ě ě í ň ó ř š ť Ť ú ů ý ž
Danish	å æ ø
Dutch	ā ä ă é è ê ë ě ē ī ĭ ij ó ò ô ō ŏ
Esperanto	ĉ ĝ ĥ ĵ ŝ ŭ
Estonian	ä č ö õ š ü ž
Finnish	å ä ö
Flemish	ë ó ij
French	á â æ ç é è ê ë î ï ô œ ù û ü
German	ä ö ß ü
Hungarian	á é í ó ö ő ü ú ű
Icelandic	á æ é ð í ó ö þ ú ý
Italian	à è ì î ò ù
Latvian	ā č ē ī ġ ļ ō š ū ž
Lithuanian	ą č ę ė į š ų ū ž
Norwegian	å æ ø
Polish	ą ć ę ł ń ó ś ź ż
Portuguese	á à â ã ç é è ê í ì ï ó ò ô õ ú û ü
Romanian	à ă â è ì î ş ţ ù
Scottish	à é è ì ó ò ù
Serbo-Croatian	č ć ď š ž
Slovak	á ä č ď é í Í ľ ň ó ô ŕ ř š ť ú ů ý ž
Spanish	á é í ñ ó ú ü
Swedish	å ä é ö
Turkish	â ç ğ ı î İ ö ş ü û
Welsh	á â ê î ï ô û ŷ

FIGURE 16.2 A summary of the accented characters used by major European languages. All those listed here have uppercase versions as well.

United States, *a.m.* and *p.m.* are often set in small caps (A.M., P.M.), the norm in Britain is to set them in lowercase only.

Often, 24-hour time is expressed without the colon to divide hours from minutes, in which case *1730,* for example, would replace *17:30.*

Note that the expression *o'clock* is used only when numbers are spelled out, so you would set *seven o'clock* but not *7:00 o'clock* or *7 o'clock.*

Currency Symbols

Most fonts that were created back in the twentieth century lack the symbol for the European currency, the euro (€). For the benefit of owners of those older fonts, most font vendors offer fonts that contain generic euro symbols in a variety of styles: serif and sans serif; roman and italic; regular weight and bold; and condensed, regular, and expanded widths. These fonts are usually free and can be downloaded from the vendor's Internet site. Even fonts without the euro symbol include the dollar sign and the British pound-sterling sign (£).

Currency symbols precede the number they modify and are not separated by a space. Because many countries use *$* as their national currency symbol (whether or not they use the name *dollar*), it's best to clarify what that symbol means if the context is at all ambiguous: Can$50 or CDN$50 (Canadian dollars); US$50 (U.S. dollars); Isr£50 (Israeli pounds); Mex$50 (Mexican pesos); UK£50 (British pounds), and so forth.

British English versus American English

Apart from the obvious differences in spelling, there are also punctuation and spacing differences between American English and British English. In general, the British approaches are more logical from a content point of view.

American and British Quotation Styles

In quoted material in American English, double quotation marks are used for the primary quote, and single quotation marks are used for quotes within quotes:

> "She called him 'weird,' and I agree."

In British English, the opposite is the rule:

> 'She called him "weird", and I agree.'

Note also in the second sample that in British English, punctuation sets outside the quotation marks unless it's a part of the material being quoted.

In American English, a period or comma is placed inside quotation marks:

> "I really must be going," she said.
>
> The senator said the legislation was "dead."

In those cases, the rules of British usage would prescribe the following settings:

> "I really must be going", she said.
>
> The senator said the legislation was "dead".

The British logic is that in these examples the punctuation is not properly part of the material within the quotes, so it should be set outside. Quite so. British rules set punctuation inside quotation marks only when it's part of the quoted matter and thus clarify the nature of the quote.

American and British Abbreviation Styles

A period in an abbreviation usually indicates where a word has been broken off and signals that what would normally follow is missing (e.g., *cont., misc.*). Nevertheless, it is also American style to add a period to titles that would not seem to need them: *Mr., Mrs.,* and so forth. In British English, periods are omitted after such titles: *Mr, Mrs, Revd, Dr,* and *St.*

American and British Temperatures

In expressions of temperature, the American style is to set the entire expression closed up: 12°C, 212°F. British style is to associate the degree sign with the temperature scale and leave a thin space or nonbreaking word space between this pair and the number of degrees: 12 °C, 212 °F. The thin or nonbreaking space prevents the expression from being divided at line's end.

French Typographic Conventions

Of all the European languages, French varies most from English (either kind) in terms of its typographic conventions. Most of these variations affect how individual characters are spaced. Unless otherwise specified in the sections below, French and English typographic conventions are the same.

French Punctuation Style

As in British English, contractions of titles do not take a period: *M (Monsieur), Mme (Madame), St (Saint),* and so forth.

En dashes are usually used the way em dashes are in English, but they're preceded and followed by a word space. (When em dashes are used, they are the shorter, *punctuating em dashes* and still take the spaces.) En dashes that in English express ranges of numbers or dates are hyphens in French:

la guerre de 1914-1918

Points of ellipsis used to indicate a break in thought or speech are set close together, so you can use the ellipsis character (...) in these situations. They are set closed up against the word they follow and are followed by a word space:

Film sur le cinéma, sur sa folie, sur ses travers, sur son cauchemar... ce qui confirme ce qu'on savait déjà: Rossi est un explorateur hors pair de l'imaginaire.

Points of ellipsis used to indicate omissions are handled as in English (see "Points of Ellipsis" in Chapter 13).

When first names are hyphenated, they retain the hyphens as initials, so *Jean-Jacques Rousseau* becomes *J.-J. Rousseau*. The linked initials in such cases are set closed up.

FRENCH QUOTATION STYLE

Increasingly, English-style quotation marks are used in French text, and they're handled just as they are in British English (see "American and British Quotation Styles" earlier in this chapter). Double *guillemets* (« »), though, are more traditionally used in place of English-style quotation marks. These are separated from the text they surround either by thin spaces or by nonbreaking word spaces that link them with the text they set next to:

> « C'est une mode », estime-t-il.

The use of punctuation alongside guillemets in French is also similar to that in British English. That is, a period or comma sets within the closing guillemets only if it belongs to the text being quoted; otherwise it sets outside them. An exception is a multiple-sentence quote that starts in mid-sentence. In this case, even though the final period of the quote may belong to the text being quoted, it is set outside the guillemets because it is thought to belong primarily to the greater sentence in which the quote occurs:

> Le sommaire a dit que son nouveau film est un « psycho-thriller au féminin qui mêle habilement la romance et l'horreur. Il s'est forgé une réputation d'œuvre choc ».

Quotes within quotes are set off with the same symbols: double guillemets. If both quotes end at the same point in the sentence (typically the end), just one set of guillemets is used—they are not doubled to indicate that both quotes are ending at once.

When quotations in dialogue are interrupted by phrases such as "he said" or "she asked," such phrases are set off by commas, and guillemets are not used internally in such sentences (as quotations marks would be used in English):

> « C'est un gouvernement de proches de Jacques Chirac, souligne François Hollande, et en matière d'ouverture, je ne crois pas que ce soit le meilleur symbole. »

In dialogue, guillemets are often dispensed with, and quotes by different speakers are introduced by an en dash (em dashes are also used in this role):

> Elle regarda, malgré elle, le siège arrière.
> — Il n'y a pas de monsieur.
> — Mais si, dit-il. Où on met les bagages. Tu sais bien.

FRENCH PUNCTUATION SPACING

Except in the following exceptional cases, punctuation spacing in French is the same as it is in English.

The following characters are preceded by a thin space or a nonbreaking word space:

%

?

!

*, †, and all other reference marks, including superior numerals

The following characters are preceded by a thin space or a nonbreaking word space and followed by a normal word space:

:

;

— (en dash, except when followed by a comma, which is set closed up)

French Accents

Accents are often omitted over capitals, especially in all-caps matter. Even in documents where it is the style to place accents over capitals, the *accent grave* over the preposition *À* is often omitted. The preference of the Imprimerie Nationale, however, is to use all accents all the time in all uppercase matter.

French Capitalization

The names of months are not capitalized, except for historical dates:

> *13 juillet* (just another day), but *14 Juillet* (Bastille Day)

Only the proper name within a street address is capitalized:

> 14 boulevard Paul Bert

Titles of books and magazines are normally set down-style, with only the first word capitalized.

French Numeric Expressions

Spans of years repeat all numerals:

1939-1945, not *1939-45*

Temperatures are set with a thin space or a nonbreaking word space:

12 °c

In numbers, the decimal point symbol used in France is a comma. Where in English a comma would be used to separate divisions of thousands in long numbers, in French a period is used:

1.000.000,00

Sometimes—particularly in tables—the periods are omitted and thin spaces used in their place:

1 000 000

When expressions such as this are set with decimal places, the decimals too get a space every three places:

6,559 67 (in English, *6.55967*)

Spanish Typographic Conventions

The aspects in which Spanish typographic practice varies from English are similar to those in French.

For quotation marks, guillemets (« ») are commonly used. They are separated from the text they surround by thin spaces or nonbreaking word spaces. When English-style quotation marks are used, punctuation follows the American style, in which commas and periods are set within the closing quotation marks.

In points of ellipsis used to indicate a break in thought or speech, the dots are set close together, so the ellipsis character (...) can be used. In these settings, the points of ellipsis are set closed up against the word that precedes them, and they're followed by a normal word space, as in French. Points of ellipsis used to indicate omissions are handled as in English (see "Points of Ellipsis" in Chapter 13).

Em dashes introducing the words of a new speaker in dialogue are set closed up. Em dashes may also be used as quotation marks, in which case they are spaced as are English-style quotation marks. When em dashes are used to set off parenthetical phrases, they are set the same way; that is, they're set closed up against the parenthetical phrase but separated from the rest of the sentence by word spaces.

Interrogatives and exclamations are introduced by inverted question marks (¿) and exclamation points (¡), respectively. A sentence that is both interrogatory and exclamatory begins with an inverted exclamation point and ends in a normal question mark.

The letter combinations *ll* and *rr* are considered single characters and cannot be divided at line's end.

Accents are optional with capital letters. The same is true in Portuguese.

Italian Typographic Conventions

Guillemets (« ») are used as quotation marks and are spaced as they are in French and Spanish, with thin spaces or nonbreaking word spaces between them and the text they enclose.

For dialogue, em dashes are usually used to introduce the words of a new speaker. In these cases, the dashes are followed by word spaces.

When points of ellipsis are used to indicate a break in thought or speech, a four-dot ellipsis is used and set closed up against the word that precedes them. In these points of ellipsis, the dots are set close, without any intervening spaces (....). They are followed by a word space. If the points of ellipsis are preceded by punctuation (e.g., a question mark), only three dots are used, but the spacing remains the same.

When an apostrophe indicating the omission of a letter follows a vowel (*Parlo un po'*), it is followed by a word space. When such an apostrophe follows a consonant (*d'italiano*), it is set closed up.

German Typographic Conventions

German sets very much like English, but with some notable exceptions.

All nouns and words that are used as nouns are capitalized.

There are several punctuation styles for quotations. One uses guillemets, which may or may not be reversed in sequence (» ... «). Double primes and double quotation marks are also used. In both of the latter cases, the opening marks center-align on the baseline while the closing marks top-align („ ... ″). When double quotation marks are used, their sequence is the reverse of that used in English („ ... "). In all cases, they're set closed up, as in English. Although base-aligned primes are not a part of the standard Windows or Macintosh character sets, base-aligned quotation marks are.

The ff, fi, and fl ligatures should be used only when both letters are part of the root of the word. For example, in words such as *auffrischen* and *aufladen*—in which the first syllable is a prefix—the ff and fl ligatures should not be used.

Em dashes are preceded and followed by word spaces.

Although the *eszett* (ß) represents a double *s,* it is not broken in half in order to hyphenate a word. Instead, the eszett is carried down to start the new line (*aufschlie-ßen*).

Text

st Paragraph
"Text" + 1st-line indent

↓

Narrow text
"1st Paragraph" + custom h&j

Germa
"Text" + Ger hyphen

HOW STYLE SHEETS WORK

CREATING AND WORKING WITH STYLE SHEETS

REMOVING STYLE SHEETS AND SETTING OVERRIDES

PARAGRAPH STYLE SHEETS AND DOCUMENT STRUCTURES

Typesetting systems have always relied on shortcuts: combinations of type-setting instructions concatenated into a single command. Current software achieves much the same effect—and similar time savings—through style sheets, which define the appearance and behavior of type at the paragraph or charac-ter level. (Another big time-saver on dedicated typesetting systems was a key-board that had plenty of extra keys to which you could assign various shortcuts. For that, we're still waiting.)

How Style Sheets Work

A style sheet is an instrument that enables you to apply many typographical formatting specifications at once. You define a style sheet the way you would define the typographic specs for any text, which usually means a tour through a series of dialog boxes. The values and settings you define are gathered into a single style sheet and given a unique name (see Figure 17.1).

The style sheets you create are listed in a pull-down menu, a dialog box, a floating palette (a small window that can stay open onscreen all the time), or all three. They can also be assigned to keyboard shortcuts, which will allow you to format text much more quickly, as you won't have to grope for the mouse.

Character Attributes	Paragraph Attributes
Typeface	Leading
Point size	Indention
Leading	Margin alignment
Baseline shift	Hyphenation-and-justification values
Kerning	Minimum/optimum/maximum letter space width
Tracking	Minimum/optimum/maximum word space width
Set height	Minimum/optimum/maximum character set width
Set width	Hyphenation on/off
Stance	Consecutive hyphens
Language	Minimum characters before hyphen
Position (normal/subscript/superscript)	Minimum characters after hyphen
Superscript size and alignment	Dictionary/algorithmic hyphenation
Subscript size and alignment	Exception dictionary
Capitalization style	Space before paragraph
Breaking/non-breaking text	Space after paragraph
Color and shade	Keeps (widow and orphan control)
Alternate character substitution	Baseline-grid alignment
	Tabs
	Rule above/below

FIGURE 17.1 A list of the most common character and paragraph attributes that you can control with style sheets. Note that leading, although called by some applications a character trait, is rarely handled as such; a leading change to one character will typically affect a whole line. Other programs consider leading to be strictly a paragraph attribute.

The floating palette has the merit of always displaying the style sheet affiliated with the current cursor position.

When you link a style sheet to a selection of text, the text takes on all the formatting you've specified in the style sheet. When you change the specifications of a style sheet in an open document, any text formatted according to that style sheet immediately follows suit, whether it's selected or not. You can change a thousand captions from 9-point to 10-point with a couple of clicks of the mouse.

Printing Style Sheets

The name *style sheet* comes from the book publisher's practice of summarizing, in a single document, all the typographic and page layout specs for a project. So it's curious (to put it generously) that programs typically do not allow you to print out the style sheets you create. These would be a great reference for future use—not to mention for projects in the works. Generally, to discover all the typographic specifications contained in an electronic style sheet, you have to wade through a long series of dialog boxes one by one to unearth all the values and settings. In addition, some of the specs may come from another style sheet upon which the current one is based, and it isn't always clear which are which. This inscrutability makes it needlessly difficult to work with the specifications in an organized way.

Since most typesetting and page layout programs are modular (they can have new functions tacked on to them), you should check with vendors of third-party plug-ins, extensions, and add-ons (mini-programs that add capabilities to a host program) to see if a style-sheet-printing capability can be added to your program. It's very handy indeed.

Paragraph versus Character Styles

A program generally offers two kinds of style sheets: *paragraph* and *character.* As alluded to in earlier chapters, individual programs vary in how they distinguish character from paragraph attributes. These distinctions are in all cases arbitrary and often at odds with traditional typographic practice.

A *template,* by comparison, is an empty document in which document-wide specifications have been defined: trim size, margins, page grids, and so forth. Templates can contain sets of style sheets specific to that document style.

To assign a paragraph style, you place the cursor anywhere within the paragraph and select the style sheet of your choice by whatever means you prefer. Keyboard shortcuts are the fastest, floating palettes the most convenient (especially for the memory challenged).

To assign a character style, you have to select the target text first and then apply the style. A character style assigned when no text has been selected will be put into effect at the current cursor position, and any ensuing text typed from that point will adopt the chosen style. If you then move the cursor before typing any text, the style-sheet assignment will be discarded; you don't have to worry about certain cursor positions on the page carrying any rogue formatting instructions. Note, however, that a word space can carry an extensive set of character-formatting instructions, including calls for fonts that may not be apparent. This can cause problems at printing time if fonts for invisible typefaces are unexpectedly required.

There are no standards for how programs handle character and paragraph style sheets. For example, leading is considered a paragraph attribute in some programs, while in others it's a character trait. In some programs you specify character attributes as you build your paragraph style sheets; others have you build character style sheets separately and then embed them in your paragraph style sheets. Check your manuals.

FOLLOW-ON PARAGRAPH STYLES

Programs usually allow you to specify not only the style for a given paragraph but also the style for the one that follows it. The *follow-on style* is applied only when you are typing directly into the program. If a heading, for example, is always followed by text in a certain format, the style sheet for the heading can point to the style sheet for the text. After you've typed that heading and hit the Return key, then, the next text you type will appear in the follow-on format. If you already have a body of text in place, though, assigning a style sheet to one paragraph will not cause any follow-on style to be assigned automatically to successive paragraphs.

Creating Style Sheets

You can create style sheets from scratch or base them on existing ones. You can also import style sheets from a document created with the same program.

To create a blank slate from which to start, programs always offer a "non-style sheet," a style sheet with no specifications assigned to it, usually somewhat sadly named "no style." When creating a style sheet from scratch, this is the one to specify when your program inevitably asks you on which existing style sheet you want to base the new one.

Normally, a style sheet you create without having a document open will be part of the style sheet library for all the documents you create thereafter. If you create a style sheet with a document open, it will be specific to that document.

To save a set of style sheets, you can save a simple document that contains those sheets (a template, in other words). From there they can be imported into other documents for reuse. If you're really organized (and have the time) the template can contain a written description of all the specs contained in the various style sheets it uses.

Parent-Child Style Sheets

Programs assume that you will be basing one style sheet on another. When you create a style sheet, the first dialog-box field you're normally expected to fill in specifies which existing style sheet the new one will be based on. Note that programs often do not use "no style" as the default style sheet on which a new one will be based, and you may have to make a conscious effort *not* to base a new style sheet on an old one. Many programs have a "normal" style as their default, and typically this style sheet cannot be deleted, only modified.

Basing one style sheet on another can be a great time-saver. Imagine, for example, that you are working on a magazine in which text can be set in three possible column widths. The text in each measure may have its own hyphenation and justification specifications and possibly unique first-line indents as well, but all other specifications are apt to be the same among all three. It's logical, then, to build one text style sheet and base the other two on it.

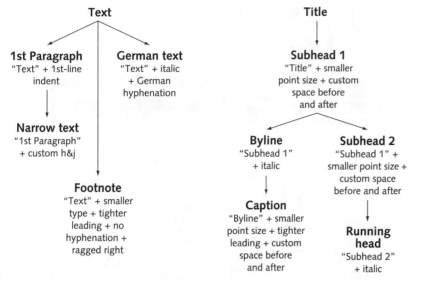

Text

1st Paragraph
"Text" + 1st-line
indent

German text
"Text" + italic
+ German
hyphenation

Narrow text
"1st Paragraph"
+ custom h&j

Footnote
"Text" + smaller
type + tighter
leading + no
hyphenation +
ragged right

Title

Subhead 1
"Title" + smaller
point size + custom
space before
and after

Byline
"Subhead 1"
+ italic

Subhead 2
"Subhead 1" +
smaller point size +
custom space
before and after

Caption
"Byline" + smaller
point size + tighter
leading + custom
space before
and after

**Running
head**
"Subhead 2"
+ italic

FIGURE 17.2 This diagram shows the relationships among members of two simple style-sheet families. Both the Text and Title style sheets pass on all their attributes to their children, each of which is endowed with certain unique qualities. The children, in turn, can beget further generations. A change to any parent is passed to its children, unless the child's attributes explicitly override such a change.

When you base one style sheet on another, you are creating a parent-child relationship between them (see Figure 17.2). The child inherits all its characteristics from the parent, and you then tweak any of its specifications as you wish or assign it unique qualities of its own. When a change occurs in a parent style sheet, that change is passed on immediately and automatically to all of its children, and its children's children (and on through the generations). These changes, in turn, are also reflected in any text formatted with these style sheets.

This ripple-through effect can save a huge amount of time when style sheets have to be updated. But it can also cause unanticipated results if changes are made to a style sheet without regard to the effect on its children. This is a particular risk in workgroups that share a set of style sheets; a thoughtless change made by one person—who may not be aware of or have access to certain generations of child style sheets—can affect the work of everyone else.

You may want to make efforts, then, to strategically build dead ends into the network of style sheets for a particular job. That is, to create style sheets that have no parents. After all, the more generations that exist between the primal style sheet and its most distant progeny, the less in common the two have. At some point, it may make sense to break the chain, so that, for example, your caption style is not based on your text style. There may be changes that you don't want rippling through every generation of a style sheet family.

If your program were able to print out a diagram of the parental relationships among style sheets, this family tree would be far less confusing. But as with printing the style sheets themselves, this feature is also among the missing, although it may be available from third-party vendors.

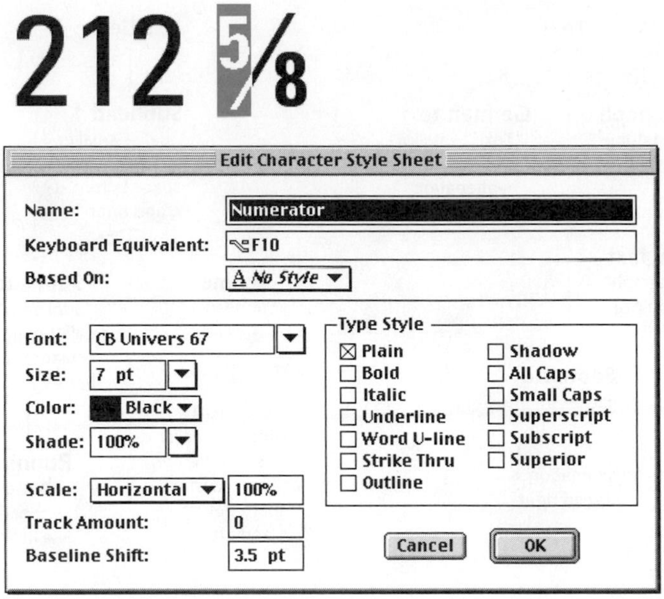

FIGURE 17.3 Creating character style sheets from existing type prevents repetitive formatting, as in the case of this fraction. Here, the numerator of a hand-built fraction has been selected and the new-style-sheet dialog box opened. All the specs for the character are read into the dialog box by the program, so all that remains to be done is to name the new style sheet.

212 ⅝

Edit Character Style Sheet

Name: **Numerator**
Keyboard Equivalent: F10
Based On: A *No Style* ▼

Font: CB Univers 67 ▼
Size: 7 pt ▼
Color: Black ▼
Shade: 100% ▼

Scale: Horizontal ▼ 100%
Track Amount: 0
Baseline Shift: 3.5 pt

Type Style
☒ Plain   ☐ Shadow
☐ Bold   ☐ All Caps
☐ Italic   ☐ Small Caps
☐ Underline   ☐ Superscript
☐ Word U-line ☐ Subscript
☐ Strike Thru ☐ Superior
☐ Outline

Cancel   OK

Creating Style Sheets from Existing Text

You can also create style sheets from existing text. When doing so, you can specify whether the new style sheet should apply to paragraphs or characters. To create a paragraph style sheet, simply place the cursor in the paragraph whose specs you want to enshrine and use your program's controls to create a new style sheet. All the specifications and settings for that paragraph will be automatically incorporated into the new style sheet.

If the paragraph text is based on an existing style sheet, that will be indicated in the new-style-sheet dialog box. If you want to sever this relationship, choose "no style" as the style upon which the new style sheet should be based. All the specifications of the text will remain intact within the new style sheet; only the link to the parent style sheet will be eliminated. This is how you would sever one style sheet from a parent style sheet, as mentioned in the previous section. More often, though, the reason for creating a style sheet this way is that the text has no style-sheet affiliation at all and you'd like to create one.

You can create new character style sheets in the same way. When doing so, select the character(s) on which you want to base the new style, as the cursor position alone can be ambiguous if it falls between characters with different type specs. Creating character style sheets this way is useful for reproducing the specifications of such labor-intensive settings as fraction numerators, accent placements, and so forth (see Figure 17.3).

Using Style Sheets

You cannot apply more than one paragraph style sheet to a single paragraph. You can't, then, create a style sheet to alter only a part of a paragraph's formatting (its H&J settings, for example) and leave the rest intact. The same is true of character style sheets.

Normally, though, you can apply a paragraph style sheet without trampling any existing character formatting that has been applied manually or via character style sheets. The program, basically, assumes that you knew what you were doing when you formatted the text the first time and that you don't want to blotto all your work. This feature is handy if, for example, you have formatted the text with a lot of hand-built fractions only to find that you have to change your typeface and leading. In such a case you could create a new paragraph style sheet (or edit the existing one), apply it, and all the point-size changes and baseline shifts that you so meticulously specified would remain intact, although the typeface would change (see Figure 17.4).

Not every program handles this situation in the same way, and in some programs certain character attributes may be overwritten by those in a paragraph style sheet that you apply later. Check your manuals to see how the capability is implemented in the programs you use. You may have to run some tests to see how your program reacts in real life, as manuals tend not to go into great detail on this subject.

Removing Style Sheets

Style sheets can multiply like rabbits. If you've inherited a document that's been set with style sheets you do not intend to use, or whose typographic formatting you plan to overhaul, you may want to strip away the old style sheets.

If the document is in word-processor format—that is, if it's one long block of running text—this is easy. Just select all the text in the document, apply "no style" to them, and delete all the old style sheets. The formatting of the document will remain intact even though the style sheets have been disconnected from the text. You can delete the style sheets without effect.

If the document in question is in a page layout program, you can first select all the running text in the document and apply the "no style" style sheet. This will leave all the typographic formatting intact but eliminate any links to style sheets. You can then use your program's search-and-replace controls (which can locate text by the style sheet they've been formatted with) to hunt down text elements that are not in the main text stream and replace their style assignments with "no style" as well.

before paragraph style sheet

Holding down the Ctrl and the Alt key simultaneously opens the Style-O-Matic® dialog box.

after paragraph style sheet

Holding down the Ctrl and the Alt key simultaneously opens the Style-O-Matic® dialog box.

FIGURE 17.4 Any character-based formatting—whether it is done manually or by means of a style sheet—is preserved when a paragraph style sheet is applied to the same text. In the sample above, two words have been put in a sans serif face for emphasis, and the trademark symbol has been reduced and top-aligned. These specifications are maintained when, below, a paragraph style sheet is applied that alters the typeface and leading.

FIGURE 17.5 In a typical style-sheet palette like this one, the name of a style sheet appears with a plus sign next to it when the cursor rests amid text that has been formatted with both the style sheet and manual overrides. This can be a quick way to check if, for example, the tracking for any part of a given passage of text has been changed.

Setting Overrides

Style sheets are not likely to cover all the formatting work you have to do in a document. In many cases, you'll do only the broad formatting strokes with style sheets and then hand-format exceptional bits here and there. The exceptional specifications you set in this way are called *overrides*—they are settings or values that override those in the style sheets. Programs typically indicate the presence of overrides by putting a plus sign (+) next to the name of the style sheet when the cursor is located amid such text (see Figure 17.5).

What the plus sign indicates, though, can be anybody's guess. If you don't remember creating an override and there are no obvious visual clues, it may be difficult to know how the text deviates from the "pure" effect of the style sheet. The plus sign could indicate that some manual character formatting (a tracking change, for example) was applied to the text. Or it could mean that a paragraph style sheet has been superimposed over a character style sheet used somewhere in the same paragraph. It could also mean that some paragraph attribute has been manually altered somewhere in the affected paragraph.

To locate the source of the override, place the cursor at the beginning of the paragraph and advance it character by character until the plus sign appears or disappears. If it never disappears, the override affects the entire paragraph.

USING STYLE SHEETS TO CREATE OVERRIDES

One of the great time-wasters of setting type is changing typefaces. Every time you scroll through a font menu you waste seconds that could be better used to shorten your working day. It's useful, then, to always call for pi fonts and expert-set fonts with character style sheets. This saves time setting small caps, footnote reference figures, old-style numbers, bullets, dingbats, and much more. Building fractions when your numerator and denominator styles are saved as style sheets is almost as fast as typing them as regular numbers.

Even simple changes of face from roman to italic may be more efficiently done with style sheets, as explained in the next section.

Searching and Replacing Styles

To avoid making a lot of changes by hand in long documents, it may be worth having a style sheet for even minor formatting changes, such as a switch from roman to italic. In fact, it may be worthwhile having several style sheets that do exactly the same thing. You can then use your program's search-and-replace controls (which can search for text formatted with a specific style sheet) to make a lot of corrections very quickly.

For example, imagine a book like this one in which the names of keys in keyboard commands are set in italic: "Then press the *return* key." It's not hard to imagine a scenario in which a design change put such commands in bold roman instead: "Then press the **return** key." If every instance of italic in the book had been set with a single style sheet called Italic, it would be a tedious procedure to sift through the entire thing with a search-and-replace command in order to decide which instances of italic (which can have many roles in a manuscript) should be changed and which left alone. If you had several style sheets for a simple change to italic—Keyboard Commands, Emphasis, Book Titles, Style-Sheet Names—you could search and replace in a much more targeted way. It may seem like a fine point, but the next time you're typesetting a 500-page book, you may think otherwise.

Paragraph Style Sheets and Document Structures

Paragraph style sheets are more than just formatting shortcuts. They are also tags that identify the hierarchical structure of your document. If you think of them this way, they'll be much more useful to you. Style sheets for titles, headings, and subheadings, for example, can be the identifiers by which programs can automatically assemble tables of contents. Likewise, caption style sheets can yield illustration lists. Words identified by a style sheet called Glossary could be extracted and used as a word list, even though they may be typographically formatted exactly like the text around them.

Importing Style Sheets

If you import a style from one document into another, most programs will simply overwrite an existing style with an imported style of the same name. You'll probably be offered the option to rename one or the other, but the assumption is that you're importing the new one because it's better than the one you have.

When you're importing style sheets, it's important that they be parent style sheets and not any style sheet's child. Otherwise you will have an incomplete, orphan style sheet that's based at least in part on a parent in another document.

HIGH-RESOLUTION OUTPUT AND PRINT-TYPE CLARITY
ADAPTING TO LOW PRINT RESOLUTIONS
WORKING WITH TYPE FOR ONSCREEN DISPLAY
TYPOGRAPHY AND THE WORLD WIDE WEB

How you set type should depend on how it will eventually be seen. The higher the resolution of the output device, the more finely the type is rendered and the finer your control over how each character is positioned. As resolution decreases, your ability to refine the spacing of type diminishes along with it. In fact, when type that's been set for output at high resolution is reproduced at low resolutions, your efforts may have made it look worse than it otherwise would. Typesetting is a resolution-dependent practice, and this chapter looks at the adaptations you have to make to accommodate that fact.

The Advantages of High-Resolution Output

The higher the resolution of the device on which your type will be rendered, the better the type will look. The higher the resolution, the smaller the dots that render the characters, and the smaller the spacing increments (in effect, blank dots) between characters. As detailed in "Output Resolution and Type Quality" in Chapter 1, different imaging technologies yield differing levels of clarity at equivalent resolutions, but in general, the higher the resolution the better.

Beyond about 1,000 dots per inch (dpi), increasing the output resolution has little effect on how well you can control the spacing of type. This resolution is

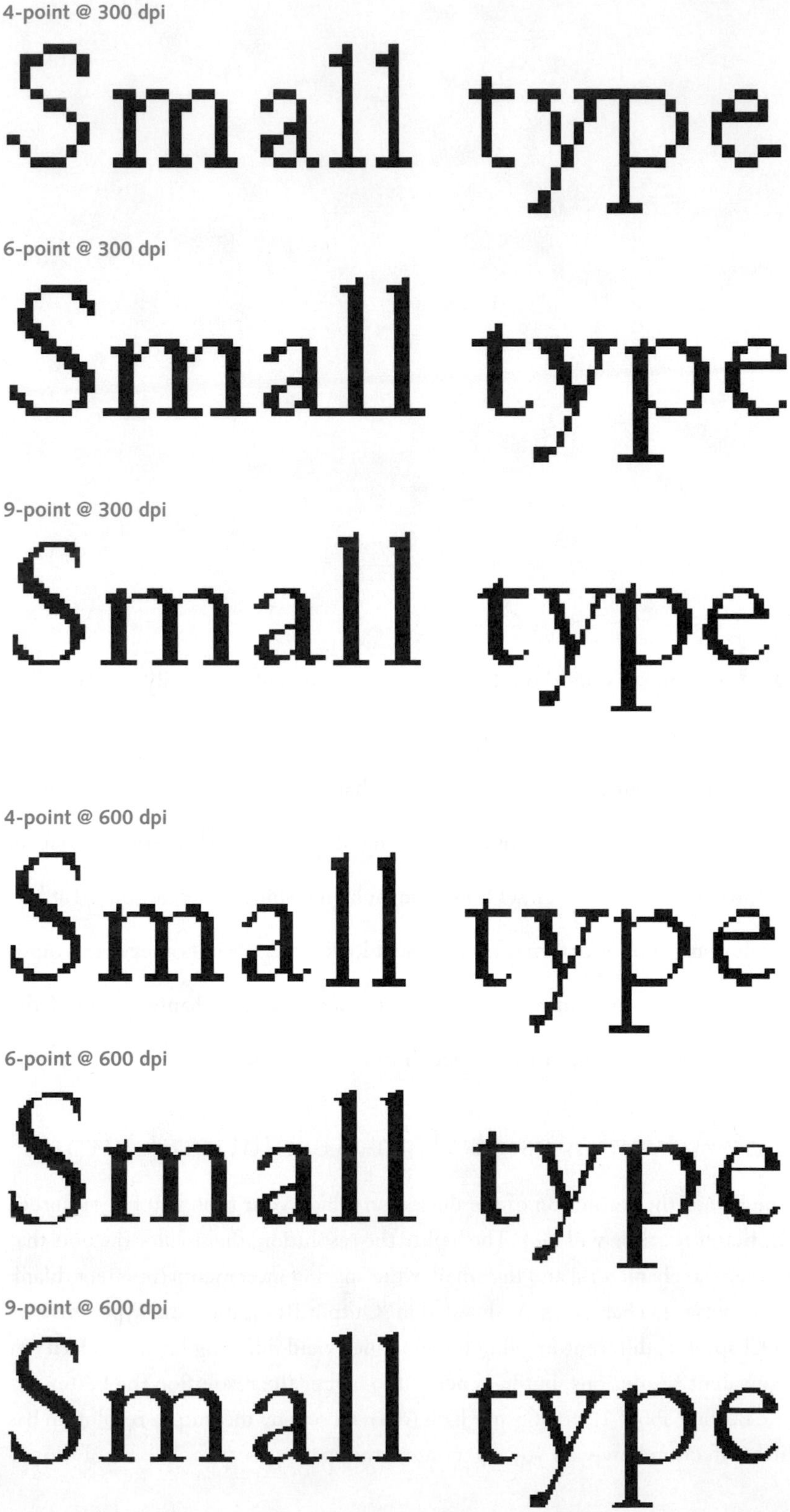

FIGURE 18.1 When character images at 300 dpi and 600 dpi are enlarged, it becomes clear how few pixels are used to render them and how crude their images are. Footnote reference marks at 4-point will be very badly rendered, and even superiors and inferiors as large as 6-point won't fare much better.

4-point @ 300 dpi

Small type

6-point @ 300 dpi

Small type

9-point @ 300 dpi

Small type

4-point @ 600 dpi

Small type

6-point @ 600 dpi

Small type

9-point @ 600 dpi

Small type

equivalent to about 14 dots per point, and $\frac{1}{14}$ point is quite a small increment. In kerning terms, a one-dot spacing adjustment at this resolution in 10-point type is equal to about $\frac{7}{1,000}$ em. This is smaller than any kerning adjustment you'd normally make and less than half the size of the smallest kerning value you're likely to find in any font's kerning table.

In typographic terms, the main reason to go beyond 1,000 dpi is for clearer type rendering, especially at very small point sizes. The differences here are subtle but noticeable. Imagesetting at resolutions higher than about 2,000 dpi is done mainly for the sake of graphics, as the quality of photographic halftoning and color blends continues to improve markedly as resolution increases.

Factors That Influence Print-Type Clarity

The clarity of the type you set is not just a function of the resolution at which it is imaged. The quality benchmark in this respect is an imagesetter using photographic film, either to create a paper positive image or a film negative. The fineness of the grain of the silver emulsion in the film assures a very *hard dot,* one that's focused and sharply defined. Direct-imaging printers—those that print directly onto plain paper—tend to create softer-edged dots, producing type that's less clear.

The paper itself plays a major role in this, as paper that's rough or absorbent can cause the imaging medium (usually ink or xerographic toner) to spread slightly, softening the dot even further. Even type that has been imaged at high resolutions on an imagesetter will lose sharpness when printed on soft, rough, or very absorbent paper. Newspaper and telephone-book printers do not take great pains refining their type, as the low quality of the paper is apt to render such efforts fruitless.

Adapting to Low Print Resolutions

For printing resolutions below 600 dpi, you have to start making a range of compensatory typographic adjustments. This is particularly true when such output is used as a photographic master from which offset-printed copies are made. The extra generation of reproduction will degrade clarity even more.

Most of the adaptations you'll have to make involve the treatment of type set below normal text size, say, 9-point and smaller (see Figure 18.1).

AVOID SMALL POINT SIZES

Type that you would normally set very small should be set slightly larger at modest resolutions. Footnotes, for example, should be set closer to text size than

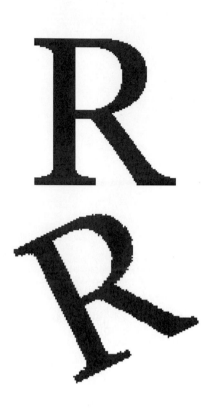

FIGURE 18.2 Grid fitting becomes difficult when characters are rotated off the pixel grid, as this illustration shows. Not only do normally vertical and horizontal features become angled and jagged, but the hints built into fonts to resolve pixel-placement problems often do not work when baselines are not horizontal. Many of the pixel positions in this rotated character seem almost random.

they would be in high-resolution settings. (In fact, you may want to boost the text size as well, just to let this smaller type gain a point size.) Likewise, text in tables should also be kept closer to text size. Reference marks for footnotes and superior and inferior figures should be set only with characters designed for that purpose. If you have your program scale text-face type down to size in these cases, you may find yourself with characters that are practically illegible, as they will be setting as small as 4- or 5-point. The problem is particularly acute with italics.

AVOID REVERSES AND TYPE OVER BACKGROUNDS

The larger dots of modest resolutions make reverses impractical except at display sizes. Small counters and hairline strokes are apt to plug with ink, and characters are likely to break up. Because screened tints are composed of much larger dots than they are at imagesetter resolutions, they will interfere more with the legibility of text set over them. Where these type effects are necessary, try to use a sans serif face or a bolder version of a seriffed face.

AVOID ANGLED TYPE AT TEXT SIZES AND BELOW

Fonts contain program instructions, or *hints,* that cause character outlines to change shape so they image more clearly at low resolutions (for more about this, see "Imaging PostScript Fonts" in Chapter 1). These instructions are particularly important for printing on desktop inkjet or laser printers. Unfortunately, the hints don't work well—or at all—when type is set on a baseline that is anything but horizontal or vertical. The instructions assume that the baseline aligns with the grid of dots on a page, and dots are normally laid down in horizontal rows as the paper advances through the printer.

Thus, text set on angled or undulating baselines does not benefit from these instructions and tends to image less clearly than it should (see Figure 18.2). Only when there are enough dots to image type clearly at any angle—without hints—will such type look as sharp as its traditional, horizontal equivalent. This happens only at well over 1,000 dpi.

Type Onscreen

Depending on your outlook, setting type for display onscreen—for the Web, CD-ROMs, or whatever—is either hopelessly depressing or wonderfully liberating. For those who really care about how type looks, setting type for display at 72 or 96 dpi is an exercise in frustration—it's almost impossible to create good-looking type at such sorry resolutions. On the upside, anything you create at such

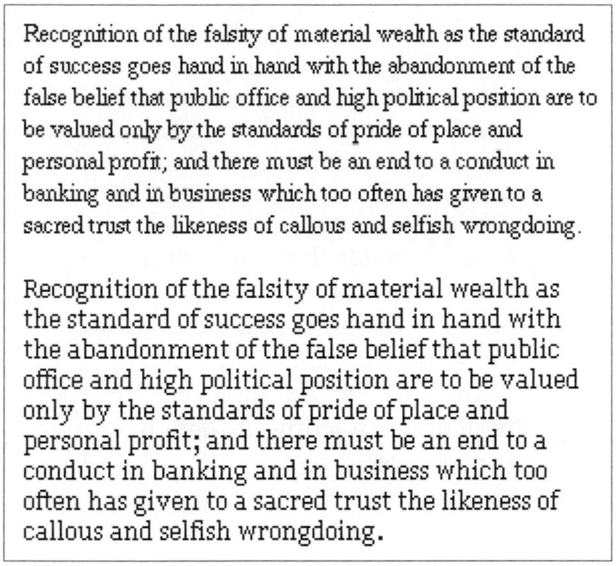

> Recognition of the falsity of material wealth as the standard of success goes hand in hand with the abandonment of the false belief that public office and high political position are to be valued only by the standards of pride of place and personal profit; and there must be an end to a conduct in banking and in business which too often has given to a sacred trust the likeness of callous and selfish wrongdoing.
>
> Recognition of the falsity of material wealth as the standard of success goes hand in hand with the abandonment of the false belief that public office and high political position are to be valued only by the standards of pride of place and personal profit; and there must be an end to a conduct in banking and in business which too often has given to a sacred trust the likeness of callous and selfish wrongdoing.

FIGURE 18.3 The usual Web-browser default typeface, Times Roman (top), is in most ways badly suited to displaying text onscreen. By contrast, Georgia (below, set at the same point size and leading) is designed for that task, and the reader benefits from its superior character fitting, larger x-height, and consistent stem weights.

resolutions is bound to look bad, so you might just as well relax and not bang your head against it.

Now that some devices such as dedicated e-book readers and tablet PCs are beginning to appear with 150-dpi resolution, there may be a chance to practice some decent typography for onscreen applications, but until screen resolutions approach 300 dpi, serious quality compromises will be the norm.

Typefaces for Screen Display

Setting type on a 72- or 96-dpi device effectively guarantees (at best) mediocre spacing, as letter spacing can vary only in whole-pixel increments. Except for the grossest spacing problems, kerning is impracticable.

Bad spacing can be partly overcome by the design of typefaces intended for display on the screen. Two good examples of this are Matthew Carter's Georgia and Verdana, created for and distributed freely by Microsoft (see Figure 18.3).

Carter created these faces by starting with bitmaps—screen fonts—at specific sizes, which he created for maximum legibility at a small number of point sizes commonly used on the Web. Normally, typefaces are designed as outlines for print reproduction, but since Georgia and Verdana's "natural" environment is the screen, Carter started with the screen type and moved backward to a design that would also look good in print. The seriffed Georgia and sans serif Verdana are both TrueType fonts.

A primary benefit of this hinting is that these typefaces' side bearings are precisely tuned to assure at least one pixel of white space between characters, preventing the unwanted ligatures that often appear in computer-displayed

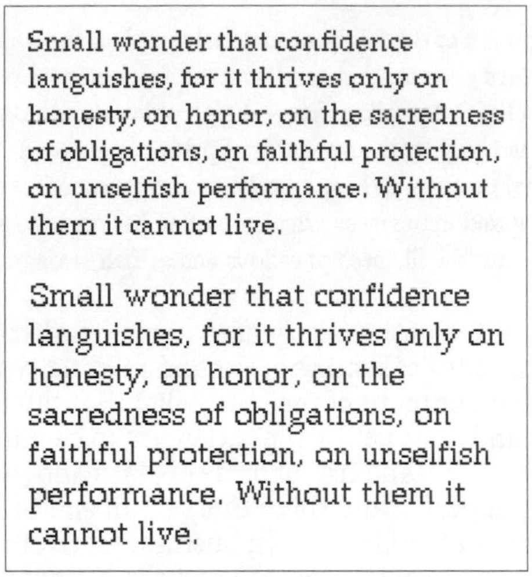

FIGURE 18.4 A shift from 12-point (top) to 14-point (below) makes a huge difference in the readability of the text. The added pixels are particularly welcome in rendering details such as serifs and lowercase counters.

Small wonder that confidence languishes, for it thrives only on honesty, on honor, on the sacredness of obligations, on faithful protection, on unselfish performance. Without them it cannot live.

Small wonder that confidence languishes, for it thrives only on honesty, on honor, on the sacredness of obligations, on faithful protection, on unselfish performance. Without them it cannot live.

text. Bad spacing—an endemic problem when print typefaces are used for Web or CD-ROM documents—makes reading onscreen needlessly tedious. Not to mention making the text just plain ugly.

Using such faces, though, forces you to choose between designing for the screen and designing for the printed page, as it throws you back on a very small selection of screen-savvy typefaces. Microsoft and other vendors offer a few dozen such fonts, but most will not look very good when printed, because they were designed for another medium. In general, their character shapes are fairly simple, since they have intentionally been stripped of the kind of subtleties (delicate curves, fine serifs, tapering stems) that are impossible to render on a low-resolution computer monitor.

When choosing print faces for screen display, look for those typefaces with large features: generous cap heights, long ascenders and descenders, and large x-heights. Sturdy sans serif faces often fare better onscreen than seriffed faces with subtle features, and issues of legibility are paramount. Screen type isn't very readable to begin with.

Other Onscreen Legibility Enhancements

The most natural solution to problems caused by low resolution is to simply make the type larger, and this definitely helps (see Figure 18.4). Not only are more pixels allotted to each character, allowing the type to be rendered better, but the letters also become big enough for readers to distinguish among different typefaces at text sizes. Even though this strategy reduces the amount of text that fits on the screen, 14-point type is often used for screen-text display. This forces a reader to scroll more, but it at least offers a reasonable level of legibility.

FIGURE 18.5 Although the anti-aliased text (lower left) is definitely smoother-looking than the black-and-white text above it, it also contains some distracting dark knots where characters touch each other, and its overall spacing looks more irregular. In the display samples on the right, the anti-aliased type is clearly superior, as the width of the fuzzy aura is less noticeable because it's so much smaller than the characters' strokes.

Another solution is anti-aliasing, in which the letters of the text are surrounded by an aura of gray pixels, which smooth out the jagged edges of the letters and make them more intelligible (see Figure 18.5). The problem with anti-aliasing is that it's hard on the eyes. Because the gray pixels give the letters a fuzzy appearance, the reader's eyes constantly, and futilely, struggle to draw the text into focus. The usual result is fatigue and eyestrain. A partial solution is to raise the point-size threshold at which anti-aliasing kicks in, keeping text-size type in crisp if jagged black and white, while display type is smoothed.

Screen resolutions can't reproduce the spacing nuances of type intended for print. As explained in "Special Tracking Situations" in Chapter 11, very loose tracking can camouflage irregular spacing at low resolutions, and screen type in general benefits from loose tracking. Exaggerating the character spacing makes words easier to read, profiting both black-and-white and grayscale, anti-aliased type (see Figure 18.6).

Typography and the World Wide Web

The main barrier to the practice of good typography on the Web is the structure of the Web itself, which was specifically designed to separate form from content. HTML (HyperText Markup Language), the programming language in which most Web pages are expressed, allows tagged content to flow from source to consumer in a compact form. The tags that identify the structural elements of the document are linked to style sheets on the consumer's computer, and only at that point does the text don its typographical garb. This separation makes specifying type over the Web quite cumbersome.

Complicating matters is that browsers contain the most rudimentary of text-composition engines, so they exercise virtually no control over the typographic qualities of text. About all they do is string one word after another.

> Stripped of the lure of profit by which to induce our people to follow their false leadership, they have resorted to exhortations, pleading tearfully for restored confidence. They know only the rules of a generation of self-seekers. They have no vision, and when there is no vision the people perish.
>
> Stripped of the lure of profit by which to induce our people to follow their false leadership, they have resorted to exhortations, pleading tearfully for restored confidence. They know only the rules of a generation of self-seekers. They have no vision, and when there is no vision the people perish.
>
> Stripped of the lure of profit by which to induce our people to follow their false leadership, they have resorted to exhortations, pleading tearfully for restored confidence. They know only the rules of a generation of self-seekers. They have no vision, and when there is no vision the people perish.
>
> Stripped of the lure of profit by which to induce our people to follow their false leadership, they have resorted to exhortations, pleading tearfully for restored confidence. They know only the rules of a generation of self-seekers. They have no vision, and when there is no vision the people perish.

FIGURE 18.6 Basing screen type on typefaces designed for print is apt to result in pinched spacing, as in the top samples here (left, black-and-white; right, anti-aliased). In the lower samples, the tracking has been opened up by .03 em.

It's common, then, for type destined for the Web to be set first in a typesetting program and then made into an image for display in Web pages. This sidesteps issues of font availability (the reader's needing the same fonts as the page creator), font embedding (assuring that a reader has the needed fonts, at the risk of bloated file sizes), and incompatibilities among Web browsers. But the reader now has a picture of text, not live, reusable text.

The Promise of Cascading Style Sheets

Cascading Style Sheets (often abbreviated css) are a standard created by the World Wide Web Consortium (w3c) to enhance html. Cascading Style Sheets promise to bring to html documents a suite of controls that let you practice the rudiments of what can really be called typography. css version 1 (css1) was quite simple when introduced, but version 2 (css2) has been fleshed out.

Unfortunately, css2 is so complex that much of it—including virtually all the typographical improvements—has never been implemented in any program. Furthermore, the specification doesn't define how things should work; it just makes them possible. That leaves the burden of execution to program vendors, who tend to resent having such burdens defined for them by others.

Take justified text margins, for example. All the css2 specification says is that justification is allowed and that text can be designated to be justified when it appears in a browser program. But it's up to the browser vendors to make it happen by building into their programs such things as hyphenation-and-justification engines, hyphenation dictionaries or algorithmic hyphenation, and a host of other H&J controls found mainly in text-composition programs. These are not trivial tasks, and there are no standards for accomplishing them.

With vendors of both Web design tools and of browsers picking and choosing among the typographic feats enabled by the Cascading Style Sheets standard (both css1 and css2), it will remain difficult to know just what "supports Cascading Style Sheets" means when software vendors make that claim.

WHAT CASCADING STYLE SHEETS CAN DO

Here is a list of what css1 and css2 can offer in a solely typographical context. Omitted are many page layout features that may have indirect typographical implications (such as text-box positioning) and features relating to colors, animation, or dancing text. The css standards allow a program to specify:

- a choice of measurement units, both fixed (points and picas, millimeters and centimeters, and inches) and relative (ems as well as percentages of line length, point size, page size, etc.)

- measure (column width)

- margin widths (either as a fixed value or relative to the size of the page)

- type size (either as a fixed value or relative to a text already set in a reference point size)

- typeface by family (either by specific typeface family or in a general sense for styles such as bold or italic, or for a "variant" such as an expert set)

- leading values, both positive and negative (either as a fixed value or as a variation by fixed value or a percentage of a "solid" set)

- a case shift (a switch to lowercase, uppercase, initial capitals, small capitals, or a reversion to a previous condition)

- unique "first line" treatment (to allow first lines of text blocks to be treated differently than the rest of the text: e.g., small capitals)

- unique "first character" treatment (to allow the first character of a text block to be treated differently than the rest of the text: e.g., a drop cap)

- indents (first line, running, and hanging, specified either by fixed values or as a percentage of line length)

- letter spacing (as a fixed positive or negative value, or as a relative unit such as .01 em)

- word spacing (as a fixed positive or negative value, or as a relative unit such as .1 em)

- underlines, overlines, and strike-throughs

horizontal offset: 3 points
vertical offset: −2 points
blur radius: 1.5 pixels
color: blue

FIGURE 18.7 The Cascading Style Sheets (version 2) standard allows some very sophisticated graphic and typographic controls in HTML files. Here a color drop shadow is specified in absolute units, but it could just as well be specified in relative units that would render the effect scalable.

- letter spacing (as a fixed positive or negative value, or as a relative unit such as .01 em)

- word spacing (as a fixed positive or negative value, or as a relative unit such as .1 em)

- underlines, overlines, and strike-throughs

- vertical alignment (subscripts, superscripts, and top, bottom, and middle alignments, all defined by percentage, relative to the baseline of some designated text that acts as a frame of reference)

- justified margins

- page-break controls (allowed break points, preferred break points, or forced breaks, with associated widow and orphan control for the bottoms and tops of pages)

- Unicode ranges for character sets (for languages with non-Latin or extended Latin character sets)

- more extensive specifications for table formatting (including better vertical alignment controls)

- bidirectional text (right to left, or left to right)

- text shadowing (with controls for density and size; see Figure 18.7)

It's only a matter of time before sophisticated text-composition tools become available for Web pages, but as long as screen resolution stays low, there's not much market pressure for them. Competitive pressures are also working against good Web typography, as standard command sets such as Cascading Style Sheets would seem to argue for competing products sharing text-composition engines. And that is a very abstract concept indeed.

Glossary

absolute measurement Measurement expressed in fixed and constant values, such as picas, inches, and millimeters. Also called fixed measurement.

Adobe Type Manager A program that works in conjunction with the operating system to generate screen type from character outlines in PostScript printer fonts. It can also render type for output on non-PostScript desktop printers. Also known as ATM.

agate (a) A 5½-point type once commonly used for classified advertising; (b) a unit of vertical measurement equal to ¹/₁₄ inch.

Aldines Old-style typefaces based on the designs popularized by Aldus Manutius (Aldo Manuzio) in the late fifteenth century. Examples include Bembo.

algorithm A mathematical rule or set of rules for solving a particular problem. In typesetting programs hyphenation, justification, and kerning may all be handled by algorithmic processes.

algorithmic hyphenation A computer hyphenation system that relies on logical rules rather than a dictionary to hyphenate words.

algorithmic kerning A computer program that relies on an analysis of the shapes of adjoining letters instead of discrete numeric values to adjust the kerning.

alphanumeric Containing letters and numbers, as a font or typeface.

alternate characters Versions of characters that vary in some way from the principal characters in a typeface. Old-style numbers, swash characters, and characters with long or short descenders are all alternate characters.

alternate font A font that complements a text font and includes alternate characters. Sometimes also called an expert-set font.

American point A unit of measure equal to ¹/₁₂ of an American pica, or .0138 inch. *See also* PostScript point.

anti-aliasing A technique for smoothing the appearance of type on a computer screen. It applies gray pixels around the edges of characters to reduce the jagged, stairstep contours apparent in black-and-white screen type. Slices of colored pixels are used to create the same effect for color anti-aliasing.

antique (a) A seriffed typeface whose strokes vary little in weight, with slightly bracketed slab serifs, such as Bookman; (b) a sans serif face in general, such as Antique Olive.

apex The top point of a character such as a capital *A,* or the point at which two strokes join, as in the center of certain *W*s.

arm A horizontal stroke of a character such as an *F.*

ascender A part of a character that rises above the height of most lowercase letters, such as the vertical stroke of a *b* or *d.*

ascender line An imaginary line to which the ascending characters of a typeface reach.

ASCII The American Standard Code for Information Interchange, it is a standard that assigns characters and certain keyboard commands to the numbers 0–127.

ASCII quotation marks *See* typewriter-style quotation marks.

ATF American Type Founders, now a part of Kingsley ATF.

ATM *See* Adobe Type Manager.

auto-activation The action of certain font-management programs to automatically install in the operating system a font that is called for when a document is opened.

automatic kerning Kerning carried out by a text-composition program as a part of hyphenation and justification.

automatic leading A leading value assigned by a program based on the size of the type being set. Automatic leading is usually set by default at 120 percent of the type's point size.

axis An imaginary line connecting the thinnest parts of the stroke of a circular character, indicating the angle of its stress.

B

bar A horizontal line that unites the stems of an *H* or *A; also* the horizontal line of an *e*.

base-align To align along the baseline of a line of type.

baseline The imaginary line on which most of the characters in a typeset line appear to be sitting.

baseline grid A page layout structure that defines where all the text baselines on a page are located. It forms an armature for the placement of graphics and text on a page.

baseline shift A typesetting control that allows a character to be raised or lowered relative to the baseline.

batch pagination Automated, rules-based page layout in which the program places all the page elements according to predefined guidelines.

beak, or beaked serif The serif form at the end of the arms of characters such as *E* and *L*.

Bézier curve A curved line whose shape is defined by a mathematical equation. It consists of two end, or anchor, points and "levers" that can control the angle at which the curve leaves the end points. It is the basic curve used in most computer drawing programs and in PostScript font outlines.

bit The basic unit of computer information, representing a single binary operation: yes or no, on or off.

bitmap An image made up of a fixed number of dots assigned to specific places on an imaginary grid. The coarser the resolution of the grid, the larger the dots and the larger the image. All digital representations—including type—are eventually imaged as bitmaps.

bitmapped font A font consisting of predrawn characters imaged as bitmaps. These are usually used for display on computer screens.

black letter Also called Fraktur or gothic, a typeface with a geometric calligraphic design associated with ecclesiastical writings and commonly used in German-speaking countries until the mid-twentieth century.

bold A version of a face with stroke weights heavier than those in the version used for setting text.

book weight A typeface weight specifically designed for long texts. Within a particular typeface family, its weight falls between light and bold.

bottom-align To align along the bottommost feature of a graphic or a character, such as a descender.

bounding box In digital fonts, an invisible rectangle that surrounds a character. Its height corresponds to the character's point size, and its width is equal to the width of the character plus its side bearings.

bowl The swelling, rounded part of certain characters such as *d* or *P.*

braces Characters used to enclose words or lines of type that are to be considered together: { } .

bracketed serif A serif that joins the main stroke of a character with a curve instead of a sharp angle.

brackets Characters used to enclose characters or words in a line of type, particularly within parentheses: [ ].

broadside A table orientation in which the rows run parallel to the binding, being rotated 90 degrees from the sense of the other pages.

C

cap height The height of the capital letters within a typeface.

capital line An imaginary line drawn along the tops of the capital letters in a typeface. As an alignment guide it is used as a ceiling against which top-aligned characters such as footnote reference marks are set.

caption A title or brief description for an illustration, graphic, or photograph. *See also* legend.

carriage return In typewriting, the action that ends the current line and positions the printing element and/or paper to start setting the next line.

cell In a spreadsheet or spreadsheet-style table, a single rectangular text frame at the intersection of a row and a column.

center-align To align two or more objects or type blocks along a common central axis of symmetry, either horizontal or vertical.

centered As a margin treatment, text set so that the leftover space on each line is divided equally, with half set along the right-hand margin and half set along the left.

chancery italic An italic typeface based on freehand calligraphic models, in particular the cancellaresca style favored by papal scribes at the beginning of the sixteenth century.

character A member of a typeface consisting of one or more glyphs. An accent, for example, is a glyph, as is the letter it modifies. The two taken together are called a character, as is a glyph itself when used individually.

character attributes Certain typographic specifications, such as typeface and point size, that can be applied to individual characters.

character fitting The process in typeface design of assigning side bearings or kerning features to individual characters to create the most natural spacing in the most common character combinations.

character set The complete collection of characters and spaces in a font.

character space The space between two adjoining characters, amounting to a total of their facing side bearings. Character spacing can be modified during hyphenation and justification or by kerning and tracking adjustments.

character width The width of the bounding box of a character, expressed in fractions of an em. *See also* set width.

cicero An absolute unit of typographic measurement equal to 12 didot points, or about 12.75 PostScript points.

Clarendons Typefaces with bracketed slab serifs and rather heavy stroke weights, such as Century Schoolbook.

closed up Descriptive of characters set next to each other without any intervening spaces.

color In typographic terms, the balance between black and white on a printed page. Type set with closer spacing and leading has a darker color than type set looser. Typefaces themselves also vary in color, based on the weight of their strokes relative to the white spaces in and around them.

column (a) On a page, a series of lines of typeset text, normally with parallel vertical margins; (b) in a table, a vertical division consisting of a series of tab entries usually surmounted by a heading.

compressed A typeface designed to have quite narrow character widths, usually narrower than those of a condensed face.

condensed A typeface designed to have narrower character widths than a typeface used for text.

contextual character switching The action of a program to substitute alternative forms of a character when it occurs in particular situations in the text.

contrast In type, a measure of the difference between the thick and thin portions of the strokes that make up a character. The difference is more marked in high-contrast faces.

control characters Nonprinting "characters" in a font that govern such program actions as return, backspace, and line feed.

core font set A basic set of fonts shared by a family of programs or devices that allows everyone using it to have a small library of fonts in common.

corrupted font A font file that has become damaged in some way through numerous readings and copyings. A corrupted font file can cause program, printing, and operating-system errors.

counter The open, negative space inside certain characters, as in the bowl of a *d* or the center of an *o*.

crossbar A horizontal stroke that crosses through the stem of a letter, as in a *t* or an *f*.

crotch The acute angle in which two strokes meet, as in a *V*.

CRT Cathode-ray tube, used for creating images in televisions, most computer monitors, and a generation of phototypesetters.

curly quotes An informal name for typographic quotation marks (" ").

cursive An inclined typeface with calligraphic qualities. The term is used to describe true italics, in contrast to oblique typefaces based on slanted versions of roman characters.

cut-in Descriptive of a text element (often a subheading) set into a multiple-line indent in a longer text.

D

de-install To remove a digital font from service. This is done by removing it from the folder or directory where the operating system expects to find it or, in the case of font-management programs, by making a font unavailable to the operating system.

decimal-alignment A tabular setting in which successive numeric entries in a column align with their decimal points in a straight vertical line.

decorative typeface A typeface designed for its evocative or decorative qualities. Decorative faces are most commonly used in advertising, as their eye-catching designs impart a message that complements the text.

dedicated system In typesetting, a computer system whose only function is to set type and compose pages. Dedicated systems offer many specialist functions not typically available in off-the-shelf consumer software, and they usually have specialist hardware as well, including custom keyboards.

default A typographic setting or specification that a program uses automatically if no other is explicitly expressed. Typesetting programs typically have default settings for such basic variables as typeface and leading, without which type cannot be set.

descender The part of a character that extends below the baseline in letters such as *p* or *y*.

descender line The imaginary line to which the descending letters of a typeface reach.

device independence This term describes software or a computer file that does not need a particular piece of hardware (a computer or printer, for example) to operate it. In terms of typography, a device-independent typeset file can be imaged on a wide range of output devices, and its formatting is not defined in any way by how that device creates its marks or draws its images.

diagonal fraction A fraction built with a sloping fraction bar separating numerator from denominator (e.g., ¼)

didot point The basic absolute measuring unit of the French didot typographic measurement system. It measures .0148 inch, compared with .0138 inch for an American point and .0139 inch for a PostScript point. Twelve didot points make up a cicero.

digital font A software-based font that describes the shapes of characters as binary data.

dingbats Utility characters—often fanciful—including icons, symbols, fleurons, and ornaments.

diphthong Two vowels merged into a single character representing a unique pronunciation (e.g., *æ, Œ*).

discretionary hyphen A hyphen that appears only when a word needs to be divided at the end of a line. It can be added either automatically by a composition program or manually. Also called a soft hyphen.

Display PostScript A version of the PostScript page description language used for creating images of text and graphics on a computer screen.

display advertising Advertising using graphics as well as text or simply text in a wide range of sizes.

display type Type used for titles, headings, subheadings, and so forth. It is typically larger than text type.

dot An accent used in languages including Basque and Lithuanian. It may appear either over or under the character it modifies.

dotless *i* A lowercase *i* with no dot, this character is used with accents to create compound characters such as *ì* and *î*. It is a standard character in Turkish. It can also be used on its own in certain display roles.

double-byte font A font whose character-numbering system is based on a two-byte counting scheme, yielding up to 65,536 possible character assignments. Double-byte fonts are commonly used for Asian ideographic languages that have very large character sets.

down style A capitalization style for display type in which only the first word and proper nouns are capitalized. Also called sentence style.

dpi Shorthand for *dots per inch,* a measure of the resolution of an imaging device such as a computer monitor, printer, or imagesetter.

drop cap An oversized first letter of a paragraph whose baseline is lower than the first baseline of the text it introduces.

dropout A problem in imaging digital type in small point sizes. It occurs when the imaging software fails to use enough pixels to create a character image, resulting in breaks in the shape of the character. Also called pixel dropout.

dropped folio A page number that appears at the bottom of a page.

dropped initial capital *See* drop cap.

Dutch typefaces Old-style typefaces of the late sixteenth and early seventeenth centuries that represent an evolution away from the popular French styles of that age (*see also* Garaldes). They have more contrast and less oblique stress than their precursors and are closely linked to the English faces of the day. They point the way to the transitional style.

dynamic font updating An action taken by certain application programs to update their font menus as soon as a new font has been installed in the operating system. Programs that do not offer this feature must be restarted to read in the updated list of fonts available from the operating system.

E

ear A small stroke that extends from the upper right of the *g* and the *r* in most seriffed roman faces.

Egyptian typefaces A name of vague definition given to certain typefaces of the nineteenth century that were deemed to have "architectural" features, including little or no contrast and sometimes slab serifs. They include faces that are sometimes called antique as well as slab-serif monoline faces and Clarendons.

ellipsis points *See* points of ellipsis.

em A relative measurement equal to the point size of the type in use.

em dash A dash 1 em wide. *See also* joining em rule, punctuating em dash.

em fraction Another name for a diagonal fraction whose nominal width (with a single-digit numerator and denominator) is 1 em.

em space A fixed space 1 em wide. Its width does not change during hyphenation and justification.

em square A square 1 em wide and 1 em tall. The em square represents the "canvas" on which typographic characters are drawn.

en A relative measurement equal to half an em.

en dash A dash 1 en wide, usually used to indicate ranges of numbers.

en fraction Another name for a horizontal fraction whose nominal width (with a single-digit numerator and denominator) is 1 en. Also called a nut fraction.

en space A fixed space 1 en wide. Its width does not change during hyphenation and justification.

encoding In a font, the assignment of numbers to particular characters. The operating system calls for characters by number, so how numbers are mapped to characters defines which characters are accessible. The most popular font encodings are Win ANSI (Windows 3.1, 95, 98, ME), MacRoman (Macintosh OS except OS X), and Unicode (Windows NT, 2000, XP; Macintosh OS X).

end mark A symbol that indicates the end of a newspaper or magazine article.

end-of-line decision During hyphenation and justification, the process of determining how a line in mid-paragraph will end: at a word space, after hyphenation, or after one of several possible line-ending characters (e.g., a dash).

end-paragraph command A typesetting command that ends the current line and starts a new paragraph.

endnotes Footnotes gathered at the end of a chapter or section rather than placed on the page where they are referenced.

English typefaces *See* Dutch typefaces.

entry-a-line index An index in which each entry or subentry starts its own line.

escapement The width of a typeset character used by a typesetting system to determine where the following character should be positioned.

eszett In German, a character representing a double *s* (ß).

exception dictionary A custom hyphenation dictionary created by the user. It can contain hyphenation guidelines that overrule the primary hyphenation dictionary as well as guidelines for words not included in that dictionary.

expanded typeface A typeface whose characters are wider than those of a normal text face, or wider than the text version of a typeface in the same family.

expert set Additional font for a typeface that contains additional or alternate characters, typically including such characters as small capitals, old-style numerals, and fractions.

extended typeface A typeface whose characters are wider than those of a normal text face or simply wider than the "regular" version in a typeface family.

extra lead Leading beyond that required for a solid set. In a solid set, the leading is the same as the point size of the type (e.g., 12-point type on 12 points of leading). A 12/14 setting (12-point type on 14 points of lead), then, uses 2 points of extra lead.

F

face *See* typeface.

family *See* font family; typeface family.

feather During vertical justification, incrementing leading slightly to spread the lines of a column to achieve some composition goal, such as filling a given space, eliminating an orphan, or creating better placement for a subhead.

figure space A fixed space the same width as the numerals in a typeface.

file format The form in which computer files are written that limits their compatibility to certain programs or operating systems. Fonts are available in several file formats, which vary according to how their information is organized and what computer system they're designed for. Application programs write their files in "native" formats that only they can read and edit. They can also write files in "exchange" formats that other applications can read but not necessarily edit.

fillet The curved line that connects a bracketed serif and the stem to which it's attached.

finial A variation of a character intended to be used as the last character of a sentence or line.

first-line indent A left indent that appears in the first line of a paragraph. Also called a paragraph indent.

fixed measurement Measurement expressed in invariable units, such as points and picas and inches and feet. Also called absolute measurement.

fixed-width typefaces Typefaces in which all the characters have the same width, as on a typewriter. Also called monospaced typefaces.

fleuron A flowerlike typographical ornament set as a single character.

flush space A variable-width space that expands to fill the space in which it's set, forcing the type on either side of it to the margins. It is similar in effect to a quad-middle command.

folio A page number. Also the total page count of a book.

font The physical source of the images of type. In metal type, a font is a collection of stamping blocks, each of which bears in high relief the image of a letter; it represents the entire character set of a typeface at a particular point size. In digital type, a font is an electronic file written in programming code that describes the shapes of some or all of the characters in a typeface. These shapes can be scaled to size as needed and imaged by rendering them as an array of tiny dots, or pixels.

font editor An application program that allows you to edit existing fonts or create new ones from scratch.

font embedding A process by which the fonts used to create a document are attached to it, allowing the document to appear correctly on any computer that reads or prints it.

font family In typography, a group of fonts that represents the members of a single typeface family. The Serifa family, for example, consists of Serifa Light, Serifa Light Oblique, Serifa Medium, Serifa Medium Oblique, Serifa Bold, and Serifa Black.

font format *See* file format.

font I.D.   A number assigned to a font and used by an operating system or application program that does not identify fonts by name. Many fonts have identical I.D. numbers, and problems, such as improper printing, can occur when fonts with identical numbers are used at the same time. Applications and font managers may automatically renumber fonts to avoid these problems.

font I.D. conflict   *See* font I.D.

font manager   A program that manages large libraries of fonts. It can organize fonts into sets that can be installed and de-installed en masse, warn of corrupted fonts, and allow more organized storage of large font collections.

font metrics   Data about the characters in a font, including their widths, the position of the baseline, and a list of kerning adjustments.

font set   *See* font manager.

footer   A repeating text element that appears at the bottom of every page, or every other page, of a document.

force-justify   To spread a line of text to completely fill its measure.

fraction bar   The diagonal line used to build em fractions.

Fraktur   *See* black letter.

frame   A graphics program construct for containing an image or passage of text. The width of a text frame normally corresponds to the measure of a column of type. Its height extends from somewhere above the first text line's ascender line to somewhere below its last line's descender line.

front end   In dedicated typesetting systems, the computer terminals and software used for the preparation of typeset text. The typesetting machine or imagesetter is the back end.

G

Garaldes   Old-style typefaces based on models from sixteenth-century France and often their Italian precursors. They have modest contrast, and their serifs are fairly steeply pitched. Examples are the many faces called Garamond.

GDI   Graphical Device Interface, a page description language the Windows operating system uses to image type onscreen and on certain printed pages.

geometric sans serif   A sans serif typeface based primarily on geometric forms, relying heavily on circles and straight lines. Stroke weight varies very little if at all. Examples are Futura and ITC Avant Garde Gothic.

glyph A typographic element that may or may not stand on its own as a type-set character. Accents are glyphs, as are the representations of the letters of the alphabet. An accent glyph can be added to a character glyph to create a unique character (e.g., ` + *a* = *à*), although that hybrid is not normally called a glyph but a character. Thus a small number of glyphs can be used to generate a large number of characters.

gothic A name given, mainly in the U.S. and starting in the nineteenth century, to sans serif faces. In Europe these faces have been called grotesques. The name *gothic* is also sometimes applied to black-letter faces.

grayscale Describes computer images created with shades of gray in addition to black and white. In type, grayscale imaging is used in anti-aliasing to smooth the jagged edges of screen type.

grid fitting During the imaging of type, the process of positioning the outlines of typeset characters on the imaginary grid of all the pixels that make up a page. Pixels whose centers fall inside the outline are imaged. Programming instructions (hints) built into the font alter the shape of the outline so that it encompasses enough pixels to create an accurate image of the character.

grotesque Another name for *sans serif*. The name arose in Europe in the nineteenth century and was originally a pejorative, although it eventually became a standard label.

guillemets A form of quotation marks that appear mainly in continental European languages (« »).

gutter A vertical band of white space that separates columns of type on a page or in a table.

H

H&J *See* hyphenation and justification.

hairline In the anatomy of typeset characters, the thinnest part of a stroke. The term is also used to describe the thin, straight serifs of modern typefaces. A hairline rule has no fixed thickness, but is usually about ¼ point.

hairline serif The thin, straight serif of a modern face such as Bodoni.

hang line An alignment guide on a page against which columns of type or illustrations top-align.

hanging character A typeset character that extends beyond the measure of a column of type or the margin of a tab entry in a table. Also any character that extends beyond the apparent margin of a column of type, as a footnote reference mark in a column of decimal-aligned numbers.

hanging indent A text alignment in which a series of lines are indented relative to the line that precedes them. Most commonly, the first line sets flush left and the lines below it are indented equally.

hanging numerals or figures *See* old-style numerals.

hanging punctuation A setting in text with justified margins in which punctuation including periods, commas, and hyphens are allowed to extend partially or wholly beyond the right-hand margin. This has the effect of making the margin look smoother and straighter.

hard hyphen A hyphen manually keyed into text.

hard return A line-ending command created by using a quad-left command or by pressing the Return key.

hard-end To create a line break manually.

head rule A rule that sets at the top of a table, above the headings row.

headline style A capitalization style for display type in which each major word is capitalized. Also called up style.

hexadecimal A base-16 counting system that uses for digits the numerals 0 through 9 plus the letters *A* through *F*.

high-bit ASCII In the ASCII encoding scheme for numbering typeset characters, those in the high-bit range are the numbers 128 through 255. High-bit ASCII characters—including accented characters—are handled in different ways by different operating systems.

hints Programming instructions added to a font that alter the shape of character outlines to assure that the optimal pixels are imaged to create a clear rendering of each character.

horizontal fraction A fraction in which the elements are stacked vertically, with a horizontal stroke for a fraction bar. Also called an en, or nut, fraction.

humanist A term usually applied to certain sans serif faces that draw their inspiration from hand-lettering rather than geometric forms. In a wider sense, it applies to all typefaces derived from hand-lettering models.

hyphenation and justification The process used by a typesetting program to compose text into lines of a fixed measure. Justification accounts for all the space on a line and may stretch or squeeze word spaces, letter spaces, and character shapes to best fill lines with type. Hyphenation aids justification by dividing words at the ends of lines, which permits type to fill lines with a minimum disturbance to spacing.

hyphenation zone An area along the right-hand margin of a column of text. If the last word of a line will not fit within the measure, it will be hyphenated only if it starts to the left of this zone. If that word starts within the hyphenation zone, it will not be hyphenated. If the hyphenation zone is made wide enough, then, it has the same effect as prohibiting hyphenation.

hyphenation Dividing words at the ends of lines so that a measure is filled more completely with type.

hypho A hyphenated widow; that is, a last line of a paragraph consisting of only part of a hyphenated word.

I

imagesetter A device for imaging type and graphics on photosensitive paper or film. An imagesetter that can create page images directly on a printing plate is called a platesetter.

indent on point A left indent on one line of type whose depth is defined by a point specified in the previous line.

indention Moving the margin of one or more lines of type to the left, to the right, or both simultaneously.

inferior In type, a character or symbol set at a reduced point size and sunk below the baseline.

ink trap *See* ink well.

ink well A feature of some typeset characters that anticipates the effect of ink filling in certain fine details during printing. The crotch of a *V*, for example, may have an exaggerated deep cleft; when plugged with ink, this cleft will yield a normally shaped character.

install To make a font available to the operating system, which in turn will serve it to application programs.

instructions *See* hints.

italic A slanted form of a typeface used as a complement, usually for emphasis or distinction. True italics have a cursive or calligraphic quality, but the term is often also applied to characters that are based on slanted versions of roman forms (also called obliques).

ITC The International Typeface Corporation, the creator of the first system-independent electronic typeface library. ITC licensed its faces to vendors of proprietary, dedicated typesetting systems so that a standard library of typefaces could be available on diverse systems. Now a digital type foundry in its own right.

J

jaggies A condition of computer graphics, including type, caused when images are created with such large pixels that a stairstep effect is visible along diagonal and curved lines.

joining em rule An em dash that is fully 1 em wide. Having no side bearings, joining em dashes connect end to end when set in a series.

jump line In a newspaper or magazine, a brief message to the reader at the end of a column of type stating where the article is continued.

jump page A page on which an article is continued in a newspaper or magazine.

justification The process of fitting type into a measure and handling any space that isn't filled with type. *See also* hyphenation and justification.

justification zone An area along the right-hand margin of a column of type. When type is being set with justified margins, the last line of a paragraph that extends into this zone will be force-justified instead of setting flush left, as it normally would.

justified margins A text alignment in which the type in each line of a column completely fills the measure. This creates straight, (usually) vertical margins on both left and right. To achieve justified margins, a composition program must flex the spaces on a line, compressing them or expanding them.

K

kern A feature of a typeset character that extends beyond its bounding box. (In metal type, a kern extended beyond the edges of its printing block.) This allows these features (such as the hook of an *f*) to slightly overlap the characters set next to them, creating a more natural spacing between the two.

kern table A list of kerning adjustments, built into a font, for specific letter pairs. The adjustments are expressed in fractions of an em.

kerning Adjusting the space between two characters to compensate for their relative shapes. A lowercase letter set after a *T,* for example, will appear too far away because of all the white space under the crossbar of the *T.* Kerning these two characters closer together restores the more natural spacing rhythm found among the characters in the rest of the text. *See also* automatic kerning, manual kerning.

kerning character A character designed with kerns, such as the fraction bar.

kerning pair A pair of letters whose shapes cause them to need a kerning adjustment. The kerning table built into a font consists of a list of kerning pairs and the adjustments they need.

keyword A principal entry in an index.

knockout The opposite of overprinting. When type is knocked out of a background, a hole is created in the shape of the type, and the type is printed into this hole. Knockouts are often necessary when printing type in a color other than black. Printing type this way calls for precise registration on the press.

L

Latin typefaces Typefaces with wedge-shaped serifs.

Latin characters The characters on which Western and most Eastern European languages are based.

leader A series of repeated characters—typically dots—used to connect type on opposite margins of a column or page. They're often seen in wide settings such as tables of contents and menus.

leading The distance, measured in points, from the baseline of one line of type to the baseline of the line that precedes it. The distance from a text baseline to a graphic above it may also be called leading. Rules, like type, have their own baselines, and their positions are also expressed in terms of leading.

legend A long explanation that sets with an illustration, photograph, or table. More commonly called a caption.

legibility The measure of the degree to which typeset characters and words can be deciphered by the eye.

letterpress printing A relief-printing process in which raised inked surfaces (such as the shapes of type characters) are pressed against paper to transfer the image. Because of this direct transfer process, the image of the raised impression must be reversed, or wrong-reading.

letterspacing The process of exaggerating the spaces between typeset characters for dramatic or artistic effect. This is not the same as letter spacing (two words), which is simply the spacing between letters in normal text.

ligature Two characters designed as one, usually to avoid difficult spacing problems, such as fi and fl.

line break The point at which one line of type ends, to be continued on the following line.

line caster A hot-metal typesetting machine that cast entire lines of type in one piece.

line feed A program command that instructs the cursor (onscreen) or imaging mechanism (in a printer) to advance one line farther down the page, usually to start imaging a new line of type.

line length *See* measure.

line space A vertical space equal to one line at the current leading setting.

line spacing *See* leading.

line-ending command Any command that causes one line of type to end and (usually) another to start.

lining numerals or figures Numerals that share a common character width and are the same height as the capital letters in a typeface.

link A connecting line between two parts of a character (such as between the bowls of a roman g) or between two characters, in the case of script typefaces.

logotype Two or more characters set together as a one-character unit, such as points of ellipsis (…).

loop The lower bowl of a *g.*

lowercase The minuscule characters: *a, b, c,* etc.

lowercase numerals or figures *See* old-style numerals.

M

MacRoman Font encoding used by versions of the Macintosh operating system that predate os x. It incorporates some characters from the Symbol font.

majuscules *See* uppercase.

manual kerning Adjusting on a case-by-case basis the spacing between specific pairs of characters.

marks of omission *See* points of ellipsis.

master In type design, a set of drawings of the characters in a typeface for imaging at a specific size. Most digital fonts contain a single set of master outlines, typically drawn for use at text size.

matrix In the Monotype metal typecasting system, a font composed of a grid of molds into which hot metal was injected to create individual printing blocks one at a time.

mean line The imaginary line that runs along the tops of nonascending lowercase letters in a particular typeface.

measure The width of a column of type, or the length over which a line of type is justified. Type set with justified margins fills the measure; lines of type set with ragged margins typically fall short of filling it.

mechanical alignment The alignment of type elements according to the measurements of a typesetting program. Because of the various shapes of typeset characters and the shapes created by different margin settings, mechanically aligned text elements may not look properly aligned. *See* optical alignment.

metrics *See* font metrics.

minuscules *See* lowercase.

modern face A typeface based on eighteenth-century models that feature high contrast between stroke weights, unbracketed hairline serifs set at right angles, and vertical stress. Examples are the many typefaces called Bodoni.

monoline Descriptive of a typeface having uniform stroke weights throughout. Monoline typefaces include many geometric sans serif faces, many slab serif faces, and most typewriter faces.

monospaced A term describing typefaces in which all the characters have the same width, as is common with typewriter faces such as Courier.

Multiple Master A variety of PostScript font invented by Adobe Systems containing two or more sets of master character outlines. Special software can interpolate between master designs to create unique varieties of a typeface. The interpolation can take place between a master designed for use at different point sizes as well as between master designs that vary in weight, serif structure, stance, etc.

N

negative leading A leading value that is less than a solid set, such as 24-point type on 20 points of lead. Negative leading is commonly used at display sizes.

no-break text A passage of type that cannot be divided at the end of a line. It typically consists of words that are not allowed to be hyphenated and that are linked by a nonbreaking space.

nonbreaking hyphen A hard hyphen that is not a legal place to end a line.

nonbreaking word space A word space that is not a legal place to end a line.

normal In terms of hyphenation and justification, *normal* describes the widths of word and letter spaces as they are defined within a font.

nut fraction *See* horizontal fraction.

O

oblique A typeface whose characters are slanted to the right and are based on the shapes of upright roman characters. Many sans serif typefaces have oblique complements instead of cursive italic ones.

offset printing A printing process in which the plates are right-reading; that is, they carry an image of the page as it is printed, not reversed as in letterpress printing. The plate is inked and the image is offset onto an intermediary roller before being printed onto paper.

old-style face A seriffed typeface based on designs popularized in late-fifteenth-century Italy. These have slight contrast; sloping, bracketed serifs; and an oblique stress. Most popular text typefaces are old-style faces.

old-style numerals Numerals that vary in height, with only the *6* and the *8* reaching cap height, and the rest reaching only the mean line. The *3, 4, 5, 7,* and *9* have descenders. Also called lowercase or hanging numerals.

OpenType A hybrid font format that can accommodate either TrueType or PostScript Type 1 font data. OpenType fonts are double-byte fonts, enabling them to contain more than 65,000 characters.

operating system The basic software on a computer that handles such functions as input (e.g., keystrokes) and output (e.g., printing), file management, and services to application programs such as supplying font metrics information and screen type.

optical alignment Alignment of graphic or type elements by eye instead of by computer program.

optical kerning Automatic kerning based on a computer analysis of character shapes rather than on a table of explicit kerning adjustment values for specific character pairs. Also called algorithmic kerning.

ordinal A typographic shorthand expression, set as a superior, that denotes degree, quality, or position in a series; for example, 2^e and 1°.

orphan A fragment of a paragraph only one or two lines long that appears at the bottom or top of a column and seems to be splintering off from the main text block.

os Abbreviation for *operating system.*

outline font An electronic font that stores the images of characters and symbols as outline drawings. These outlines are described mathematically and can be scaled to any size before being imaged.

overprint To print type (usually in black ink) over a colored or tinted background. Overprinting avoids registration problems.

override A typographic setting that varies from the formatting created by the application of a style sheet.

overstrike *See* strike-through type.

P

page description language A programming language used for describing the appearance of entire pages. A page description language can ideally represent any typographic or graphic event that occurs on a printed or projected page.

page grid An underlying structure for a page that includes alignment and placement guidelines for such elements as text, graphics, running heads, and folios and defines such geometry specifications as margins and trim size.

paragraph attribute A typographic attribute associated with entire paragraphs, such as first-line indents.

paragraph indent An indent from the left margin assigned to the first line in a paragraph. Also called a first-line indent.

path In computer graphics, the trace of a line or curve. The path itself has no width, only direction, and becomes visible only when it is stroked (assigned a rule weight) or filled.

PDL *See* page description language.

photographic font   A font that takes the form of a photographic negative. The images of the characters are clear on a black background, and a light is flashed through them to cast images of the characters on photosensitive paper or film. Also called filmstrip font.

phototypesetting   The use of light to create images of type on photosensitive paper or film, which is then developed.

pi font   A font containing nonalphabetic characters, symbols, utility characters, and so forth.

pica   An absolute typographic measurement consisting of 12 points. Six American picas equal .9936 inch. A PostScript pica is slightly larger, so that there are exactly six to an inch.

pixel   Shorthand for *pic*ture *el*ement, a pixel is one dot of a digital image.

plain   In the language of word processors and desktop computer programs, text is plain when it has been assigned a typeface only. It has had no additional "style" (e.g., underscoring) applied to it, nor has it been altered with "style" controls to make it italic or bold.

platform   The type of computer or computer system that a program is running on. Usually, the term refers to the operating system being used, rather than a specific kind of hardware. A Macintosh running the Windows operating system, then, would from this standpoint be a Windows platform, not a Mac.

point   An absolute typographic measurement, 12 of which make up a pica. An American point is .0138 inch, whereas a PostScript point is .0139 inch. *See* pica.

point size   The measurement in points of type set at a given size, expressed visually as the distance from just above the ascender line to just below the descender line. The point size is in fact the height of the characters' bounding boxes, as in metal type it was once the height of the face of the printing block a letter's image was cast on.

points of ellipsis   A series of dots, or periods, used to indicate an omission of text or a suspension in the flow of the text. Three-dot ellipses are used in mid-sentence, while four-dot ellipses are used at the ends of sentences.

points of suspension   *See* points of ellipsis.

pop cap   *See* standing cap.

PostScript   A page description language used by most imagesetters to create printed versions of electronically composed pages. PostScript treats all marks—

including type—as graphics. Characters in PostScript fonts are created with the same drawing technology as that found in PostScript illustration software.

PostScript font A font that was designed for use with the PostScript page-imaging technology.

PostScript interpreter A software program (often running on a dedicated computer) that reads page descriptions written in the PostScript programming language and translates them into an array of dots for imaging on an output device such as a computer screen, desktop printer, or imagesetter.

PostScript point An adaptation of the traditional American typographic point to make it more compatible with the English measuring scheme. A PostScript point is exactly $1/72$ inch, so 6 PostScript picas equal 1 inch.

"PostScript-flavored" OpenType font An OpenType font containing PostScript Type 1 font data.

primes Typographic symbols (′ ″) used to indicate inches and feet, and hours and minutes. A single prime is used to indicate typographic points.

proportional Term describing typefaces whose characters have unique widths, as opposed to monospaced typefaces, whose characters are all the same width.

punctuating em dash An em dash with side bearings, making it slightly less than a full em wide. The extra spacing makes it useful in text, where full-width em dashes may set too close to adjoining characters. *See also* joining em rule.

Q

quad In metal type, a nonprinting block of metal used as a spacing element.

quad center A typesetting command that ends a line of type and centers it within its measure (by adding quads—real or virtual—before and after it).

quad left A typesetting command that instructs the system to end a line of type and set it flush left, filling the rest of the line with quads (real or virtual).

quad middle A typesetting command that instructs the system to insert enough quads (real or virtual) at the point it was issued to drive the text on either side of it to set flush against the right and left margins.

quad right A typesetting command that instructs the system to end a line of type and set it flush right, filling the rest of the line with quads (real or virtual).

QuickDraw A page description language used to draw screen images in versions of the Macintosh operating system before os x. os x uses Display PostScript.

R

ragged left A text margin treatment in which all lines end hard against the right-hand margin but are allowed to begin short of the left-hand margin. On lines that do not fully fill the measure (nearly all of them), any leftover space is deposited along the left-hand margin. This creates an irregular margin along the left side of the text column.

ragged right A text margin treatment in which all lines begin hard against the left-hand margin but are allowed to end short of the right-hand margin. On lines that do not fully fill the measure (nearly all of them), any leftover space is deposited along the right-hand margin. This creates an irregular margin along the right side of the text column.

range kerning Another term for tracking.

ranging numerals *See* lining numerals.

ranked hyphenation In a hyphenation dictionary, a system of preferring certain hyphenation points in a word to others. There may be several degrees of preference, with the goal being to divide a word so that it is most comprehensible to the reader: *re-educate,* and not *reed-ucate,* for example.

raster image processor A program (often running on a dedicated computer) that translates instructions written in a page description language into an array of dots that can be imaged on a computer screen, digital printer, or other digital output device. Also called a RIP.

rasterize To render programming code for a page description language into a series of dots for imaging.

readability A measure of how easy and pleasant it is to read a given body of text.

recto A right-hand page (or the front side of a single-page document).

reference mark A symbol, number, or letter indicating a footnote or endnote.

regular A term often used to describe the text-weight version in a typeface family, frequently the version that gives the entire family its name. This face may be called "regular" to differentiate it from its italic, lighter, or bolder kin, although the word is not usually a part of its official name.

relative indent An indent based on another indent. An absolute indent is measured from the margin of the text column, but a relative indent is added to another. A first-line indent is normally a relative indent, so that if the entire text block is indented from the left, the first-line indent is still in effect, being added onto the running left indent.

relative measurement A typographic measurement whose dimension varies according to the size of the type. The most common relative measurements are ems and ens.

rendering *See* rasterize.

resolution A measure of the size of the dots used in digital imaging devices, expressed in dots per inch (or centimeter). The higher the resolution, the smaller the dots and the crisper the image.

return A computer keyboard command derived from the typewriter carriage return. The return command immediately ends the current line and begins a new one, which is usually the start of a new paragraph as well.

reverse Type set white on a black or colored background.

reverse leading *See* negative leading.

right-reading In terms of film or printing plates, an image that appears as it will on the printed page, with text reading from left to right.

RIP *See* raster image processor.

river A series of word spaces in consecutive lines that stack one upon the other to create the appearance of a fissure in the text.

romain du roi A typeface, designed for Louis XIV of France at the end of the seventeenth century, that was the precursor to the modern typeface style.

roman A typeface with upright letters, normally used for long texts.

row In a table, a horizontal division consisting of a set of tab entries.

rule A typographic line used to separate or enclose. The thinnest is a hairline (about ¼ point thick). Rule weights are measured in points or halves of points.

rule fill A command that links two points in a typeset line with a rule of a specific weight.

run-in A kind of subhead that shares the baseline of the first line of the paragraph it introduces.

runaround A margin treatment in which the text follows the shape of a graphic or other page element.

running head A repetitive heading that appears above the text area of the pages in a publication.

running indent An indent assigned to two or more consecutive lines.

running text The main text on a page, usually organized into paragraphs.

runover line The continuation of type from a previous line.

S

sans serif A typeface whose strokes end in blunt terminals, lacking the flared forms known as serifs. Sans serif faces have little if any contrast between thick and thin strokes.

Scotch typefaces Typefaces derived from the modern style and popularized in Scottish print works in the nineteenth century. They have a sturdier look than classical moderns but the two share fine serifs and a vertical stress.

Scotch rule A double rule, the upper one of which is usually heavier.

screen font Bitmapped font intended for screen display. Being drawn in advance by hand, characters from a bitmapped screen font are more legible at small point sizes than screen type generated automatically from font outlines.

script typeface A face designed to imitate handwriting. Consecutive characters are typically joined by links, in the handwritten style.

sentence style A capitalization style in display type in which only the first word and proper names are capitalized. Also called down style.

serif A crossing feature at the end of the principal character strokes of certain typefaces. Serifs aid in character recognition and also have a decorative quality.

seriffed typeface A face whose characters contain serifs.

set width The width of an imaged character as it appears in print or onscreen.

shaped margin A margin treatment in which the text follows the shape of a graphic or other page element.

shaped rag An intentional or accidental arrangement of line endings in ragged-margin copy that gives the margin a smooth shape.

shoulder A curved character stroke with a convex shape, as in an *h* or *m*.

side bearing The space between the outer edge of a character and the edge of its bounding box (digital type) or type block (metal type). The side bearings of two adjoining characters combine to create the letter space between them.

side-head Another name for subhead.

single-byte font A font containing a maximum of 256 characters.

skew An arrangement of type set with a straight but nonvertical margin.

slab serif A serif that has a blocklike appearance with squared-off ends.

slur serif A serif that is rounded, bulbous, or ill defined.

small capitals Capital letters that are shorter than normal capitals, often as short as x-height.

smoothing *See* anti-aliasing.

soft hyphen A hyphen set manually or by a computer program that appears only when a word has to be divided at the end of a line. If the text reflows and the word ends up in midline, the soft hyphen disappears.

soft return A modified return command that starts a new line without starting a new paragraph. The equivalent of a quad-left or quad-right command, depending on the margin alignment in effect.

solid A leading configuration in which the leading value is the same as the point size of the type in use.

solidus Another name for the virgule, or slash (/).

solidus fraction In typewriting tradition, a fraction built with full-size lining numerals separated by a solidus (e.g., *2/3*).

sorts In metal type, a generic term for the small printing blocks that carry images of characters and that are properly distributed in their assigned drawers in the type cabinet.

space band Another name for a word space.

space-after Extra lead added after a paragraph.

space-before Extra lead added before a paragraph.

spine The central part of the main stroke of an *S*.

spread Two facing pages in a publication taken as a whole.

square serif *See* slab serif.

stance The angle at which a character stands. Roman characters have an upright stance; italics have an inclined or oblique stance.

standoff The specification that defines how far away text should set from an object being wrapped.

standard-width typeface A typeface whose lowercase alphabet, set without spaces, is 13 ems long.

standing cap A large initial capital letter at the start of a paragraph that shares the baseline of the first line of the text.

standing initial capital *See* standing cap.

stem The principal upright stroke of a character such as a *T* or an *L.*

straddle entry In a table, a tab entry that spans more than one column.

straddle head In a table, a heading that spans more than one column, each of which normally has its own subhead.

stress A thickening in the stroke weight of a character either caused by or in imitation of the effect of a wide-nibbed pen. In a round letter such as an *o,* a line connecting the thin portions of the stroke reveals the angle of the stress.

strikeout *See* strike-through type.

strike-through type Type over which have been superimposed a series of dashes to indicate that the text ought to be omitted or is going to be omitted in a future draft of the document.

stroke A principal element of a character, representing the movement of a pen as the letter would be drawn.

stroked path In a computer program, a line, or a path (which can have direction without mass) that has been assigned a rule weight.

stub column In a table, the leftmost column when it contains headings or descriptions amplified by entries in the columns to its right.

style sheet A named set of typographical specifications that can be applied simultaneously to a body of text. Typographic style sheets are normally divided into those that can be applied at the character level and those that can be applied only to whole paragraphs.

subentry A secondary heading in an index, subordinate to a keyword.

subheading A heading that divides running text into sections.

subscript *See* inferior.

subsetting The process of embedding into an electronic document only those characters used in the document. This reduces file size at the expense of editability, as complete versions of the fonts have not been included.

suitcase In the Macintosh operating system, a special kind of folder for holding TrueType fonts or PostScript screen fonts.

superior In type, a character or symbol set at a reduced point size and top-aligned, usually along the ascender line.

superscript *See* superior.

swash character A decorative alternate character (usually a capital) that has certain dramatically extended strokes often called flourishes.

T

tab cycle In a table, an entire row's worth of tab entries taken as a whole.

tab entry In a table, a block of text that occurs at the intersection of a row and a column.

tab stop In a word processing program, a point at which text advanced with the Tab key will align. When no text is present, pressing the Tab key will advance the cursor from one tab stop to the next, as on a typewriter.

tab value In table-setting software, a point along the measure of the table that defines the margin of a tab column.

tail The descending part of certain letters such as *Q* or *y*.

tail rule A rule that sets below a table.

template An empty electronic document formatted with page specifications that contains style sheets for text to be added later.

terminal The end of a character stroke, which may or may not be adorned with a serif.

terminal character *See* finial.

text on a path Text set on a curved baseline or a baseline that follows a shape.

text face A typeface designed for use in long texts, particularly books. Text faces are generally seriffed, with modest contrast, generous character widths, and fairly light stroke weights.

thin space A fixed space normally equal to ¼ em, or about that of a word space. Often a typesetting program allows a custom definition of a thin space.

tight rag An arrangement in ragged-margin copy in which all the lines are fairly close to being the same length.

titling face A typeface proportioned specifically for use in large point sizes. Titling faces often consist only of capital letters.

top-align To align objects of different sizes against a common "ceiling."

track kerning Another name for tracking.

tracking The measure of the overall spacing between characters in a passage of text. Tightening the tracking draws characters together by the same proportional amount. Loosening the tracking enlarges the spaces between characters.

transitional face Literally, any typeface whose design places it on the cusp between two design trends. Usually, though, the term refers to certain faces, such as Baskerville, seen as precursors to the modern style.

trim size The size of a publication's pages after it has been bound and trimmed.

TrueType font A font in the highly extensible, programmable format created principally by Apple Computer. TrueType fonts are close enough in function to PostScript fonts to work with most PostScript interpreters.

TrueType GX font One of the fonts based on an extension of the TrueType font format and supported only (for a short time) by the Macintosh operating system. Few GX fonts were made, and the Mac os no longer supports them.

turn line *See* runover line.

Type 1 font *See* PostScript font.

type area The part of a page populated by the main text and usually defined by the top, bottom, outside, and binding margins.

type size *See* point size.

typeface A collection of characters, numerals, accents, and related symbols that share a common design motif.

typeface family In typography, a group of typefaces that share a common root name and common design characteristics. The Serifa family, for example, consists of Serifa Light, Serifa Light Oblique, Serifa Medium, Serifa Medium Oblique, Serifa Bold, and Serifa Black.

typeset quality A standard of type-rendering quality based on the clarity and sharpness of images created by a phototypesetter.

typographic quotation marks The traditionally shaped quotation marks used in English text (" " ' ') that have distinct opening and closing forms. Often referred to in Britain as inverted commas.

typewriter-style quotation marks Direction-neutral quotation marks designed for the typewriter (" '); they are part of the ASCII character set.

U

unbracketed serif A serif joined to the main stroke at a sharp angle.

underscore A rule set beneath a passage of text.

Unicode A multilingual typographic character encoding (character-identification scheme) that assigns numbers to specific characters. It can accommodate more than 1 million characters.

unshift The keyboard setting that allows the typing of lowercase characters.

up style A capitalization style for display type in which every major word is capitalized. Also called headline style.

uppercase The capital letters in a typeface. Also called majuscules.

V

variable dot size A technology used in certain desktop printers that allows the size of a printed dot to vary. Setting smaller dots around the edge of a typeset character, for example, gives it a smoother appearance.

Venetian faces Typefaces based on the earliest designs for movable type created in the late fifteenth century in Italy, and particularly Venice. They are old-style faces that have little contrast, steeply angled serifs, oblique stress, and a signature slanted bar in the *e*. An example is Jenson.

vector In computer graphics, a direction from one point to another that can be either stroked (assigned a rule weight) or filled (used as a boundary or container for a color or image).

vector font *See* outline font.

verso A left-hand page (or the back side of a single-page document).

vertical justification Filling columns of type by altering leading to avoid such layout problems as short copy, orphans, and poor subhead placement.

vertical space band A space between typeset lines at which a vertical-justification program is allowed to alter leading.

virgule Another name for the solidus character (/). Also called a slash.

visual alignment *See* optical alignment.

W

wedge serif A triangular serif. It is a hallmark of so-called Latin typefaces.

weight A measure of the thickness of the strokes that make up the characters of a typeface. Typeface weights range from extra light through light, medium, and book, to bold, heavy, extra bold, and beyond.

white space In type, the space in and around typeset characters. Much of the practice of typography is based on the control of white space.

widow A very short last line of a paragraph that creates the visual effect of a line space between paragraphs.

width table In an electronic font, a table that assigns a width—expressed in fractions of an em—to every character. The operating system feeds these widths to application programs, which use them to calculate where to position characters on a line and how much type will fit within a given measure.

width-compatible typefaces Typefaces of different (although usually similar) designs whose corresponding characters have exactly the same width. A document set using one such font, then, will compose identically when a width-compatible font is substituted. The core set of fonts used by the Windows and Macintosh operating systems are width compatible.

wild rag An arrangement in ragged-margin copy in which the lengths of the typeset lines vary widely.

Win ANSI The font encoding used by versions of the Windows operating system that do not support Unicode: Windows 3.x, 95, 98, and ME.

word space A blank character created by pressing the spacebar on a keyboard. Its width is defined within the font in use, but that width may be altered during hyphenation and justification to attain certain composition goals.

wrap (a) Text that has turn lines or runover lines is said to wrap. Adding or deleting text in a paragraph will cause the lines to rewrap, or break at new places. (b) Text whose margin is shaped to follow the contours of another page element is also often called a wrap.

WYSIWYG Shorthand for "what you see is what you get," a reference to computer screen displays that give a preview of how something will look when printed.

X

x-height The distance from the baseline to the mean line, a measure of the height of the lowercase characters in a typeface. The *x* is used as a gauge because it has both a flat top and a flat bottom.

Index

Symbols

Accents

′ (acute accent), 58, 208, 260
˘ (breve), 208, 260
¸ (cedilla), 208, 260
ˆ (circumflex), 58, 208, 260
¨ (dieresis, or umlaut), 58, 208, 260
″ (double acute), 208
` (grave accent), 58, 208, 260
ˇ (haček), 208, 260
¯ (macron), 208, 260
˛ (ogonek), 208, 260
° (ring), 208, 260
˜ (tilde), 58, 208, 260

Currency symbols

¢ (cent sign), 210
$ (dollar sign), 210, 261–262
€ (euro sign), 261
£ (pound-sterling sign), 261

Footnote reference symbols

* (asterisk), 191, 210, 230
† (dagger), 191, 231
‡ (double dagger), 231
§ (section mark), 209, 231
¶ (paragraph symbol), 209, 231

Mathematic symbols

≈ (approximately equal to sign), 209
° degree sign), 210
÷ (division sign), 209
= (equals sign), 23, 209
> (greater than sign), 209
≥ (greater than or equal to sign), 209
< (less than sign), 209
≤ less than or equal to sign), 209
− (minus sign), 208, 209, 210
× (multiplication sign), 208, 209
≠ (not equal to sign), 209
% (percent sign), 210
+ (plus sign), 209, 210, 278
± (plus or minus sign), 210
× (powers of magnitude), 210
′ ″ (primes). *See* primes
/ (virgule). *See* virgule (/)

Punctuation

{ } (braces), 190, 296
[ ] (brackets), 190, 296
. . . (ellipsis, three-dot), 205–206
. . . . (ellipsis, four-dot), 206
—— (em dash). *See* em dashes
– (en dash). *See* en dashes
« » (guillemets). *See* guillemets (« »)
- (hyphen). *See* hyphens
( ) (parentheses), 190
. (period), 80, 263
' ' " " (quotation marks). *See* quotation marks
; (semicolon), in indexes, 233
/ (virgule). *See* virgule (/)

Other symbols

& (ampersand), 209
@ (at sign), 209
• (bullet), 190, 207, 209
© (copyright symbol), 209
(number or pound sign), 210
® (registered trademark symbol), 209, 210
™ (trademark symbol), 210

A

abbreviations
    acronyms, 198
    A.D., B.C., B.C.E., 198
    A.M., P.M., 198, 260–261

abbreviations *(continued)*
in British English, 263
in French, 201, 263
of Latin terms, 72
n/a, N.A., 255
with periods, 198
absolute measurements
in Cascading Style Sheets, 289
defined, 293
in typography, 21–24
accented characters
escapements for, 7
in European languages, 259, 265
on Macintosh systems, 58–59,
overview of, 208–209
See also names of specific characters
acronyms
preventing hyphenation of, 144
small caps for, 198
See also abbreviations
acute accent (´), 58, 208, 260
Ad Lib typeface (ATF), 75
Adobe Garamond typeface, 60, 70, 131, 230
Adobe InDesign, 57, 153
Adobe PageMaker, 172
Adobe Systems, Inc.
development of OpenType, 40, 53
development of PostScript, 13, 21–22
font hinting, 16
Multiple Master font format, 39
Adobe Type Manager (ATM)
defined, 293
missing fonts and, 98
PostScript interpreters and, 52
screen display and, 93
advertising type
agates in, 293
decorative typefaces in, 75
display advertising, 44, 69, 189–190, 300
dotless *i* in, 209
spacing of type in, 107
agates, 27, 293
aircraft names, italics for, 72
Akzidenz Grotesque typeface
(Berthold), 69
Aldine types
defined, 293
roman capitals and, 42
See also italics

algorithmic hyphenation, defined, 293
versus dictionary-based hyphenation,
142–143
end-of-line decisions and, 135
algorithmic kerning, 170, 293
alignment
base alignment, 204, 295
bottom alignment, 188, 190, 244, 296
center alignment, 190, 244, 296
characters and text blocks, 187
decimal alignment, 244, 252–253, 298
hanging characters and, 190–191
mechanical alignment, 311
outline formats, 221
page and baseline grids and, 187–188
of tables, 244
text frames and, 188
top alignment, 189
vertical alignment, 188–189
See also optical alignment
alphanumeric fonts, 51, 293
alternate characters, 60, 293
alternate fonts
defined, 294
overview of, 59–60
See also expert sets
A.M., conventions for setting, 260–261
American English typographic conventions,
262–263
abbreviation style, 263
hyphenation, 260
quotation styles, 262
temperature expressions, 263
American point, 21–22, 294
American Standard Code for Information
Interchange. *See* ASCII (American
Standard Code for Information
Interchange)
American Type Founders (ATF), 75, 294
Americana typeface (Kingsley ATF),
x-height of, 32
ampersand (&), 209
angled type, imaging problems with, 284
anti-aliasing
defined, 294
overview of, 18–19
screen display, 287
See also color anti-aliasing

Antique Olive typeface (M. Olive), 32, 74, 294

antique typeface, defined, 294

apex, of character
  defined, 294
  and point size, 23

apostrophe
  with italic word, 72, 169
  Italian conventions, 267
  in letterspaced text, 153

Apple Computer
  and PostScript, commercial use of, 13
  and TrueType, development of, 16, 52–54, 95
  TrueType GX technology of, 39
  See also Macintosh computers

approximately equal to sign (≈), 209

Arabic numerals, 222

Arial typeface (Monotype), similarity to Helvetica (Linotype), 54, 98

arm, of character
  defined, 294
  illustrated, 33

Arrighi, Ludovico, 42

arrows (pi characters), 207

artwork, italics for names of, 72

ascender line, defined, 294
  See also top alignment

ascenders
  defined, 294
  illustrated, 33
  leading and, 131
  superior characters and, 201–202
  typeface design and, 36

ASCII (American Standard Code for Information Interchange)
  character sets, 55
  comma-delimited, 245
  defined, 294
  font encoding and, 56
  high-bit, 56, 306
  PostScript written in, 13
  quotation marks, 294

Asian languages
  MacRoman encoding, 59
  Unicode fonts and, 55

asterisk (*), 191, 210, 230

asymmetrical leading, in display type, 127

at sign (@), 24, 209

ATF (American Type Founders), 75, 294

ATM. *See* Adobe Type Manager (ATM)

author names, in bibliographies, 234–235

auto-activation, of fonts, defined, 294

automatic kerning, 166
  defined, 294
  turning off, 131, 171, 198, 205

automatic leading
  avoiding, 122–123
  defined, 294

Avant Garde Gothic typeface (ITC), 32, 73, 74, 304
  similarity to Century Gothic (Monotype), 98

axis
  defined, 294–295
  horizontal, 189
  in Multiple Master font, 39

B

backgrounds
  effect on typography, 75–76, 173, 255, 284
  output resolution and, 284

ballot boxes, setting, 207

bar, of character
  defined, 295
  illustrated, 33

base alignment
  defined, 295
  of virgule, 204

baseline shift
  defined, 295
  leading and, 126–127
  and top alignment, 190

baselines
  alignment by, 37, 188–189
  defined, 295
  grids and, 187
  leading and, 31, 120–121
  table rules and, 248
  text on a path and, 174–175
  x-height and, 32

Baskerville, John, 41

Baskerville typeface
  compared with Bodoni, 70–71
  in historical classifications, 46
  specifying, issues in, 47

batch pagination, 159, 295
Bauhaus design school, 40–41
Bauhaus typeface (ITC), 75
beaked serif, defined, 295
Bell Centennial typeface (Linotype), 37
Bembo typeface (Monotype), 46, 70, 293
benchmarks, 154
Benton, M. F., 75
Bernhard Fashion typeface (EF), 75
Bézier curves, 15, 295
bibliographies
    author names in, 234–235
    formats for, 234
    works cited in, 235
bidirectional type, 290
Big Caslon typeface (Carter and Cone),
    74, 95
binary operations, defined, 295
bitmapped fonts
    defined, 295
    use of, 49–50
bitmaps
    defined, 295
    graphics and, 49–50
    compared with scalable graphics, 14
bits, of computer data, 14, 49, 295
black box translator. *See* raster image
    processors (RIPS)
black letter
    defined, 295
    gothic type and, 305
    as text typeface, 68
blank line
    as extra lead, 188
    as improper line space, 125
blank spaces
    Gutenberg's system, 4
    letterpress printing, 10
    offset lithography, 11
    on printed page, 5
    ragged-margin text, 162–163
    in tables, 255
blocks of type, 3–4
Bodoni, Giambattista, 47
Bodoni typeface
    compared with Baskerville, 70–71
    hairline serifs and, 305
    in historical classifications, 46
    loose tracking and, 173

specifying, issues in, 47
    x-height of, 32
bold type
    in bibliographies, 234
    in Cascading Style Sheets, 289
    defined, 295
    for emphasis, 71–72
    headings and, 72, 218
    jump lines and, 226
    in indexing illustrations, 72, 232
    and low resolutions, 284
    synthesized by computer, 51, 52, 94–95
    tables and, 243
    in typeface families, 43, 94
    and typeface weight, 41
    typewriting versus typesetting, 84
    uses of, 71–72
    See also semibold type
bold italics
    jump lines and, 226
    subheads and, 218, 219
    synthesized by computer, 51, 52, 94–95
    in typeface families, 43, 94
Book Antigua typeface (Monotype),
    similarity to Palatino (Linotype), 98
book titles, 72
    See also titles
book, typeface weight, 42, 295
    variations in, 130
Bookman Light typeface (ITC), 41, 130
Bookman Old Style (Monotype), 98
Bookman typeface (ITC)
    as example of antique typeface, 294
    obliqued italic of, 42
    similarity to Bookman Old Style
        (Monotype), 98
books
    citation of, in bibliographies, 235
    H&J in composing, 138
    standard type sizes for, 120
    titles, 72, 216
    tracking in CD-ROM versions of, 173
    typefaces for, 130
bottom alignment
    defined, 296
    descender line and, 190
    in tables, 244
    text frames and, 188

bottom rules. *See* tail rules

bounding boxes
    character proportions and, 129
    defined, 296
    em dashes and, 24, 205
    point size and, 23
    tracking and, 136
    type design and, 5

bowl, of character
    defined, 296
    illustrated, 33

braces ({ }), 190, 296

bracketed serifs, 34–35, 296

brackets ([ ]), 190, 296

breve (˘), 208, 260

British English typographic conventions,
    262–263
    abbreviation style, 263
    hyphenation, 260
    pound-sterling sign, 261
    quotation styles, 262
    temperature expressions, 263

broadside orientation, of tables, 238, 296

browsers, text-composition abilities of, 288

bullet (•), 190, 207, 209

C

calligraphy
    as basis for Gutenberg's system, 5–6
    cursive typefaces and, 298
    influence on typeface design, 32–33
    swash characters and, 201

cancellaresca lettering, 296
    See also chancery italics

cap height
    defined, 296
    and type size, apparent, 129

capital line, defined, 296

capitalization
    French, 265–266
    headings, 217
    headline (up) style, 217, 306, 323
    sentence (down) style, 217, 226, 318
    titles, 266
    See also capitals, full;
        caps and small caps

capitals, full
    author names, in bibliographies, 234

chapter headings, 217
    initial capitals, 210–213
    in outline formats, 222
    compared with small caps, 197

caps and small caps
    author names, in bibliographies, 234
    captions and legends, 227–228
    chapter headings, 217

captions
    condensed faces and, 73
    contrasted with legends, 227
    defined, 296
    format of, 227–228
    and style sheets, 279
    in tables, 244

carriage returns
    defined, 296, 317
    hard returns, 306
    typewriting versus typesetting, 81–82
    See also soft returns

Carta font (Adobe), 44, 207

Carter, Matthew, 285

Cascading Style Sheets (CSS), 289–291
    See also style sheets

case. *See* lowercase; uppercase

case shift, in Cascading Style Sheets, 290

Caslon typeface, 46, 47
    Caslon 540 typeface (Linotype), 36,
        70, 74

Caslon, William, 46, 69

catalogs, leading in, 128

cathode ray tubes (CRTs)
    defined, 298
    and electronic fonts, 12
    raster images on, 14

CD-ROM manuals, tracking and, 173

cedilla (¸), 208, 260

cells, table
    adjusting/formatting, 241–243,
        253–254
    defined, 296
    grid structure and, 240

center alignment
    of characters, 190
    defined, 189, 296
    of headings and subheads, 111,
        191–192, 220
    in tables, 244–245, 249–252

centered subheads, 220

centered text

    defined, 296

    problems with visual alignment of, 192

    See also vertical justification

cent sign (¢), 210

Century Expanded typeface (Kingsley ATF), 70, 173

Century Gothic typeface (Monotype),

    similarity to ITC Avant Garde

    Gothic, 98

Century Old Style typeface (Kingsley ATF), 44, 69

Century typefaces

    similarities between Century

        Schoolbook (Monotype) and

        New Century Schoolbook

        (Linotype), 98

    width of, 69, 73

chancery italics, 42, 296

    See also italics

chapter headings, 216–217

    See also headings

character attribute

    controlling with style sheets, 272

    defined, 297

    leading as, 126

character-by-character calculation, in H&J, 136–137

character fitting

    decorative typefaces and, 75

    defined, 297

Character Map, Windows

    accented characters, 208–209

    character sets and, 57–58

character sets, 57–61

    Character Map (Windows), 57–58

    defined, 51, 297

    economics of large sets, 195

    European, 259–260

    expert sets, 59–60

    font encoding and, 56

    font formats and, 55

    Key Caps (Macintosh), 57–58

    Latin 1, 55

    OpenType, 54

    PostScript Type 1, 52

    TrueType, 53

    Unicode, 55, 60–61

character spacing

    characters followed by a space, 209

    characters not followed by a space, 210

    characters preceded and followed by

        spaces, 209

    defined, 297

    See also spacing issues

character style sheets

    applying, 273

    creating from existing text, 276

    formats, 277

    including expert and pi fonts with, 278

    See also style sheets

character switching, contextual, 53, 297

character width

    defined, 297, 318

    flexing, 152–153

    legibility and, 43

    measured in em-based units, 24–25

    Monotype machines and, 10

    typefaces and, 69, 130

characters

    control characters, defined, 298

    defined, 297

    followed by a space, 209

    hanging, 190–191

    not followed by a space, 210

    oversized, 193

    preceded and followed by spaces, 209

    type size changes and, 38

    typewriting versus typesetting, 85

    varying weight with size, 41

    See also special characters

Cheltenham typefaces, 74

Chinese language, 55

ciceros, 27, 297

circumflex (ˆ), 58, 208, 260

Clarendon typefaces, 34, 297

    from Bitstream, 35

    from Linotype, 74

Clearface typeface (ITC, Linotype), 75

closed-up characters, 209, 210, 297

code-driven text-processing, 91

color

    high resolution and, 283

    text typefaces and, 75–76

color anti-aliasing, defined, 294

color, type. *See* type color

columns
  defined, 297
  gutters between, 128–129
  leading in multicolumn applications, 128
  measuring width in picas, 23
  narrow-measure problems and, 110
  page-setup options, 116
  single-column limit in typewriters, 79
  tables of contents and, 223
columns, in tables, 237–238
  balancing column width and gutters,
      246–247
  defining, 239–240
  specifying, 245–246
  stub column and, 237
comma-delimited ASCII, 245
compatibility issues, with fonts, 54–56
composition
  hyphenation, 155
  letterpress type and, 11
  line-by-line H&J versus multiline,
      138–139
  line spacing, 154–156
  masking problems by loose spacing, 107
  paragraph color, 156–157
  ragged right margins, 162–163
  rivers, 161–162
  vertical justification, 159–161
  widows and orphans, 157–159
compressed typefaces. See condensed
    typefaces
computer typesetting, 89–101
  font copyrights, 101
  font embedding, 99–100
  font management, 95–99
  replacing word processors and
      dedicated typesetting machines,
      89–91
  screen display and, 92–95
  WYSIWYG (what you see is what you
      get), 91–92
condensed typefaces
  defined, 297
  drop caps and, 211
  legends and, 228
  legibility and, 43
  synthesized by computer, 73–74
  uses of, 73–74

contextual character switching
  defined, 297
  TrueType fonts and, 53
continued from, 226
contraction of titles, British English, 263
contraction of titles, French, 263
contrast
  defined, 298
  between thick and thin portion of
      strokes, 45–46
control characters, defined, 298
Cooper Black typeface (ATF), 74
copyright symbol (©), 209
copyrights, font, 101
core font set
  defined, 298
  Windows and Macintosh computers,
      54, 98
Corel Ventura Publisher, 182
corrupted fonts, 96–97, 298
counter, of character
  defined, 298
  illustrated, 33
  low resolution and, 284
  master designs and, 38
Courier typeface
  highlighting errors with, 9
  as monospaced typeface, 8, 79, 311
  as replacement font for missing fonts, 98
  similarity to New Courier
      (Monotype), 98
crossbar, of character
  defined, 298
  illustrated, 33
crotch, of character
  defined, 298
  illustrated, 33
  ink wells and, 37
  in specific letters, 36–37
CRTS. See cathode ray tubes (CRTS)
CSS (Cascading Style Sheets), 289–291
  See also style sheets
curly quotes (' ' " "), 86, 298
currency symbols
  aligning in tables, 254–255
  aligning in text, 190
  language-specific conventions, 261–262
  spacing with, 171, 261
cursiva humanistica, 42

cursive typefaces
  defined, 298
  versus oblique, 42
cut-in subheads, 221
cut-ins, defined, 298
cutline, 227
  See also legends

D

dagger (†), 191, 231
dashes, 204–205
  centering on x-height, 190
  typewriting versus typesetting, 85
  See also em dashes; en dashes; hyphens;
    3-em dash
decimal alignment
  defined, 298
  justification and, 244
  numeric tables, 252–253
decorative typefaces
  defined, 298
  initial capitals and, 210
  overview of, 44
  uses of, 75
dedicated typesetting systems
  assigning typographic attributes with,
    90, 91, 271
  compared with digital typesetting
    systems, 17–18
  compared with word processors, 89
  defined, 299
  escapement and, 7
  leading and, 126
  quadding commands and, 82–83
  ragged margins, control of, 162
  tables, tools for setting, 19
  vertical space bands and, 126
  word spacing and, 80
default settings
  defined, 299
  leading, 122–123
default style sheets, 154, 274
definitions, use of italics for, 72
degree sign (°), 210
de-install, digital fonts, 298
denominators, in fractions, 203
descender line
  bottom alignment and, 190

defined, 299
descenders
  defined, 299
  illustrated, 33
  typeface design and, 36
design
  Bauhaus design school, 40–41
  bounding boxes and, 5
  legibility and readability and, 104
  role of typography in, 215
  of tables, 239
  type design and, 5
  See also typeface design
desktop computers, 13
desktop publishing, 13–16
  benefits of, 13
  device independence and, 14–15
  lack of quadding commands in, 83
  PostScript fonts, 15
  PostScript images, 15–16
  PostScript model and, 13–14
  raster image processing and, 14
device drivers, printers, 98
device independence, 13–15
  defined, 299
  desktop publishing and, 14–15
  PostScript fonts and, 13–14
diagonal fractions, 203, 299
dialog boxes
  assigning typographic attributes with, 90
  style sheets and, 271
  as typesetting interface, 18
dialogue, punctuation of
  British English conventions, 262
  French conventions, 264–265
  German conventions, 267–268
  Italian conventions, 267
  Spanish conventions, 267
  See also quotation marks
dictionary-based hyphenation. *See*
  hyphenation dictionary
didot points, 27, 299
dieresis (¨), 58, 208, 260
digital fonts
  de-installing, 298
  defined, 299
  master designs, 38
  outline characters and, 12–13
  proportional widths, 25

digital images, defined, 295
digital type
    dot basis of, 16
    limitations of, 38–39
    compared with metal type, 4
digital typesetting systems, 17–18
dingbats, 207, 299
    See also pi fonts
diphthongs, 200, 299
direct-input typesetting, 10
discretionary hyphens
    among types of hyphens, 143
    defined, 299
    instead of hard hyphens, 155
display. *See* screen display
display advertising, 44, 69, 74–75, 107, 189–190, 209, 300
Display PostScript, 93, 299
display type, versus text type, 6
display typefaces
    asymmetrical leading in, 127
    kerning and, 168
    letterspacing and, 151
    ligatures in, 201
    overview of, 44
    sans serif as standard for, 69
    uses of, 74
division sign (÷), 209
document structures
    chapter headings, 217
    cut-in subheads, 217–218
    extracts, 221
    outline formats, 222
    overview of, 215–217
    style sheets and, 279
    subheads, 217–220
    tables of contents, 223
dollar sign ($), 210, 261–262
Dom Casual typeface (ATF), 74
dot (·), 260
dot, of character, 33, 300
    defined, 300
    illustrated, 33
dot matrix printers, 92–93
dotless *i,* 209, 300
dots
    creating images from, 49
    output resolution and, 281

variable dot size, 323
    See also pixels
dots, as leader, 309
dots per inch (dpi)
    defined, 300
    digital type and, 16
    resolution and, 14
double acute (″), 208
double-byte fonts, 55, 300
double dagger (‡), 231
double-hyphenated words, 144
double quotation marks (" "). *See* quotation marks
double *s. See* eszett
double word spaces, ending sentences with, 80–81
down (sentence) capitalization style
    defined, 300
    newspaper headlines and, 217
    titles of books and magazines, 266
dpi. *See* dots per inch (dpi)
drivers, printer, 98
drop caps
    aligning, 193
    defined, 210, 300
    overview of, 211
    problem characters for, 211
    readability issues, 212
    visual alignment and, 110–111
dropout
    defined, 300
    pixels and, 16
dropped folio, 224, 300
dropped initial capital. *See* drop caps
duplicate fonts, 99
Dutch typefaces, defined, 300
dynamic font updating, 96, 300

E

e-book readers, 285
ear, of character
    defined, 301
    illustrated, 33
Eastern European languages, 208
Egyptian typefaces, 69, 301
electronic fonts
    condensing/expanding type and, 73–74
    scalability of type and, 12–13

ellipsis points, 24, 205–207
    defined, 301
    ellipsis character (...), 206
    four-dot ellipsis (....), 206
    French conventions, 263–264
    Italian conventions, 267
    line breaks and, 206–207
    Spanish conventions, 267
    three-dot ellipsis (...), 205–206
em
    character width and, 24–25
    defined, 24, 301
    in letterspaced text, 152
    relation to *M,* 24
    tracking and kerning calibrations based
        on, 26, 51, 156, 165
    white-space adjustments, 25–26
    word space and, 26–27
em dashes, 24, 85
    defined, 301
    French conventions, 263
    as line-break points, 139
    for missing or void tab entries, 255
    punctuating em dash, 205
    spacing issues, 210
    Spanish conventions, 267
    types of, 204–205
    uses of, 205
em fractions, 203, 301
em square
    baselines and, 30–31
    character width and, 43
    defined, 301
    typeface design and, 30
embedding fonts, 99–100
emphasis
    boldface for, 72
    italics for, 72
    typeface use and, 71
    typewriting versus typesetting, 84–85
    See also highlighting
en
    defined, 301
    em basis of, 26
    relation to *N,* 26
    word spaces and, 80
en dashes, 85
    defined, 301
    French conventions, 263

    as line-break points, 139
    spacing issues, 210
    uses of, 204
en fractions, 203, 301
en spaces, 26, 80, 152, 247
encoding
    ASCII, 56
    defined, 301
    font encoding, 56
    MacRoman, 56, 59, 202
    Unicode, 60–61
    Win ANSI, 56, 58
end-line command, 81–82, 310
end marks, 226, 301
end-of-line decisions, 134–136, 301
end-paragraph command, 81, 301
endnotes
    defined, 301
    compared with footnotes, 228–229
    See also footnotes
English measurements, 22, 24
English ordinals, 202
English typefaces, defined, 300
English typographic conventions, 262–263
    abbreviation styles, 263
    hyphenation, 260
    measurements, 22, 24
    quotation styles, 262
    temperature expressions, 263
entry-a-line index, 233, 302
equals sign (=), 23, 209
escapement
    defined, 302
    monospaced type and, 8
    typewriters and, 7
eszett (ß), 268, 302
euro sign (€), 261
European languages
    euro sign and, 261
    Latin alphabet and, 259
    See also specific languages
exception dictionary, 144, 302
expert sets
    in Cascading Style Sheets, 289
    defined, 294, 302
    including in style sheets, 278
    overview of, 59–60
extended character sets, 195–196

extended or expanded typefaces
    defined, 302
    legibility and, 43
    synthesized by computer, 73–74
    uses of, 73–74
extra condensed typefaces. *See* condensed
    typefaces
extra lead
    as aid to readability, 108, 119
    in bibliographies, 234
    calculating, 121–122
    captions and, 228–229
    defined, 121, 302
    with drop caps, 211
    extracts and, 221
    footnotes and, 229, 230
    jump lines and, 226
    with running indents, 179
    subheads and, 31, 124–126, 219–220
    table of contents and, 223
    tables and, 247, 248
    typefaces and, 36, 131
    in vertical justification, 160
extracts (quoted text), 221

F

face. *See* typefaces
family. *See* typeface family
feathering leading, 160, 302
feet, indicating with prime, 86, 208
Fenice typeface (ITC), 35
figure space
    currency symbols and, 254–255
    defined, 302
    em basis of, 26
filename extensions
    .otf (OpenType), 62
    .pfb and .pfm (PostScript Type 1), 62
    .ttf or .ttc (TrueType), 62
file formats
    defined, 302–303
    font compatibility and, 54
    Macintosh and Windows, 52
    native, 245
    See also font formats
fillet, bracketed serifs, 34, 303
film fonts. *See* photographic fonts
finials, 196–197, 201, 303

first-line indents
    defined, 303
    footnotes and, 230
    relative indents and, 316
    standing caps and, 212
    tables and, 244
    See also paragraph indents
fixed measurements
    in Cascading Style Sheets, 289
    defined, 303
    typographic measurements and, 21
fixed spaces
    em spaces, 26, 80, 247
    en spaces, 26, 80
    figure spaces, 26, 254
    in letterspacing, 152
    for paragraph indents, avoiding, 180
    thin spaces, 26, 152, 254
fixed-width typefaces, defined, 303
    See also monospaced type
fleurons
    defined, 303
    ornaments and, 196
    pi characters and, 207
floating palettes, 271–272
flourished characters, 201
    See also swash characters
flush space, 151, 303
folios, 223–224
    defined, 303
    dropped folio, 224, 300
    jump lines and, 225
    page grid and, 188
    point size of, 224
    positioning, 223–224
    running heads and, 224, 225
    tables of contents and, 223
follow-on style sheets, 273–274
font editors
    customizing kerning, 170
    defined, 303
    font use and, 64–65
font embedding
    computer typesetting and, 99–100
    defined, 303
font encoding, 56
    See also encoding
font family, defined, 303

font formats
   defined, 52
   identifying, 61–63
   OpenType, 53–54
   PostScript, 15, 52
   TrueType, 16, 53
   See also file formats
font I.D. conflicts, 99–100, 304
font management, 64, 95–99
   corrupted fonts, 96–97
   duplicate fonts, 99
   font-storage locations and, 96
   missing fonts, 97–98, 273
   operating systems and, 95–96
font manager, defined 304
font metrics, 24–25, 51, 304
   See also character width
font sets, 64
   See also font manager
fonts, 10–13, 49–65
   corrupted, 96–97
   defined, 29, 303
   and device independence, 15
   duplicates, 99
   electronic, 12–13
   historical evolution of, 10–11
   information contained in, 51
   installing, 307
   kerning tables and, 166–167
   master character designs, 38–39
   metric measurements, 30, 304
   missing, 94, 97–98, 273
   Monotype machine, 11
   nonalphabetic, 44–45
   photographic, 12
   versus typefaces, 29–30
fonts, working with, 49–65
   character sets, 57–61
   cross-platform compatibility issues,
      54–56
   font-editing programs, 64–65
   font formats, 52–54
   font managers, 64
   identifying font formats, 61–63
   information contained in fonts, 51
   outline fonts and bitmapped fonts, 49–50
footers, defined, 304
footnotes
   alignment, 230

function of, 228–229
hanging characters and, 191, 254
jump lines and, 225
low-resolution adjustments for,
      282–284
placement, 229
point size and leading, 229–230
semibold typefaces and, 229–230
style sheets and, 278
symbols, 230–231, 282, 284
in tables, 253, 255
forced justification, 151–152, 304
foreign words and phases
   hyphenation of, 260
   italics for, 72
   See also language issues
formats
   converters, 245
   multiple meanings of, 52
   using style sheets to change, 279
   See also file formats; font formats
four-dot ellipsis (. . . .), 206
Fournier typeface, 46
fraction bar (/)
   defined, 304
   as kerning character, 166
   typewriting versus typesetting, 86
   compared with virgule, 203
   in Windows, 87
fractions
   as alternate characters, 196–197
   building by hand, 203–204
   closed-up setting, 204
   denominator and numerator figures, 203
   diagonal, 203, 299
   forms of, 204
   horizontal, defined, 306
   inferior numerals and, 202
   punctuation after, 204
   semibold typefaces and, 203
   solidus, 203, 319
   space after, 204
   types of, 202–203
   typewriting versus typesetting, 86–87
Fraktur type, 68, 295
   See also black letter
frame-at-a-time vertical justification,
      160–161

frames, text
    alignment and, 188
    defined, 304
    drawing/specifying width of, 116
    leading and, 123–124
Franklin Gothic typeface (ATF), 74
French typographic conventions, 263–266
    abbreviations, 201, 263
    accents, 265
    capitalization, 265–266
    numeric expressions, 266
    punctuation style, 263–264, 265
    quotation style, 264–265
Friz Quadrata typeface (ITC), 24, 74
front ends
    defined, 304
    word processors as, 19
Frutiger typeface (Linotype), 131
Futura typeface (Bauer)
    as example of sans serif, 41
    geometric sans serif and, 40, 304
    for text, 131
    weights of, 41
    x-height of, 32

G

Galliard typeface (ITC), 36, 70, 196
Garalde typefaces
    defined, 304
    Dutch typefaces and, 300
    old-style and, 45
Garamond, Claude, 45
Garamond typeface
    Adobe Garamond, 60, 70, 131, 230
    as book typeface, 69, 130
    condensed versions of, 73
    expert font set, 60
    in historical classifications, 45–46
    ITC Garamond, 41, 73, 94
    Monotype Garamond 3, 130
    screen display of, 94
    specifying, issues in, 47
    Stempel Garamond, 42, 45, 69
    weights of, 41, 94
GDI (Graphical Device Interface), 92, 304
genus/genera, use of italics for, 72
geometric sans serif, 40, 304
Georgia typeface (Microsoft), 285–286

German typographic conventions, 267–268
Gill Sans typeface (Monotype), 42–43
    x-height of, 32
glossary, style sheets and, 279
glyphs
    characters and, 297
    defined, 305
    em square and, 30
    fonts and, 50–51
    typeface as collection of, 29
gothic type, 295, 305
Goudy Old Style typeface
    from Kingsley ATF, 70, 173
    from Monotype, 36
graphic design. See design
Graphical Device Interface (GDI), 92, 304
graphical user interfaces (GUIS)
    assigning typographic attributes
        with, 90
    limitations for typographic formatting, 18
    selections and, 91
graphics
    bitmaps and, 49–50
    bitmaps versus vector-based, 14
    frames, 184
    high resolution and, 283
    measuring in picas, 23
    role of typography in, 215
    text wrapping and, 110
grave accent (`), 58, 208, 260
grayscale, defined, 305
greater than or equal to symbol (≥), 209
greater than symbol (>), 209
grid approach, to tables, 240–243
    gutters, 241–242
    horizontal rules, 242
    limitations of, 241
    WYSIWYG compatibility and, 240
grid fitting
    defined, 305
    PostScript and, 15–16
grid, page. See page grid
Griffo, Francesco, 45
grotesque typefaces, 69, 305
    See also sans serif typefaces
GUI. See graphical user interfaces (GUIS)
guillemets (« »)
    defined, 305
    French quotation style, 264

guillemets (« ») *(continued)*
     German quotation style, 268
     Italian quotation style, 267
     Spanish quotation style, 266
Gutenberg, Johannes, 3–4
Gutenberg's Bible, 6
gutters
     around wraps, 183–184
     between columns, 128–129
     defined, 305
     grid-defined, 187
     vertical, 185
gutters, in tables
     balancing with column width in tables,
          246–247
     table-setting tools and, 241, 242
     white space and, 238

H

H&J. *See* hyphenation and justification (H&J)
haček (ˇ), 208, 260
hairline, of character
     defined, 305
     illustrated, 33
     low-resolution adjustments and, 284
     modern typefaces and, 46
hairline serifs, 34–35, 305
halftones, 283
handset type, 6
hang line, 188, 256, 305
     See also top alignment
hanging characters
     alignment and, 190–191
     defined, 305–306
     in numeric tables, 253–254
hanging figures, 199
     See also old-style numerals
hanging indents, 181–182, 306
hanging punctuation, 190, 306
     See also hanging characters
hard ending, defined, 306
hard hyphens
     controlling hyphenation, 141–142
     defined, 306
     versus discretionary hyphens, 155
     headings and, 217
     typewriting versus typesetting, 85
hard return, defined, 306

head rules
     defined, 306
     in tables, 244–245
headings
     bold type for, 71–72
     capitalization of, 217
     chapter headings, 216–217
     grid structure and, 187
     as signposts, 216
     style sheets and, 279
     compared with titles, 216
     visual alignment and, 111
     See also running heads; subheads; titles
headings, of tables
     alignment, 192, 250–252
     heading row, 238
     multiple-line, 246–247
     overview of, 238
     straddle heads, 238
headline (up) capitalization style, of display
          type and headings, 217, 306, 323
headlines
     master typeface designs for, 38
     photographic fonts and, 12
Helvetica font, possibility of duplicates, 98
Helvetica typeface (Linotype)
     Akzidenz Grotesque and, 69
     as example of proportionally spaced
          typeface, 8
     as example of sans serif, 40
     obliqued italic of, 42
     popularity in early desktop publishing, 68
     range of weights in, 42
     similarity to Arial (Monotype), 54, 98
hexadecimal numbers, 306
high-bit ASCII, 56, 306
high-resolution output, 281–283
highlighting
     pi characters and, 207
     problem lines and spacing problems, 154
     See also emphasis
hints
     defined, 306
     fonts and, 16
     low resolution and, 284
     screen display and, 286
     TrueType and, 53
historical designations, small caps for, 198
horizontal axis, 189

horizontal fractions, 203, 306

horizontal rules, tables

    centering text, 249

    leading and, 248

    rule types and, 244

HTML (HyperText Markup Language)

    Cascading Style Sheets and, 289

    type specification and, 288

humanist sans serifs, 40, 306

hyphenation

    defined, 133

    dictionary-based versus algorithmic, 142–143

    double-hyphenation, avoiding, 144

    frequency of, 141

    headings, avoiding in, 217

    indexes and, 232

    language-specific conventions, 260

    restrictions on, 141–144, 148

      of German eszett, 268

      of Spanish *ll, rr,* 267

    table headings and, 247

    zones, 142–143, 307

    See also algorithmic hyphenation; hyphenation dictionary

hyphenation algorithms. *See* algorithmic hyphenation

hyphenation and justification (H&J), 133–163

    adding to hyphenation dictionary, 144–145

    algorithmic hyphenation, 142–143, 293

    character-by-character calculations, 136–137

    character width and, 152–153

    controlling hyphenation, 141–142

    defined, 133, 307

    end-of-line decisions and, 134–136

    forced justification and, 151–152

    hyphenation zones and, 142–143

    justified margins and, 146–150

    letter-space ranges and, 147–152

    letterspacing and, 151–152

    line-at-a-time calculations, 137–139

    measure and, 145

    paragraph attributes and, 154

    ragged margins and, 145–146

    restrictions, 143–144

    selecting means of, 142–143

    style sheets and, 276

    testing specifications, 154

    word-space ranges and, 145–150

    word spacing, 140–141

hyphenation dictionary

    adding to, 144–145

    algorithmic hyphenation and, 142–143

    end-of-line decisions and, 135

    language-specific conventions and, 260

    ligatures and, 200

    ranked hyphenation, 316

hyphenation zones

    defined, 307

    H&J and, 142–143

hyphens

    centering on x-height, 190

    in French first names, 264

    spacing issues, 210

    types of, 143, 204

    typewriting versus typesetting, 85

    uses of, 204

hypho, 307

I

IBM Selectric typewriters, 83

icons, font identification and, 62

images. *See* graphics

imagesetters

    defined, 307

    high resolutions and, 283

    PostScript interpreters and, 52

    resolutions of, 14

    typesetting machines as, 13

import filters, 245

importing data, into tables 245

importing style sheets, 279

inches, indicating with primes, 208

indent-on-point, 178, 182, 307

indentation. *See* indention

indention

    Cascading Style Sheets and, 290

    defined, 177, 307

    first-line indents, 180–181

    folios, 223–224

    hanging indents, 181–182

    indents as paragraph attribute, 178

    indents on a point or character, 178, 182

    indexes and, 232–233

    measuring, 23

indention *(continued)*
    outline formats, 221
    relative indents, 316
    running indents, 179–180
    subheads, 220
    in tables, 244
    tabs and, 87
    types of, 177–178
    word spaces and, 80, 181
    See also paragraph indents
indents on a point or character, 178,
        182, 307
InDesign, Adobe, 57, 153
indexes
    bold page numbers in, 72
    entry-a-line index, 302
    formats, 231–232
    indention styles, 232–233
    keywords, 309
    leading in, 128
    overview of, 231–232
    page breaks, 233–234
    subentries, 320
    typefaces and point sizes, 232
inferior characters. *See* subscripts
inferior numerals, in fractions, 202
initial capitals, 210–213
    drop caps, 211–212
    standing caps, 212–213
    types of, 210–211
ink wells (ink traps), 36–37, 307
inkjet printers, 16–17, 284
installing and uninstalling fonts, 298, 307
instructions, for fonts. *See* hints
interfaces. *See* graphical user interfaces (GUIS)
international font standards, 55
International Typeface Corporation (ITC),
        207, 308
Italian Old Style typeface (Monotype), as
        example of Venetian face, 45
Italian typographic conventions, 267
italics
    in Cascading Style Sheets, 289
    defined, 308
    jump lines and, 226
    kerning transitions with roman
            type, 169
    low-resolution adjustments and, 284
    overview of, 42

for punctuation, 72
replaces underscoring, 85
reversed type and, 76
subheads and, 218, 219
synthesized by computer, 51, 52, 94–95
in typeface families, 43, 94
uses of, 72, 232, 235
ITC. *See* International Typeface
        Corporation (ITC)
ITC Avant Garde Gothic typeface, 73,
        74, 304
    similarity to Century Gothic
            (Monotpe), 98
ITC Bookman typeface
    as example of antique typeface, 294
    obliqued italic of, 42
    similarity to Bookman Old Style
            (Monotype), 98
ITC Bauhaus typeface, 75
ITC Bookman Light typeface, 130
ITC Fenice typeface, 35
ITC Friz Quadrata typeface, 24, 74
ITC Galliard typeface, 36, 70, 196
ITC Garamond typeface, 41, 73, 94
ITC Korinna typeface, 74
ITC New Baskerville typeface, 36, 70
ITC Novarese typeface, 42
ITC Souvenir typeface, 74
ITC Zapf Chancery Medium Italic,
        similarity to Monotype Corsiva, 98
ITC Zapf Dingbats font, 45, 98, 207
    MacRoman and, 59
    pi characters and, 44–45, 207
    similarity to Monotype Sorts, 98
    Unicode and, 196

J

jaggies, 308
Janson typeface (Monotype), x-height
        of, 32
Japanese language, 55
Jenson, Nicholas, 45, 323
joining em rule, 205, 308
journals
    citation in bibliographies, 235
    standard type sizes for, 120
jump lines, 225–226, 308
jump pages, 225, 308

justification
    defined, 10, 133, 308
    forced justification, 151–152
    justified margins in tables, 244
    vertical justification, 124, 159–161
    word spaces and, 27
    See also hyphenation and justification
        (H&J); justified margins
justification zones, 151, 308
justified margins
    in Cascading Style Sheets, 290
    defined, 308
    end-of-line decisions and, 135
    measure problems and, 109
    spacing and, 134
    in tables, 244
    word-space ranges and, 146–150
    See also justification

K

keeps
    orphans and, 159
    vertical justification and, 160
kern, defined, 308
kern table, 170–171, 308
kern-table editor, QuarkXPress, 170–171
kerning
    algorithmic, 170, 293
    applying, 166–168
    automatic, 131, 171, 198, 205, 294
    on curved baselines, 175
    custom kerning tables, 170–171
    defined, 165–166, 309
    H&J and, 136–137
    italic to roman transitions, 169
    manual, 168–169
    numerals, 171–172
    small cap to full-size capital
        transitions, 198
    small caps, 198
    standing caps, 213
    using em units to express, 25–26
kerning character, 309
    illustrated, 5, 166
kerning pair metrics, 26
kerning pairs
    assigning new values to, 171
    caps and small caps, 198

contained in fonts, 170
    defined, 309
    difficult pairs, 169
    manual kerning and, 168
    metrics, 26
kerning tables, 51, 166–167, 170–171
Key Caps, Macintosh
    accented characters in, 208–209
    overview of, 58
    Unicode and, 59
keyboard shortcuts
    for kerning, manual 168
    for paragraph styles, 273
    style sheets and, 271
keyboards
    computer keyboard based on
        typewriter, 79
    typesetting limitations of, 271
keywords, 232, 309
Kingsley ATF, 294
knockout, 76, 309
Korinna typeface (ITC), 74

L

language issues, 259–268
    British English versus American
        English, 262–263
    character sets, 259–260
    currency symbols, 261–262
    French, 263–266
    German, 267–268
    hyphenation of foreign words, 260
    Italian, 267
    italics for foreign words, 72
    Spanish, 266–267
    time expressions, 260–261
language-specific fonts, 208
    Asian languages, 55, 59
laser printers
    output compared with photographic
        film, 16–17
    desktop publishing and, 13
    font hinting and, 284
    variable dot size and, 17
Latin 1 character set, 55
Latin alphabet
    character sets and, 259
    defined, 309

Latin alphabet *(continued)*
  predominance of seriffed forms in, 40
  width of characters in, 8
Latin typefaces, 34, 309
layout. *See* page layout
leaders (dots), 223, 309
leading, 120–128
  ascenders and descenders and, 36
  asymmetrical, in display type, 127
  automatic, 122–123
  baseline shift and, 126–127
  for bibliographies, 234
  calculating, 121
  for captions and legends, 228
  for catalogs, 128
  changing as type size changes, 124–125
  in Cascading Style Sheets, 290
  defined, 309
  for endnotes and footnotes, 229–230
  for extracts (quoted text), 221
  feathering, 160, 302
  fineness of adjustments, 122
  historical derivation of term, 4
  line spaces versus space bands, 125–126
  measuring from baseline to baseline, 31
  measuring in points, 23
  multicolumn applications, 128
  negative leading, 121, 312
  non-text applications, 128
  overview of, 120–122
  as paragraph attribute, 126
  Return key and, 81
  reverse leading, 317
  and reversed type, 127
  and running heads, 225
  setting measure too wide for, 109
  subheads, 124–125, 220
  for table of contents, 223
  tall ascenders and, 36
  text frames and, 123–124
  tight leading, 108–109
  two-story characters and, 209
  typefaces and, 131
  x-height and, 131
  See also line spacing; spacing issues
leading, in tables, 247–248
  overview of, 247
  rule leading, 248
  white space and, 243

left indents, 179
legends
  contrasted with captions, 227
  defined, 309
  format of, 227–228
  See also captions
legibility
  character width and, 43
  defined, 103–104, 309
  display typefaces and, 74
  screen display and, 32, 285, 287
  seriffed typefaces and, 34
  tight spacing and, 146
  type size and, 37
  x-height and, 130
  See also readability
less than or equal to symbol (≤), 209
less than symbol (<), 209
letter pairs. *See* kerning pair
letter spaces
  Cascading Style Sheets and, 290
  comparisons of various settings,
    117–119, 141
  end-of-line decisions and, 135–136
  H&J and, 140–141
  specifying ranges, 147–152
letterforms
  classical and Renaissance, 40
  flexing character widths and, 153
  seriffed and sans serif, 40
  stress and, 32
  strokes and, 33
letterpresses
  composition on, 11
  defined, 309
  printing process on, 10
letters
  italics for individual letters, 72
  measuring spaces between, 25
  names of parts of, 33
  straight-legged, 33
  varying shapes and widths of, 8
  See also letterforms
letterspacing
  defined, 310
  display typefaces and, 151
  forced justification and, 151–152
licenses, fonts, 101
Life typeface (Simoncini), 131

ligatures
    automatic substitution, 200–201
    defined, 199, 310
    display typefaces and, 201
    expert or alternate fonts, 60
    Latin 1 character set and, 55
    most common, 200
    as special characters, 196
light, typeface weight, 41
    variations in, 130
line-at-a-time H&J, 137–139
    line breaks and, 139
    versus multiline, 138–139
    problems with, 137
line breaks
    defined, 310
    ellipsis points and, 206–207
    H&J and, 139
    hard-ending, 306
    See also line-break points
line-break points
    improper, 143–144
    legal, 139, 206–207
line caster, 10, 310
line-ending commands, 81–83, 310
line endings, typewriting versus
        typesetting, 81–82
line feed, 81, 310
line length, 115–120
    overview of, 115–116
    point size and, 116–120
    readability and, 108–109
    typewriting versus typesetting, 79–80
    See also measure
line printers, 83
line spacing
    creating with Return key, 125–126
    defined, 310
    measuring from baseline to baseline, 31
    measuring in points, 23
    tweaking, 155–156
    See also leading; spacing issues
lines. *See* rules
lines, long, 108–109
lining numerals
    with all-caps headings, 217
    defined, 310
    numbers in text, 199
    proportional, 196

link, of character
    defined, 310
    illustrated, 33
Linotype fonts
    in core set for Macintosh, 54
    and PostScript, 13
Linotype machines, 9–12
lists
    bulleted lists, 207
    leading in, 128
Lithos typeface (Adobe), 74
logotypes, 199–200, 310
loop, of character
    defined, 310
    illustrated, 33
loose spacing
    H&J and, 154–155
    intentional, 107
    screen display and, 287
low resolution, adjusting type for, 283
lowercase
    defined, 310
    as gauge for typeface width, 130
    historical development of, 6, 210
    x-height and, 32, 130
lowercase figures, 199, 310
    See also old-style numerals

M

M
    as drop cap, 211
    relation to em, 24
    strokes of (illustration), 33
Macintosh computers
    core font set, 54, 98
    dynamic font updating, 96, 300
    file formats, 52
    font compatibility, 54
    font encoding, 56
    font formats, 62
    font-storage locations, 95–96
    Key Caps, 58–59
    ligatures and, 200
    missing fonts, 97
    nonbreaking spaces, 139
    primes, minus signs, and multiplication
        signs, 208
    QuickDraw, 92

Macintosh computers *(continued)*
    WYSIWYG interface, 91
Macintosh OS X
    font formats supported by, 93
    fraction characters, 203
    and support for Unicode, 55, 59, 259
MacRoman encoding
    accented characters, 208
    defined, 310
    dotless *i* and, 209
    European languages and, 259
    ordinals, 202
    overview of, 59
    three-dot ellipsis (...), 206
    Windows compatibility with, 56
macron (¯), 208, 260
magazines
    citations in bibliographies, 235
    down-style headings, 217
    end marks and, 226
    jump lines in, 225–226
    loose spacing of type in, 107
    multiline H&J and, 138–139
    standard type sizes for, 120
    use of italics for titles, 72
majuscules (capitals), 6
    See also capitals; uppercase
manual kerning, 168–169, 311
Manutius, Aldus, 42, 293
margins
    centered text, 296
    Cascading Style Sheets and, 290
    justified, 146–150
    measuring in picas, 22–23
    page-setup options for, 116
    ragged, 145–146
    ragged right, 162–163
    skewed, 182–183
    tab values of table column margins, 239
marks of omission. *See* ellipsis points
master character designs, 38–39
    defined, 311
    photographic fonts and, 12
    type sizes and, 6–7
mathematical formulas, inferiors and
        superiors in, 202
matrices, of fonts, 10, 311
m-dash. *See* em dash

mean line
    aligning rounded characters to, 37
    ascenders and descenders and, 36
    defined, 311
    measuring from, 32
    overshoot and, 37
measure
    in Cascading Style Sheets, 290
    defined, 311
    H&J and, 134, 145
    interdependence with point size and
        leading, 109
    overview of, 115–116
    point size and, 116–120
    sans serif typefaces and, 131
    seriffed typefaces and, 129
    See also line length
measurement
    in Cascading Style Sheets, 289
    fixed or absolute, 21
    indicating with primes, 208
    relative units, 24
    units of, for character design, 25
    See also metric measurements;
        typographic measurement
mechanical alignment, 311
medium-weight type, 42
Memphis typeface (Linotype), 35
menu-based typesetting, 18
Mergenthaler-Linotype, 13
Mergenthaler VIP phototypesetter, 12
Meridien typeface (Linotype), 35
metal type
    compared with digital type, 4
    foundries, 6
    replaced by phototypesetting, 11
metric measurements
    fonts, 30, 304
    point conversion to, 22
    typographic, 24
Microsoft Corporation
    development of OpenType, 40, 53
    development of TrueType, 16, 52–54, 95
Microsoft Windows computers. *See*
        Windows computers
military time, 260
minus sign (−), 208, 209, 210

minuscules, 6
  See also lowercase
minutes, indicating with primes, 86, 208
missing entries, in tables, 255
missing fonts, 94, 97–98, 273
modern typefaces
  defined, 311
  hairline serifs and, 34
  strokes in, 46–47
monitors. *See* screen display
monoline
  strokes, 34
  typefaces, 311
monospaced type
  defined, 303, 311
  escapement and, 8
  modern applications of, 8–9
  replacing with proportional type, 9
Monotype casting machines, 9–12
  early evolution of fonts and, 11, 24–25
Monotype Corsiva typeface, similarity to
    ITC Zapf Chancery Medium Italic, 98
Monotype fonts, as core set for Microsoft
    Windows, 54
Monotype Sorts font, 45, 207
  similarity to ITC Zapf Dingbats, 98
mouse-based typesetting, 18
movable type, 3–4
multiline H&J, 138–139
Multiple Master font format, 39–40, 311
multiplication sign (✕), 208, 209

N

N
  as drop cap, 211
  relation to en space, 26
n/a, N.A., 255
name ambiguities, of typefaces, 47
narrow-measure page layout, 109–110
narrow typefaces. *See* condensed typefaces
native file formats, 245
navigation tools, 223–226
  end marks, 226
  folios, 223–224
  jump lines, 225–226
  running heads, 224–225
n-dash. *See* en dash

negative indention, 182
negative leading, 121, 312
New Baskerville typeface (ITC), 36, 70
New Century Schoolbook typeface
    (Linotype), 30
  See also Century typefaces
New Courier typeface (Monotype),
    similarity to Courier, 98
newsletters, H&J and, 138–139
newspapers
  jump lines in, 225–226
  multiline H&J and, 138–139
  narrow-measure problems, 109–110
  typefaces for, 130
  up style of headlines, 217
nibbed pens, 32–33
no-break text, 312
nonalphabetic fonts, 44–45
nonbreaking hyphens
  among types of hyphens, 143
  defined, 312
  H&J and, 139
nonbreaking spaces
  defined, 312
  French punctuation and, 265
  H&J and, 139
  with ellipsis points, 206
  in PostScript Type 1 character set, 51
  in temperature expressions, 263
nonhyphenation zones, 142
normal H&J, 312
normal style, 274
normal word spaces, 140
not equal to sign (≠), 209
Novarese typeface (ITC), 42
number or pound sign (#), 210
numbers, page. *See* folios
numerals
  as footnote reference marks, 230
  French conventions, 266
  hanging, 306
  kerning, 171–172
  lining, 196, 199, 310
  old-style, 60, 196, 199, 310
  ranges of, 205
  See also fractions; outlines, formats of;
      ordinal characters; roman
      numerals; subscripts; superscripts

numerator figures, fractions, 203
numeric tables
    aligning, 252–253
    hanging characters in, 253–254
nut fractions, 203, 306

O

O
    as illustration of overshoot, 37
    as drop cap, 211
oblique typefaces, 42–43, 312
office typesetting, 7
offset lithography
    benefits of, 11
    defined, 312
    paper grades and, 36
ogonek (ͺ), 208, 260
old-style numerals, 199
    with all-caps headings, 217
    as alternate characters, 293
    defined, 312
    expert or alternate fonts, 60
    illustrated, 196
old-style typefaces, 45–46, 312
OpenType font
    characters in, 195
    defined, 312
    font formats and, 53–54
    origins of, 40
    "PostScript-flavored" OpenType, 315
operating systems
    defined, 312
    font-storage locations and, 95–96
    graphical user interfaces and, 91–92
    See also Macintosh computers; Windows
        computers
optical alignment
    centered text and, 192
    correction for bad mechanical
        alignment, 110–111
    defined, 312
    leading, 127
    oversized characters, 193
    ragged margins, 191–192
    tables, 250–251
    typeface design, 37
    See also alignment

optical kerning
    defined, 313
    versus table-based, 170
Optima typeface (Linotype), 40, 225
ordinal characters
    defined, 313
    English ordinals, 202
    superior ordinals, 202
ornament characters, 207
orphans
    defined, 313
    H&J and, 157–159
    running indents and, 179
    vertical justification and, 160
os. *See* operating systems
.otf filename extension (OpenType), 62
out of sorts, 6
outdents. *See* hanging indents
outline characters, digital fonts, 12–13
outline fonts, 49–50, 313
outlines, formats of, 222
output resolution, 281–291
    advantages of high resolution, 281–283
    angled type and, 284
    low resolution, adjusting type for, 283
    point size and, 283–284
    print-type clarity and, 281–283
    reverses and type over backgrounds, 284
    screen display and, 284–287
    World Wide Web and, 288–291
    See also resolution
overprinting, 76, 313
overrides
    defined, 313
    style sheets and, 278
overshoot, 37
oversized characters, alignment of, 193
overstrike, 85, 313

P

P. T. Barnum typeface (ATF), 75
page breaks, 233–234, 290
page description languages (PDLS), 13, 313
page grid, 188–189, 313
page layout programs
    building tables, 256–257
    forced justification, 151
    fraction characters, 203

grid options, 116

H&J defaults, 154

legacy of word processors, 19

ligatures, 200

manual kerning, 168

narrow measures, problems with, 109–110

orphans, 159

spacing specifications, 150

style sheets, 277

table rules, 248

text frames, 123, 188

wraps or runarounds, 183

page numbers. *See* folios

PageMaker, Adobe, 172

pages

    folio placement, 187, 300, 303

    margin and column measurements, 23

    measuring in picas, 22–23

    trim size, 24, 116, 322

    typewriting versus typesetting, 79–80

Palatino font, as part of Macintosh core set, 98

Palatino typeface (Linotype), 42, 57, 69, 71, 230

    similarity to Book Antiqua (Monotype), 98

Palo Alto Research Center (PARC), 13

paper

    economizing on, with use of narrow typefaces, 70

    impact on print quality, 283

    wove paper, 41

paragraph attributes

    assigning in dialog boxes, 90

    controlling with style sheets, 272

    defined, 313

    end-paragraph command, 81

    H&J and, 154

    indents as, 178, 179

    leading as, 126

    "space after" control, 121, 124–125

    "space before" control, 121, 124–125

    of subheads, 124–125 (*see also* subheads)

paragraph indents

    creating with tabs or word spaces, avoiding, 80, 87, 181

    defined, 178, 313

    measuring in points, 23

    overview of, 180–181

    rag-left text and, 181

    sidestepping, 181

    See also indention

paragraph mark (¶), 209, 231

paragraph style sheets

    applying, 273

    creating from existing text, 276

paragraphs

    aesthetic rags, 162–163

    not hyphenating last word of, 143–144

    spacing issues, 137

    type color issues, 156–157

    widows and orphans, 157–159

PARC (Xerox Palo Alto Research Center), 13

parent-child style sheets, 274–275, 279

parentheses

    alignment of, 190

    kerning with italic characters, need for, 169

Parisian typeface (ATF), 75

paths

    curved (vectors), 13, 14

    defined, 313

    stroked paths, 248

    See also rules

patterned backgrounds, 173

PC typesetting. *See* computer typesetting

pens, nibbed, 32–33

percent sign (%), 210

period

    in abbreviations, 263

    with American, British, French, and Spanish quotation marks, 262, 264

    with ellipsis points, 206

    in French numeric expressions, 264

    spacing of, 80

periodicals. *See* magazines

personal computer typesetting. *See* computer typesetting

per-thousand sign (‰), 24

.pfb, .pfm filename extensions (PostScript Type 1), 62

photocomposition, 14

    See also photographic fonts

photographic film

    as benchmark for high-resolution output, 283

    typesetting and, 16–17

photographic fonts, 11–12
   benefit of, 12
   defined, 314
   replaces metal type, 11
photographic plates, offset lithography, 11
Photon typesetting machine, 166
phototypesetting
   defined, 314
   compared with Linotype and Monotype
      machines, 12
pi fonts
   characters in, 44–45
   defined, 314
   highlighting with, 207
   in style sheets, 278
   primes and, 86
picas
   defined, 314
   history of, 22
   notation conventions, 23
   units of measurement and, 21
   uses of, 22–23
picture elements. *See* pixels
pixels
   defined, 314
   dropout and, 16, 300
   jaggies, 308
   PostScript interpreter and, 15–16
   resolution and, 16–17, 32
   screen display and, 18–19, 50
plain text, 314
platforms, computer, 314
   See also Macintosh computers; Windows
      computers
plus or minus sign (±), 210
plus sign (+), 209, 210, 278
P.M., conventions for setting, 260–261
point size
   for bibliographies, 234
   calculating, 120
   for captions and legends, 228
   defined, 23, 314
   for endnotes and footnotes, 229–230
   for extracts (quoted text), 221
   of folios, 224
   for indexes, 232
   interdependence with line length and
      leading, 108
   jump lines, 226

kerning and, 51, 168
Mac interpolation for screen display, 93
measure and, 109, 116–120
output resolution and, 283–284
for running heads, 225
sans serif typefaces and, 131
selecting, 83–84
seriffed typefaces and, 129
for subheads, 218
for tables, 243
tracking and, 172
typographic measurement of, 23
points
   American, 21–22, 294
   defined, 314
   didot, 27, 297, 299
   notation conventions, 23
   PostScript, 22, 315
   as unit of measurement for type, 21
   uses of, 22–23
   See also typographic measurement
points of ellipsis. *See* ellipsis points
points of suspension. *See* ellipsis points
pop caps. *See* standing caps
"PostScript-flavored" OpenType fonts, 315
PostScript fonts
   blocking the embedding of, 100
   character set of, 51
   defined, 314–315
   device independence and, 13–14
   em units and, 25
   filename extensions (.pfb, .pfm), 62
   ligatures and, 200
   native support in Windows 2000/XP, 93
   overview of, 52
   screen display and, 93
PostScript interpreter
   Adobe Type Manager as, 52
   converting page description to print
      image, 14
   defined, 315
   pixels and, 15–16
PostScript points, 22, 315
PostScript Type 1 font. *See* PostScript fonts
pound or number sign (#), 210
pound-sterling sign (£), 261
powers of magnitude sign (×), 210
presses. *See* printing presses

primes (′ ″)
    defined, 315
    keystrokes for, 208
    measurements with, 208
    set closed up, 210
    single prime (′) as symbol for points, 23
    typewriting versus typesetting, 86
print-type clarity, 281–283
printer drivers, 98
printers
    dot matrix, 92–93
    inkjet, 16–17
    laser, 13, 16–17
    line, 83
    PostScript interpreters and, 52
printing presses
    letterpresses, 10–11
    matching type to, 14
    offset lithography, 11
Private Use range, Unicode, 60–61
proofreading
    spotting rivers, 161
    spotting visual alignment problems, 111
proportional type, 9, 315
pull-down menus, style sheets, 271
punctuating em dashes, 205, 315
    See also em dashes
punctuation
    British English versus American
        English, 262–263
    in center alignment, 193
    as component of typeface, 29
    after fractions, 294
    French conventions, 263–266
    German conventions, 267–268
    hanging, 191
    Italian conventions, 267
    italics for, 72
    in monospaced type, 8
    Spanish conventions, 266–267
    thin space as placeholder for, 255
    See also individual punctuation marks

Q

quadding commands
    defined, 315
    overview of, 82–83
    typewriting versus typesetting, 82

QuarkXPress, 170–171
QuickDraw
    defined, 315
    Macintosh computers and, 92
    QuickDraw GX, 53
quotation marks
    ASCII, 86, 294
    British English versus American
        English, 262
    defined, 322
    extracts and, 221
    French, 264–265
    German, 267–268
    Italian, 267
    on keyboard, hidden, 86
    Spanish, 266–267
    typewriter style
        defined, 323
        improper uses of, 86
quoted text. See extracts

R

rag right. See ragged right margins
ragged left margins
    defined, 316
    paragraph indents and, 181
ragged margins
    aesthetics of, 162–163
    headings with, visual alignment of,
        111, 191–192
    H&J and, 145–146
    shaped rags, 318
    wraps and, 184
ragged right margins
    defined, 316
    footnotes, 230
    hyphenation zones and, 142
    indexes, 231
    justification and, 134
    legends and, 228
    measure and, 199, 115
rags. See ragged margins
Raleigh typeface (Linotype), 36
range kerning, 316
ranging numerals. See lining numerals
ranked hyphenation, 316
raster image processors (RIPs)
    defined, 316

raster image processors (RIPS) *(continued)*
  overview of, 14–15
  PostScript fonts and, 52
  TrueType fonts and, 53
rasterized images
  CRTS and, 14
  defined, 316
  illustration of, 15
readability
  anti-aliased type and, 19
  defined, 103–104, 316
  drop caps and, 212
  screen displays, 286
  seriffed typefaces and, 34
  tight spacing and, 105–106
  type size and, 37
  typeface selection for, 67–68
  wrapped margins and, 183
recto, defined, 316
reference marks
  defined, 316
  indicating footnotes with, 230–231
  low resolution, adjusting type for, 284
registration
  color printing and, 76
  overprinting and, 76, 313
registered trademark symbol (®), 209, 210
regular weight
  component of typeface families, 43
  defined, 316
  setting text in, 71
relative indents, 316
relative measurements
  in Cascading Style Sheets, 289
  defined, 316
  versus fixed spaces, 26
  kerning and, 25–26, 168
  typographic measurement and, 24
Remington typewriters, 7
rendering. *See* rasterized images
Renner, Paul, 41
resolution
  bitmaps and, 49–50
  defined, 317
  digital type, 16–19
  dots per inch (dpi), 14
  tracking and, 173
  See also output resolution

Return key
  leading and, 81
  line spaces versus space bands and,
    125–126
  paragraph indents and, 181
  See also carriage returns
reverse indents. *See* hanging indents
reverse leading, 317
reversed type
  defined, 317
  leading and, 127
  output resolution and, 284
  sans serif typefaces and, 76–77
  semibold typefaces and, 76–77
  tracking and, 173
rewrapping lines, 155, 163
  See also wraps
Rialto typeface (dfType), 35
right indents, 179
right-reading images
  defined, 317
  offset lithography and, 11
ring (°), 208, 260
RIPS. *See* raster image processors (RIPS)
rivers
  defined, 317
  H&J and, 161–162
romain du roi, 46, 317
roman numerals, 222
roman typefaces
  defined, 317
  kerning transition with italics, 169
  old-style and, 45
  overview of, 42
Rosewood typeface (Adobe), 75
rows, tables
  defined, 317
  overview of, 237–238
  specifying, 245–246
rubber stamps, compared with movable
    type, 4
rule fill
  command, 84
  defined, 317
rules
  baselines of, 248
  centering text between, 249–250
  defined, 317
  leading of, 248

reserving for complex tables, 244

specifying horizontal rules, 242

types of, 244

use with straddle heads, 238

weights of, 245

run-in heads, 317

run-in index style, 232, 233

run-in subheads, 219–220

runarounds. *See* wraps

running heads, 187, 317

folios and, 224, 225

function of, 224–225

using in pairs, 225

See also headings

running indents

defined, 178, 317

orphans and, 179–180

overview of, 179

running text, defined, 318

runover lines

controlling, 239, 240

defined, 318, 322

footnotes and, 230

in indexes, 234

outline formats and, 222

in tables, 244

S

Sabon typeface (Linotype), 70, 116–119

sans serif typefaces

color and, 75

defined, 318

display use of, 44, 74

drop caps and, 211

geometric, 40, 304

jump lines and, 226

ligatures and logotypes, 199

low resolution and, 284

point size and measure and, 131

readability, 68

reversed type, 77

screen display and, 286

versus seriffed typefaces, 33, 40–41

tight spacing and, 106

traditional uses, 68–69

weights of, 44

scaling type, 24

Scotch rule, 245, 318

Scotch typefaces, 318

screen display, 92–95

anti-aliasing type, 18–19, 294

bitmapped fonts, 92–93, 295

Display PostScript and, 93, 299

inaccuracy of screen images, 18–19

increasing type size, 287

legibility of, 32, 287

loose tracking and, 174

low resolution as norm on, 284–285

output resolution and, 284–287

PostScript and Adobe Type Manager
and, 93

rendering type when fonts are
missing, 94

resolution on, 49

Style menu and, 94

TrueType and, 95

typefaces for, 285–286

screen fonts, 318

See also bitmapped fonts

script typefaces

defined, 318

tracking and, 173–174

seconds, using primes to indicate, 86, 208

section headings, books, 216

section mark (§), 209, 231

See also references, in indexes, 232

selections, GUIs versus traditional
typesetting, 91

semibold type

footnotes and, 229–230

fractions and, 203

reversed type and, 76–77

small caps and, 198

superiors and, 190, 202

semicolon (;), in indexes, 233

semi-oblique typefaces, 42–43

sentence (down) capitalization style

defined, 318

newspaper headlines and, 217

titles of books and magazines, 266

sentences, double-space convention
following periods, 80

seriffed typefaces

benefits of, 33–34

character width, 130

color and, 75

condensing, 73

seriffed typefaces *(continued)*
    defined, 318
    point size and measure and, 129
    readability, 68
    reversed type, 77
    versus sans serif typefaces, 40–41
    stroke weight, 130
    typeface categories and, 33
    types of, 34–35
    uses of, 68–69
    x-height, 129–130
serifs
    bracketed, 34–35
    defined, 318
    hairline, 34–35, 305
    illustrated, 33
    slur, defined, 319
    unbracketed, 34–35
    wedge, 34–35
    variations of, 34
servers, font storage and, 96
set width. *See* character width
shaped margins
    defined, 318
    margin types, 182–183
shaped rags, 318
Shift, typewriters, 85
ship names, italics for, 72
shoulder, of character
    defined, 318
    illustrated, 33
side bearing
    defined, 318
    screen display and, 286
    source of alignment problems,
        110–111, 187, 193
    type design and, 5
side-head. *See* subheads
Silentium Pro Open Type typeface
    (Adobe), 61
single-byte font, 259–260, 318
single prime (′). *See* primes
single quotation marks (' '). *See* quotation
    marks
size changes, typeface design and, 37–38
skewed margins
    defined, 182, 319
    setting, 183

skews. *See* skewed margins
slab serifs, 34–35, 319
slash. *See* virgule (/)
slur serif, defined, 319
small capitals, 196–198
    in captions and legends, 227–228
    in chapter headings, 217
    defined, 319
    expert or alternate fonts for, 60
    overview of, 196–197
    semibold typefaces and, 198
    setting straddle heads in, 243
    transitions to full-size capitals, 198
    unique proportions of, 197–198
    uses of, 198
    See also caps and small caps
smoothing type. *See* anti-aliasing
soft hyphens
    defined, 319
    typewriting versus typesetting, 85
    uses of, 143
soft returns
    aesthetic rags and, 163
    defined, 319
    first-line indents and, 181
    typewriting versus typesetting, 82
solid-set type, 120, 319
solidus
    defined, 319
    fractions, 86, 203, 319
    line breaks and, 139
sorts, type
    defined, 319
    out of sorts, 6
Souvenir typeface (ITC), 74
spaces. *See* character spacing; fixed spaces;
    letter spaces; nonbreaking spaces;
    word spaces
"space after" paragraph control, 124–125, 319
space band. *See* word spaces
"space before" paragraph control, 124–125
spacing issues
    characters, 25, 209–210
    em dashes, 205
    H&J and, 140–142, 145–156, 159–161
    loose word and character spacing, 107
    metal type and, 4
    subheads, leading of, 219–220

tight word and character spacing, 105–107

loose and tight lines, 155–156

type color and, 104–105

typesetting and, 5

unbalanced spacing, 107–108

See also character spacing; kerning; kerning pairs; line spacing; tracking; word spaces

Spanish typographic conventions, 266–267

special characters

accented characters, 208–209

dashes, 204–205

ellipsis points, 205–207

extended character sets, 195–196

fractions, 203–204

hard-to-find characters, 207–208

initial capitals, 210–213

ligatures, logotypes, and diphthongs, 199–201

old-style numbers, 199

pi characters, 207

small capitals, 196–198

spacing issues, 209

superiors, inferiors, and ordinals, 201–202

swash characters, 201

See also symbols

species, use of italics for, 72

spelling dictionary, 200–201

spine, of character

defined, 319

illustrated, 33

spread, 225, 319

spreadsheet approach. *See* grid approach, to tables

spur, of character, illustrated, 33

square serifs. *See* slab serifs

stance

defined, 319

roman typefaces and, 42

standard-width typefaces, 69, 130, 320

standards

Unicode and ASCII, 55

See also Cascading Style Sheets

standing caps

defined, 210, 320

overview of, 212

problem characters for, 213

standing initial capitals. *See* standing caps

standoff distance, wraps, 183–184, 319

stem, of character

defined, 320

illustrated, 33

Stencil typeface (ATF), 75

straddle entries

defined, 320

example of, 239

in tables, 238

straddle heads

defined, 320

setting in caps or small caps, 243

in tables, 238

use of rules with, 238

straight quotes, 86

stress

defined, 320

in old-style typefaces, 45

type styles and, 32

strike-through type

in Cascading Style Sheets, 290

defined, 313

typewriting versus typesetting, 85

strikeout. *See* strike-through type

stroke weight

applying, 71–72

bold, 41, 43, 71–72, 295

bold italic, 43

book, 42, 295

defined, 324

effect of, 130

italics, 42–43, 72, 308

light, 41

regular, 43, 71, 316

type size and, 129

stroked paths, 248, 313, 320

strokes, character

defined, 320

illustrated, 33

modern typefaces and, 46–47

monoline, 34

old-style typefaces and, 45

type color and, 38, 105

type size and, 129

stub columns

defined, 320

in tables, 237, 238

Style menu, 94
style sheets, 271–279
    applying, 276–277
    creating from existing text, 276
    creating from other style sheets,
        274–275
    defined, 320
    document structures and, 279
    follow-on styles, 273–274
    functioning of, 271–272
    H&J and, 154
    importing, 279
    overrides, 278
    paragraph versus character styles, 273
    printing, 272–273
    removing, 277–278
    searching and replacing, 279
subentries, indexes, 232, 320
subheads
    bold type for, 71–72
    cut-in subheads, 217–218
    defined, 320
    functions of, 217
    hierarchy of, 216
    indention, 220
    leading and, 124–125
    level-A, level-B, and level-C, 217–218
    run-in, 317
    spacing, 219–220
    style sheets and, 279
    in tables, 243
    weight of, 218
subscripts
    alignment and, 189
    defined, 307, 320
    in expert sets, 253
    low-resolution adjustments and, 284
    overview of, 201–202
subsets, of fonts, 100, 320
suitcase icon, TrueType fonts, 62, 321
superior characters. *See* superscripts
superior ordinals, 202
superscripts
    alignment and, 189
    defined, 321
    in expert sets, 189–190, 196, 231, 253
    low-resolution adjustments and, 282, 284
    overview of, 201–202
    semibold typefaces and, 190, 202

suspension points. *See* ellipsis points
swash characters
    defined, 321
    expert sets or alternate fonts, 60
    special characters, 196, 201
Symbol font
    duplicates, possibility of, 98
    MacRoman encoding and, 56, 59
    multiplication and minus signs, 208
    pi characters and, 44–45, 207
    primes and, 86, 208
    Unicode and, 196
symbols
    currency, 254–255, 261–262
    indicating footnotes with, 230–231
    on Macintosh computers (*see* Key Caps)
    spaces with, 209–210
    Unicode numbers of, 261–262
    on Windows computers
        (*see* Character Map)
    See also accented characters; pi fonts,
        special characters; *names of specific
        symbols; Symbols section at beginning
        of Index*

T

tab cycle, 321
tab entries, tables
    aligning, 250–252
    balancing with column width and
        gutters, 246
    defined, 321
    horizontal and vertical alignment of, 244
    leading and, 237–238
    missing or void, 255
    narrow example, 246
    spanning columns (straddle heads), 238
Tab key
    indention and, 80
    for indention, improper use of, 87, 181
    word processors and, 239
tab stops
    defined, 321
    typewriters, 87
tab values
    alignment problems and, 251
    defined, 321
    table margins, 239

table. *See* tables

table-based kerning, 170

table-setting techniques, 245–256

    column width, balancing with gutters, 246–247

    currency symbol alignment, 254–255

    data imports, 245

    hanging characters, 253–254

    heads and tab entries, 250–252

    leading, 247–248

    numeric tables, 252–253

    setting from scratch, 245–246

    text centering, 249–250

    void or missing entries, 255

table-setting tools

    grid approach, 240

    limitations of, 237, 256

    versus page layout programs, 256–257

tables, 237–257

    alignment, 244

    complexity of, 237

    and Cascading Style Sheets, 290

    designing, 239

    grid (spreadsheet) approach to, 240–243

    hanging characters and, 191

    headings, 192, 238

    indention, 244

    leading, 128, 243

    low resolution, adjusting type for, 284

    point sizes, 243

    rows and columns, 237–238

    rules, 244–245

    small caps for headings, 198

    structures of, 239–240

    typeface choice, 243

    visual alignment and, 250

tables of contents (TOCs)

    automatic generation of, 222

    format of, 223

    style sheets and, 279

tablet PCs, 285

tabs

    aligning in tables, 250–252

    for indention, improper use of, 87, 181

    typewriting versus typesetting, 87

    typographic versus word processing, 239

tail, of character

    defined, 321

    illustrated, 33

tail rules, in tables, 244–245, 321

technical terminology, use of italics for, 72

temperature, expressions of, American versus British, 263

templates

    defined, 321

    compared with style sheets, 273–274

terminal characters, 197, 201, 303

terminal, of character

    defined, 321

    illustrated, 33

text

    alignment, 80

    blocks, 187

    creating style sheets from existing, 276

    hierarchical elements of, 215–216

    letter spaces and, 147–151

    low-resolution adjustments and, 284

    plain text, 314

    sans serif typefaces used for, 131

text frames. *See* frames, text

text on a path, 174, 321

text-processing, code-driven, 91

text, quoted. *See* extracts

text shadowing, in Cascading Style Sheets, 290

text type, versus display type, 6

text typefaces

    common features of, 69–71

    defined, 321

    overview of, 44

    seriffed as standard for, 68

text wrapping. *See* wraps

thin spaces

    aligning table entries, 254–255

    with bullets, 207

    defined, 26, 321

    with ellipsis points, 206

    em basis of, 26

    fixed spaces and, 152

    in French typography, 264–266

    in letterspacing, 152

    in Italian typography, 266

    in Spanish typography, 266

    in temperature expressions, 263

thin typefaces. *See* stroke weight

three-dot ellipsis (. . .), 205–206

3-em dash, 235

tight leading, 108–109

tight rag, 145, 321
  See also ragged margins
tight spacing
  H&J and, 154–155
  problems created by, 105–107
  See also spacing issues
tilde (˜), 58, 208, 260
time expressions
  language-specific conventions, 260–261
  military time, 260
Times (London), 69–70
Times font, possibility of duplicates, 98
Times New Roman typeface (Monotype)
  popularity of, 69–70
  readability problems with, 70, 105
  size sensitivity of, 39
  similarity to Times Roman (Linotype), 97, 98
  Small Text, 39
  type color and, 105
Times Roman typeface (Linotype)
  character width, 69, 130
  compatibility problems of early fonts, 95
  as example of seriffed typeface, 40
  popularity of, 69–70
  readability problems with, 70, 105
  screen display and, 285
  similarity to Times New Roman (Monotype), 97, 98
  type color and, 105
titles
  compared with headings, 216
  master typeface designs for, 38
  style sheets and, 279
  use of italics for, 72
titles, French, 263
titling characters, 196
titling typefaces
  defined, 322
  type size changes and, 38
  uses of, 74
  See also display typefaces
toggle controls, 90
top alignment
  defined, 322
  in tables, 244
  varieties of, 189
top rules (head), tables, 244–245
track kerning. *See* tracking

tracking
  controlling, 172–173
  correcting composition faults, 155–157, 161
  defined, 166, 322
  display typefaces and, 74
  H&J and, 136–137
  at low resolutions, 173
  patterned backgrounds and, 173
  of script faces, 173–174
  special situations, 173
trademark symbol (™), 210
transitional typefaces, 45–46, 322
trim size, pages
  defined, 322
  measuring, 24
  page-setup options for, 116
TrueType font
  characters in, 195
  defined, 322
  development of, 16
  em units and, 25
  filename extensions (.ttf or .ttc), 62
  font formats and, 53
  ligatures and, 200
  screen display and, 95
TrueType GX technology, 39, 322
Trump Mediæval typeface (Linotype), 35, 69
.ttf or .ttc filename extensions (TrueType), 62
Turkish text, 209
turn lines
  controlling, 239, 240
  defined, 318, 322
  footnotes and, 230
  in indexes, 234
  outline formats and, 222
  in tables, 244
Type 1, PostScript font. *See* PostScript font
type area, page grids, 187, 322
type color
  defined, 297
  evenness of, 38
  leading and, 128, 131
  overview of, 5
  paragraph color problems, 156–157
  type qualities and, 104–105
  See also tracking
Type Founders Association, U.S., 21

type qualities, 103–111
   legibility and readability, 103–104
   long lines and tight leading, 108–109
   loose spacing, 107
   narrow measures, 109–110
   optical effects and alignment, 110–111
   tight spacing, 105–107
   trusting visual appearance, 111
   type color, 104–105
   unbalanced spacing, 107–108
type size
   in Cascading Style Sheets, 290
   leading and, 124–125
   measuring in points, 23
   See also point size
typeface design
   ascenders and descenders, 36
   baselines, 30–31
   calligraphic influences on, 32–33
   ink wells, 36–37
   master character designs, 38–39
   multiple master fonts, 39–40
   proportional sizing and, 5
   role of em square in, 30
   serifs, 33–35
   size changes and, 37–38
   visual appearance versus mechanical
      correctness, 37
   x-height, 32
typeface family, 43, 322
typefaces
   captions and legends, 228
   in Cascading Style Sheets, 290
   classifications of, historical, 45–47
   condensed (*see* condensed typefaces)
   decorative (*see* decorative typefaces)
   defined, 29, 322
   digital type, limitations of, 38–39
   display (*see* display typefaces)
   endnotes and footnotes and, 229
   extended (*see* extended or expanded
      typefaces)
   families, 43–44, 322
   fixed-width, defined, 303
   compared with fonts, 29–30
   indexes and, 232
   jump lines, 226
   leading and, 131
   modern, 34, 46–47, 311

name ambiguities and, 47
nonalphabetic fonts, 44–45
oblique, 42–43, 312
old-style, 45–46, 312
point size and measure and, 129–131
roles performed by, 44
roman (*see* roman typefaces)
sans serif (*see* sans serif typefaces)
for screen display, 285–286
script, 173–174, 318
selecting, 83–84
semi-oblique, 42–43
seriffed (*see* seriffed typefaces)
specifying, issues in, 47
standard-width, 69, 130, 320
style sheets and, 279
subheads and, 218
tables and, 243
text (*see* text typefaces)
titling (*see* titling typefaces)
tracking values and, 172
transitional, 45–46, 322
weight of, 41–42
width-compatible, defined, 324
width of, 43
See also names of specific typefaces
typefaces, working with, 67–77
   bold faces, 71–72
   color, use of, 75–76
   condensed and extended faces, 73–74
   decorative faces, 75
   display faces, 74
   expressing emphasis, 71
   italics, 72
   readability and, 67–68
   reverses, 76–77
   seriffed and sans serif types, 68–69
   text faces, 69–71
   type weight and, 71–72
typeset quality, 16, 322
typesetting, historical overview, 3–20
   bounding boxes and spaces, 5
   calligraphy and, 5–6
   desktop publishing and, 13–16
   device independence and, 15
   digital type resolution and quality, 16–19
   fonts, 10–13
   handset type, 6
   Linotype machines, 10

typesetting, historical overview *(continued)*
  monospaced type, 8–9
  Monotype machines, 9–10
  movable type, 3–4
  proportional type, 9
  typewriters, 7
  word processors, 19
typesetting systems
  dedicated *(see* dedicated typesetting
    systems)
  personal computers *(see* computer
    typesetting)
  typesetting versus typewriting *(see*
    typewriting versus typesetting)
typesetting with style sheets. *See* style
  sheets
typewriters, 7–9
  escapement and, 7
  IBM Selectric, 83
  monospaced type and, 8–9
  Remington, 7
  See also typewriting versus typesetting
typewriting versus typesetting, 79–87
  character availability, 85
  emphasis and highlighting, 84–85
  fractions, 86–87
  hyphens and dashes, 85
  line endings and carriage returns, 81–82
  page sizes and line lengths, 79–80
  periods, space after, 80
  primes, 86
  quadding commands, 82–83
  quotation marks, 86, 323
  tabs, 87
  typeface and point-size selection, 83–84
  word spaces, 80–81
typographic attributes, assigning in
  dedicated systems, 90
typographic measurements, 21–27
  agates, 27
  American point, 21–22
  ciceros and didot points, 27
  em-based units, 24–26
  English and metric units, 24
  fixed and absolute, 21
  notation conventions, 23
  picas and points, 22–23
  PostScript point, 22
  relative units, 24

word space, 26–27
typographic quotation marks. *See* quotation
  marks

U

ultra condensed typefaces. *See* condensed
  typefaces
umlaut (¨), 58, 208
  See also dieresis
unbalanced spacing, 107–108
unbracketed serifs, 34–35, 323
underscoring
  in Cascading Style Sheets, 290
  defined, 323
  for emphasis, 84–85
Unicode
  accented characters, 208–209
  assigning Unicode numbers to
    symbols, 196
  Character Map and, 58
  in Cascading Style Sheets, 290
  defined, 323
  encoding issues with, 60–61
  European languages and, 260
  fraction characters, 203
  hard-to-find characters and, 207–208
  Mac OS X and, 55, 59, 259
  operating systems support, 55,
    58–59, 259
  primes, coding for, 208
uninstalling and installing fonts, 298, 307
Univers typeface (Haas), 41, 131
Universal News with Commercial Pi font
  (Linotype), 207
unshift, typewriters, 85, 323
up (headline) capitalization style, 217, 323
uppercase
  defined, 323
  historical derivation of term, 6
  See also capitals
user interfaces. *See* graphical user
  interfaces (GUIs)

V

variable dot size
  defined, 323
  laser printers and, 17

vector-based objects, 14

vector fonts. *See* outline fonts

vectors

    defined, 50, 323

    outline fonts and, 50

    in PostScript, 14

Venetian typefaces, 45, 323

    See also old-style typefaces

Verdana typeface (Microsoft), 285–286

verso, defined, 323

vertical alignment, 188–189, 290

vertical justification

    controls, 139

    defined, 323

    frame-at-a-time, 160–161

    text frames and, 124

    vertical space bands and, 159–160

vertical rules, 244

vertical space bands

    defined, 323

    text frames and, 124

    vertical justification and, 160

video presentations, loose tracking and, 173

Vineta typeface (VG), 75

virgule (/)

    base alignment of, 204

    defined, 323

    compared with fraction bar, 203

    fractions and, 86

    as line-break point, 139

visual alignment. *See* optical alignment

void entries, in tables, 255

W

Web browsers, text-composition abilities

    of, 288

Web, typography on, 173, 288–291

wedge serifs, 34–35, 324

weight

    stroke thickness and, 41–42, 71–72, 324

    of subheads, 218

    of table rules, 245

    type size and, 129

    See also stroke weight

Western European languages, accents

    for, 208

what you see is what you get. *See* WYSIWYG

    (what you see is what you get)

white space

    defined, 324

    em units, 25–26

    kerning and, 168

    point size and, 121

    screen-display typefaces and, 286

    table gutters and, 238

    tables and, 243

    type size and, 37–38

widows

    defined, 324

    caused by deep indents, 181

    causes and cures, 157–159

width-compatible typefaces, 324

    See also core font set

width tables

    defined, 324

    as part of font, 51

widths

    of Monotype machine characters, 10

    of typefaces, 43

    See also character width

wild rag, 145, 324

    See also ragged margins

Win ANSI

    accented characters, 208

    defined, 324

    dotless *i,* 209

    encoding, 56, 58

    European languages and, 259

    fraction characters, 203

    fractions, 87

    ligatures, 200

    Macintosh compatibility with, 56

    ordinal superior characters, 202

    three-dot ellipsis character and (. . .), 206

Windows 2000/XP, native support for

    PostScript, 93

Windows computers

    core font set, 54, 98

    file formats, 52

    font compatibility and, 54

    font encoding and, 56

    font-storage locations, 95–96

    fractions and, 87

    Graphical Device Interface (GDI), 92

    graphical user interfaces and, 91

    identifying font formats, 62–63

    ligatures, 200

Windows computers *(continued)*
  minus sign, 208
  missing fonts, 97
  multiplication sign, 208
  nonbreaking space, 139
  primes, 208
  and support for Unicode, 55, 58, 259
Wingdings font (Microsoft), 207
word-division rules, 260
  See also hyphenation and justification
    (H&J)
word processors
  leading as paragraph attribute in, 126
  legacy of, 19
  ligatures, 200
  orphans, 159
  page size, 80
  removing style sheets, 277
  tabs, 87, 239, 240
  traditional typesetting and, 17
  typesetting limitations of, 19, 89–90
  typographic attributes, 90
  word spaces and, 80
word spaces
  aligning table entries, 255
  with bullets, 207
  defined, 26, 324
  with ellipsis points, avoiding, 206
  em basis of, 26–27
  formatting instructions contained in, 273
  after fractions, 204
  Gutenberg's system, 4
  for indention, improper use of, 80, 181
  in indexes, 232
  as line-break point, 139
  nonbreaking, 139
    with ellipsis points, 206
    in expressions of temperature,
      263, 266
    with guillemets and other
      punctuation, 264, 266, 267
  in PostScript Type 1 character set, 51
  compared with thin space, 152
  in typewriting versus typesetting,
    80–81
word spacing
  balancing with letter spaces, 107
  in Cascading Style Sheets, 290

comparisons of various H&J settings,
  117–119, 141
  end-of-line decisions and, 135–136
  justification and, 27, 140–141
  normal, 140
  ranges of, 145–150
  tight versus loose, 105–107, 146
World Wide Web, output resolution and,
  288–291
wove paper, 41
wraps, 182–187
  cut-in subheads and, 221
  defined, 182, 317, 324
  drop caps and, 212
  H&J and, 137
  irregularly shaped, 186–187
  narrow measures and, 110
  rectangular, 184–186
  rewrapping lines, 155, 163
  setting, 183–184
  standoff distance, 183–184, 319
WYSIWYG (what you see is what you get)
  computer typesetting and, 91–92
  defined, 324
  desktop publishing and, 13
  kerning and, 169
  limitations of, 17–19
  table formats compatible with, 240

X

x-height
  ascenders and descenders and, 36
  defined, 324
  leading and, 131
  seriffed typefaces, 129–130
  type color and, 105
  type size and, 129
  typeface design and, 32
Xerox Palo Alto Research Center (PARC), 13

Z

Zapf Dingbats font (ITC), 45, 98, 207
  MacRoman and, 59
  pi characters and, 44–45, 207
  similarity to Monotype Sorts, 98
  Unicode and, 196
Zapf, Hermann, 152

Further Reading

The Elements of Typographic Style, by Robert Bringhurst (Hartley & Marks, Vancouver, 1996). Typography for the book, from a design perspective rather than a typesetting one. A thorough and thoughtful treatment of typographic aesthetics.

Stop Stealing Sheep & Find Out How Type Works, Second Edition, by Erik Spiekermann and E.M. Ginger (Peachpit Press, Berkeley, Ca., 2002). A fresh and engaging look at how and why type works, by a leading graphic and typeface designer. A clever, insightful, and eye-opening tour de force of the typographic arts.

Anatomy of a Typeface, by Alexander Lawson (David R. Godine, Boston, 1990). Lovely and very informative histories of several dozen exemplary typeface designs and design styles. Includes an excellent bibliography on the subjects of type and printing.

Printing Types, by Alexander Lawson and Dwight Agner (Beacon Press, Boston, 1990). A lucid, compact introduction to the complex subject of typeface classification and identification.

The History and Technique of Lettering, by Alexander Nesbitt (Dover, New York, 1998). Nominally a textbook for students of lettering technique, but also a terrific history of letterforms and type from a practical perspective. Contains many good type samples. Written in 1950, reprinted in 1998.

Hart's Rules for Compositors and Readers, 39th Edition (Oxford University Press, Oxford, 1983). This style guide for the Oxford University Press packs an enormous amount of typographic wisdom into a very small package. While very British in typographic style, it offers wonderful attention to detail.

Words into Type, 3rd Edition (Prentice-Hall, Englewood Cliffs, N.J., 1974). The granddaddy of reference works for the typographically savvy copyeditor. Contains more about type than most books about type.